Fodor's 94 Paris

D0710149

Fodor's Travel Publications, Inc.
New York • Toronto • London • Sydney • Auckland

Fodor's Paris

Editor: Suzanne De Galan
Editorial Contributors: Bob Blake, Alice Brinton, David Downie, Corinne LaBalme, Valerie Martone, Sheila Mooney, Robert Noah, Marcy Pritchard, Alexandra Siegel
Creative Director: Fabrizio La Rocca
Cartographer: David Lindroth
Illustrator: Karl Tanner
Cover Photograph: Daniel Barbieri/Stockphotos, Inc.

Design: Vignelli Associates

Special Sales

Contents

Maps and Plans

Foreword

While every care has been taken to ensure the accuracy of the information in this guide, the passage of time will always bring change, and consequently, the publisher cannot accept responsibility for errors that may occur.

All prices and opening times quoted here are based on information supplied to us at press time. Hours and admission fees may change, however, and the prudent traveler will avoid inconvenience by calling ahead.

Fodor's wants to hear about your travel experiences, both pleasant and unpleasant. When a hotel or restaurant fails to live up to its billing, let us know and we will investigate the complaint and revise our entries where the facts warrant it.

Send your letters to the editors of Fodor's Travel Publications, 201 East 50th Street, New York, NY 10022.

Highlights'94 and Fodor's Choice

Highlights '94

Visitors to Paris have even more reasons to head straight for the Louvre—about twice as many, in fact. By the time the **Grand Louvre** project is completed in 1996, the museum (now officially named the Grand Louvre, though it's doubtful anyone will call it that) will have doubled its exhibition space. At press time, most of the facades had been cleaned, dozens of paintings had been restored, and substantial space had been allotted for displaying 18th- and 19th-century French art. More than 30 more rooms were scheduled to open in the north wing by the end of 1993. Other additions include the underground Carrousel du Louvre concourse, housing scores of glossy showcases for French luxury-goods manufacturers and a permanent space for the presentation of French fashion collections. Construction of an underground garage has also begun.

As François Mitterand's presidency draws toward its close in 1995, the ambitious building campaign that included the Louvre project, as well as the Opéra Bastille and the Arche de la Défense, enters its final phase. His (personal and political) health permitting, Mitterand will inaugurate the **Bibliothèque de France,** the last major monument of his mandate, shortly before his term ends. At press time, the controversial library's four transparent towers—shaped like open books—had already surged 250 feet upward, taking their considerable place in the Paris skyline.

The TGB (*Très Grande Bibliothèque*), as it is called, anchors the city's burgeoning southeast. Though not a tourist attraction in the usual sense, this area (the Quai de la Gare on the Left Bank in the 13th arrondissement and the Quai de Bercy on the Right Bank in the 12th arrondissement) will soon be a must-see for visitors interested in urban planning. By 1996, this far-flung sector—known as **Seine Rive Gauche**—will be linked to central Paris and points west by the express **Météor** métro line; the area is already being touted as the "Latin Quarter of the next millennium." Covering nearly half a mile of riverfront, it will include, along with the TGB, a university, a graphic-arts center, student housing, artists' studios, and cultural facilities.

Directly across the river at Bercy, the stunning, offbeat **American Center,** designed by architect Frank Gehry, was set to open its new headquarters in September 1993 (it was formerly located on the Left Bank). Europe's largest American cultural institute offers everything from English lessons to dance performances and seems poised to play an even larger role in the city's creative arts scene than before. Practically next door, an immense international **Food and Wine business complex** is rising from the rubble of the old wine merchants' quarter, the Entrepôts de Bercy. A vestige of that ramshackle, charming district, the Cour St-Emilion, has been preserved as a shopping center.

The **Centre National d'Art et de Culture Georges-Pompidou,** better known as the **Beaubourg,** is benefitting from a much-needed brushup. Since 1977 more than 20,000 visitors a day have tramped through the museum, straining the already fragile structure and facilities. Architect Renzo Piano, who with Richard Rogers designed the center, ordered a fresh coat of paint for the museum's skeletal shell, and is supervising the current full-scale renovation of the interior.

More from the facelift department: A year-long restoration completed in December 1992 left the regal **place Vendôme** with a sparkling granite pavement and twice its previous number of Second Empire–style street lamps (they create a magic glow on misty nights). Better still, motor traffic is now confined to two lanes, and parking (even for the privileged patrons of the Ritz, Chanel, and Cartier's) is restricted to an underground lot.

On the economic front, the French franc—unlike the devalued currencies of Italy, Great Britain, and Spain—has continued fairly strong againt the U.S. dollar. (At press time, the exchange rate was 5.3 francs to $1). However, a recession within France has kept prices down, and U.S. visitors will find their money goes further in Paris stores and restaurants than it has in recent years. Dining can be particularly affordable, as the trend toward budget bistros shows no signs of abating. Parisians are flocking to these informal eateries for traditional dishes such as pot au feu, mashed potatoes, and crème brûlée—comfort foods for an uncertain *fin de siècle*.

Outside Paris, the much-ballyhooed **Euro Disney Resort** was struggling at press time with slack attendance and less-than-enthusiastic crowds. Europeans, it seems, are balking at the high restaurant and hotel prices, especially since 1992's devaluation of the lira, the peseta, and the pound. Additional hotel rooms at the resort, as well as film studios, a second theme park, and another golf course, have been postponed until 1996 at the earliest.

Fodor's Choice

No two people will agree on what makes a perfect vacation, but it's fun and helpful to know what others think. We hope you'll have a chance to experience some of Fodor's Choices yourself while visiting the City of Light. For detailed information about each entry, refer to the appropriate chapters within this guidebook.

Views

The back of St-Gervais-St-Protais church from the Seine (angle of the Quai de l'Hôtel de Ville and rue des Barres)

Ile de la Cité from the Pont des Arts

The towering twin columns of place de la Nation from the Cours de Vincennes

Paris spread out beneath the Sacré-Coeur at Montmartre

Notre Dame from the Square Jean XXIII

Walks

Along the banks of the Seine between place de la Concorde and the Ile St-Louis

Along the Canal St-Martin in east Paris

Around the banks of the Lac Inférieur in the Bois de Boulogne

From the Arc de Triomphe to the Louvre, via the Champs-Elysées, place de la Concorde, and the Tuileries Gardens

Monuments

Arc de Triomphe

Eiffel Tower

Louvre's glass pyramid(s)

The bronze column on place Vendôme

Works of Art

Géricault's *Raft of the Medusa* in the Louvre

The *Lady and the Unicorn* tapestries at the Musée de Cluny

Manet's *Déjeuner sur l'Herbe* in the Musée d'Orsay

Monet's *Water Lilies* at the Musée de l'Orangerie

The royal tombs in the basilica of St-Denis

Museums

Musée d'Orsay

Musée Rodin

Musée Marmottan

Musée des Monuments Français

The Louvre, with plenty of time on your hands

Churches

Notre Dame Cathedral

St-Germain-des-Prés

Sainte-Chapelle

St-Eustache

Dôme Church at the Invalides

Times to Treasure

Coffee and croissants outside a café on a sunny morning

Fête de la Musique: impromptu street concerts (June 21)

The French Open Tennis Championships at Roland Garros in May

An early evening aperitif at Café Beaubourg, admiring the street performers in front of the Pompidou Center

Bastille Day (July 14)

Restaurants

La Tour d'Argent, 5e (*Very Expensive*)

Taillevent, 8e (*Very Expensive*)

Au Trou Gascon, 12e (*Expensive*)

Benoît, 4e (*Expensive*)

Le Relais du Parc, 16e (*Expensive*)

Chez Philippe/Pyrénées-Cévennes, 11e (*Moderate*)

La Fermette Marbeuf, 8e (*Moderate*)

Le Petit Bourbon, 1er (*Moderate*)

Baracane, 4e (*Inexpensive*)

Chez Jenny, 3e (*Inexpensive*)

Jacques Mélac, 11e (*Inexpensive*)

Hotels

Crillon, 8e (*Very Expensive*)

Ritz, 1er (*Very Expensive*)

Deux-Iles, 4e (*Expensive*)

Hôtel d'Angleterre, 6e (*Expensive*)

Grands Ecoles, 5e (*Moderate*)

Marronniers, 6e (*Moderate*)

Place des Vosges, 4e (*Moderate*)

Argenson, 8e (*Inexpensive*)

Castex, 4e (*Inexpensive*)

Shopping

Rue du Faubourg St-Honoré and avenue Montaigne (designer clothes)

The Marais and place des Victoire (avant-garde designer clothes)

Place Vendôme (jewelry)

Trocadéro–Victor Hugo area (second-hand shops)

Au Printemps (department store)

Louvre des Antiquaires complex (antiques)

Rue Lepic, rue de Buci, and rue Mouffetard (street markets)

Open-air bookstalls along the Seine

N

PORTE D'AUBERVILLIERS
PORTE DE LA VILLETTE

Canal de l'Ourcq

PORTE DE CLIGNANCOURT
Blvd. Ney

PORTE DE LA CHAPELLE

Blvd. Macdonald

R. Ordener

Blvd. Ormano

R. de la Chapelle

R. Riquet

R. d'Aubervilliers

R. de Flandre

LA VILLETTE

MONTMARTRE
aulaincourt

R. Custine

Blvd. Barbès

R. Marx Dormoy

Bassin de la Villette

PORTE DE PANTIN

LE PRÉ-ST-GERVAIS

Sacré Coeur

Blvd. de Rochechouart

Blvd. de la Chapelle

lichy

R. du Faubourg St-Martin

Canal St-Martin

Gare du Nord

Blvd. de la Villette

BUTTES-CHAUMONT

PORTE DES LILAS

Gare de l'Est

R. La Fayette

Blvd. de Magenta

Blvd. de la Villette

du Temple

BELLEVILLE

d. des aliens Montmartre
Blvd. Poissonniere

Blvd. St-Denis

Blvd. St-Martin

R. du Faubourg

Blvd. de Belleville

PORTE DE BAGNOLET

Palais Royal

R. du Louvre

Blvd. de Sébastopol

R. de Turbigo

Pl. de la République

Av. de la République

Cimetière du Pere Lachaise

Louvre

R. Rambuteau

Beaubourg

MARAIS

Blvd. Beaumarchais

Blvd. Richard Lenoir

Blvd. Voltaire

Blvd. de Ménilmontant

Av. Philippe Auguste

PORTE DE MONTREUIL

Hôtel de Ville

R. de Rivoli

Pl. des Vosges

Ile de la Cité

Notre Dame

Ile St-Louis

Pl. de la Bastille

R. du Faubourg St-Antoine

Rollin

St-Germain

Palais du Luxembourg

R. Monge

Av. Ledru

PORTE DE VINCENNES

Cours de Vincennes

Pl. de la Nation

Jardin du Luxembourg

Sorbonne

Panthéon

Blvd. Diderot

Av. Daumesnil

PORTE DE ST-MANDÉ

Blvd. St-Michel

R. Gay Lussac

Gare d'Austerlitz

Gare de Lyon

Blvd. de Bercy

Pl. Félix Eboué

Blvd. St-Marcel

Blvd. de l'Hôpital

R. de Dijon

PORTE DE PICPUS

Parc Zoologique

Blvd. Arago

Av. des Gobelins

Blvd. de la Gare

R. de Tolbiac

Quai de Bercy

Seine

Quai de la Gare

PORTE DE CHARENTON

Bois de Vincennes

Blvd. St-Jacques

Blvd. A. Blanqui

Pl. d'Italie

PORTE DE BERCY

R. d'Alésia

R. Bobilot

Av. de Choisy

Av. d'Italie

Av. d'Ivry

Blvd. de Masséna

R. de Paris

rdan

Blvd. Kellerman

IVRY-SUR-SEINE

PORTE D'ITALIE

PORTE D'IVRY

GENTILLY

PORTE DE CHOISY

Paris Arrondissements

ST. OUEN

CLICHY

COURBEVOIE

LEVALLOIS-PERRET

Blvd. Berthier

Av. de Clichy

Av. de St. Ouen

LA DEFENSE

Pt. de Neuilly

Av. Charles de Gaulle

NEUILLY-SUR-SEINE

17e

Av. de Villiers

Blvd. des Batignolles

Blvd. Bessières

R. d'Amsterdam

Blv

Av. de Wagram

Blvd. de Courcelles

Parc Monceau

Gare St-Lazare

Av. de la Grande Armée

Blvd. Friedland

Blvd.

Haussmann

Arc de Triomphe

Av. des Champs

8e

La Madeleine

Opéra

Av. Foch

Av. Kléber

Av. Marceau

Av. George V

-Elysées

Av. F. D. Roosevelt

Pl. Vendôme

Av. Victor Hugo

Pl. de la Concorde

R. de Rivoli

Bois de Boulogne

Pl. du Trocadéro

Av. du Pres. Wilson

Jardin des Tuileries

Quai d'Orsay

Palais de Chaillot

Eiffel Tower

Av. de la Bourdonnais

7e

16e

PASSY

Av. du Pres. Kennedy

Av. de Suffren

Av. de Breteuil

Hôtel des Invalides

Blvd.

Blvd. de Grenelle

Av. du Général Sarrail

Blvd. Murat

Blvd. Exelmans

AUTEUIL

R. de Sèvres

Blvd. Raspail

6e

Blvd. Exelmans

Av. Emile Zola

R. de la Convention

R. Lecourbe

R. de Vaugirard

Blvd. du Montparnass

Av. F. Faure

15e

R. de Vaugirard

Gare Montparnasse

Blvd. Victor

R. de Vaugirard

MONTPARNASSE

Blvd. Galleni

R. Ernest Renan

R. d'Alésia

14e

Av. du Maine

Av. du Gl. Leclerc

Blvd. Lefebvre

Blvd. Brune

Blvd.

Av. Victor Cresson

VANVES

ISSY-LES-MOULINEAUX

MONTROUGE

World Time Zones

+12 +13 -9 -4 -3

-10 -7 -5 -4 -3:30

-11 -8 -6

-10

+11

+12

-4

-5

-4 -3

-5

-4

-3

-3

International Date Line

MONDAY SUNDAY

Clock positions across the top

| +11 | +12 - | -11 | -10 | -9 | -8 | -7 | -6 | -5 | -4 | -3 | -2 |

Numbers below vertical bands relate each zone to Greenwich Mean Time (0 hrs.).
Local times frequently differ from these general indications,
as indicated by light-face numbers on map.

Algiers, **29**	Berlin, **34**	Delhi, **48**	Istanbul, **40**
Anchorage, **3**	Bogotá, **19**	Denver, **8**	Jerusalem, **42**
Athens, **41**	Budapest, **37**	Djakarta, **53**	Johannesburg, **44**
Auckland, **1**	Buenos Aires, **24**	Dublin, **26**	Lima, **20**
Baghdad, **46**	Caracas, **22**	Edmonton, **7**	Lisbon, **28**
Bangkok, **50**	Chicago, **9**	Hong Kong, **56**	London (Greenwich), **27**
Beijing, **54**	Copenhagen, **33**	Honolulu, **2**	Los Angeles, **6**
	Dallas, **10**		Madrid, **38**
			Manila, **57**

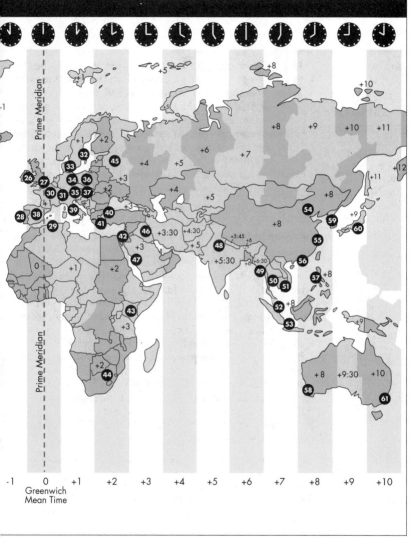

Introduction

*By John G.
Morris*

*John G. Morris
has worked as a
journalist for
major American
newspapers and
magazines—the*
Washington Post,
The New York
Times, Life,
Ladies' Home
Journal, *and*
National
Geographic. *He
now contributes
regularly to the*
International
Herald Tribune.

I t is often said that Paris isn't what it used to be. Of
course not. When I first came to Paris in 1944, there was
still shooting in the streets. I looked out on the sleepy
city from a balcony of the Hôtel Scribe, early on a September morning, and the air was heavy with suspense. Paris
had just emerged from 50 months of German occupation.
There was an ominous, audible rumble of war to the north
and east. During the night there had been occasional small-
arms fire, as the *résistance* rounded up German soldiers
still in hiding—and settled scores with their collaborators.

I had checked into the Scribe, headquarters for Allied war
correspondents, in the middle of the night, after hitching
rides in jeeps and command cars all the way from Normandy. My mission was to help *Life* magazine reestablish a Paris bureau. I had never been in Paris before, and my French
was strictly from high school. How was I to manage in the
vast, unfamiliar, and malfunctioning city? *Life* photographer Robert Capa, with whom I had shared both perilous
and frivolous moments in Normandy, came to my rescue.
At breakfast he said, "I have a French friend who will show
you around, a photographer named Henri Cartier-Bresson.
He's been living underground in Paris ever since he escaped
from a German prison camp. He went to Oxford, so I think
you'll understand him." At the door of the Scribe, I was in-
troduced to a slight, blue-eyed young man, shy but friendly.
He held a bicycle with one hand, his pants clipped to avoid
the gears; with the other he greeted me. Certainly, Paris
isn't what it used to be.

These days I can sit in a café with a *crème* or a *thé au citron*,
reading the paper to the tinkling musical background of the
pinball machine. I can sit there for hours, in the sun or
shade, and the waiter will not even fidget. I look up and
watch the people around me. Just to my left a couple is making love across the table, elbows firmly planted and hands
clasped together, faces virtually invisible. The young man
over there is obviously waiting for someone. He alternates
coffee and cigarettes. Finally she comes, hands him a little
note, and leaves without a word. What has happened between them? The old man on the right orders tea with milk.
He unwraps the sugar cube, touches it to his tongue, wraps
it again, and puts it in his pocket. How long will it last him?
A strolling *accordéoniste* comes by, plays just enough not to
become a nuisance, passes the hat, and quietly goes on . . .
followed by a girl selling red roses and, a bit later, by a
bare-chested black man who swallows flaming swords.

You have heard it said that "Paris would be great if it
weren't for the Parisians." If a Frenchman says it, it means

that he is determined to be provincial. But if it comes from a foreigner, it probably means that he or she has had an unfortunate linguistic encounter. It takes a certain nerve to try out one's French, no matter one's level. A former *New York Times* Paris bureau chief told me he got by only because his French was "audacious." Many foreigners, and I am one, are afraid of being laughed at. The cure for this is to make a faux pas so ridiculous that you can tell it on yourself. A young photographer friend of mine, for example, was trying to tell some French friends about his first date with a girl of good family and prim reputation. He thought he was telling them that he had kissed her good night—the polite peck. Instead, he was saying that he had bedded her the first night. They were impressed but incredulous.

My own greatest blooper came in our local mom-and-pop produce store. We had noticed that it was possible to order a spit-roasted chicken, and one Sunday morning I was dispatched to place such an order. After rehearsing my speech, I pushed my way past the line of fruit-and-vegetable customers to the rear of the shop and said, *"Madame, je voudrais commander un chien rôti"* (I should like to order a roast dog). With perfect *politesse* she replied, *"Un chien rôti?"* Immediately realizing what I had said, I broke up—as did the entire line of customers. If only I had had the presence to continue, *"Mais oui, madame, vous savez bien que les Américains aiment les hot dogs"* (Of course, madame, you know very well that we Americans love hot dogs!).

Paris is the city where, once you are known, shopkeepers greet you coming and going and proprietors shake your hand as you leave their restaurants. It is the city where bus drivers may reopen the door for you if you come on the run, and where bellmen are sometimes too proud to linger for a tip.

Not that Parisians are perfect. There are the usual shady characters who populate our urbanized world. There are pickpockets, just to make you feel at home. *En garde!* Weapons are not often used in Paris crime, but thieves can be ingenious. A friend from Manhattan was the victim of a classic ploy. Sensing that his wallet had been lifted while he was standing in awe of Notre Dame, he whirled on the probable thief, a girl of about 12. To attest her innocence, she lifted her dress, revealing a totally naked brown body. Our friend was too flustered to pursue the matter further.

Paris is not France, but France would be unimaginable without Paris. Here, past and present coexist, sometimes comfortably, sometimes uneasily. Children play house in the playground of the Cluny museum, on the spot where Romans took their leisure in baths 100 meters long.

Called Lutetia by the Romans but renamed for the Parisii, a Celtic tribe, Paris has been a settlement on the Seine for more than two millennia. Blood has flowed here as constantly as the river. Crossing the place de la Concorde, one still shivers at the thought of the 1,344 persons beheaded there by the guillotine, including King Louis XVI and Marie Antoinette. Tourists flock to the Sacré-Coeur, at once the ugliest and boldest church in Paris. It stands on a hill named Montmartre, for the Christian martyrs; one of them, Saint Denis, is said to have carried his severed head in his hands as he walked north out of the city in the third century. Joan of Arc was wounded in Paris in 1429, but it was another woman, Geneviève, a shepherdess from Nanterre, who became the special saint of Paris, having rallied the city against Attila the Hun. Today, students at the Sorbonne study in a reading room as long as a football field and high enough for a dropkick, in the library of her name. A department store, La Samaritaine, backs up against the church of St-Germain l'Auxerrois, from whose tower bells rang on the night of August 24, 1572, to signal the prearranged massacre of 3,000 Huguenots. A short walk away, at a Jewish restaurant called Goldenberg's in the heart of the Marais district, a mini-massacre, on August 9, 1982, took the lives of six people at lunchtime.

If the French have a knack of putting the past into perspective (they take their time about naming streets for statesmen; artists and scientists have a better chance), they nevertheless have a problem with the turbulent present. In Paris, the tourist may have an opportunity not only to observe history but also to participate in it. Scarcely a month goes by without a *manifestation* (demonstration) of some kind, and sometimes they get out of hand. The city, too, has its share of terrorist activities—the occasional bomb or an Algerian remembering past wrongs, the normal *va-et-vient* of European life.

For those of us who lived through World War II, Paris is full of poignancy. Around the corner from where I used to live on the Ile St-Louis, there is a large apartment house. A plaque near the front door says: "*A la mémoire des 112 habitants de cette maison dont 40 petits enfants deportés et morts dans les camps allemands en 1942*" (To the memory of 112 residents of this building, of whom 40 were little children, deported to and died in German camps in 1942). On April 28, the National Day of the Deportation, a silent little parade forms at the synagogue just across from here, in the Marais. With bared heads, muffled drums, and tricolored sashes, the marchers—no doubt including relatives of those 112 residents—file across to the Ile de la Cité, on whose point, facing up the Seine, is the Memorial to the Deported. There the Unknown Deportee sleeps in a bed of stone as the river flows silently by on both sides. It is a moving and little-visited shrine, only a stone's throw from the gardens of Notre Dame.

Only London and Rome can even come close to holding such treasures of the past as does Paris. Hitler, furious with the retreat of his forces in World War II, ordered the city burned, but his own commander failed him and Allied forces swept in. To sense the grandeur that would have been lost, try sitting on a bench above the Seine on the pedestrian Pont des Arts, which offers a kind of gracious scaffolding over the river. Face downstream and set your watch by the clock of the Institut Français on the Left Bank as the rays of the sun, setting into the muddy green river, gild the towers of the Louvre on your right. Or look upstream at the Pont Neuf as it crosses the prow of the Ile de la Cité. Beyond but out of sight is the Ile St-Louis, perhaps the world's most perfect village, standing almost exactly as it began—a real estate development built on pastures of the 17th century.

Paris has a museum for every period and taste. Parisians argue museums as Americans fight over baseball teams. They tend either to loathe or love the Beaubourg, its red and blue insides exposed like an oil refinery. And unlike almost any other city, Paris's artistic life is closely tied to its political realities. The battle royal between Jacques Chirac (in his role as mayor) and President François Mitterrand's cultural impresario of the early 1980s, Jack Lang, raged up and down the avenues and boulevards, and the evidence of their struggle is still around, notably in the Buren Pillars at the Palais-Royal. The exciting Musée d'Orsay is dedicated to the art of the period 1848–1914 and houses the great collection of Impressionists that was formerly in the Jeu de Paume.

I first entered the Louvre in 1944, only to find it virtually empty. The foresighted French had evacuated and hidden most of the great masterpieces at the onset of war. All that remained of the *Mona Lisa* was a chalk scrawl to indicate its normal hanging place. Nevertheless, the Grande Galérie of the Louvre was just as staggering a spectacle as it is today. The Louvre is a palace so vast that one can make a fresh discovery on every visit.

Great exhibitions are not limited to museums. The Grand Palais, a marvel of turn-of-the-century iron and glass construction, and its little neighbor of the same vintage, the Petit Palais, occasionally attract lines that stretch far down avenue Winston Churchill. As if those are not enough, the city has built another huge complex, a kind of fairground of halls, playgrounds, and theaters (one of which is enclosed in a shining sphere) on the site of the former slaughterhouses of La Villette, on the city's outskirts.

There are another dozen or so art museums. The Musée Guimet has Oriental art; the Marmottan is a mansion containing Monets and others. Museums have been created in the studios of Rodin, Delacroix, and Brancusi. Paris has major museums of anthropology, natural history, history, and science, and smaller ones dealing with everything from advertising and bread to urban transport and wine. The Musée Grévin, the waxworks museum on the boulevard Montmartre and in the Forum des Halles, is perhaps the most amusing of all.

If you're a nosy type, one who loves to poke and peek, a certain amount of respectful audacity will take you far in Paris. Instead of taking the guided tour at the Bourse, or stock exchange, you can try to talk your way into a look at the trading floor. Nearby, at the Bibliothèque Nationale, without a reader's card, you can look into the main reading room or the equally impressive periodicals room. For lawyers, a place of interest is the Palais de Justice, with courtrooms where black-robed judges and *avocats* hear and plead cases all day long. Just walking the halls there is a spectacle; one can tiptoe into courts in session. In the waiting rooms of the nearby Préfecture de Police, you will find scenes of poverty and desperation reminiscent of Daumier.

Notre Dame is just a bit farther; for your first visit, try entering through the north portal instead of through the nave, as most tourists do. You will then immediately confront the most glorious of the three rose windows. Stay for a mass or an organ concert.

Finally, if you are fascinated by the celebration of life eternal, as are the Catholic French, you can quietly visit Père Lachaise, one of the world's most famous cemeteries and well worth seeing for its exotic and nostalgic monuments to the *célèbres*.

Some come to Paris just to eat. They come laden with research, with starred lists, credit cards, and calculated appetites. Many have done their homework well, with one or more of the useful books that devote themselves to mouth-watering descriptions of Parisian delicacies. My own approach is more casual; to my way of thinking, it's rather difficult to get a *bad* meal in Paris.

The sheer profusion of places to eat in Paris is staggering. There are, for example, 12,000 places where one can get a cup of tea or coffee—*or* a glass of wine or beer—a convenience that is one of the finer attributes of French civilization. I go sometimes by hearsay, sometimes by looks, often by ambience. The *carte* posted at the door offers further clues, especially as to price. The same rules apply in Paris as elsewhere: One tends to pay for name and fame. Some places seem so cheap that one gets suspicious, but there is often more fun in a bistro than in an elegant two-star.

The French Government Tourist Office, that most helpful, overworked institution on the Champs-Elysées near the Arc de Triomphe, offers a listing of 600 Paris restaurants. Like many of the good things in Paris, it is free—and in English. In a line or two, it charts 10 attributes of each place. The least snobbish of restaurant guides, it gives equal linage to the most expensive restaurants and the cheapest (several in Paris offer menus of 50 francs or less). Among specialties, you will find not only pig's feet béarnaise but also milkshakes, macrobiotic food, stuffed carp, "60 kinds of crêpe," and "exotic sherbets," not to mention the conventional gourmet dishes. As for ambience, you can dine in a cellar or in a high rise, in a former stable or in a former monastery. You may have the elegant surroundings of Louis XV or the Second Empire, the bustle of a railroad station, or the calm of a farmhouse. You may look out on the Louvre, on the Tour Eiffel, or on Notre Dame. Or you may look up at them as you glide along aboard a Bateau Mouche *au restaurant*. For entertainment with dinner, you can have flamenco or karaoke, polkas or cancan. For music, it can be violins, accordions, or oompah bands. The listed restaurants represent only a small fraction of what Paris has to offer when it comes to food and drink. In addition, there are the thousands of wine bars, bistros, and cafés. It's fun to make your own discoveries. At cafés and wine bars, and at most brasseries, no reservations are required. If the table has no tablecloth, you can normally just sit down. Your best chance of getting a table, if you have not called ahead, is to go early, but not before 7:30 PM or you will find the staff eating. Go a little before 8, when the first diners arrive. Some restaurants take credit cards, and almost any business establishment in Paris will take a Eurocheck in francs. Don't hurry, and when you leave, shake hands with the proprietor.

Next to dining, entertainment is the most appealing industry of Paris. The week begins on Wednesday with the appearance of *Pariscope*, one of the three weekly bibles for those who go out often. A typical issue will list the 300 films that play the 384 cinemas in Paris and environs in an average week. That total includes 98 revivals, but not the films playing in the 14 film festivals or the 43 films screened free at the film libraries of the subsidized Beaubourg and Palais de Chaillot, or the 23 "special screenings" of various kinds.

In this same typical week, there are 18 works being performed in the 10 publicly supported theaters (Comédie Française, the Opéra, etc.). Another 101 theatrical pieces are being performed on 76 commercial stages, including works by Shakespeare, Strindberg, Brecht, Aristophanes, Chekhov, Sartre, Neil Simon, and Sam Shepard—most, but not all, in French. Another 160 cafés, cabarets, music halls, discos, and nightclubs offer programs ranging from political satire to striptease, New Orleans jazz, and the traditional cancan. Churches often offer chamber music. In this typical week, 96 concerts and 13 ballets are performed.

There is an easy informality about attending Paris theaters. Many are small and intimate. One can normally get tickets at the last minute, except for hit shows, and prices are low. Take one night at the Opéra. Early one New Year's Eve, Nureyev was dancing. We didn't bother to call; we simply went to the box office 10 minutes before curtain time. "What do you have?" I asked. "Standing room, no view, 20 francs," was the quick reply. We bought two, and climbed the onyx and marble staircase under the chandeliered dome with its ceiling painted by Chagall. Checking our coats, we rented opera glasses and were ushered to a box right over the stage. For the first act, we stood, looking down over the shoulders of those in the first row. At the interval, hoping to do better, we climbed to the Opéra's top circle. There we found a series of little pie-shaped loges; one was open and empty—save for one chair. My wife planted herself there while I scavenged for another. Then, after a quick trip to the bar for a demi of champagne and two glasses, we enjoyed the second and third acts with a full view of the stage. The *soirée* in our little aerie had cost the equivalent of $12 for the evening. "Paris is a moveable feast."

Paris is the home of the exile. It is here that Chopin came to compose, Picasso to paint, Joyce to write *Ulysses*. In Paris, even more than in London and New York, it is possible to live as a citizen of the world. It is almost possible to forget one's race, one's religion, almost possible to believe all men are brothers. Burnoose and sari, blue jeans and haute couture walk side by side. Gallic cynicism and *la vie en rose* go together. Victor Hugo aptly stated the message of Paris:

Cities are bibles of stone. This city possesses no single dome, roof, or pavement that does not convey some message of alliance and of union, and that does not offer some lesson, example, or advice. Let the people of all the world come to this prodigious alphabet of monuments, of tombs, and of trophies to learn peace and to unlearn the meaning of hatred. Let them be confident. For Paris has proven itself. To have once been Lutèce and to have become Paris—what could be a more magnificent symbol! To have been mud and to have become spirit!

1 Essential Information

Before You Go

Government Tourist Offices

Contact the French Government Tourist Office for free information.

In the United States 610 5th Ave., New York, NY 10020, tel. 212/315–0888 or 212/757–1125; 645 N. Michigan Ave., Chicago, IL 60611, tel. 312/337–6301; 2305 Cedar Springs Rd., Dallas, TX 75201, tel. 214/720–4010; 9401 Wilshire Blvd., Beverly Hills, CA 90212, tel. 213/271–6665; 1 Hallidie Plaza, Suite 250, San Francisco, CA 94102, tel. 415/986–4174.

In Canada 1981 McGill College Ave., Suite 490, Montreal, Quebec H3A 2W9, tel. 514/288–4264; 1 Dundas St. W, Suite 2405, Box 8, Toronto, Ontario M5G 1Z3, tel. 416/593–4723.

In the United Kingdom 178 Piccadilly, London W1V 0AL, tel. 071/629–1272.

Tours and Packages

Should you buy your travel arrangements packaged or do it yourself? There are advantages either way. Buying packaged arrangements saves you money, particularly if you can find a program that includes exactly the features you want. You also get a pretty good idea of what your trip will cost from the outset. Generally, two types of packaged travel arrangements are available. **Escorted tours** are one option if you don't mind having limited free time and traveling with strangers. Escorted tours are most often via motorcoach, with a tour director in charge. Your baggage is handled, your time rigorously scheduled, and most meals planned. Escorted tours are therefore the most hassle-free way to see a destination, as well as generally the least expensive. **Independent packages** allow plenty of flexibility. They generally include airline travel and hotels, with certain options available, such as sightseeing, car rental, and excursions. Independent packages are usually more expensive than escorted tours, but your time is your own.

While you can book directly through tour operators, you will pay no more to go through a travel agent, who will be able to tell you about tours and packages from a number of operators. Whatever program you ultimately choose, be sure to find out exactly what is included: taxes, tips, transfers, meals, baggage handling, ground transportation, entertainment, excursions, sports or recreation (and rental equipment if necessary). Ask about the level of hotel used, its location, the size of its rooms, the kind of beds, and its facilities and amenities, such as pool, room service, or programs for children. Find out the operator's cancellation penalties. Nearly everyone charges them, and the only way to avoid them is to buy trip-cancellation insurance (*see* Insurance, *below*). Also ask about the single supplement, a surcharge assessed to solo travelers. Some operators do not make you pay it if you agree to be matched up with a roommate of the same sex, even if one is not found by departure time. Remember that a program that has features you won't use may not be the most cost-wise choice.

Fully Escorted Tours Escorted tours are usually sold in three categories: deluxe, first-class, and tourist or budget class. The most important differences are the price, of course, and the level of accommodations. Some operators specialize in one category, while others offer a range. Programs that include Paris generally spend two nights and only one full day in Paris; most are first-class, among them **American Express Vacations** (300 Pinnacle Way, Norcross, GA 30093, tel. 800/241–1700), **Globus-Gateway** (95-25 Queens Blvd., Rego Park, NY 11374, tel. 800/221–0090 or 718/268–7000), **Olson-Travelworld** (Box 10066, Manhattan Beach, CA 90226, tel. 800/421–5785 or 310/546–8400), and **Trafalgar Tours** (21 E. 26th St., New York, NY 10010, tel. 800/854–0103 or 212/689–8977).

Most itineraries are jam-packed with sightseeing, so you see a lot in a short amount of time (usually one place per day). To judge just how fast-paced the tour is, review the itinerary carefully. If you are in a different hotel each night, you will be getting up early each day to head out, travel to your next destination, do some sightseeing, have dinner, and go to bed, then you'll start all over again. If you want some free time, make sure it's mentioned in the tour brochure; if you want to be escorted to every meal, confirm that any tour you consider does that. Also, when comparing programs, be sure to find out if the motorcoach is air-conditioned and has a restroom on board. Make your selection based on price and stops on the itinerary.

Independent Packages Independent packages, which travel agents call FITs (for foreign independent travel), are offered by airlines, tour operators who may also do escorted programs, and any number of other companies from large, established firms to small, new entrepreneurs. Their programs come in a wide range of prices based on levels of luxury and options—in addition to hotel and airfare, sightseeing, car rental, transfers, admission to local attractions, and other extras. The **French Experience** (370 Lexington Ave., New York, NY 10017, tel. 212/986–1115), has a wide selection of Paris programs. Airline packages, typically including hotel, round-trip airfare, and limited sightseeing, are available through **Air France** (tel. 800/237–2747), **American Airlines Fly AAway Vacations** (tel. 800/321–2121), **Continental Airlines' Grand Destinations** (tel. 800/634–5555), and **Delta Dream Vacations** (tel. 800/328–6877). **Globus-Gateway** and **Trafalgar Tours** (*see above*) offer Paris and London–Paris programs with accommodations, airfare, and some sightseeing.

When to Go

The major tourist season in France stretches from Easter to mid-September, but Paris has much to offer at every season. Paris in the early spring can be disappointingly damp; June is delightful, with good weather and plenty of cultural and other attractions. July and August can be sultry and dusty. Moreover, many restaurants, theaters, and small shops close for at least four weeks in summer.

September is ideal. Cultural life revives after the summer break and sunny weather often continues through the first half of October. The ballet and theater are in full swing in November, but the weather is part wet-and-cold, part bright-and-sunny.

December is dominated by the *fêtes de fin d'année* (end-of-year festivities), with splendid displays in food shops and restaurants and a busy theater, ballet, and opera season into January.

February and March are the worst months, weatherwise, but with the coming of Easter, Paris starts looking beautiful again.

Climate What follow are the average daily maximum and minimum temperatures for Paris.

Jan.	43F	6C	May	68F	20C	Sept.	70F	21C
	34	1		49	10		53	12
Feb.	45F	7C	June	73F	23C	Oct.	60F	16C
	34	1		55	13		46	8
Mar.	54F	12C	July	76F	25C	Nov.	50F	10C
	39	4		58	14		40	5
Apr.	60F	16C	Aug.	75F	24C	Dec.	44F	7C
	43	6		58	14		36	2

Information Sources For current weather conditions for cities in the United States and abroad, plus the local time and helpful travel tips, call the **Weather Channel Connection** (tel. 900/WEATHER; 95¢ per minute) from a touch-tone phone.

National Holidays (1993) With 11 national holidays (*jours feriés*) and five weeks of paid vacation, the French have their share of repose. In May there is a holiday nearly every week, so be prepared for stores, banks, and museums to shut their doors for days at a time. Bastille Day (July 14) is observed in true French form, with an annual military parade down the Champs-Elysées and a fireworks display at the Eiffel Tower.

January 1 (New Year's Day); April 3 (Easter Monday); May 1 (Labor Day); May 8 (VE Day); May 12 (Ascension); May 23 (Pentecost Monday); July 14 (Bastille Day); August 15 (Assumption); November 1 (All Saints); November 11 (Armistice); December 25 (Christmas).

Festivals and Seasonal Events

Top seasonal events in Paris include the French Open Tennis Championships in May, the Festival du Marais in June through July, July's Bastille Day, the Festival Estival musical event in the summer, and the September Autumn Festival.

Feb. **Foire à la Feraille de Paris** is an antiques and bric-a-brac fair held in the Parc Floral de Paris and the Bois de Vincennes in the 12th arrondissement.

Mar. **Salon du Livre,** the international book exposition, is held annually at the Grand Palais at the end of the month.

Late Mar.–Apr. The **Prix du Président de la République** takes place at the Auteuil Racecourse.

Apr.–late Oct. The **Son et Lumière des Invalides** is a sound and light show in the courtyard of the Hôtel des Invalides; there are separate English and French versions.

May–late Sept. **Grandes Eaux Musicales** is a fountain display at the Château de Versailles. Sundays only.

Mid-May **International Marathon of Paris** leaves from the place de la Concorde and ends at the Château de Vincennes.

Late May– early June **Festival de Jazz de Boulogne-Billancourt** attracts big names and varied styles of jazz in the suburbs of Boulogne-Billancourt. Some jazz movies, too.

Late May– early June	**French Open Tennis Championships** take place at Roland-Garros Stadium.
Mid-June–mid-July	**Festival du Marais** features everything from music to dance to theater in the churches and historic mansions of the Marais.(Tickets: 44 rue François-Miron, 4e, tel. 48–87–60–08.)
June	**Paris Air Show,** which takes place in odd-numbered years only, is a display of old and new planes and an update on worldwide technological developments in the aeronautical industry, at Le Bourget Airport.
Mid-June	**Grand Steeplechase de Paris** is a popular horse race at Auteuil Racecourse. The **Course des Garçons de Café** is an entertaining race through the streets of Paris by waiters bearing full trays of drinks. It begins and ends at the Hôtel de Ville.
June 21	**Fête de la Musique de Paris** celebrates the summer solstice with parades, street theater, and live bands throughout the city.
Late June	**Grand Prix de Paris,** a major test for three-year-old horses, isheld at Longchamp Racecourse.
July 14	**Bastille Day** celebrates the storming of the Bastille prison in 1789. This national holiday is commemorated throughout France. In Paris, there's a military parade along the Champs-Elysées in the morning and fireworks at night above Trocadéro.
Mid-July– late Sept.	**Festival Estival of Paris** features classical music concerts in churches, museums, and concert halls throughout the city. (Tickets: 20 rue Geoffroy-l'Asnier, 4e, tel. 48–04–98–01.)
Late July	**Tour de France,** the world's leading bicycle race, finishes on the Champs-Elysées.
Late July– end Aug.	**Musique en l'Ile** is a series of concerts held in the picturesque 17th-century Eglise St-Louis on the Ile St-Louis. (Tel. 45–23–18–25 for details.)
Mid-Sept.– end Dec.	**Festival d'Automne,** with concerts, plays, dance, and exhibitions throughout Paris. (Tickets: 156 rue de Rivoli, 1er, tel. 42–96–96–94.)
Early Oct.	**Prix de l'Arc de Triomphe,** one of Europe's top horse races, takes place at Longchamp Racecourse. The **Fêtes des Vendanges,** held the first Saturday of the month, marks the grape harvest in the Montmartre Vineyard, at the corner of rue des Saules and rue St-Vincent.
Oct.	**Paris Motor Show** (even-numbered years only) features the latest developments in the international automobile industry.
Mid-Oct.–Early Nov.	**Festival de Jazz de Paris** is a two-week celebration that includes lots of big-name jazz artists. (Tel. 47–83–33–58 for information.)
Oct.–Nov.	**Festival d'Art Sacré** features concerts and exhibitions held in churches throughout the city. (Tel. 42–77–92–26 for information.)
Nov. 11	**Armistice Day** ceremonies at the Arc de Triomphe include a military parade down the Champs-Elysées.
Dec.	**Christmas** in Paris is highlighted by illuminations throughout the city, particularly on the Champs-Elysées, avenue Montaigne, and boulevard Haussmann.

What to Pack

Clothing   Pack light: Baggage carts are scarce at airports, and luggage restrictions on international flights are tight. What you pack depends more on the time of year than on any particular dress code. It can rain a fair amount in Paris, even in the summer, so consider bringing a raincoat and umbrella. Otherwise, pack as you would for a major American city: formal clothes for formal restaurants and nightclubs, casual clothes elsewhere. Jeans are as popular in Paris as anywhere and are perfectly acceptable for sightseeing and informal dining. However, a jeans-and-sneakers outfit will raise eyebrows at the theater, at expensive restaurants, and when visiting French families. Note that men and women wearing shorts will not be allowed in many churches and cathedrals.

Wear sturdy walking shoes for sightseeing: Paris is full of cobblestone streets, and many historic buildings are surrounded by gravel paths. To protect yourself against purse snatchers and pickpockets, take a handbag with long straps that you can sling across your body, bandolier-style, with a zippered compartment for your money and passport—French law requires that you carry identification at all times.

Miscellaneous   If you have a health problem that requires you to take a prescription drug, pack enough to last the duration of the trip or have your doctor write a prescription using the drug's generic name, as brand names vary widely from country to country. If you're staying in budget hotels, take along small bars of soap. And don't forget to pack a list of the addresses of offices that supply refunds for lost or stolen traveler's checks.

Luggage *Regulations*   Free baggage allowances on an airline depend on the airline, the route, and the class of your ticket. In general, on domestic flights and on international flights between the United States and foreign destinations, you are entitled to check two bags—neither exceeding 62 inches, or 158 centimeters (length + width + height), or weighing more than 70 pounds (32 kilograms). A third piece may be brought aboard as a carryon; its total dimensions are generally limited to less than 45 inches (114 centimeters), so it will fit easily under the seat in front of you or in the overhead compartment. There are variations, so ask in advance. The single rule, a Federal Aviation Administration safety regulation that pertains to carry-on baggage on U.S. airlines, requires only that carryons be properly stowed and allows the airline to limit allowances and tailor them to different aircraft and operational conditions. Charges for excess, oversize, or overweight pieces vary, so inquire before you pack.

If you are flying between two foreign destinations, note that baggage allowances may be determined not by the piece method but by the weight method, which generally allows 88 pounds (40 kilograms) of luggage in first class, 66 pounds (30 kilograms) in business class, and 44 pounds (20 kilograms) in economy. If your flight between two cities abroad *connects* with your transatlantic or transpacific flight, the piece method still applies.

Safeguarding Your Luggage   Before leaving home, itemize your bags' contents and their worth; this list will help you estimate the extent of your loss if your bags go astray. To minimize that risk, tag them inside and out with your name, address, and phone number. (If you use your home address, cover it so that potential thieves can't see it.) At check-in, make sure that the tag attached by baggage handlers bears the correct three-letter code for your destination. If your bags do not arrive with you, or if you detect damage, do not leave the airport until you've filed a written report with the airline.

Electricity The electrical current in Paris is 220 volts, 50 cycles alternating current (AC); the United States runs on 110-volt, 60-cycle AC current. Unlike wall outlets in the United States, which accept plugs with two flat prongs, outlets in France take plugs with two round prongs.

Adapters, To plug in U.S.-made appliances abroad, you'll need an adapter
Converters, plug. To reduce the voltage entering the appliance from 220 to
Transformers 110 volts, you'll also need a converter, unless it is a dual-voltage appliance, made for travel. There are converters for high-wattage appliances (such as hair dryers), low-wattage items (such as electric toothbrushes and razors), and combination models. Hotels sometimes have outlets marked "For Shavers Only" near the sink; these are 110-volt outlets for low-wattage appliances; don't use them for a high-wattage appliance. If you're traveling with a laptop computer, especially an older one, you may need a transformer—a type of converter used with electronic-circuitry products. Newer laptop computers are auto-sensing, operating equally well on 110 and 220 volts (so you need only the appropriate adapter plug).

Taking Money Abroad

Traveler's Checks The most widely recognized are **American Express, Barclay's, Thomas Cook,** and those issued by major banks such as **Citibank** and **Bank of America.** American Express also issues *Traveler's Cheques for Two*, which can be signed and used by you or your traveling companion. Some checks are free; usually the issuing company or the bank at which you make your purchase charges 1% of the checks' face value as a fee. Be sure to buy a few checks in small denominations to cash toward the end of your trip, when you don't want to be left with more foreign currency than you can spend. Always record the numbers of checks as you spend them, and keep this list separate from the checks.

Currency Banks and bank-operated exchange booths at airports and rail-
Exchange road stations are usually the best places to change money. Hotels, stores, and privately run exchange firms typically offer less favorable rates.

Before your trip, pay attention to how the dollar is doing vis-à-vis French currency. If the dollar is losing strength, try to pay as many travel bills as possible in advance, especially the big ones. If it is getting stronger, pay for costly items overseas, and use your credit card whenever possible—you'll come out ahead, whether the exchange rate at which your purchase is calculated is the one in effect the day the vendor's bank abroad processes the charge, or the one prevailing on the day the charge company's service center processes it at home.

To avoid lines at airport currency-exchange booths, arrive in France with a small amount of the local currency already in your pocket—a so-called tip pack. **Thomas Cook Currency Ser-**

vices (630 5th Ave., New York, NY 10111, tel. 212/757–6915) supplies foreign currency by mail.

Getting Money from Home

Cash Machines   Automated-teller machines (ATMs) are proliferating; many are tied to international networks such as **Cirrus** and **Plus.** You can use your bank card at ATMs away from home to withdraw money from your account and get cash advances on a credit-card account (providing your card has been programmed with a personal identification number, or PIN). Check in advance on limits on withdrawals and cash advances within specified periods. Ask whether your bank-card or credit-card PIN number will need to be reprogrammed for use in the area you'll be visiting—a possibility if the number has more than four digits. Remember that you pay interest on cash advances from the time you get your money from ATMs just as you do from tellers. And note that, although transaction fees for ATM withdrawals abroad will probably be higher than fees for withdrawals at home, Cirrus and Plus exchange rates tend to be good.

Plan ahead. Though ATMs in Paris work pretty much the same way as in the United States, not all have English prompts. Learn the French equivalents for key words, such as *withdraw, how much?, amount, transaction, okay,* and *clear* before you go. Also obtain ATM locations and the names of affiliated cash-machine networks before departure. For specific foreign Cirrus locations, call 800/4–CIRRUS; for foreign Plus locations, consult the Plus directory at your local bank.

American Express Cardholder Services   The company's **Express Cash** system lets you withdraw cash and/or traveler's checks from a worldwide network of 57,000 American Express dispensers and participating bank ATMs. You must *enroll first* (call 800/CASH–NOW for a form and allow two weeks for processing). Withdrawals are charged not to your card but to a designated bank account. You can withdraw up to $1,000 per seven-day period on the basic card, more if your card is gold or platinum. There is a 2% fee (minimum $2.50, maximum $10) for each cash transaction, and a 1% fee for traveler's checks (except for the platinum card), which are available only from American Express dispensers. At AmEx offices, cardholders can also cash personal checks for up to $1,000 in any seven-day period (21 days abroad); of this $200 can be in cash, more if available, with the balance paid in traveler's checks, for which all but platinum cardholders pay a 1% fee. Higher limits apply to the gold and platinum cards.

Wiring Money   You don't have to be a cardholder to send or receive an **American Express MoneyGram** for up to $10,000. To send one, go to an American Express MoneyGram agent, pay up to $1,000 with a credit card and anything over that in cash, and phone a transaction reference number to your intended recipient, who need only present identification and the reference number to the nearest MoneyGram agent to pick up the cash. There are MoneyGram agents in more than 60 countries (call 800/543–4080 for locations). Fees range from 5% to 10%, depending on the amount and how you pay. You can't use American Express, which is really a convenience card—only Discover, MasterCard, and Visa credit cards.

You can also use **Western Union.** To wire money, take either cash or a check to the nearest office. (Or you can order money sent by phone, using a credit card.) Fees are roughly 5%–10%. Money sent from the United States or Canada will be available for pick up at agent locations in Paris within minutes. (Note that once the money is in the system it can be picked up at *any* location. You don't have to miss your train waiting for it to arrive in City A, because if there's an agent in City B, where you're headed, you can pick it up there, too.) There are approximately 20,000 agents worldwide (call 800/325–6000 for locations).

French Currency

The unit of currency in France is the franc, which is divided into 100 centimes. The bills are 500, 200, 100, and 50 francs. Coins are 20, 10, 5, 2, and 1 francs and 50, 20, 10, and 5 centimes. At press time (mid-1993), the exchange rate was 5.2 francs to the dollar and 8.5 francs to the pound.

What It Will Cost

Inflation in France has continued to average a modest annual 3%–3½% increase in recent years.

As in most capital cities, life in Paris is more expensive than anywhere else in the country (except the Riviera). Yet, unlike, say, central London, Paris is a place where people live as well as work; Parisians, who shop and lunch locally, are not prepared to pay extravagant rates, and visitors who avoid the obvious tourist traps will not have to pay those rates, either.

Prices tend to reflect the standing of an area in the eyes of Parisians; much sought-after residential arrondissements such as the 7th, 16th, and 17th—of limited tourist interest—are far more expensive than the student-oriented, much-visited Latin Quarter. The tourist area where value for money is most difficult to find is the 8th arrondissement, on and around the Champs-Elysées. Places where you can be virtually certain to shop, eat, and stay without overpaying include the streets surrounding Montmartre (not the Butte, or hilltop, itself); the St-Michel/Sorbonne area on the Left Bank; the mazelike streets around the Halles and Marais in central Paris; and Bastille and eastern Paris.

Taxes All taxes must be included in affixed prices in France. Restaurant and hotel prices must by law include taxes and service charges: If these appear as additional items on your bill, you should complain. VAT (value added tax, known in France as TVA), at a standard rate of 18.6%, is included in the price of many goods, but foreigners are often entitled to a refund (*see* Shopping, Chapter 4).

Sample Costs A cup of coffee, standing at a bar, costs from 4 francs; if you sit, it will cost from 7 francs. A glass of beer costs from 6 francs standing at the bar and from 9 francs if you're seated; a soft drink costs between 6 francs and 10 francs. A ham sandwich will cost between 12 francs and 15 francs. Expect to pay 25–30 francs for a short taxi ride.

Passports and Visas

If your passport is lost or stolen abroad, report it immediately to the nearest embassy or consulate and to the local police. If you can provide the consular officer with the information contained in the passport, he or she will usually be able to issue you a new passport. For this reason, it is a good idea to keep a copy of the data page of your passport in a separate place, or to leave the passport number, date, and place of issuance with a relative or friend at home.

U.S. Citizens All U.S. citizens, even infants, need a valid passport to enter France for stays of up to 90 days.

You can pick up new and renewal application forms at any of the 13 U.S. Passport Agency offices and at some post offices and courthouses. Although passports are usually mailed within two weeks of your application's receipt, it's best to allow three weeks for delivery in low season, five weeks or more from April through summer. Call the Department of State Office of Passport Services' information line (1425 K St. NW, Washington, DC 20522, tel. 202/647-0518) for details.

Canadian Citizens Canadian citizens need a valid passport to enter France. Application forms are available at 23 regional passport offices as well as post offices and travel agencies. Whether applying for a first or subsequent passport, you must apply in person. Children under 16 may be included on a parent's passport but must have their own passport to travel alone. Passports are valid for five years and are usually mailed within two weeks of an application's receipt. For more information in English or French, call the passport office (tel. 514/283-2152).

U.K. Citizens Citizens of the United Kingdom need a valid passport to enter France. Applications for new and renewal passports are available from main post offices as well as at the six passport offices, located in Belfast, Glasgow, Liverpool, London, Newport, and Peterborough. You may apply in person at all passport offices, or by mail to all except the London office. Children under 16 may travel on a parent's passport when accompanying them. All passports are valid for 10 years. Allow a month for processing.

A British Visitor's Passport is valid for holidays and some business trips of up to three months to France. It can include both partners of a married couple. A British visitor's passport is valid for one year and will be issued on the same day that you apply. You must apply in person at a main post office.

Customs and Duties

On Arrival If you're coming from a European Community (EC) country, you may import duty free: (1) 300 cigarettes or 150 cigarillos or 75 cigars or 400 grams of tobacco; (2) 5 liters of table wine and, in addition, (a) 1.5 liters of alcohol over 22% volume (most spirits) or (b) 3 liters of alcohol under 22% volume (fortified or sparkling wine) or (c) 3 more liters of table wine; (3) 90 milliliters of perfume and 375 milliliters of toilet water; and (4) other goods to the value of 2,000 francs (400 francs for those under 15).

If you're coming from anywhere else, you may import duty free: (1) 200 cigarettes or 100 cigarillos or 50 cigars or 250 grams of tobacco (twice that if you live outside of Europe); (2) 2 liters of wine and, in addition, (a) 1 liter of alcohol over 22% volume (most spirits) or (b) 2 liters of alcohol under 22% volume (fortified or sparkling wine) or (c) 2 more liters of table wine; (3) 60 milliliters of perfume and 250 milliliters of toilet water;

and (4) other goods to the value of 2,400 francs (620 francs for those under 15).

Any amount of French or foreign currency may be brought into France, but foreign currencies converted into francs may be reconverted into a foreign currency only up to the equivalent of 5,000 francs.

Returning Home
U.S. Customs Provided you've been out of the country for at least 48 hours and haven't already used the exemption, or any part of it, in the past 30 days, you may bring home $400 worth of foreign goods duty free. So can each member of your family, regardless of age; and your exemptions may be pooled, so one of you can bring in more if another brings in less. A flat 10% duty applies to the next $1,000 of goods; above $1,400, the rate varies with the merchandise. (If the 48-hour or 30-day limits apply, your duty-free allowance drops to $25, which may not be pooled.) Please note that these are the *general* rules, applicable to most countries, including France.

Travelers 21 or older may bring back 1 liter of alcohol duty-free, provided the beverage laws of the state through which they reenter the United States allow it. In addition, 100 non-Cuban cigars and 200 cigarettes are allowed, regardless of your age. Antiques and works of art more than 100 years old are duty-free.

Gifts valued at less than $50 may be mailed duty free to stateside friends and relatives, with a limit of one package per day per addressee (do not send alcohol or tobacco products, nor perfume valued at more than $5). These gifts do not count as part of your exemption, unless you bring them home with you. Mark the package "Unsolicited Gift" and include the nature of the gift and its retail value.

For a copy of "Know Before You Go," a free brochure detailing what you may and may not bring back to the United States, rates of duty, and other pointers, contact the **U.S. Customs Service** (Box 7407, Washington, DC 20044, tel. 202/927–6724).

Canadian Customs Once per calendar year, when you've been out of Canada for at least seven days, you may bring in $300 worth of goods duty-free. If you've been away less than seven days but more than 48 hours, the duty-free exemption drops to $100 but can be claimed any number of times (as can a $20 duty-free exemption for absences of 24 hours or more). You cannot combine the yearly and 48-hour exemptions, use the $300 exemption only partially (to save the balance for a later trip), or pool exemptions with family members. Goods claimed under the $300 exemption may follow you by mail; those claimed under the lesser exemptions must accompany you on your return.

Alcohol and tobacco products may be included in the yearly and 48-hour exemptions but not in the 24-hour exemption. If you meet the age requirements of the province through which you reenter Canada, you may bring in, duty free, 1.14 liters (40 imperial ounces) of wine or liquor *or* two dozen 12-ounce cans or bottles of beer or ale. If you are 16 or older, you may bring in, duty free, 200 cigarettes, 50 cigars or cigarillos, and 400 tobacco sticks or 400 grams of manufactured tobacco. Alcohol and tobacco must accompany you on your return.

Gifts may be mailed to Canada duty-free. These do not count as part of your exemption. Each gift may be worth up to $60—label the package "Unsolicited Gift—Value under $60." There are no limits on the number of gifts that may be sent per day or per addressee, but you can't mail alcohol or tobacco.

For more information, including details of duties on items that exceed your duty-free limit, ask the Revenue Canada Customs and Excise Department (Connaught Bldg., MacKenzie Ave., Ottawa, Ont., K1A OL5, tel. 613/957–0275) for a copy of the free brochure "I Declare/Je Déclare."

U.K. Customs If your journey was wholly within EC countries, you no longer need to pass through customs when you return to the United Kingdom. According to EC guidelines, you may bring in 800 cigarettes, 400 cigarillos, 200 cigars, and 1 kilogram of smoking tobacco, plus 10 liters of spirits, 20 liters of fortified wine, 90 liters of wine, and 110 liters of beer. If you exceed these limits, you may be required to prove that the goods are for your personal use or are gifts.

For further information or a copy of "A Guide for Travellers," which details standard customs procedures as well as what you may bring into the United Kingdom from abroad, contact HM Customs and Excise (New King's Beam House, 22 Upper Ground, London SE1 9PJ, tel. 071/620–1313).

Traveling with Cameras, Camcorders, and Laptops

About Film and Cameras Pack some lens tissue and an extra battery for your built-in light meter, and invest in an inexpensive skylight filter, to both protect your lens and provide some definition in hazy shots. Store film in a cool, dry place—never in the car's glove compartment or on the shelf under the rear window.

Films above ISO 400 are more sensitive to damage from airport security X-rays than others; very high speed films, ISO 1,000 and above, are exceedingly vulnerable. To protect your film, don't put it in checked luggage; carry it with you in a plastic bag and ask for a hand inspection. Such requests are honored at American airports and up to the inspector abroad. Don't depend on a lead-lined bag to protect film in checked luggage—the airline may very well turn up the dosage of radiation to see what you've got in there. Airport metal detectors do not harm film, although you'll set off the alarm if you walk through one with a roll in your pocket. Call the Kodak Information Center (tel. 800/242–2424) for details.

About Camcorders Invest in a skylight filter to protect the lens, and check the lithium battery that lights up the LCD (liquid crystal display) modes. As for the rechargeable nickel-cadmium batteries that are the camera's power source, take along an extra pair, so while you're using your camcorder you'll have one battery ready and another recharging. Most newer camcorders are equipped with the battery (which generally slides or clicks onto the camera body) and, to recharge it, with what's known as a universal or worldwide AC adapter charger (or multivoltage converter) that can be used whether the voltage is 110 or 220. All that's needed is the appropriate plug.

About Videotape Unlike still-camera film, videotape is not damaged by X-rays. However, it may well be harmed by the magnetic field of a walk-through metal detector. Airport security personnel may want you to turn the camcorder on to prove that that's what it is, so make sure the battery is charged when you get to the airport.

About Laptops Security X-rays do not harm hard-disk or floppy-disk storage. Most airlines allow you to use your laptop aloft but request that you turn it off during takeoff and landing so as not to interfere with navigation equipment. Make sure the battery is charged when you arrive at the airport, because you may be asked to turn on the computer at security checkpoints to prove that it is what it appears to be. If you're a heavy computer user, consider traveling with a backup battery. For international travel, register your laptop with U.S. Customs as you leave the country, providing it's manufactured abroad (U.S.-origin items cannot be registered at U.S. Customs); when you do so, you'll get a certificate, good for as long as you own the item, containing your name and address, a description of the laptop, and its serial number, that will quash any questions that may arise on your return. If your laptop is U.S.-made, call the consulate of the country you'll be visiting to find out whether it should be registered with customs in that country upon arrival. Some travelers do this as a matter of course and ask customs officers to sign a document that specifies the total configuration of the system, computer and peripherals, and its value. In addition, before leaving home, find out about repair facilities at your destination, and don't forget any transformer or adapter plug you may need (*see* Electricity, *above*).

Staying Healthy

Finding a Doctor The **International Association for Medical Assistance to Travellers** (IAMAT, 417 Center St., Lewiston, NY 14092, tel. 716/754–4883; 40 Regal Rd., Guelph, Ontario N1K 1B5; 57 Voirets, 1212 Grand-Lancy, Geneva, Switzerland) publishes a worldwide directory of English-speaking physicians whose qualifications meet IAMAT standards and who have agreed to treat members for a set fee. Membership is free.

Assistance Companies Pretrip medical referrals, emergency evacuation or repatriation, 24-hour telephone hot lines for medical consultation, dispatch of medical personnel, relay of medical records, up-front cash for emergencies, and other personal and legal assistance are among the services provided by several membership organizations specializing in medical assistance to travelers. Among them are **International SOS Assistance** (Box 11568, Philadelphia, PA 19116, tel. 215/244–1500 or 800/523–8930; Box 466, Pl. Bonaventure, Montréal, Qué. H5A 1C1, tel. 514/874–7674 or 800/363–0263), **Near Services** (450 Prairie Ave., Suite 101, Calumet City, IL 60409, tel. 708/868–6700 or 800/654–6700), and **Travel Assistance International** (1133 15th St. NW, Suite 400, Washington, DC 20005, tel. 202/331–1609 or 800/821–2828), part of Europ Assistance Worldwide Services, Inc. Because these companies will also sell you death-and-dismemberment, trip-cancellation, and other insurance coverage, there is some overlap with the travel-insurance policies discussed below, which may include the services of an assistance company among the insurance options or reimburse travelers for such services without providing them.

Insurance

For U.S. Residents   Most tour operators, travel agents, and insurance agents sell specialized health-and-accident, flight, trip-cancellation, and luggage insurance as well as comprehensive policies with some or all of these features. But before you make any purchase, review your existing health and homeowner policies to find out whether they cover expenses incurred while traveling.

Health-and-Accident Insurance   Supplemental health-and-accident insurance for travelers is usually a part of comprehensive policies. Specific policy provisions vary, but they tend to address three general areas, beginning with reimbursement for medical expenses caused by illness or an accident during a trip. Such policies may reimburse anywhere from $1,000 to $150,000 worth of medical expenses; dental benefits may also be included. A second common feature is the personal-accident, or death-and-dismemberment, provision, which pays a lump sum to your beneficiaries if your die or to you if you lose one or both limbs or your eyesight. This is similar to the flight insurance described below, although it is not necessarily limited to accidents involving airplanes or even other "common carriers" (buses, trains, and ships) and can be in effect 24 hours a day. The lump sum awarded can range from $15,000 to $500,000. A third area generally addressed by these policies is medical assistance (referrals, evacuation, or repatriation and other services). Some policies reimburse travelers for the cost of such services; others may automatically enroll you as a member of a particular medical-assistance company.

Flight Insurance   This insurance, often bought as a last-minute impulse at the airport, pays a lump sum to a beneficiary when a plane crashes and the insured dies (and sometimes to a surviving passenger who loses eyesight or a limb); thus it supplements the airlines' own coverage as described in the limits-of-liability paragraphs on your ticket (up to $75,000 on international flights, $20,000 on domestic ones—and that is generally subject to litigation). Charging an airline ticket to a major credit card often automatically signs you up for flight insurance; in this case, the coverage may also embrace travel by bus, train, and ship.

Baggage Insurance   In the event of loss, damage, or theft on international flights, airlines limit their liability to $20 per kilogram for checked baggage (roughly about $640 per 70-pound bag) and $400 per passenger for unchecked baggage. On domestic flights, the ceiling is $1,250 per passenger. Excess-valuation insurance can be bought directly from the airline at check-in but leaves your bags vulnerable on the ground.

Trip Insurance   There are two sides to this coin. **Trip-cancellation-and-interruption insurance** protects you in the event you are unable to undertake or finish your trip. **Default** or **bankruptcy insurance** protects you against a supplier's failure to deliver. Consider the former if your airline ticket, cruise, or package tour does not allow changes or cancellations. The amount of coverage to buy should equal the cost of your trip should you, a traveling companion, or a family member get sick, forcing you to stay home, plus the nondiscounted one-way airline ticket you would need to buy if you had to return home early. Read the fine print carefully; pay attention to sections defining "family member" and "preexisting medical conditions." A characteristic quirk of default policies is that they often do not cover default by travel agencies or default by a tour operator, airline, or cruise line if you bought your tour and the coverage directly from the firm in question. To reduce your need for default insurance, give preference to tours packaged by members of the United States Tour Operators Association (USTOA), which maintains a fund to reimburse clients in the event of member defaults. Even better, pay for travel arrangements with a major credit card, so that you can refuse to pay the bill if services have not been rendered—and let the card company fight your battles.

Comprehensive Policies Companies supplying comprehensive policies with some or all of the above features include **Access America, Inc.,** underwritten by BCS Insurance Company (Box 11188, Richmond, VA 23230, tel. 800/284–8300); **Carefree Travel Insurance,** underwritten by The Hartford (Box 310, 120 Mineola Blvd., Mineola, NY 11501, tel. 516/294–0220 or 800/323–3149); **Tele-Trip** (Mutual of Omaha Plaza, Box 31762, Omaha, NE 68131, tel. 800/228–9792), a subsidiary of Mutual of Omaha; **The Travelers Companies** (1 Tower Sq., Hartford, CT 06183, tel. 203/277–0111 or 800/243–3174); **Travel Guard International,** underwritten by Transamerica Occidental Life Companies (1145 Clark St., Stevens Point, WI 54481, tel. 715/345–0505 or 800/782–5151); and **Wallach and Company, Inc.** (107 W. Federal St., Box 480, Middleburg, VA 22117, tel. 703/687–3166 or 800/237–6615), underwritten by Lloyds, London. These companies may also offer the above types of insurance separately.

U.K. Residents Most tour operators, travel agents, and insurance agents sell specialized policies covering accident, medical expenses, personal liability, trip cancellation, and loss or theft of personal property. Some policies include coverage for delayed departure and legal expenses, winter-sports, accidents, or motoring abroad. You can also purchase an annual travel-insurance policy valid for every trip you make during the year in which it's purchased (usually only trips of less than 90 days). Before you leave, make sure you will be covered if you have a preexisting medical condition or are pregnant; your insurers may not pay for routine or continuing treatment, or may require a note from your doctor certifying your fitness to travel.

For advice by phone or a free booklet, "Holiday Insurance," that sets out what to expect from a holiday-insurance policy and gives price guidelines, contact the **Association of British Insurers** (51 Gresham St., London EC2V 7HQ, tel. 071/600–3333; 30 Gordon St., Glasgow G1 3PU, tel. 041/226–3905; Scottish Provincial Bldg., Donegall Sq. W, Belfast BT1 6JE, tel. 0232/249176; call for other locations).

Car Rentals

There's no reason to rent a car if you plan to stay in the Paris area. Traffic is almost always heavy, parking is impossible, and unpleasant confrontations with Parisian drivers will not contribute to a favorable impression of the city. On the other hand, taxis are a relatively good deal, and public transportation is generally fast and efficient; RER trains go directly to Versailles and Euro Disney, and other trains depart frequently for Fontainebleau and Giverny. For more information on other transportation options, *see* Getting Around Paris, *below.*

All major car-rental companies are represented in Paris, including **Avis** (tel. 800/331–1212, 800/879–2847 in Canada); **Bud-**

get (tel. 800/527–0700); **Dollar** (tel. 800/800–4000); **Hertz** (tel. 800/654–3131, 800/263-0600 in Canada); **National** (tel. 800/227–7368), known internationally as InterRent and Europcar (tel. 800/227–7368); and **Thrifty** (tel. 800/367–2277). Rates range from $40 per day for an economy car to $80 for a mid-size car with automatic transmission, weekly unlimited-mileage rates range from $200 to $430. This does not include VAT tax, which in France is among the highest in Europe, 18.6%.

Requirements Your own driver's license is acceptable. An International Driver's Permit, available from the American or Canadian Automobile Association, is a good idea.

Extra Charges Picking up the car in one city or country and leaving it in another may entail drop-off charges or one-way service fees, which can be substantial. The cost of a collision or loss-damage waiver (*see below*) can be high, also. Automatic transmissions and air-conditioning are not universally available abroad; ask for them when you book if you want them, and check the cost before you commit yourself to the rental.

Cutting Costs If you know you will want a car for more than a day or two, you can save by planning ahead. Major international companies have programs that discount their standard rates by 15%–30% if you make the reservation before departure (anywhere from two to 14 days), rent for a minimum number of days (typically three or four), and prepay the rental. Ask about these advance-purchase schemes when you call for information. More economical rentals are those that come as part of fly/drive or other packages, even those as bare-bones as the rental plus an airline ticket (*see* Tours and Packages, *above*).

Budget companies with offices in town may cost less than major companies with an airport outlet; but you could waste time trying to locate it in return for only a small savings. If you're arriving and departing from different airports, look for a one-way car rental with no return fees.

Other sources of savings are the several companies that operate as wholesalers—companies that do not own their own fleets but rent in bulk from those that do and offer advantageous rates to their customers. Rentals through such companies must be arranged and paid for before you leave the United States. Among them are **Auto Europe** (Box 1097, Camden, ME 04843, tel. 207/236–8235 or 800/223–5555, 800/458–9503 in Canada), **Connex International** (23 N. Division St., Peekskill, NY 10566, tel. 914/739–0066, 800/333–3949, 800/843–5416 in Canada), **Europe by Car** (mailing address, 1 Rockefeller Plaza, New York, NY 10020; walk-in address, 14 W. 49th St, New York, NY 10020, tel. 212/581–3040 or 212/245–1713; 9000 Sunset Blvd., Los Angeles, CA 90069, tel. 213/252–9401 or 800/223–1516 in CA), **Kemwel** (106 Calvert St., Harrison, NY 10528, tel. 914/835–5555 or 800/678–0678), and **Foremost Euro-Car** (5430 Van Nuys Blvd., Suite 306, Van Nuys, CA 91401, tel. 818/786–1960 or 800/272–3299). Always ask whether the prices are guaranteed in U.S. dollars or foreign currency and if unlimited mileage is available. Find out about any required deposits, cancellation penalties, and drop-off charges, and confirm the cost of the collison damage waiver (CDW). One last tip: Remember to fill the tank when you turn in the vehicle, to avoid being charged for refueling at what you'll swear is the most expensive pump in town.

Requirements Your own driver's license is acceptable. An International Driver's Permit, available from the American or Canadian Automobile Association, is a good idea.

Insurance and Collision Damage Waiver The standard rental contract includes liability coverage (for damage to public property, injury to pedestrians, etc.) and coverage for the car against fire, theft (not included in certain countries), and collision damage with a deductible—most commonly $2,000–$3,000, occasionally more. In the case of an accident, you are responsible for the deductible amount unless you've purchased the CDW, which costs an average $12 a day, although this varies depending on what you've rented, where, and from whom.

Because this adds up quickly, you may be inclined to say "no thanks"—and that's certainly your option, although the rental agent may not tell you so. Planning ahead will help you make the right decision. By all means, find out if your own insurance covers damage to a rental car while traveling (not simply a car to drive when yours is in for repairs). And check whether charging car rentals to any of your credit cards will get you a CDW at no charge. Note before you decline that deductibles are occasionally high enough that totaling a car would make you responsible for its full value.

Rail Passes

The **French Flexipass** (formerly the France-Vacances Rail Pass) is a good value for those planning to do a lot of traveling by train. The pass allows you to stagger your train travel time instead of having to use it all at once. For example, the four-day pass ($175 in first class, $125 in second) may be used on any four days within a one-month period. Travelers may also add on up to five days of travel for $38 a day in first class and $27 in second class. Air-and-rail passes, rail-and-car rental passes, and air-rail-car rental passes are also available. All must be purchased before leaving for France, and are sold by travel agents and by **Rail Europe** (226–230 Westchester Ave., White Plains, NY 10604, tel. 914/682-5172 or 800/848-7245 from the East and 800/848-7245 from the West).

Many travelers with rail passes do not realize that on some trains, such as the high-speed TGVs, seat reservations are required. Getting them in advance through Rail Europe costs $10, more than in France, but assures you of a seat. On most other trains, while you don't need a seat reservation, you may want to get one anyway if you want to be guaranteed a seat. Reservations are always required for overnight sleeping accommodations.

Student and Youth Travel

Students are a noticeable presence in the capital, where intellectuals are the French equivalent of American movie stars. The area surrounding the Sorbonne in the bohemian Latin Quarter is filled with students discoursing in smoke-filled cafés, or browsing in crowded bookshops. Visiting students should have no trouble meeting their Parisian counterparts.

In keeping with a tradition of subsidizing education, Paris offers a variety of student discounts. Most museums and movie theaters offer students a **tarif réduit** of 20%–50%. An International Student Identity Card (*see below*) entitles you to significant discounts on train and airplane travel, theater, and youth hostels. For a detailed listing of deals for students in Paris, ask for the brochure *Jeunes à Paris* from the main tourist office (127 av. des Champs-Elysées, tel. 47–23–61–72). Also try **Usit Voyages** (12 rue Vivienne, tel. 42–96–15–88), a travel agency specializing in youth travel, for current information.

Travel Agencies The foremost U.S. student travel agency is **Council Travel,** a subsidiary of the nonprofit Council on International Educational Exchange. It specializes in low-cost travel arrangements, is the exclusive U.S. agent for several discount cards, and, with its sister CIEE subsidiary, **Council Charter,** is a source of airfare bargains. The Council Charter brochure and CIEE's twice-yearly *Student Travels* magazine, which details its programs, are available at the Council Travel office at CIEE headquarters (205 E. 42nd Street, New York, NY 10017, tel. 212/661–1450) and at 37 branches in college towns nationwide (free in person, $1 by mail). The **Educational Travel Center** (ETC, 438 N. Francis St., Madison, WI 53703, tel. 608/256–5551) also offers low-cost rail passes, domestic and international airline tickets (mostly for flights departing from Chicago), and other budgetwise travel arrangements. Other travel agencies catering to students include **Travel Management International** (TMI, 18 Prescott St., Suite 4, Cambridge, MA 02138, tel. 617/661–8187) and **Travel Cuts** (187 College St., Toronto, Ont. M5T 1P7, tel. 416/979–2406).

Discount Cards For discounts on transportation and on museum and attractions admissions, buy the **International Student Identity Card** (ISIC) if you're a bona fide student, or the **International Youth Card** (IYC) if you're under 26. In the United States the ISIC and IYC cards cost $15 each and include basic travel accident and sickness coverage. Apply to **CIEE** (*see* address *above,* tel. 212/661–1414; the application is in *Student Travels*). In Canada the cards are available for $15 each from **Travel Cuts** (*see above*). In the United Kingdom they cost £5 and £4 respectively at student unions and student travel companies, including Council Travel's London office (28A Poland St., London W1V 3DB, tel. 071/437–7767).

Hosteling An International Youth Hostel Federation (IYHF) membership card is the key to more than 5,300 hostel locations in 59 countries; the sex-segregated, dormitory-style sleeping quarters, including some for families, go for $7–$20 a night per person. Membership is available in the United States through American Youth Hostels (AYH, 733 15th St. NW, Washington, DC 20005, tel. 202/783–6161), and costs $25 for adults 18–54, $10 for those under 18, $15 for those 55 and over, and $35 for families. Volume 1 of the two-volume *Guide to Budget Accommodation* lists hostels in Europe and the Mediterranean ($13.95, including postage). IYHF membership is available in Canada through the Canadian Hostelling Association (CHA, 1600 James Naismith Dr., Suite 608, Gloucester, Ont. K1B 5N4, tel. 613/748–5638) for $26.75, and in the United Kingdom through the Youth Hostel Association of England and Wales (Trevelyan House, 8 St. Stephen's Hill, St. Albans, Herts. AL1 2DY, tel. 0727/55215) for £9.

Traveling with Children

Despite their reputed chilliness, most Parisians regard children warmly. Many restaurants serve children's portions and have high chairs, and larger hotels will provide cribs free to guests with young children. (This is often not the case in *pensions* and smaller hotels.) Paris has plenty of diversions for the young (*see* What to See and Do with Children in Chapter 3), and almost all museums and movie theaters offer discounted rates to children.

Getting around Paris with a stroller can be a challenge. Not all métro stations have escalators, and many museums will require you to check the stroller at the entry. Buses are a better bet, since they are often not as crowded as the métro and have adequate space for strollers and carriages. You won't have a problem finding items such as diapers (*couches à jeter*) or baby food. Supermarkets carry several major brands of each, and after-hours pharmacies provide the essentials.

Publications *Family Travel Times,* published 10 times a year by **Travel With**
Newsletter **Your Children** (TWYCH, 45 W. 18th St., 7th Floor Tower, New York, NY 10011, tel. 212/206–0688; annual subscription $55), covers destinations, types of vacations, and modes of travel; an airline issue comes out every other year (the last one, February/March 1993, is sold to nonsubscribers for $10). On Wednesday, the staff answers subscribers' questions on specific destinations.

Books *Great Vacations with Your Kids,* by Dorothy Jordan and Marjorie Cohen ($13; Penguin USA, 120 Woodbine St., Bergenfield, NJ 07621, tel. 800/253–6476) and, *Traveling with Children—And Enjoying It,* by Arlene K. Butler ($11.95 plus $3 shipping per book; Globe Pequot Press, Box 833, Old Saybrook, CT 06475, tel. 800/243–0495, or 800/962–0973 in CT), both help you plan your trip with children, from toddlers to teens. *Innocents Abroad: Traveling with Kids in Europe,* by Valerie Wolf Deutsch and Laura Sutherland ($15.95 or $4.95 paperback, Penguin USA, *see above*), covers child and teen friendly activities, food, and transportation.

Tour Operators **GrandTravel** (6900 Wisconsin Ave., Suite 706, Chevy Chase, MD 20815, tel. 301/986–0790 or 800/247–7651) offers international and domestic tours for grandparents traveling with their grandchildren. The catalogue, as charmingly written and illustrated as a children's book, positively invites armchair traveling with lap-sitters aboard. **Families Welcome!** (21 W. Colony Pl., Suite 140, Durham, NC 27705, tel. 919/489–2555 or 800/326–0724) packages and sells family tours to Europe. **Rascals in Paradise** (650 5th St., Suite 505, San Francisco, CA 94107, tel. 415/978–9800, or 800/872–7225) specializes in programs for families. Another family travel arranger that can even set up short-term rentals is **The French Experience** (370 Lexington Ave., New York, NY 10017, tel. 212/986–3800).

Hotels The **Novotel** chain (international reservations, tel. 800/221–4542) allows up to two children under 15 to stay free in their parents' room, and many properties have playgrounds. **Sofitel** hotels (international reservations, tel. 800/221–4542) offer a free second room for children during July and August and over the Christmas period.

Getting There
Air Fares On international flights, the fare for infants under 2 not occupying a seat is generally 10% of the accompanying adult's fare; children ages 2–11 usually pay half to two-thirds of the adult fare.

Baggage In general, infants paying 10% of the adult fare are allowed one carry-on bag, not to exceed 70 pounds or 45 inches (length + width + height). The adult baggage allowance applies for children paying half or more of the adult fare. Check with the airline for particulars, especially regarding flights between two foreign destinations, where allowances for infants may be less generous than those above.

Safety Seats The FAA recommends the use of safety seats aloft and details approved models in the free leaflet **"Child/Infant Safety Seats Recommended for Use in Aircraft"** (available from the Federal Aviation Administration, APA–200, 800 Independence Ave. SW, Washington, DC 20591, tel. 202/267–3479). Airline policy varies. U.S. carriers must allow FAA-approved models, but because these seats are strapped into a regular passenger seat, they may require that parents buy a ticket even for an infant under 2 who would otherwise ride free. Foreign carriers may not allow infant seats, may charge the child's rather than the infant's fare for their use, or may require you to hold your baby during takeoff and landing, thus defeating the seat's purpose.

Facilities Aloft Airlines do provide other facilities and services for children, such as children's meals and freestanding bassinets (to those sitting in seats on the bulkhead, where there's enough legroom to accommodate them). Make your request when reserving. The annual February/March issue of *Family Travel Times* gives details of the children's services of dozens of airlines (*see above*). "Kids and Teens in Flight" (free from the U.S. Department of Transportation, tel. 202/366–2220) offers tips for children flying alone.

Baby-sitting Services First check with the hotel concierge for recommended child-care arrangements. Local agencies include: **Ababa,** 8 av. du Maine, 15e, tel. 45–49–46–46; **Allô Service Maman,** 21 rue de Brey, 75017 Paris, tel. 42–67–99–37; **Allo Maman Poule,** 4 rue Greffulhe, Levallois, tel. 47–48–01–01; **Baby Sitting Service,** 18 rue Tronchet, 75008 Paris, tel. 46–37–51–24; and **Home Service,** 5 rue Yvon-Villarceau, 75016 Paris, tel. 45–00–82–51. All can provide English-speaking baby-sitters with just a few hours notice. *L'Officiel des Spectacles* lists babysitting agencies under "Gardes d' Enfants." Expect to pay between 28 and 35 francs per hour, plus an additional 50-franc agency fee.

Miscellaneous Contact the **CIDJ** (Centre d'Information et de Documentation pour la Jeunesse, 101 quai Branly, 75015 Paris, tel. 45–67–35–85) for information about activities and events for youngsters in Paris.

Hints for Travelers with Disabilities

Though it has a long way to go, Paris ranks above many European cities in its ability to accommodate travelers with mobility impairments. Most sidewalks now have low curbs, and most arrondissements have public restrooms and telephone boxes that are wheelchair-accessible. Taxi drivers are required by law to assist travelers with disabilities in and out of their vehicles; specially adapted taxis are available by calling 48–37–85–85.

In addition, most métro stations are wheelchair-accessible; an RER and métro access guide is available from the Paris Transit Authority (RATP) office (Pl. de la Madeleine, 8e, tel. 40–46–42–17). Ask for the free brochure *Touristes Quand Même* at the main tourist office (127 av. des Champs-Elysées) for detailed information about wheelchair accessibility.

Organizations Several organizations provide travel information for people with disabilities, usually for a membership fee, and some publish newsletters and bulletins. Among them are the **Information Center for Individuals with Disabilities** (Fort Point Pl., 27–43 Wormwood St., Boston, MA 02210, tel. 617/727–5540 or 800/462–5015 in MA between 11 and 4, or leave message; TDD/TTY tel. 617/345–9743); **Mobility International USA** (Box 3551, Eugene, OR 97403, voice and TDD tel. 503/343–1284), is the U.S. branch of an international organization based in Britain and present in 30 countries; **MossRehab Hospital Travel Information Service** (1200 W. Tabor Rd., Philadelphia, PA 19141, tel. 215/456–9603, TDD tel. 215/456–9602); the **Society for the Advancement of Travel for the Handicapped** (SATH, 347 5th Ave., Suite 610, New York, NY 10016, tel. 212/447–7284, fax 212/725–8253); the **Travel Industry and Disabled Exchange** (TIDE, 5435 Donna Ave., Tarzana, CA 91356, tel. 818/368–5648); and **Travelin' Talk** (Box 3534, Clarksville, TN 37043, tel. 615/552–6670).

In the United Kingdom Main sources include the **Royal Association for Disability and Rehabilitation** (RADAR, 25 Mortimer St., London W1N 8AB, tel. 071/637–5400), which publishes travel information for the disabled in Britain, and **Mobility International** (228 Borough High St., London SE1 1JX, tel. 071/403–5688), the headquarters of an international membership organization that serves as a clearinghouse of travel information for people with disabilities.

Travel Agencies and Tour Operators **Directions Unlimited** (720 N. Bedford Rd., Bedford Hills, NY 10507, tel. 914/241–1700), a travel agency, has expertise in tours and cruises for the disabled. **Evergreen Travel Service** (4114 198th St. SW, Suite 13, Lynnwood, WA 98036, tel. 206/776–1184 or 800/435–2288) operates Wings on Wheels Tours for those in wheelchairs, White Cane Tours for the blind, and tours for the deaf, and makes group and independent arrangements for travelers with any disability. **Flying Wheels Travel** (143 W. Bridge St., Box 382, Owatonna, MN 55060, tel. 800/535–6790 or 800/722–9351 in MN), a tour operator and travel agency, arranges international tours, cruises, and independent travel itineraries for people with mobility disabilities. **Nautilus**, at the same address as TIDE (*see above*), packages tours for the disabled internationally.

Publications Several free publications are available from the Consumer Information Center (Pueblo, CO 81009): "New Horizons for the Air Traveler with a Disability," a U.S. Department of Transportation booklet describing changes resulting from the 1986 Air Carrier Access Act and those still to come from the 1990 Americans with Disabilities Act (include Department 608Y in the address), and the Airport Operators Council's *Access Travel: Airports* (Dept. 5804), which describes facilities and services for the disabled at more than 500 airports worldwide.

Twin Peaks Press (Box 129, Vancouver, WA 98666, tel. 206/694–2462 or 800/637–2256) publishes the *Directory of Travel*

Agencies for the Disabled ($19.95), listing more than 370 agencies worldwide; *Travel for the Disabled* ($19.95), listing some 500 access guides and accessible places worldwide; the *Directory of Accessible Van Rentals* ($9.95) for campers and RV travelers worldwide; and *Wheelchair Vagabond* ($14.95), a collection of personal travel tips. Add $2 per book for shipping.

Hints for Older Travelers

Older travelers to Paris enjoy most of the same discounts offered students. Museums and movie theaters offer a 20%–50% discount for people over 60. Seniors traveling outside Paris can take advantage of the French rail system's 30%–50% reduced fare (*Carte Vermeil*) when making at least four train trips within either France or Europe.

Organizations The **American Association of Retired Persons** (AARP, 601 E St. NW, Washington, DC 20049, tel. 202/434–2277) provides independent travelers the Purchase Privilege Program, which offers discounts on hotels, car rentals, and sightseeing, and the AARP Motoring Plan, provided by Amoco, which furnishes domestic trip-routing information and emergency road-service aid for an annual fee of $39.95 per person or couple ($59.95 for a premium version). AARP also arranges group tours, cruises, and apartment living through AARP Travel Experience from American Express (400 Pinnacle Way, Suite 450, Norcross, GA 30071, tel. 800/927–0111); these can be booked through travel agents, except for the cruises, which must be booked directly (tel. 800/745–4567). AARP membership is open to those 50 and over; annual dues are $8 per person or couple.

Two other membership organizations offer discounts on lodgings, car rentals, and other travel products, along with such nontravel perks as magazines and newsletters. The **National Council of Senior Citizens** (1331 F St. NW, Washington, DC 20004, tel. 202/347–8800) is a nonprofit advocacy group with some 5,000 local clubs across the United States; membership costs $12 per person or couple annually. **Mature Outlook** (6001 N. Clark St., Chicago, IL 60660, tel. 800/336–6330), a Sears Roebuck & Co. subsidiary with 800,000 members, charges $9.95 for an annual membership.

Note: When using any senior-citizen identification card for reduced hotel rates, mention it when booking, not when checking out. At restaurants, show your card before you're seated; discounts may be limited to certain menus, days, or hours. If you are renting a car, ask about promotional rates that might improve on your senior-citizen discount.

Tour Operators **Saga International Holidays** (222 Berkeley St., Boston, MA 02116, tel. 800/343–0273), which specializes in group travel for people over 60, offers a selection of variously priced tours and cruises covering five continents as well as a Road Scholar program of educational tours, mostly to European destinations. If you want to take your grandchildren, look into **GrandTravel** (*see* Traveling with Children, *above*).

Further Reading

For a look at the American expatriates in Paris between the wars, read *Sylvia Beach and the Lost Generation* by Noel R.Fitch, or *A Moveable Feast* by Ernest Hemingway.

Flaubert's *Sentimental Education* includes excellent descriptions of Paris and its environs, as do many Zola novels. Other recommended titles include Charles Dickens's *A Tale of Two Cities*, Henry James's *The Ambassadors*, Colette's *The Complete Claudine*, and Hemingway's *The Sun Also Rises*. George Orwell's *Down and Out in Paris and London* gives a stirring account of life on a shoestring in these two European capitals between the world wars. For those who like it hot, try Henry Miller's *Tropic of Cancer* or *The Diary of Anaïs Nin*, by Miller's errant lover. For a racy read about three generations of women in Paris, take along *Mistral's Daughter* by Judith Krantz. Helen MacInnes's *The Venetian Affair* is a well-known spy thriller that winds through Paris.

Arriving and Departing

From North America by Plane

Flights are either nonstop, direct, or connecting. A **nonstop** flight requires no change of plane and makes no stops. A **direct** flight stops at least once and can involve a change of plane, although the flight number remains the same; if the first leg is late, the second waits. This is not the case with a **connecting** flight, which involves a different plane and a different flight number.

Airlines The airlines that serve Paris from various major U.S. cities include **Air France** (tel. 800/237–2747, tel. 45–35–61–61 in Paris), **TWA** (tel. 800/892–4141, tel. 47–20–62–11 in Paris), **American Airlines** (tel. 800/433–7300, tel. 42–89–05–22 in Paris), **Delta** (tel. 800/241–4141, tel. 47–68–92–92 in Paris), **United** (tel. 800/ 538–2929, tel. 48–97–82–82 in Paris), **Continental** (tel. 800/ 231–0856, tel. 42–99–09–09 in Paris), **Northwest** (tel. 800/225– 2525, tel. 42–66–90–00 in Paris) and **USAir** (tel. 800/428–4322, tel. 49–10–29–00 in Paris). Most local reservations offices are closed on Sundays.

Flying Time From New York: 7 hours. From Chicago: 9½ hours. From Los Angeles: 11 hours.

Cutting Flight Costs The Sunday travel section of most newspapers is a good source of deals. When booking, particularly through an unfamiliar company, call the Better Business Bureau to find out whether any complaints have been registered against the company, pay with a credit card if you can, and consider trip-cancellation and default insurance (*see* Insurance, *above*).

Promotional Airfares Most scheduled airlines offer three classes of service: first class, business class, and economy or coach. To ride in the first-class or business-class sections, you pay a first-class or business-class fare. To ride in the economy or coach section—the remainder of the plane—you pay a confusing variety of fares. Most expensive is full-fare economy or unrestricted coach, which can be bought one-way or round-trip and can be changed and turned in for a refund.

All the less expensive fares, called promotional or discount fares, are round-trip and involve restrictions. The exact nature of the restrictions depends on the airline, the route, and the season and on whether travel is domestic or international, but you must usually buy the ticket—commonly called an APEX (advance purchase excursion) when it's for international travel—in advance (seven, 14, or 21 days are usual). You must also respect certain minimum- and maximum-stay requirements (for instance, over a Saturday night or at least seven and no more than 30, 45, or 90 days), and you must be willing to pay penalties for changes. Airlines generally allow some changes for a fee. But the cheaper the fare, the more likely the ticket is nonrefundable; it would take a death in the family for the airline to give you any of your money back if you had to cancel. The cheapest fares are also subject to availability; because only a certain percentage of the plane's total seats will be sold at that price, they may go quickly.

Consolidators Consolidators or bulk-fare operators—also known as bucket shops—buy blocks of seats on scheduled flights that airlines anticipate they won't be able to sell. They pay wholesale prices, add a markup, and resell the seats to travel agents or directly to the public at prices that still undercut the airline's promotional or discount fares. You pay more than on a charter but ordinarily less than for an APEX ticket, and, even when there is not much of a price difference, the ticket usually comes without the advance-purchase restriction. Moreover, although tickets are marked nonrefundable so you can't turn them in to the airline for a full-fare refund, some consolidators sometimes give you your money back. Carefully read the fine print detailing penalties for changes and cancellations. If you doubt the reliability of a company, call the airline once you've made your booking and confirm that you do, indeed, have a reservation on the flight.

The biggest U.S. consolidator, C.L. Thomson Express, sells only to travel agents. Well-established consolidators selling to the public include **UniTravel** (Box 12485, St. Louis, MO 63132, tel. 314/569–0900 or 800/325–2222); **Council Charter** (205 E. 42nd St., New York, NY 10017, tel. 212/661–0311 or 800/800–8222), a division of the Council on International Educational Exchange and a longtime charter operator now functioning more as a consolidator; and **Travac** (989 6th Ave., New York, NY 10018, tel. 212/563–3303 or 800/872–8800), also a former charterer.

Charter Flights Charters usually have the lowest fares and the most restrictions. Departures are limited and seldom on time, and you can lose all or most of your money if you cancel. (Generally, the closer to departure you cancel, the more you lose.) The charterer, on the other hand, may legally cancel the flight for any reason up to 10 days before departure; within 10 days of departure, the flight may be canceled only if it becomes physically impossible to operate it. The charterer may also revise the itinerary or increase the price after you have bought the ticket, but if the new arrangement constitutes a "major change," you have the right to a refund. Before buying a charter ticket, read the fine print for the company's refund policy and details on major changes. Money for charter flights is usually paid into a bank escrow account, the name of which should be on the contract. If you don't pay by credit card, make your check payable to the escrow account (unless you're dealing with a travel agent, in which case, his or her check should be payable to the escrow account). The Department of Transportation's Consumer Affairs Office (I–25, Washington, DC 20590, tel. 202/366–2220) can answer questions on charters and send you its "Plane Talk: Public Charter Flights" information sheet.

Charter operators may offer flights alone or with ground arrangements that constitute a charter package. Well-established charter operators include **Council Charter** (205 E. 42nd St., New York, NY 10017, tel. 212/661–0311 or 800/800–8222), now largely a consolidator, despite its name, and **Travel Charter** (1120 E. Long Lake Rd., Troy, MI 48098, tel. 313/528–3570 or 800/521–5267), with Midwestern departures. **DER Tours** (Box 1606, Des Plains, IL 60017, tel. 800/782–2424), a charterer and consolidator, sells through travel agents.

Discount Travel Clubs Travel clubs offer their members unsold space on airplanes, cruise ships, and package tours at nearly the last minute and at well below the original cost. Suppliers thus receive some revenue for their "leftovers," and members get a bargain. Membership generally includes a regular bulletin or access to a toll-free telephone hot line giving details of available trips departing anywhere from three or four days to several months in the future. Packages tend to be more common than flights alone, so if airfares are your only interest, read the literature before joining. Reductions on hotels are also available. Clubs include **Discount Travel International** (114 Forrest Ave., Suite 203, Narberth, PA 19072, tel. 215/668–7184; $45 annually, single or family), **Moment's Notice** (425 Madison Ave., New York, NY 10017, tel. 212/486–0503; $45 annually, single or family), **Travelers Advantage** (CUC Travel Service, 49 Music Sq. W, Nashville, TN 37203, tel. 800/548–1116; $49 annually, single or family), and **Worldwide Discount Travel Club** (1674 Meridian Ave., Miami Beach, FL 33139, tel. 305/534–2082; $50 annually for family, $40 single).

Enjoying the Flight Because the air aloft is dry, drink plenty of beverages while on board; remember that drinking alcohol contributes to jet lag, as do heavy meals. Sleepers usually prefer window seats to curl up against; restless passengers ask to be on the aisle. Bulkhead seats, in the front row of each cabin, have more legroom, but since there's no seat ahead, trays attach awkwardly to the arms of your seat, and you must stow all possessions overhead. Bulkhead seats are usually reserved for the disabled, the elderly, and people traveling with babies.

Smoking Since February 1990, smoking has been banned on all domestic flights of less than six hours duration; the ban also applies to domestic segments of international flights aboard U.S. and foreign carriers. On U.S. carriers flying to Paris and other destinations abroad, a seat in a no-smoking section must be provided for every passenger who requests one, and the section must be enlarged to accommodate such passengers if necessary as long as they have complied with the airline's deadline for check-in and seat assignment. If smoking bothers you, request a seat far from the smoking section.

Foreign airlines are exempt from these rules but do provide no-smoking sections, and some nations have gone as far as to ban smoking on all domestic flights; other countries may ban smoking on flights of less than a specified duration. The International Civil Aviation Organization has set July 1, 1996, as the date to ban smoking aboard airlines worldwide, but the body has no power to enforce its decisions.

Between the	The easi͏
Airports and	urban ͏
Downtown	vette-
Charles de Gaulle	stat͏
(Roissy)	H͏

RER-B line, the sub-
͏-look for the word *na-*
͏uildings and the train
͏ns to central Paris (Les
͏e every 15 minutes. The
͏33 francs, and journey time
͏   every 20 minutes between
Cha͏.   ͏ Arc de Triomphe, with a stop
at the A͏.   at Porte Maillot. The fare is 48
francs, and ͏.   ͏bout 40 minutes. The **Roissybus**,
operated by the ͏   ͏sit Authority, has buses every 15
minutes to rue Scribe͏ ͏e Opéra; cost is 30 francs. Rush-hour
traffic can make this trip slow and frustrating. **Taxis** are readily
available. Journey time is around 30 minutes, depending on the
traffic, and the fare is around 200 francs.

Orly Airport   The easiest way to get into Paris is on the **RER-C** line, the suburban express train. Again, there's a free shuttle bus from the
terminal building to the train station. Trains to Paris leave every 15 minutes. The fare is 42 francs, and journey time is about
25 minutes. A shuttle-train service, **Orlyval**, runs between the
Antony RER-B station and Orly airport every 7 minutes. The
fare from downtown Paris is 42 francs during peak periods, or
32 francs daily 11 AM–3 PM and after 9 PM, and Sat. noon–
Sun. noon. **Buses** run every 12 minutes between Orly airport
and the Air France air terminal at Les Invalides on the Left
Bank. The fare is 32 francs, and journey time is between 30
and 60 minutes, depending on traffic. The Paris Transit
Authority's **Orlybus** leaves every 15 minutes for the Denfert-
Rochereau métro station; cost is 23 francs. **Taxis** take around 25
minutes in light traffic; the fare will be about 160 francs.

From the United Kingdom

By Plane   **Air France** (tel. 081/742–6600) and **British Airways** (tel. 081/
897–4000) together offer service from London's Heathrow Air-
port to Paris every hour to two hours. The cost of round-trip
tickets is almost halved if you purchase them 14 days in advance
and stay over on a Saturday night. There are three **British Airways** and up to five **Air France** flights daily, except weekends,
to Paris from London's most central airport, London City, in
the Docklands area.

Other airlines with regular scheduled flights from London to
Paris include **British Midland** (tel. 081/754-7321), **TAT European** (tel. 0293–567955), and **Dan Air** (tel. 081/759-1818). Except
on Sundays, there are several daily flights (mostly Air France
and BA) direct to Paris from Manchester, Bristol, and Bir-
mingham, and up to four from Glasgow, Edinburgh, Aberdeen,
Cardiff, Belfast, Newcastle, and Southampton.

The Paris Travel Service (115 Buckingham Palace Rd., London
SW1 V9SJ, tel. 071/2337892) operates a good-value weekly
Paris Express from Gatwick to Beauvais (a 40-minute flight
and a one-hour bus ride into central Paris). Departure is on Friday, and return is the following Monday.

By Car   There are a number of different driving routes to Paris. The
Dover–Calais route includes the shortest Channel crossing;
the Newhaven–Dieppe route requires a longer Channel crossing but a shorter drive through France.

Dover–Calais   Ticket prices for ferries vary widely depending on the number of passengers in a group, the size of the car, the season and time of day, and the length of your trip. Call one of the ferry service reservation offices for more exact information. **P&O European Ferries** (Channel House, Channel View Rd., Dover, Kent CT17 9TJ, tel. 081/575–8555) has up to 15 sailings a day; the crossing takes about 75 minutes. **Sealink** (Charter House, Park St., Ashford, Kent TN24 8EX, tel. 0233/646801) operates up to 18 sailings a day; the crossing takes about 90 minutes. **Hoverspeed** (Maybrook House, Queens Gardens, Dover, Kent CT17 9UQ, tel. 0304/240241) operates up to 23 crossings a day, and the crossing (by Hovercraft) takes 35 minutes.

Dover–Boulogne   **P&O European Ferries** has up to six sailings a day with a crossing time of 100 minutes. Fares are the same as for the Dover–Calais crossing. **Hoverspeed** also operates on this route, with six 40-minute crossings a day. The fares are the same as for the Dover–Calais route.

Ramsgate–   **Sally Line** (Argyle Centre, York St., Ramsgate, Kent CT11
Dunkerque   9DS, tel. 0843/595522) has up to five 2½-hour crossings a day.

Newhaven–Dieppe   **Sealink** has up to four sailings a day; the crossing takes four hours.

Portsmouth–   **P&O European Ferries** has up to three sailings a day, and the
Le Havre   crossing takes 5¾ hours by day, 7 by night.

Driving distances from the French ports to Paris are as follows: **from Calais,** 290 kilometers (180 miles); **from Boulogne,** 243 kilometers (151 miles); **from Dieppe,** 193 kilometers (120 miles); **from Dunkerque,** 257 kilometers (160 miles). The fastest routes to Paris from each port are via the N43, A26, and A1 from Calais; via the N1 from Boulogne; via the N15 from Le Havre; via the D915 and N1 from Dieppe; and via the A25 and A1 from Dunkerque.

By Train   **British Rail** has four departures a day from London's Victoria Station, all linking with the Dover–Calais/Boulogne ferry services through to Paris. There is also an overnight service using the Newhaven–Dieppe ferry. Journey time is about eight hours. Round-trip fare is around £65 (five-day excursion). Credit card bookings are accepted by phone (tel. 071/834–2345) or in person at a British Rail Travel Centre.

The Channel Tunnel, destined for trains only (with cars taken on board), which will slash the Paris–London journey time to under four hours, pushed back its scheduled opening date to spring 1994. Fare details were not available at press time.

Train Stations   Paris has six international rail stations: **Gare du Nord** (northern France, northern Europe, and England via Calais or Boulogne); **Gare St-Lazare** (Normandy, England via Dieppe); **Gare de l'Est** (Strasbourg, Luxembourg, Basle, and central Europe); **Gare de Lyon** (Lyon, Marseille, the Riviera, Geneva, Italy); and **Gare d'Austerlitz** (Loire Valley, southwest France, Spain). Note that **Gare Montparnasse** has taken over as the main terminus for trains bound for southwest France since the introduction of the new TGV-Atlantique service. For train information from any station, call 45–82–50–50. You can reserve tickets in any Paris station, irrespective of destination. Go to the **Grandes Lignes** counter for travel within France and to the **Billets Internationaux** desk if you're heading out of France.

By Bus **Eurolines** (52 Grosvenor Gardens, London SW1W 0AU, tel. 071/730–0202) operates a nightly service from London's Victoria Coach Station, via the Dover–Calais ferry, to Paris. Departures are at 9 AM, arriving at 6:15 PM; 12 noon, arriving at 9:45 PM; and 9 PM, arriving at 7:15 AM. Fares are £52 round-trip (under-25 youth pass £49), £31 one-way.

Hoverspeed (Maybrook House, Queen's Gardens, Dover, Kent CT17 9UQ, tel. 0304/240241) offers a faster journey time with up to five daily departures from Victoria Coach Station. The fare is £25 one-way, £43 round-trip.

Both the Eurolines and Hoverspeed services are bookable in person at any **National Express** office or at the **Coach Travel Centre,** 13 Regent Street, London SW1 4LR. Credit card reservations can be made by calling 071/824–8657.

Staying in Paris

Important Addresses and Numbers

Tourist Information The main **Paris Tourist Office** (127 av. des Champs-Elysées, 75008 Paris, tel. 47–23–61–72) is open daily 9–8. There are also offices at all main train stations, except Gare St-Lazare. Dial 47–20–88–98 for recorded information in English. All of these offices—and certain métro stations—sell museum passes (*Carte Musées et Monuments*), which offer unlimited access to more than 60 museums and monuments in Paris over a one-, three-, or five-day period; cost, respectively, is 55, 110, or 160 francs.

Embassies **U.S. Embassy** (2 av. Gabriel, 8e, tel. 42–96–12–02). **Canadian Embassy** (35 av. Montaigne, 8e, tel. 44–43–32–00). **British Embassy** (35 rue du Fbg St-Honoré, 8e, tel. 42–66–91–42).

Emergencies **Police** (tel. 17). **Ambulance** (tel. 15 or 45–67–50–50). **Doctor** (tel. 47–07–77–77). **Dentist** (tel. 43–37–51–00).

Hospitals **The American Hospital** (63 blvd. Victor Hugo, Neuilly, tel. 46–41–25–25) has a 24-hour emergency service. **The Hertford British Hospital** (3 rue Barbès, Levallois-Perret, tel. 47–58–13–12) also offers a 24-hour service.

Pharmacies **Dhéry** (Galerie des Champs, 84 av. des Champs-Elysées, 8e, tel. 45–62–02–41) is open 24 hours. **Drugstore Publicis** (corner of blvd. St-Germain and rue de Rennes, 6e) is open daily till 2 AM. **Pharmacie des Arts** (106 blvd. Montparnasse, 14e) is open daily till midnight.

Tour Operators **American Express** (11 rue Scribe, 9e, tel. 47–77–70–00). **Air France** (119 av. des Champs-Elysées, 8e, tel. 42–99–23–64). **Wagons-Lits** (8 rue Auber, 9e, tel. 42–66–90–90).

Telephones

To call Paris from the United States, dial 011–33–1 and then the local eight-digit number.

Local Calls The French telephone system is modern and efficient. A local call costs 73 centimes plus 12 centimes per minute. Call-boxes are plentiful; they're found at post offices and often in cafés.

Most French pay phones are now operated by cards *(télécartes)*, which you can buy from post offices and some *tabacs* (cost is 40 francs for 50 units; 96 francs for 120). These cards will save you money and hassle. In cafés you can still find pay phones that operate with 50-centime, 1-, 2-, and 5-franc coins (1 franc minimum). Lift the receiver, place your coin(s) in the appropriate slots, and dial. Unused coins are returned when you hang up. All French phone numbers have eight digits; a code is required only when calling Paris from outside the city (add 16–1 for Paris) and when calling outside the city from Paris (add 16, then the number). Note that the number system was changed in 1985, so you may come across some seven-figure numbers in Paris and some six-figure ones elsewhere. Add 4 to the start of such Paris numbers, and add the former two-figure area code to the provincial numbers.

International Calls Dial 19 and wait for the tone, then dial the country code (1 for the United States and Canada, 44 for the United Kingdom) and the area code (minus any initial 0) and number. Expect to be overcharged if you make calls from your hotel. Approximate daytime rates, per minute, are 9.36 francs to the United States and Canada; 4.50 francs to the United Kingdom; reduced rates, per minute, are 5.71 francs (2 AM–noon) to the United States and Canada or 7.17 francs (8 PM–2 AM weekdays, noon–2 AM Sun. and public holidays); and 3 francs to the United Kingdom (before 8 AM and after 2 PM).

AT&T's USA Direct program allows callers to take advantage of AT&T rates by connecting directly with the AT&T system. To do so from France dial 19-0011. You can then either dial direct (area code + number), billing the call to a credit card, or make a collect call.

Operators and Information To find a number within France or to request information, dial 12. For international inquiries, dial 19–33 plus the country code.

Mail

Post offices, or PTT, are scattered throughout every arrondissement, and are recognizable by a yellow sign. They are usually open weekdays 8 AM–noon and 2:30–7 PM, Sat. 8 AM–noon. The main office, 52 rue du Louvre, 1er, is open 24 hours.

Rates Airmail letters to the United States and Canada cost 4.00 francs for 20 grams, 7.30 francs for 30 grams, 7.60 francs for 40 grams, and 7.90 francs for 50 grams. Letters to the United Kingdom cost 2.50 francs for up to 20 grams, as they do within France. Postcards cost 2.30 francs within France and to Canada, the United States, the United Kingdom, and EC countries; 3.70 francs if sent to North America by airmail. Stamps can be bought in post offices and cafés sporting a red TABAC sign.

Receiving Mail If you're uncertain where you'll be staying, have mail sent to **American Express** (if you're a card member), or to **Poste Restante** at any post office.

Getting Around Paris

Paris is relatively small as capital cities go, and most of its prize monuments and museums are within easy walking distance of one another. Walking also lets you participate in the French national sport of people-watching, and gives you an appetite (and an excuse) for that next memorable meal. The most convenient form of public transportation is the métro, with stops every few hundred yards. Buses are a slower alternative, though you do see more of the city. Taxis are relatively inexpensive and convenient, but not always easy to hail. Private car travel within Paris is best avoided;parking is extremely difficult.

Maps of the métro/RER network are available free from any métro station and in many hotels. They are also posted on every platform, as are maps of the bus network. Bus routes are also marked at bus stops and on buses. To help you find your way around Paris, we suggest you buy a *Plan de Paris par arrondissement* (about 20 frs), a city guide with separate maps of each district, including the whereabouts of métro stations and an index of street names. They're on sale in newsstands, bookstores, stationers, and drugstores.

By Métro   Métro stations are recognizable either by a large yellow M within a circle or by the distinctive curly green Art Nouveau railings and archway bearing the full title (Métropolitain). The métro is the most efficient way to get around Paris and is so clearly marked at all points that it's easy to find your way around without having to ask directions.

There are 13 métro lines crisscrossing Paris and the suburbs, and you are seldom more than 500 yards from the nearest station. It is essential to know the name of the last station on the line you take, as this name appears on all signs. A connection (you can make as many as you like on one ticket) is called a *correspondance*. At junction stations, illuminated orange signs bearing the name of the line terminus appear over the correct corridors for each *correspondance*. Illuminated blue signs marked *sortie* indicate the station exit.

The métro service starts at 5:30 AM and continues until 1:15 AM, when the last train on each line reaches its terminus. Some lines and stations in the less salubrious parts of Paris are a bit risky at night; in particular Lines 2 and 13. But in general, the métro is relatively safe throughout, providing you don't walk around with your wallet hanging out of your back pocket or (especially women) travel alone late at night. The biggest nuisances you're likely to come across will be the wine-swigging *clochards* (tramps) blurting out drunken songs as they bed down on platform benches.

The métro network connects at several points in Paris with the **RER** network. RER trains, which race across Paris from suburb to suburb, are a sort of supersonic métro and can be great time-savers.

All métro tickets and passes are valid for RER *and* bus travel within Paris. Métro tickets cost 6.50 francs each, though a carnet (10 tickets for 39 francs) is better value. If you're staying for a week or more and plan to use the métro frequently, the best deal is the weekly *(coupon jaune)* or monthly *(carte orange)* ticket, sold according to zone. Zones 1 and 2 cover the entire métro network; tickets cost 59 francs a week or 208 francs a month. If you plan to take suburban trains to visit places in the Ile-de-France, we suggest you consider a four-zone (Versailles, St-Germain-en-Laye; 109 francs a week) or six-zone (Rambouillet, Fontainebleau; 142 francs a week) ticket. For these weekly/monthly tickets, you will need a pass (available from rail and major métro stations) and two passport-size photographs.

Alternatively, there are one-day (*Formule 1*) and two-, three-, and five-day (*Paris Visite*) unlimited travel tickets for the métro, bus, and RER. Their advantage is that, unlike the *coupon jaune*, which is good from Monday morning to Sunday evening, *Formule 1* and *Paris Visite* passes are valid starting any day of the week and also give you discounts on a limited number of museums and tourist attractions. The price is 36 (one-day), 65 (two-day), 90 (three-day), and 145 (five-day) francs for Paris only; 85, 150, 200, and 275 francs, respectively, for suburbs including Versailles, St-Germain-en-Laye, and Euro Disney.

Access to métro and RER platforms is through an automatic ticket barrier. Slide your ticket in and pick it up as it pops out. Keep your ticket during your journey; you'll need it to leave the RER system.

By Bus Travel by bus is a convenient, though slower, way to get around the city. Paris buses are green single-deckers; route number and destination are marked in front and with major stopping-places along the sides. Most routes operate from 6 AM to 8:30 PM; some continue to midnight. Ten night buses operate hourly (1:30–5:30 AM) between Châtelet and various nearby suburbs; they can be stopped by hailing them at any point on their route. The brown bus shelters, topped by red and yellow circular signs, contain timetables and route maps.

The bus accepts métro tickets, or you can buy a single ticket on board. You need to show (but not punch) weekly, monthly, and *Paris-Visite/Formule 1* tickets to the driver as you get on. If you have individual yellow tickets, you should state your destination and be prepared to punch one or more tickets in the red and gray machines on board the bus.

By Taxi Paris taxis may not have the charm of their London counterparts—there is no standard vehicle or color—but they're cheaper. Daytime rates (7 AM till 7 PM) within Paris are around 2.80 francs per kilometer, and nighttime rates are around 4.50 francs. There is a basic hire charge of 11 francs for all rides, and a 5-franc supplement per piece of luggage. Rates outside the city limits are about 40% higher. Waiting time is charged at roughly 100 francs per hour. You are best off asking your hotel or restaurant to ring for a taxi, or going to the nearest taxi station (you can find one every couple of blocks); cabs with their signs lit can be hailed, but are annoyingly difficult to spot. Note that taxis seldom take more than three people at a time. Tip the driver about 10%.

By Bike You can hire bikes in the Bois de Boulogne (Jardin d'Acclimatation), Bois de Vincennes, some RER stations, and from the Bateaux-Mouches embarkation point by place de l'Alma. Or try **Paris-Vélo** (2 rue du Fer à Moulin, 5e, tel. 43–37–59–22). Rental rates vary from about 90 to 140 francs per day, 160 to 220 francs per weekend, and 420 to 500 francs per week, depending on the type of bike. There is about a 1,000-franc deposit for rental.

Guided Tours

Orientation Tours Bus tours of Paris offer a good introduction to the city. The two largest operators are **Cityrama** (4 pl. des Pyramides, 1er, tel. 42–60–30–14) and **Paris Vision** (214 rue de Rivoli, 1er, tel. 42–60–31–25). Their tours start from the place des Pyramides, across from the Louvre end of the Tuileries Gardens. Tours are generally in double-decker buses with either a live or tape-re-

32

Paris Métro

33

corded commentary (English, of course, is available) and last three hours. Expect to pay about 150 francs.

The **RATP** (Paris Transport Authority, tel. 40–46–42–17) has many guide-accompanied excursions in and around Paris. Inquire at its Tourist Service on the place de la Madeleine, 8e (to the right of the church as you face it) or at the office at 53 bis quai des Grands-Augustins, 6e. Both are open daily 9–5.

Special-Interest Tours **Cityrama** and **Paris Vision** (*see* OrientationTours, *above*) offer a variety of thematic tours ("Historic Paris," "Modern Paris," "Paris-by-Night") lasting from 2½ hours to all day and costing between 150 and 300 francs (more if admission to a cabaret show is included).

Bike Tours **Paris by Cycle** (99 rue de la Jonquiere, 17e, tel. 42–63–36–63) organizes daily bike tours around Paris and its environs (Versailles, Chantilly, and Fontainebleau) for about 180 francs (an additional 95 francs for bike rental).

Boat Trips Boat trips along the Seine, usually lasting about an hour, are a must for the first-time visitor. Many boats have powerful floodlights to illuminate riverbank buildings; on some, you can also lunch or wine and dine—book ahead. The following services operate regularly throughout the day and in the evening.

Bateaux-Mouches has departures from Pont de l'Alma (Right Bank), 8e, tel. 42–25–96–10. Boats depart 10–noon, 2–7, and 8:30–10:30. The price is 30 francs (40 francs after 8 PM; 15 francs children under 14). Lunch is served on the 1 PM boat and costs 300 francs (150 francs children under 14). Dinner on the 8:30 service costs 500 francs (reservations required; no children). Wine and service are included in the lunch and dinner prices.

Vedettes du Pont Neuf has departures from Square du Vert Galant (Ile de la Cité), 1er, tel. 46–33–98–38. Boats depart 10–noon, 1:30–6:30, and 9–10:30 every half hour. The price is 40 francs during the day (20 francs children under 10 and 40 francs at night).

Bateaux Parisiens–Tour Eiffel has departures from Pont d'Iéna (Left Bank), 7e, tel. 44–11–33–44. Boats depart at 10 and 11 AM and 12, 2, 3, 4, 5, and 6 PM. The price is 40 francs during the day (20 francs children under 12). Lunch service costs 300 francs (200 francs children under 12). Dinner cruises on the 8 PM service cost 550 francs (no children). Wine and service are included in the lunch and dinner prices.

Canauxrama (tel. 42–39–15–00) organizes leisurely half-day canal tours in flat-bottom barges along the picturesque but relatively unknown St-Martin and Ourcq Canals in East Paris. Departures are from 5 bis quai de la Loire, 19e (9:15 and 2:45), or from Bassin de l'Arsenal, 12e (9:45 and 2:30), opposite 50 boulevard de la Bastille. The price is 70 francs (60 francs for students and senior citizens and on weekend afternoons; 45 francs children under 12).

Food Tours If you have more than a passing interest in French cuisine, you may be interested in **Paris en Cuisine** (49 rue de Richelieu, 1er, tel. 42–61–35–23). American Robert Noah leads individuals and groups on walking tours of the Rungis wholesale food market, as well as various restaurant and tasting outings.

Walking Tours There are plenty of guided tours of specific areas of Paris, often concentrating on a historical or architectural topic—"Restored

Mansions of the Marais," "Private Walled Gardens in St-Germain," or "Secret Parts of the Invalides." Tours are often restricted to 30 people and are popular with Parisians as well as tourists. They are accompanied by guides whose enthusiasm and dedication is invariably exemplary, though most are French and may not be able to communicate their enthusiasm to you in English. These potential linguistic problems are more than outweighed by the chance to see Paris in a new light and to visit buildings and monuments that are not usually open to the public. Charges vary between 35 and 50 francs, depending on fees that may be needed to visit certain buildings. Tours last around two hours and are generally held in the afternoons, starting at 2:30 or 3. Details are published in the weekly magazines *Pariscope* and *L'Officiel des Spectacles* under the heading "Conférences." In most cases, you must simply turn up at the meeting point (usually listed as "RV" or "rendezvous"), but it's best to get there early in case of restriction on numbers. You can get information on walking tours by contacting the **Caisse Nationale des Monuments Historiques** (Bureau des Visites/Conférences, Hôtel de Sully, 62 rue St-Antoine, 4e, tel. 44–61–20–00), which publishes a small booklet every two months listing all upcoming tours. For visits to some private mansions, you may be asked to show identification, so be sure to have your passport with you.

Personal Guides   **Espaces Limousine** (18 rue Vignon, 9e, tel. 42–65–63–16) and **Executive Car** (25 rue d'Astorg, 8e, tel. 42–65–54–20) have limousines and minibuses (taking up to seven passengers) that will take you around Paris and environs for a minimum of three hours. Reservations are required. The cost is about 250 francs per hour.

Opening and Closing Times

Banks are open weekdays, but there's no strict pattern to their hours of business. Generally, they're open from 9:30 to 4:30 or 5. Some banks close for lunch between 12:30 and 2.

Most Paris **museums** close one day a week—usually either Monday or Tuesday—and on national holidays. Usually, they're open from 10 to 5 or 6. Many museums close for lunch (12 to 2) and are open Sundays only in the afternoon.

Large **shops** are open from 9 or 9:30 to 6 or 7 and don't close at lunchtime. Smaller shops often open earlier (8 AM) but take a lengthy lunch break (1 to 4); small food shops are often open Sunday mornings, 9 to 1. Some corner grocery stores will stay open until about 10 PM. Most shops close all day Monday.

Tipping

Bills in bars and restaurants must, by law, include service, but it is customary to leave some small change unless you're dissatisfied. The amount of this varies—from 30 centimes for a beer to a few francs after a meal. In expensive restaurants, it's common to leave an additional 5% of the bill on the table.

Tip **taxi drivers** and **hairdressers** about 10% of the bill. Give theater and cinema **ushers** a couple of francs. In some theaters and hotels, **cloakroom attendants** may expect nothing (*pourboire interdit*—no tip); otherwise, give them 5 francs. **Washroom at-**

tendants usually get 2–5 francs, though the sum is often posted.

If you stay more than two or three days in a hotel, it is customary to leave something for the **chambermaid**—about 10 francs per day. Expect to pay about 10 francs (5 francs in a moderately priced hotel) to the person who carries your bags or who hails you a taxi. In hotels providing room service, give 5 francs to the waiter (this does not apply if breakfast is routinely served in your room). If the chambermaid does some pressing or laundering for you, give her 5–10 francs on top of the bill.

Service station attendants get nothing for gas or oil, but 5 or 10 francs for checking tires. Train and airport **porters** get a fixed sum (6–10 francs) per bag. **Museum guides** should get 5–10 francs after a guided tour. It is standard practice to tip **bus drivers about 10 francs** after an excursion.

Participant Sports

Biking The Bois de Boulogne and the Bois de Vincennes, with their wide leafy avenues, are good places for biking. Bikes can be rented from **Paris Vélo** (2 rue du Fer à Moulin, 5e, tel. 43–37–59–22) for around 80 francs a day or 160 francs a weekend.

Hotel Fitness Centers Paris's classic hostelries have the edge in ambience, but the best fitness facilities are in the newer hotels on the edges of the city center. The Vitatop Club on the top floors of the **Sofitel Paris** (8 rue Louis-Armand, 15e, tel. 45–54–79–00) offers a 15-meter pool, a sauna, a steam room, and a Jacuzzi, plus a stunning view of the Paris skyline; the club is free to hotel guests. Next door lies the **Parc Suzanne Lenglen,** with plenty of room for running, plus indoor and outdoor tennis courts. The **Nikko** hotel (61 quai de Grenelle, 15e, tel. 45–75–25–45) has a 17-meter pool; guests must pay 20 francs to use it. The **Bristol** (112 rue du Fbg. St-Honoré, 8e, tel. 42–66–91–45) provides its guests with a large, elegant pool, plus a sauna.

Jogging The best inner-city running is in the **Champs de Mars,** next to the Eiffel Tower, measuring 1½ miles around the perimeter. Shorter and more crowded routes are found in the **Luxembourg Gardens,** with a 1-mile loop just inside the park's fence; in the **Tuileries,** again measuring about 1 mile; and in the **Parc Monceau,** which has a loop of two-thirds of a mile. The **Bois de Boulogne,** on the western edge of Paris, offers miles of trails through woods, around lakes, and across grassy meadows. The equally bucolic **Bois de Vincennes,** on the eastern side of the city, offers a 9-mile circuit or a 1-mile loop around the Château de Vincennes itself.

Physical Fitness Several gyms and clubs in Paris offer one-day or short-term memberships. Facilities are generally less up-to-date than in American gyms, but nonetheless provide a satisfactory way to work off croissants. **Espace Vit'Halles** in the 1st arrondissement offers a broad range of aerobics classes (30 francs per class, 700 francs for 10), exercise machines, sauna, and steam room (60 francs a day, 10-franc towel rental). *Place Beaubourg, 48 rue Rambuteau, 1er, tel. 42–77–21–71. Open weekdays 9 AM–10 PM; Sat. 11–7, Sun. 11–3.*

Club Quartier Latin boasts a 30-meter skylighted pool, a climbing wall, squash courts, and exercise equipment. Sixty francs per day entitles you to use of the gym and pool; add another 60 francs per hour for squash (raquets, 15-franc rental). *19 rue de Pontoise, 5e, tel. 43–54–82–45. Open Mon.–Thurs. 10 AM–midnight, Fri. 10–10, weekends 9:30–7:30.*

One of the oldest health clubs in Paris, **Club Jean de Beauvais** is also one of the best. An entire floor is devoted to cardiovascular and strength-training equipment, and the range of programs includes low-impact aerobics and special back-care classes. Cost is 150 francs for a one-day pass; 400 francs per week. The club also rents gymwear and shoes for a small fee. *5 rue Jean-de-Beauvais, 5e, tel. 46–33–16–80. Open weekdays 7 AM–10:30 PM; Sat. 8:30–7, Sun. 9:30–5.*

Tennis Tennis courts within Paris are few and far between. Your best bet is to try the public courts in the **Luxembourg Gardens.** There is also a large complex of courts at the "Polygone" sports ground in the **Bois de Vincennes.** It's a 20-minute walk down route de la Pyramide from Château de Vincennes métro, so you might want to take a taxi.

Spectator Sports

Cricket There are cricket grounds in the **Bois de Boulogne** (Bagatelle), **Bois de Vincennes** (Belle Etoile), and at **Château de Thoiry,** with games most weekends during summer. Admission is free.

Horse Racing Paris and its suburbs are remarkably well-endowed with racetracks. The most beautiful is **Longchamp** in the Bois de Boulogne, stage for the prestigious (and glamorous) Prix de l'Arc de Triomphe in October. Also in the Bois de Boulogne, and easier to get to (by métro to Porte d'Auteuil) is **Auteuil** racetrack. Other grass tracks *(hippodromes)* close to Paris are at **St-Cloud, Chantilly,** and **Enghien-les-Bains.** Vincennes has a cinder track for trotting races. Admission is usually between 35 and 50 francs. Details can be found in the daily press.

Ice Hockey Although this is hardly a national sport, the Français Volant steam flies the Paris flag with matches every other Saturday afternoon in winter at the **Bercy Sports Palace** (8 blvd. de Bercy, 12e; take the métro to Bercy). Tickets range from 30 to 75 francs. Call the club at 43–46–98–37 for details.

Rugby The Racing Club de France, one of France's leading teams, plays Saturday afternoons in winter at **Colombes,** just north of Paris (trains from St-Lazare to Le Stade station).

Soccer As in most European countries, soccer is the sport that pulls in the biggest crowds. The main Paris club is Paris St-Germain, which plays at the **Parc des Princes** stadium in southwest Paris; take the métro to Porte de St-Cloud. Matches are usually on Saturday evenings with an 8:30 kickoff. Admission prices vary from 25 to 200 francs.

Tennis The highlight of the season—in fact the second most important European tennis tournament after Wimbledon—is the **French Open,** held during the last two weeks in May at the **Roland Garros Stadium** on the eastern edge of the Bois de Boulogne. (Take the métro to Porte d'Auteuil.) Center-court tickets are difficult to obtain; try your hotel or turn up early in the morning (play starts at 11) and buy a general ground ticket. Tickets range from 80 to 300 francs. The Bercy Indoor Tournament in November is one of the richest in the world and attracts most of the top players.

2 Portraits of Paris

Paris at a Glance:
A Chronology

Paris

c 200 The Parisii—Celtic fishermen—live on the Ile de la Cité.

52 BC Romans establish a colony, Lutetia, on the Ile de la Cité, which soon spreads to both Seine banks. Under the Romans, Paris becomes a major administrative and commercial center, its situation on a low, defensible crossing point on the Seine making it a natural communications nexus.

c AD 250 St-Denis, first bishop of Paris and France's patron saint, is martyred in Christian persecutions.

451 The hordes of Attila the Hun are said to have been halted before reaching Paris by the prayers of Saint Geneviève (died 512); in fact they are halted by an army of Romans and mercenaries. Few traces of the Roman era in Paris remain. Most of those that do are from the late empire, including the catacombs of Montparnasse and the baths that form part of the Cluny Museum.

486–751 **The Merovingian Dynasty**

507 Clovis, king of the Franks and founder of the Merovingian dynasty, makes Paris his capital. Many churches are built, including the abbey that will become St-Germain-des-Prés. Commerce is active; Jewish and Oriental colonies are founded along the Seine.

751–987 **The Carolingian Dynasty**

Under the Carolingians, Paris ceases to be the capital of France and sinks into political insignificance, but it remains a major administrative, commercial, and ecclesiastical center—and, as a result of the latter, one of the foremost centers of culture and learning west of Constantinople.

845–887 Parisians restore the fortifications of the city, which are repeatedly sacked by the Vikings (up to 877).

987–1328 **The Capetian Dynasty**

987 Hugh Capet, Count of Paris, becomes king. Paris, once more the capital, grows in importance. The Ile de la Cité is the seat of government, commerce makes its place on the Right Bank, and the university develops on the Left Bank.

1140–63 The Gothic style of architecture appears at St-Denis: Notre Dame, begun in 1163, sees the style come to maturity. In the late 12th century, the streets are paved.

1200 Philippe-Auguste charters the university, builds walls around Paris, and constructs a fortress, the first Louvre.

1243–46 The Sainte-Chapelle is built to house the reputed Crown of Thorns brought by Louis IX (St. Louis) from Constantinople.

1253 The Sorbonne is founded, to become a major theological center.

The World

221 BC Ch'in dynasty under Shih Huang-ti unites China.

AD 30 Jesus is crucified in Jerusalem.

50 First human images of Buddha appear in central India.

271 First use of the magnetic compass (China).

449 Anglos, Saxons, and Jutes begin colonization of Britain.

500 Teotihuacán in central Mexico is now sixth-largest city in the world, with a population of 299,000.

632 Death of Mohammed; Islam begins.

732 Printing invented in China. Arabs advance through Spain and France to Poitiers.

800 Charlemagne crowned Holy Roman Emperor in Rome.

c 1000 Vikings arrive in America (via Greenland).

1050 The Chinese learn to print from moveable type.

1096 First European Crusade to the Holy Land.

1161 Chinese use gunpowder in warfare.

1206 Mongols under Genghis Khan begin the conquest of Asia.

1275 Marco Polo reaches China.

Paris

1328–1589 The Valois Dynasty

1348–49 The Black Death and the beginning of the Hundred Years War bring misery and strife to Paris.

1364–80 Charles V works to restore prosperity to Paris. The Bastille is built to defend new city walls. The Louvre is converted into a royal palace.

1420–37 After the battle of Agincourt, Henry V of England enters Paris. Joan of Arc leads an attempt to recapture the city (1429). Charles VII of France drives out the English (1437).

1469 The first printing house in France is established at the Sorbonne.

1515–47 François I imports Italian artists, including Leonardo da Vinci, to work on his new palace at Fontainebleau, bringing the Renaissance to France. François resumes work on the Louvre and builds the Hôtel de Ville in the new style.

1562–98 In the Wars of Religion, Paris remains a Catholic stronghold. On August 24, 1572, Protestant leaders are killed in the St. Bartholomew's Day Massacre.

1589–1789 The Bourbon Dynasty

1598–1610 Henri IV begins his reign after converting to Catholicism: "Paris is worth a mass." He embellishes Paris, laying out the Renaissance place des Vosges, first in a new Parisian style of town planning that will last till the 19th century. In 1610, Henri is assassinated. His widow, Marie de Médicis, begins the Luxembourg Palace and Gardens.

1643–1715 Reign of Louis XIV, the Sun King. Paris rebels against him in the Fronde risings (1648–52). During most of his reign, he creates a new palace at Versailles, away from the Paris mobs. It is the largest royal complex in Europe, the symbolic center of a centralized French state. His minister of finance, Colbert, establishes the Gobelins factory/school for tapestries and furniture (1667). André Le Nôtre transforms the Tuileries Gardens and lays out the Champs-Elysées (1660s). Louis founds the Hôtel des Invalides (1670).

1715–89 During the reigns of Louis XV and Louis XVI, Paris becomes the European center of culture and style. Aristocrats build town houses in new fashionable quarters (Faubourg St-Honoré). The Rococo style gains popularity.

1783 New outer walls of Paris are begun, incorporating customs gate-houses to control the flow of commerce into the city. The walls, which include new parks, triple the area of Paris.

1789–1814 The Revolution and the First Empire

1789–99 The French Revolution begins as the Bastille is stormed on July 14, 1789. The First Republic is established. Louis XVI and his queen, Marie Antoinette, are guillotined in the place de la Concorde. Almost 2,600 others perish in the same way during the Terror (1793–94).

The World

1348	Europe is ravaged by the Black Death (Bubonic Plague) originating in Asia—75 million die in four years.
1368	Ming dynasty is established in China.
1445	Gutenberg prints the first book in Europe.
1492	Columbus sails to the Caribbean and "discovers" the New World. The Moors are finally expelled from Spain.
1493	Treaty of Tordesillas divides the New World between Spain and Portugal.
1521	Martin Luther is excommunicated—the Protestant Reformation begins.
1532	Inca Empire is destroyed by Pizarro.
1571	The Spanish conquer the Philippines.
1607	First permanent English settlement in America at Jamestown, Virginia.
1608	Quebec founded by the French.
1620	The *Mayflower* arrives off New England.
1625	New Amsterdam is founded by Dutch colonists.
1632	The Taj Mahal is built at Agra in India.
1645	Tasman, a Dutch mariner, circumnavigates Australia and discovers New Zealand.
1656	St. Peter's in Rome is finished.
1703	St. Petersburg, capital of the Russian Empire, is founded.
1759–60	The British win New France—Quebec in 1759, Montreal in 1760.
1775–76	The American Revolution and the Declaration of Independence.
1798–1812	The Napoléonic Wars spread French domination across Europe and into Russia.
1803	The United States is nearly doubled in size by the Louisiana Purchase.

Paris

1799–1814 Napoléon begins to convert Paris into a neo-Classical city—the Empire style. The Arc de Triomphe and the first iron bridges across the Seine are built.

1815 The Congress of Vienna ensures the restoration of the Bourbon dynasty following the fall of Napoléon.

1828 Urban and political discontent causes riots and demonstrations in the streets; further outbreaks in 1833 and 1842.

1848 Europe's "Year of Revolutions" brings more turmoil to the Paris streets.

1852–70 **The Second Empire**

In 1852, further additions to the Louvre are made. Under Napoléon III, the Alsatian town planner, Baron Haussmann, guts large areas of medieval Paris to lay out broad boulevards linking important squares. Railroad stations and the vast covered markets at Les Halles are built.

1870–71 Franco-Prussian War; Paris is besieged by Prussian troops; starvation is rampant—each week during the winter, 5,000 people die. The Paris Commune, an attempt by the citizens to take power in 1871, results in bloody suppression and much damage to property.

1889 The Eiffel Tower is built for the Paris World Exhibition.

1900 The International Exhibition in Paris popularizes the curving forms of Art Nouveau with the entrance for the newly opened Paris Métro.

1910 Sacré-Coeur (Montmartre) is completed.

1914–18 World War I. The Germans come within nine miles of Paris (so close that Paris taxis are used to carry troops to the front).

1918–39 Between the wars, Paris attracts artists and writers, including Americans Ernest Hemingway and Gertrude Stein. Paris nourishes Existentialism, a philosophical movement, and major modern art movements—Constructivism, Dadaism, Surrealism.

1939–45 World War II. Paris falls to the Germans in 1940. The French government moves to Vichy and collaborates with the Nazis. The Resistance movement uses Paris as a base. The Free French Army, under Charles de Gaulle, joins with the Allies to liberate Paris after D-Day, August 1944.

The World

1807 The Slave Trade is abolished in the British Empire.

1819 The United States buys Florida from Spain.

1823 Promulgation of the Monroe Doctrine.

1840 Britain introduces the first postage stamp.

1846 Beginning of the Mexican War.

1848 Marx and Engels publish the *Communist Manifesto*.

1857 The Indian Mutiny.

1861–65 The American Civil War.

1867 Establishment of the Dominion of Canada.

1869 Suez Canal is completed. First U.S. transcontinental railroad is opened.

1880s The European powers (Germany, Belgium, Britain) seize control of most of central Africa.

1898 The Spanish-American War.

1899 The Boer War begins in southern Africa.

1900 The Boxer Rebellion breaks out in China.

1914–17 World War I. In 1917, the United States enters the war. A Jewish homeland in Palestine is promised by the Balfour Declaration.

1922 Mussolini comes to power in Italy.

1929 The Wall Street crash brings on the Great Depression.

1933 President Roosevelt introduces the New Deal. Hitler becomes German Chancellor; the Nazi era begins.

1937 War begins between Japan and China.

1939–45 World War II. In 1941, the United States enters the war after Pearl Harbor; in 1944, the Allies land in Normandy; 1945 brings the defeat of Germany, and the atom bomb is dropped on Japan.

1958–69	De Gaulle is President of the Fifth Republic.
1960s–70s	Paris undergoes physical changes: Dirty buildings are cleaned, beltways are built around the city, and expressways are driven through the heart of the city, even beside the Seine, in an attempt to solve traffic problems. Major new building projects (especially La Défense) are banished to the outskirts.
1962	De Gaulle grants Algeria independence; growth of immigrant worker problem in Paris and other cities.
1968	Parisian students declare the Sorbonne a commune in riots that lead to de Gaulle's resignation.
1969	Les Halles market is moved and its buildings demolished.
1970s	Paris, with other Western capitals, becomes the focus of extreme leftist and Arab terrorist bomb outrages.
1977	The Beaubourg (Centre Pompidou) opens to controversy, marking a high point in modern political intervention in the arts and public architecture.
1981	François Mitterrand is elected President. Embarks on a major building program throughout the city.
1986	Musée d'Orsay opens, housing hitherto scattered collections of 19th-century art and design.
1988	President Mitterrand is elected to a second term.
1989	Paris celebrates the bicentennial of the French Revolution. Grande Arche (La Défense) and Opéra Bastille completed. Louvre's glass pyramid completed.
1990	Cognacq-Jay museum reopens in the Marais.
1991	Edith Cresson becomes France's first female Prime Minister.
1992	Euro Disney opens in Marne-la-Vallée near Paris.

The World

1946–49 Civil war in China.

1947 India and Pakistan gain independence.

1948 The State of Israel is established.

1950 Beginning of the Korean War.

1953 Death of Stalin.

1956 Suez Crisis; Russia stamps out the Hungarian revolt.

1961 Berlin Wall is constructed.

1962 Cuban Missile Crisis.

1963 President Kennedy is assassinated.

1966 Cultural Revolution in China.

1969 Man lands on the moon.

1973 United States abandons the Vietnam War. Britain joins EEC.

1974 President Nixon resigns.

1979–84 The decline of world leaders—the Shah of Iran falls (1979); Yugoslavia's Marshall Tito dies (1980); President Sadat of Egypt is assassinated (1981); President Brezhnev of the U.S.S.R. dies (1982); Indira Gandhi of India is assassinated (1984).

1982 The Falklands War between Argentina and Britain.

1985 Mikhail Gorbachev comes to power in the Soviet Union.

1986 The Chernobyl nuclear reactor disaster.

1989 Ruling Communist parties ousted in Poland, East Germany, Czechoslovakia, Bulgaria, and Romania.

1990 German reunification. Iraq invades Kuwait.

1991 War in the Persian Gulf. Republics separate from U.S.S.R., forming independent countries. Mikhail Gorbachev falls from power, despite withstanding an unsuccessful coup against his government. Civil war in Yugoslavia.

Why Paris Works

By Steven
Greenhouse

Steven
Greenhouse was a
correspondent in
the New York
Times Paris
bureau for five
years.

In a hidden, walled-off area, just west of the Boulevard
St.-Michel, Paul Rissel looks like a figure borrowed
from the 19th century as he opens the door to the lush
greenhouse. Wearing a rough brown tweed sport coat and a
long camel-colored scarf, he pushes past some ficus and
stops next to a dozen unobtrusive black trays. These trays,
he points out, are one of the secrets behind the ageless
beauty of Paris's ornate Jardin du Luxembourg, which was
built for Queen Marie de Médicis some 370 years ago.
Rissel, one of the two chief gardeners, explains that the
trays produce seedlings for the tens of thousands of geraniums, dahlias and petunias that the Jardin's 80 gardeners
meticulously replant each May around the majestic central
fountain.

The resplendent array of flowers gives the garden the idyllic air of a Renoir painting. During the gentle rains of
spring, lovers stroll hand in hand, and when the sun breaks
through, 5-year-olds scamper around the fountain to chase
after their toy sailboats.

"People just love this garden," says Rissel, with a pride
nurtured by 38 years of working at the Jardin. "In most big
cities, the natives lack contact with nature, and that's what
we're trying to give them."

A soft-spoken man with soft hands and long gray side-
burns, Rissel heads a small army of gardeners. Each year
they plant or transplant 350,000 flowers, and each spring
they cart out 150 palm and orange trees, some of them 200
years old, that were lovingly sheltered from the winter
cold.

At a time when cities from Lagos to Los Angeles are af-
flicted by homelessness, crime and budget traumas, Paris's
famed garden is an oasis from urban turmoil. Mayors
around the world may be screaming for cash, but the Jardin
du Luxembourg is awash in money. It boasts more than one
gardener per acre, which allows for an attention to detail
and beauty that is rare in modern cities. One gardener devoted two full months to scooping out the rot from the trunk
of a beech tree that the gardeners were eager to save because it stood eloquently alongside a small Bartholdi Statue
of Liberty. "We function like the gardeners of an old house
of the bourgeoisie," Rissel says. "We do much more by
hand."

Rissel and the garden he nurses are just one gilded strand
in the tapestry of cobbled streets, quaint quays and medieval churches that make Paris one of the world's most beautiful, best-run cities. Although many cities appear to be

breaking down from poverty and decaying infrastructure, Paris seems to be improving with age.

For many of the city's 2.2 million residents and many of the 20 million tourists who visit each year, Paris remains a magical, even transcendent, place. While many Americans shun their own cities as if they were places suffering from the plague, Paris is a city with which countless people still have a passionate love affair.

The people who run Paris know that if their city relied on just the charms of its past, it would lose its magic. Thus, they have sought to superimpose a smoothly running, modern metropolis on the city bequeathed them by medieval kings and 18th-century revolutionaries. And they have succeeded royally.

Garbage is picked up seven days a week, mail is delivered three times a day and all of Paris's 800 miles of streets are swept by hand each day. At rush hour, the subways come once every 80 seconds, and many Métro stops are decorated with mosaics and murals. Affluent families are rushing not to flee for the suburbs, but to buy apartments in Paris's choicest neighborhoods and to send their children to public schools.

There is no single explanation for why Paris works so well. Rather, Paris has become a shining model for urban planners thanks to numerous ingredients lacking in many other cities: ample financing, sound administration, farsighted planning, technological ingenuity, a flair for design and an ambition to always improve.

It would be wrong to single out Paris from other French cities as a success story, because Toulouse, Lyons, Nice, Bordeaux and Strasbourg have worked just as hard to keep their beauty, build a vibrant cultural life and remain attractive for families. Nonetheless, Paris, whose metropolitan area includes 10.5 million people (one-fifth of France's population), is undeniably the Olympus of French cities.

Parisians have two major complaints. Traffic congestion has created a miasma of noise, pollution and stress, helping to make Paris's high-strung population even more irritable. The other is that crime is growing, although the roughest parts of Paris seem no more dangerous than the safest parts of many American cities. Paris had 80 murders last year, compared with 482 in Washington, which has about one-fourth the population.

Homelessness is another problem, although it does not seem one of the Parisians' main concerns, perhaps because the city has long romanticized the *clochards* who sleep along the Seine. The homeless, estimated at between 6,000 and 15,000, can stay for up to six months in 60 government-run or private shelters where they receive free room, board, medical care and job training. Most go to these shelters voluntarily, but the police often round up sleeping drunks to protect them from the cold.

"Paris's streets are cleaner than American cities, its garbage is picked up more regularly, its streets are paved more often and its bureaucracy is more efficient," says Michel Rousseau, an economics professor who studies urban problems. "But all this costs a lot of money."

Fortunately for Paris, the national Government contributes more than half the city's revenues. Because the state pays so much, Paris's affluent families do not shoulder a huge fiscal burden of caring for the immigrants and poor living in the city. This is one reason Paris has not suffered from the middle-class flight that has hurt so many American cities.

As one urban planner puts it: "One reason Paris has so few problems is that the type of people who make problems can't afford to live in Paris." Economic realities force the poor to live in suburbs ringing Paris, but even there, in the *banlieue*, the levels of poverty, violence and drugs are a fraction of those in American cities.

"Because of France's republican traditions, there is a real sense of solidarity, a real desire to help the less-well-off," says Roland Castro, director of the national Government's efforts to help the suburbs. "People often point to American cities as a model to avoid. They say, 'That can happen to us if we let things slide.'"

At one of the 50 mahogany tables under the gaze of two austere Chinese statues, François Dupin is scribbling on a napkin to explain why his cafe, Les Deux Magots, remains a mecca for Paris's beau monde. "The Chamber of Deputies is over there," says the short, dapper cafe manager, drawing a short black arrow to the west. "The students come from over there," he says, aiming an arrow to the east. "And all the artists and antique dealers come from down there." His last arrow points north to the Seine.

On the cream-colored wall behind him is a photograph of Simone de Beauvoir hunched over a table, writing at the famed cafe on the Boulevard St.-Germain. Nearby is a photo of a debonair, mustached young Ernest Hemingway, reading a newspaper at the cafe. Partly to imbibe the legend of such famous writers, partly to taste its flavorful coffee and atmosphere, camera-toting Japanese tourists, chain-smoking French intellectuals and lanky American Hemingway-wannabes crowd into Les Deux Magots each day. Many rush to the sidewalk tables, next to artists selling lithographs and in the shadow of the 12th-century towers of the church of St.-Germain-des-Prés.

"We're in a privileged neighborhood," Mr. Dupin says.

In one way or another all of Paris's 20 *arrondissements*, or districts, are privileged. The first arrondissement has the Palais Royal and Louvre; the fourth has the Place des Vosges and the Île St.-Louis; the fifth has the Sorbonne; the sixth, the Jardin du Luxembourg and École des Beaux-Arts; the seventh, the Invalides and the Eiffel Tower. The eighth is known for the Champs-Élysées, the Élysée Palace and world-famous shops like Hermès and Christian Lacroix. The ninth has the grandiose 19th-century Palais Garnier opera house, and the plush 16th is renowned for its opulent fin-de-siècle mansions.

Everyone wants to live in these neighborhoods, but only the privileged few need apply. One reason is that Paris is small, about half the size of Brooklyn. Rents have been pushed sky-high by limits on building heights and a shortage of land for new housing, caused in part by all the space used for parks, businesses and government. Not wanting Paris to become Manhattan-sur-Seine, the city's planners have generally limited building heights to seven stories in the historic center and relegated skyscrapers to the outskirts.

A two-bedroom apartment in central Paris often costs $2,500 a month, about the same as in Manhattan and some 60 percent more than in Chicago. Parking a car costs about $250 a month, roughly the same as in Manhattan. Cleaning a suit is around $15 and a good chicken runs $2.30 a pound. About the only things cheaper in Paris than in America are baguettes, Beaujolais and Christian Dior gowns.

"I love to live in Paris—I love the possibilities it offers," says Françoise Romand, a 36-year-old film maker. "The Métro is great, the buses are great and the city's very safe. If you get lost anywhere, there's hardly any risk."

In her view, there is nowhere else to live in France for people in film. Paris gives her the cultural fix she needs day after day. She recently went to a dance concert by Dominique Bagouet's French troupe, an experimental farce about a restaurant, "Lapin Chasseur," and a rock concert at the Cigalle, one of Paris's hottest nightclubs. She also visited Sophie Calle's photography exhibit at the Museum of Modern Art and Nicholas Garnier's avant-garde show at an art gallery near the Boulevard Montparnasse.

And that's not to mention exhibitions at the Grand Palais, Louvre, Picasso Museum and Musée d'Orsay. The money the national and city governments spend on Paris's cultural life is probably equal to the overall budgets of some third world nations.

"The French remain very attached to the idea of culture and education," says Françoise Cachin, director of the Musée d'Orsay. She says that both the left and the right agree it is important to finance museums generously to improve Paris's cultural life and to keep the tourists coming.

"There is a rivalry between the national and city governments about who can sponsor the best shows," Cachin says. "It's very positive for the museums and museumgoers."

Notwithstanding the impressive array of museums and municipal services, Parisians' local taxes are not astronomical. The reason: L'État, the national Government, pays 40 percent of the city's $23 billion operating budget. The national Government also pays half of most large projects, like schools, sewers and day-care centers. In addition, the state finances Paris's public hospitals, covers almost all welfare costs and pays the salaries of Paris's 24,650 teachers and 26,000 police officers and firefighters.

"In almost every European country, the central Government plays an important role in supporting the cities," says Leo van den Berg, director of the European Institute for Comparative Urban Research at the University of Rotterdam. "Europe's cities are very dependent on central money, and not so much on local fiscal circumstances."

That the cost of running Paris is spread throughout France means the city's residents are not socked with exorbitant taxes, although overall the French pay a greater share of their income for national taxes than Americans do. Indeed, the main taxes in Paris—the apartment tax and the business tax—are lower than in many country towns, causing some provincial politicians to complain that they are subsidizing Paris's elite.

Paris is probably far more spoiled by the state than are other European cities because it is the seat of Government and the capital of French finance, industry, entertainment and mass communication. Not only that, it is the cradle of French culture and history, the city of Voltaire, Napoleon, Pasteur, Hugo, Proust, de Gaulle and Sartre.

No one will ever see a headline like "Mitterrand to Paris: Drop Dead," because one of President François Mitterrand's preoccupations is adding new baubles to the capital. The French press has dubbed him Mitterramses I because of the huge monuments he has built, including the $400 million Bastille Opera, the I. M. Pei glass pyramid at the Louvre, the gigantic new finance ministry and the 350-foot-tall Grande Arche de la Défense. And that doesn't include the $1.3 billion Bibliothèque de France that Mitterrand has commissioned, which is slated to be the world's largest library.

Mitterrand's presidential projects, with a price tag of $3 billion, follow similarly grandiose schemes by his predecessors: Valéry Giscard d'Estaing masterminded the Musée d'Orsay and the Cité des Sciences museum, while Georges Pompidou fathered the Pompidou Center, the hugely popular art museum.

Although many critics deride these buildings as monuments to presidential egos, these projects have undeniably increased Paris's stature as a city of art, culture and architecture. The Musée d'Orsay, for instance, attracts almost four million visitors a year, and art critics from around the world have hailed its recent exhibitions on Seurat, Munch and Gauguin. The museum, which used to be a train station, was slated for demolition until President Giscard d'Estaing moved to save it. "It was a project that couldn't be done without the will of the State," says Cachin, the museum's director. "I can only rejoice."

Tourists strolling along Quai de Montebello near Notre Dame often pass a man in a green uniform who is intently sweeping the street with what looks like a large twig broom. Street cleaners like him are ubiquitous in Paris—of the city's 38,000 employees, 4,500 are sweepers, most of them Arab or African immigrants. They sweep each of Paris's streets daily, and heavily trafficked business and tourist streets are swept twice.

All this work by hand shows Paris's efficiency, obsession with detail and willingness to spend money to achieve its goals. Each year Paris spends 10 percent of its budget, or about $2.2 billion, on cleanliness, which translates to $1,000 for every resident.

"The broom remains irreplaceable," says Alain Le Troquet, technical director for Paris's department of sanitation and the environment. "You can't do everything with a machine."

Astute observers will notice a curious thing. The brooms no longer have crude brown branches, but instead bright green plastic fingers. Engineers in Paris's sanitation department had long appreciated how efficiently peasants' twig brooms swept debris along, but they were frustrated by how much the brooms cost and how often the twigs broke.

So Paris's sanitation department, considered Europe's most innovative, asked manufacturers to develop a broom that used sturdy plastic fingers rather than wood. The new plastic brooms cost one-fifth as much as the wooden ones and last seven times as long.

This is just one way Paris's administrators have demonstrated their technological ingenuity. The city's water system churns out a foot-wide stream that runs alongside the city's curbs to wash away litter. Paris has worked with industry to develop a vehicle to clean up the animal oil left from all the poultry, rabbit and beef sold at open-air markets. *Voilà*, the Gyrolave squirts steaming, swirling soapy water onto the pavement and then sweeps the street.

Another truck shoots compressed water under cars to remove the litter beneath them, while a second vehicle has long arms with five joints to pick up leaves. The newest vehicle has an elephantlike trunk that vacuums up sidewalk litter. The city soon hopes to introduce a robotic, unmanned version of this contraption.

"You have to give the French credit for being innovative," says van den Berg, the urban expert in Rotterdam.

Parisians say the city has become much cleaner since 1977 when Jacques Chirac became their first democratically elected mayor in a century. Previously Paris had been run by a prefect appointed by the Interior Minister, but residents often argued that a mayor held accountable in regular elections would be more attentive to their needs. (The prefect still runs the police department.)

When Parisians talk about cleanliness, their main complaint is canine excrement, notwithstanding the city's vaunted new motor scooters that vacuum up dog droppings. Not wanting to alienate dog owners, who represent a powerful voting bloc, the city for years refused to fine owners who did not clean up after their poodles. But with complaints growing, Philippe Galy, director of the department of sanitation and the environment, started ordering fines in May: $110 for the first offense and $230 for the second. "It's absurd," he says. "With all the serious environmental problems, like global warming, the ozone layer, Chernobyl and nuclear waste, it's unbelievable that the No. 1 subject of conversation at every Paris dinner party is dog doo."

A public high school like Lycée Janson-de-Sailly, built with busts of Pascal, Hugo and other luminaries along its majestic 200-yard facade, simply does not exist in an American city. The 109-year-old institution is in the 16th arrondissement, the Paris equivalent of Park Avenue, and the bankers, diplomats and high government officials who live there scurry to send their children to Janson.

Janson has 3,200 students, a lengthy waiting list and a substantial number of students from Paris's rich western suburbs, who are attracted by the school's reputation. The school has 250 teachers, several of them accomplished novelists and historians. Janson's alumni include former President Giscard d'Estaing, former Prime Minister Laurent Fabius and the Attali twins—Jacques, president of the European Bank for Reconstruction and Development, and Bernard, chairman of Air France.

Its paint may be peeling, its long, primitive desks may be gnarled from decades of use and abuse, but its student body continues to excel. About 95 percent of Janson's graduates pass the forbidding, all-important *baccalauréat* examination that is the ticket to a university.

"The school is excellent in many ways," says Françoise Rietsch, who heads one of Janson's parent associations.

"There is a lot of discipline, self-discipline, among the students."

Sitting behind the old wooden desk in her tidy office, Yvonne Cluzet, the school's earnest principal, makes clear that her main concern is academics and not the woes often associated with urban schools.

"Drugs just aren't a problem here," she says. "And we don't have problems with teen-age pregnancy. Our students are mature." The biggest problem she could think of was that two years ago bands of teen-agers from the suburbs stole pocketbooks, wallets and expensive coats from Janson students as they left school. The police quickly stopped it.

Janson and other Parisian schools do not suffer from a vicious cycle in which the middle class pulls its children out of public schools, tilting the balance toward poorer immigrant children and causing more middle-class families to send their children elsewhere.

Jean-Marie Demade, manager at a metallurgy company, moved his family from Rueil-Malmaison, a suburb, back to Paris so his son Julien could attend Janson. "I returned because of the quality of the education," he says. "And life for children is more interesting and lively in Paris, with the movies, museums, theaters and concerts, than it is in the suburbs."

Twenty-four percent of Paris's high-school students go to private schools. Parents choose those schools because they want their children to receive a religious education or because they have underachieving children and think that private schools will be stricter. The overachievers are sent to public schools like Janson, which, good as it is, doesn't even rank at the top of Paris's public lycées. Most teachers rate Louis-le-Grand and Henri IV even higher.

"The middle class flocking to private schools just isn't a problem here," says Michèle Gendreau-Massalou, the rector of Paris's school system. "In terms of passing the *baccalauréat*, public schools produce better results than private schools."

Schools are just one of the quality services that keep families in Paris. The city has begun building moderately priced three-bedroom apartments because many couples have complained that once they have two or three children they can no longer afford Parisian rents. The city issues a "Paris-Famille" card to parents of three or more children entitling them to $400 in annual discounts on a range of activities, including transport, school meals and college tuition.

Another magnet for families is the city-run day-care system, which cares for 20,000 children a day, attracting rich and poor alike. The day-care center at 54 rue St.-Maur is typical of the 250 city-run centers except for its bold architecture: it has a spiraling concrete facade that resembles the Guggenheim Museum. Its front is windowless to keep out street noise and pollution, while its back is filled with sun-drenched floor-to-ceiling windows.

The center on the rue St.-Maur has a staff of 25 to watch over 87 children, aged 3 months to 3 years. Each of its three floors has a glass-enclosed nap area, and the staff has painted pink and blue rabbits and stars on the see-through walls. Each week, one of the center's aides stages a marionette show; the city offers special courses to teach day-care workers how to do such shows.

"I can afford my own au pair, but I much prefer the day-care center," says Patricia Fayet, a radiologist, as she watches her 1-year-old son, Yann, play in a bright blue plastic tub filled with hundreds of striped balls. "At the day-care center, the children get professional care and learn how to live with others."

Each center has a director who lives on the site and is trained as a licensed nurse and specialist in early child development. All the day-care workers must have spent a year in college studying care of children under age 3. A doctor visits each center once a week.

At the center on the rue St.-Maur, parents can leave their children from 7:30 A.M. to 6:30 P.M., but France Galas, the director, chides parents who leave a child for more than eight hours. Payments are on a sliding scale, ranging from $30 to $400 a month per child, with the city picking up half the cost of running the centers.

The centers are so successful that there is a waiting list of thousands of children, and the city is struggling to keep up by building one new daycare center a month.

"A few years ago mothers thought it was bad to put their children in a public day-care center because they felt guilty they weren't doing enough for their kids," says Elisabeth Allaire, director of social services, children and health for Paris. "Now mothers have heard so many good things about our day-care centers that they think they are bad mothers if they *don't* send their kids to our centers."

I n many ways, Paris is a tale of two cities. There is the Paris of the travel guides: the city of three-star restaurants and Yves Saint Laurent boutiques, the city of the 2.2 million privileged souls who live within the 22-mile ring road, the Boulevard Périphérique.

Then there is the other Paris, the outer ring where the working classes live, often in anonymous 1960's tower blocks. These are the suburbs where gangs of immigrant teen-agers clash with the police, where the sons of Algerian and Moroccan workers have a 25 percent jobless rate and where the native French tilt heavily toward Jean-Marie Le Pen, the far-right, anti-immigrant leader. These suburbs include Sartrouville, Montfermeil, Mantes-la-Jolie and Gennevilliers.

"One important reason why Paris is successful is that it's a fantastically elitist city," says Christopher Brooks, an economist specializing in urban issues at the Organization for Economic Cooperation and Development in Paris. "While a lot of people would like to live there, lots of people can't afford to. The social composition is skewed as a result. The poor are forced to live in the outskirts."

The Quartier du Luth in Gennevilliers is neither the worst nor the best of the banlieue. It is a United Nations of immigrants from Algeria, the Antilles, the Ivory Coast, Morocco, Tunisia, Turkey, Zaire and a dozen other countries. About 40 percent of its 10,000 residents are immigrants, and fewer than half the children finish high school. Teachers complain that they find syringes near the school gates.

"This isn't the greatest neighborhood," says Ahmet Ersoy, a 30-year-old unemployed refugee from Turkey. "We'd like to move on to another neighborhood eventually." Ersoy lives in a nondescript, 14-story, 500-yard-long block that could have won a Stalinist design contest. Its graffiti-splattered walls say "Momo" and "Chaka Chaoui." Social agencies steer immigrants to districts like the Luth, four miles northwest of Paris, because they have the cheapest housing in the region. A modest two-bedroom apartment is $350, about one-seventh the cost in central Paris.

In the Luth, France's activist Government works hard to improve living conditions. There are playgrounds with bright red swings and slides, and an office has been set up where four social workers counsel the Luth's residents.

The district has been designated a "Priority Education Zone." This means its schools receive extra money and teachers to help integrate immigrant children and provide special help to the laggards. At Guy Moquet Middle School, Claude Naveau, the principal, is proud that his school, filled with Botticelli and Manet posters, has a computer room and its own radio station.

"We have a lot of children who don't have a good family environment, who don't have someone asking them, 'Are you doing your homework?'" says Naveau, whose heavy glasses and thick beard make him look like an archetypal intellectual. "Children love our school because it's an oasis from the chaos outside."

To be sure, Paris proper also has its less chic neighborhoods, most notably the 18th, 19th and 20th arrondissements in the north and east. These have a large North African population, much of it second generation, many of whom work in small businesses, especially textiles.

The epicenter of Arab Paris is Barbès-Rochechouart, the intersection of two bustling avenues, which seems a cross between a Moroccan souk and Manhattan's 14th Street. Elevated trains rumble by as people squeeze past a 200-yard line of sidewalk stalls. Nearby, young toughs wait until sundown to begin their purse snatchings.

"A lot of young kids come up from the Maghreb, can't find jobs and start creating trouble," says Youssef Karoui, who runs the Eslem restaurant.

The problem in these neighborhoods, residents say, is not violent crime, but purse-snatchings, burglaries and car thefts. Fortunately for Paris, crack has not made inroads and drug addiction is far less prevalent than in American cities.

The entrance to the concrete, 1960's building on the Boulevard Bourdon, 250 yards south of the Bastille, could not be more nondescript. There isn't even a nameplate. But deep inside, behind the security guards, is a cavernous room filled with display panels and flashing lights that looks like the Pentagon's war room.

Welcome to the central command post for Paris's subway system, an intricate web with 434 stations, 686 escalators and 1.6 billion riders a year.

At rush hour, 560 trains snake through the city, and on the command center's 13 display panels, each as long as a baseball scoreboard, orange lights show the location and progress of every single train. If there is a subway fire or someone jumps in front of a train—there are about 150 such suicides each year—a subway line manager leaps up from his console and runs to his display panel to switch off power for his line.

"We have already extended this display panel to include some new stations that we still haven't opened," says Jean-Pierre Renard, a longtime manager at the command center. The panel shows two stations to be added when line No. 1 is extended under the Seine to La Défense, the ultramodern office district west of Paris.

Probably better than anything else, the Métro demonstrates Paris's devotion to constant improvement: to improve through planning, bold engineering and a willingness to spend money. The Métro recently added a conductorless train that connects Orly Airport with the main subway line. The express suburban rail system, known as the R.E.R., has been extended east to Euro-Disneyland, which opened in April. There are plans for a six-mile-long tramway that will connect blue-collar suburbs north of Paris and for an express subway connecting the southernmost part of Paris to the St.-Lazare train station on the right bank.

The budget for these and other transit projects—which are selected by a regional transportation board—will total $3 billion over the next five years. The financing comes from ticket revenues and from the city, regional and national governments.

Thanks to a solid flow of funds, the subway cars undergo maintenance once a week, and as a result mechanical failures are responsible for less than a third of line shutdowns. Usually the problem is human failures, like fights between passengers or pranksters pulling the emergency cord.

"If our trains ran without passengers, we'd hardly have any problems," jokes Renard, a short, dapper man in a blue bow tie and charcoal-striped suit.

Like many Parisian civil servants, Renard exudes an extreme pride in his work and his city. He boasts about a new varnish that helps keep the Métro graffiti-free. He brags about the system's safety record, saying he cannot remember the last time there was a fatal accident.

"I'm a modest man, so don't expect me to say that our Métro is the best in the world," he says, with a twinkle in his eye. "Let's just say it's one of the best.

"We plan to keep it that way."

3 Exploring Paris

Paris is a city of vast, noble perspectives and winding, hidden streets. This combination of the pompous and the intimate is a particularly striking and alluring feature of Paris. The French capital is also, for the tourist, a practical city: It is relatively small as capitals go, with many of its major sites and museums within walking distance of one another.

In fact, the best method of getting to know Paris is on foot, although public transportation—particularly the métro subway system—is excellent. Buy a *Plan de Paris* booklet: a city map-guide with a street-name index that also shows métro stations. Note that all métro stations have a detailed neighborhood map just inside the entrance.

Paris owes both its development and much of its visual appeal to the river Seine, which weaves through its heart. Each bank of the Seine has its own personality; the Rive Droite (Right Bank), with its spacious boulevards and haughty buildings, generally has a more sober and genteel feeling to it than the more carefree and bohemian Rive Gauche (Left Bank) to the south.

Paris's historical and geographical heart is Notre Dame Cathedral on the Ile de la Cité, the larger of the Seine's two islands (the other is the Ile St-Louis). The city's principal tourist axis is less than 4 miles long, running parallel to the north bank of the Seine from the Arc de Triomphe to the Bastille.

Monuments and museums are sometimes closed for lunch, usually between 12 and 2, and one day a week, usually Monday or Tuesday. Check before you set off. And don't forget that cafés in Paris are open all day long. They are a great boon to foot-weary tourists in need of a coffee, a beer, or a sandwich. *Boulangeries* (bakeries) are another reliable source of sustenance.

We've divided our coverage of Paris into six tours, but there are several "musts" that any first-time visitor to Paris is loath to miss: the Eiffel Tower, the Champs-Elysées, the Louvre, and Notre Dame. It would be a shame, however, not to explore the various *quartiers*, or districts, each with its own personality and charm.

The Historic Heart

Numbers in the margin correspond to points of interest on the Historic Heart map.

Of the two islands in the Seine—the Ile St-Louis (*see* The Marais and Ile St-Louis, *below*) and Ile de la Cité—it is the Ile de la Cité that forms the historic heart of Paris. It was here, for obvious reasons of defense, and in the hope of controlling the trade that passed along the Seine, that the earliest inhabitants of Paris, the Gaulish tribe of the Parisii, settled in about 250 BC. They called their little home Lutetia, meaning "settlement surrounded by water." Whereas the Ile St-Louis is today largely residential, the Ile de la Cité remains deeply historic, the result not just of more than 2,000 years of habitation, but of the fact that this is the site of the most important and one of the most beautiful churches in France—the great brooding cathedral of Notre Dame. Few of the island's other medieval buildings have survived to the present, most having fallen victim to town planner Baron Haussmann's ambitious rebuilding of the

Paris Exploring *(Boxes Refer to Detail Maps)*

LEVALLOIS-PERRET

NEUILLY-SUR-SEINE

Blvd. Bessier

Av. de Clichy

Av. de St. Ouen

Blvd. Berthier

Blvd. des Batignolles

Av. de Wagram

Av. de Villiers

Arc de Triomphe to

Blvd. de Courcelles

Parc Monceau

Gare St-Lazare

Av. de La Grande Armée

Blvd. Friedland

Blvd.

Haussmann

Opéra

Av. Foch

Arc de Triomphe

Av. Marceau

Av. George V

Av. F. D. Roosevelt

La Madeleine

Pl. Vendôn

Av. Kléber

Av. des Champs

-Elysées

Pl. de la Concorde

R. de Rivoli

Av. Victor Hugo

Wilson

Jardin des Tuileries

Pl. du Trocadéro

Av. du Pres.

Quai d'Orsay

Palais de Chaillot

PASSY

Eiffel Tower

Av. de la Bourdonnais

Blvd.

Av. de Suffren

Hôtel des Invalides

Av. du Pres. Kennedy

Blvd. de

Grenelle

Av. de Breteuil

R. de Sèvres

Orsay to Trocadéro

Av. Emile Zola

R. de la Convention

R. Lecourbe

Blvd. du Montparnasse

Blvd. Raspail

R. de Vaugirard

Gare Montparnasse

Av. du Maine

Av. F. Faure

Av. F. Faure

Blvd. Victor

R. de Vaugirard

R. d'Alésia

The Left Bank

city in the mid-19th century. But among the rare survivors are the jewel-like Sainte-Chapelle, a vision of shimmering stained glass, and the Conciergerie, the grim former city prison.

Another major attraction on this tour—the Louvre—came into existence in the mid-13th century, when Philippe-Auguste built it as a fortress to protect the city's western flank. It was not until pleasure-loving François I began a partial rebuilding of this original rude fortress in the early 16th century that to-day's Louvre began gradually to take shape. A succession of French rulers was responsible for this immense, symmetrical structure, now the largest museum in the world, as well as the easiest to get lost in.

If Notre Dame and the Louvre represent Church and State, re-spectively, the third major attraction we cover—Les Halles (pronounced *lay al*)—stands for the common man. For centur-ies, this was Paris's central market, replenished by an army of wagons and later, trucks, which caused astounding traffic jams in the city's already congested streets. The market was closed in 1969 and replaced by a striking shopping mall, the Forum. The surrounding streets have since undergone a transforma-tion, much like the neighboring Marais, with shops, cafés, res-taurants, and chic apartment buildings. However, the vast public spaces here have attracted a large vagrant population to the area, and general shabbiness has emerged.

Old and new blend and clash in Paris, contrasts that are hard to escape as you follow this tour. The brash modernity of the Fo-rum, for example, stands in contrast to the august church of St-Eustache nearby. The Louvre itself has not been spared controversy: While Louis XIV's harmoniously imposing Cour Carrée, one of the supreme architectural achievements of his reign, has been painstakingly restored and thousands of cob-blestones have been laid in place of tarmac, a mixture of awe and outrage has greeted the glass pyramid on the opposite side of the complex. Similarly, the incongruous black-and-white columns in the classical courtyard of Richelieu's neighboring Palais Royal present a further case of architectural vandal-ism—or daring modernity, depending on your point of view. The Parisians take seriously their role as custodians of a glori-ous heritage, but they are not content to remain mere guardi-ans of the past. If the city is to remain in the forefront of urban change, it is imperative that present generations bequeath something to the future. Well, so some say.

Toward the Louvre

The tour begins at the western tip of the Ile de la Cité, at the sedate **Square du Vert Galant.** Nothing is controversial here, not even the statue of the Vert Galant himself, literally the vig-orous—by which was really meant the amorous—adventurer, Henri IV, sitting foursquare on his horse. Henri, King of France from 1589 until his assassination in 1610, was some-thing of a dashing figure, by turns ruthless and charming, a stern upholder of the absolute rights of monarchy, and a notori-ous womanizer. He is probably best remembered for his cynical remark that *Paris vaut bien une messe* ("Paris is worth a mass"), a reference to his readiness to renounce his Protestant-ism as a condition of gaining the throne of predominantly Cath-olic France, and indeed of being allowed to enter the city. A measure of his canny statesmanship was provided by his enactment of the Edict of Nantes in 1598, by which French Protestants were accorded (almost) equal rights with their Catholic counterparts. It was Louis XIV's renunciation of the Edict nearly 100 years later that led to the massive Huguenot exodus from France, greatly to the economic disadvantage of the country. The square itself is a fine spot to linger on a sunny afternoon. It is also the departure point for the glass-topped *vedette* tour boats on the Seine.

Crossing the Ile de la Cité, just behind the Vert Galant, is the oldest bridge in Paris, confusingly called the **Pont Neuf**, or New Bridge. It was completed in the early 17th century and was the first bridge in the city to be built without houses lining either side. Turn left onto it. Visible to the north of the river is the large-windowed **Samaritaine** department store. Once across the river, turn left again and walk down to rue Amiral-de-Coligny. Opposite you is the massive eastern facade of the Louvre. It is Baroque dignity and coherence with no frills, a suitably imposing entrance to the rigorous classicism of the Cour Carrée beyond.

However, before heading for the Louvre, stay on the right-hand sidewalk and duck into the church of **St-Germain l'Auxerrois.** This was the French royal family's Paris church, used by them right up to 1789, in the days before the Revolution, when the Louvre was a palace rather than a museum. The fluid stonework of the facade reveals the influence of 15th-century Flamboyant Gothic, the final, exuberant fling of the Gothic before the classical takeover of the Renaissance. Notice the unusually wide windows in the nave, light flooding through them, and the equally unusual double aisles. The triumph of classicism is evident, however, in the fluted columns around the choir, the area surrounding the altar. These were added in the 18th century and are characteristic of the desire of 18th-century clerics to dress up medieval buildings in the architectural raiment of their day.

The Louvre

The best times to visit the Louvre are during lunchtime between 12:30 and 2:30 or on Monday and Wednesday evenings, when it stays open till 9:45.

In 1984, President François Mitterrand launched his Grand Louvre Project, a plan for restoration of the museum that includes the extension and modernization of the museum interior, renovation of the Palais du Louvre, and the restoration of the Carrousel gardens between the museum and the Tuileries Gardens. By 1993, the bicentennial of the opening of the Louvre, most of the facades had been cleaned, the museum's collection extended into the Richelieu wing, and construction of an underground garage and shopping arcade begun. The project is not scheduled for completion until 1996, so don't be surprised to see construction crews and steam shovels marring the otherwise superb locale when you visit.

The Louvre colonnade across the road from St-Germain l'Auxerrois screens one of Europe's most dazzling courtyards, the **Cour Carrée,** a monumental, harmonious, and superbly rhythmical ensemble. It has something of the assured feel of an Oxford or Cambridge quadrangle, though on a much grander

66

2e

Rue Réaumur

0 — 220 yards
0 — 200 meters

Rue d' Aboukir

17

R. Etienne Marcel

R. de Turbigo

R. des Petits-Champs

19

R. Pierre Lescot

R. St-Denis

Blvd. de Sébastopol

3e

18

1er

R. du Louvre

R. St-Honoré

R. Berger

20

R. Rambuteau

R. Beaubourg

R. de Rivoli

R. Amal.-de-Coligny

3

R. du Pont Neuf

R. des Halles

R. St-Denis

Sq. des Innocents

Beaubourg
(Pompidou Center)

R. St-Martin

R. du Renard

4e

R. de Rivoli

21

2

1

Pont Neuf

Conti

Dauphine

Quai des Grands Augustins

Pont au Change

Pont au Change

Pl. du Châtelet

Pont Notre Dame

22 23

24

Pl. Lépine

Blvd. du Palais

R. de Lutèce

25

R. de la Cité

Pont d'Arcole

Ile de la Cité

Pont St-Michel

Pl. St-Michel

Rue des Arts

Pl. du Parvis

27

Petit Pont

R. du Cloître Notre Dame

29

26

Pont Louis Philippe

Ile St-Louis

Blvd. St-Michel

R. St-Jacques

Pont au Double

28

Pont St-Louis

30

Quai de Montebello

Pont de l'Archevêché

5e

scale. In the **crypt** under it, excavated in 1984, sections of the defensive towers of the original, 13th-century fortress can be seen.

If you enter the museum via the quai du Louvre entrance, saunter through the courtyard and pass under the **Pavillon de l'Horloge**—the Clock Tower—and you come face to face with the Louvre's most controversial development, I. M. Pei's notorious **glass pyramid,** surrounded by three smaller pyramids. It's more than just a grandiloquent gesture, a desire on the part of Mitterrand, who commissioned it, to make his mark on the city. First, the pyramid marks the new, and much needed, entrance to the Louvre; it also houses a large museum shop, café, and restaurant. Second, it acts as the terminal point for the most celebrated city view in Europe, a majestic vista stretching through the Arc du Carrousel, the Tuileries Gardens, across place de la Concorde, up the Champs-Elysées to the towering Arc de Triomphe, and ending at the giant modern arch at La Tête Défense, 2½ miles more to the east. Needless to say, the architectural collision between classical stone blocks and pseudo-Egyptian glass panels has caused a furor. Adding insult to injury, at least as far as many Parisians are concerned, is the shocking fact that Pei isn't even a Frenchman! Before making up your mind, however, it may help to remember that the surrounding buildings in this part of the Louvre are mainly earnest 19th-century pastiche, whose pompous solemnity neither jars nor excites. Furthermore, though it may seem a coherent, unified structure, today's Louvre is the end product of many generations of work. The earliest parts of the building date from the reign of François I at the beginning of the 16th century. Down the years, Henri IV (1589–1610), Louis XIII (1610–1643), Louis XIV (1643–1715), Napoléon (1804–1814), and Napoléon III (1852–1870) have all contributed to the construction. Before rampaging revolutionaries burned part of it down during the bloody Paris Commune of 1871, the building was even larger. The open section facing the Tuileries Gardens was originally the Palais des Tuileries, the main Paris residence of the royal family.

The uses to which the building has been put have been almost equally varied. Though Charles V (1364–1380) made the Louvre his residence, later French kings preferred to live elsewhere, mainly in the Loire Valley. Even after François I decided to make the Louvre his permanent home, and accordingly embarked on an ambitious rebuilding program (most of which came to nothing), the Louvre never became more than a secondary palace. When, in 1682, Louis XIV decided to move the French court out of the city to Versailles, despite having previously initiated a major program of rebuilding at the Louvre, it seemed that the Louvre would never be more than a home for minor courtiers. Indeed, during the remainder of Louis's reign, the palace underwent a rapid decline. Its empty apartments were taken over by a rabble of artists; little shacklike shops were set up against the walls; and chimneys projected higgledy-piggledy from the severe lines of the facades. Louis XV (1715–1774), thanks in large measure to the financial shrewdness of his chief minister, Marigny, then inaugurated long-overdue renovations, though he, too, preferred to live at Versailles. The Louvre's association with the French crown was not to last much longer. It was from the Tuileries Palace that Louis XVI and Marie Antoinette fled in 1791, two years after the start of the Revolution, only to be arrested and returned to Paris for their executions. The palace was taken over by the Revolutionary leaders—the Convention first, then the Directory. At the very end of the century, Napoléon, initially as first consul, subsequently as emperor, initiated a further program of renovation and rebuilding and established the Louvre, first and foremost, as a museum rather than as a palace. This did not, however, prevent the three remaining French kings—Louis XVIII (1814–1824), who has the dubious distinction of having been the only French monarch to have died in the Louvre; Charles X (1824–1830); and Louis-Philippe (1830–1848)—from making the Louvre their home. The latter pair suffered the indignity of expulsion at the hands of the dreaded Paris mob in the uprisings of 1830 and 1848, respectively.

Today, of course, you'll want to see the Louvre not just to walk through a central part of French history, or even to marvel at the French gift for creating buildings that convey the pomp and prestige they consider their nation's due; rather, you'll be drawn here to see the extraordinary collections assembled under its roofs. Paintings, drawings, antiquities, sculpture, furniture, coins, jewelry—the quality and the sheer variety are intimidating. The number-one attraction for most is Leonardo da Vinci's enigmatic *Mona Lisa*, "La Joconde" to the French. But there are numerous other works of equal quality. The collections are divided into seven sections: Oriental antiquities; Egyptian antiquities; Greek and Roman antiquities; sculpture; paintings, prints, and drawings; furniture; and objets d'art. What follows is no more than a selection of favorites, chosen to act as key points for your exploration. If you have time for only one visit, they will give some idea of the riches of the museum. But try to make repeat visits—the Louvre is half-price on Sundays. With the rearrangement of the museum far from complete—the rue de Rivoli wing, which used to house the French Finance Ministry, is to become part of the museum by 1994—it's not possible to say with certainty just what works will be on display where. Study the plans at the entrance to get your bearings, and pick up a map to take with you.

Paintings: French paintings dominate the picture collection. Here are the highlights, in chronological order:

The Inspiration of the Poet, by Poussin (1594–1665), is a sturdy example of the Rome-based painter's fascination with the classical world and of the precision of his draftsmanship. The coloring, by contrast, is surprisingly vivid, almost Venetian.
Cleopatra Landing, by Claude (1600–1682), presents an altogether more poetic vision of the ancient world, delicately atmospheric, with the emphasis on light and space rather than on the nominal subject matter.
The Embarkation for the Island of Cythera, by Watteau (1684–1721), concentrates on creating an equally poetic mood, but there is an extra layer of emotion: The gallant gentlemen and their courtly women seem drugged by the pleasures about to be enjoyed, but disturbingly aware of their transitory nature, too.
The Oath of the Horatii, by David (1748–1825), takes a much sterner view of classical Rome; this is neo-Classicism—severe, uncompromising, and austere. The moral content of the painting takes precedence over purely painterly qualities; it also

held an important political message for contemporaries, championing the cause of Republicanism.

La Grande Odalisque, by Ingres (1780–1867), is the supreme achievement by this habitually staid "academic" artist; sensuous yet remote and controlled. Here, exoticism and the French classical tradition gel to produce a strikingly elegant image.

The Raft of the Medusa, by Gericault (1791–1824), presages a much more gloomily Romantic view of the human state, nightmarish despite its heroism and grand scale.

The Massacre at Chios, by Delacroix (1798–1863), is a dashing example of the painter's brilliant coloring and free handling. The rigid orthodoxies of French academic painting are decisively rejected in favor of a dramatically Romantic approach.

Among works by non-French painters, pride of place must go to the *Mona Lisa,* if only by virtue of its fame. The picture is smaller than you might expect and kept behind protective glass; it is invariably surrounded by a crowd of worshipers. The Italian Renaissance is also strongly represented by Fra Angelico, Mantegna, Raphael, Titian, and Veronese. Holbein, Van Eyck, Rembrandt, Hals, Brueghel, and Rubens underline the achievements of northern European painting. The Spanish painters El Greco, Murillo, Velázquez, and Goya are also well represented.

Sculpture: Three-dimensional attractions start with marvels of ancient Greek sculpture such as the soaring *Venus of Samothrace,* from the 3rd century BC, and the *Venus de Milo,* from the 2nd century BC. The strikingly realistic *Seated Scribe* dates from around 2000 BC. Probably the best-loved exhibit is Michelangelo's pair of *Slaves,* intended for the unfinished tomb of Pope Julius II.

Furniture and Objets d'Art: The number-one attraction is the **French crown jewels,** a glittering display of extravagant jewelry, including the 186-karat Regent diamond. Among the collections of French furniture, don't miss the grandiose 17th- and 18th-century productions of Boulle and Riesener, marvels of intricate craftsmanship and typical of the elegant luxury of the best French furniture. The series of immense Gobelins tapestries may well be more to the taste of those with a fondness for opulent decoration. *Tel. 40–20–50–50. Palais du Louvre. Admission: 35 frs adults, 20 frs 18–25 years, over 60, and Sun.; children under 18 free. Open Thurs.–Sun. 9–6, Mon. and Wed. 9 AM–9:45 PM. Some sections open some days only.*

Time Out To reflect and recharge, visit the **Café Mollien,** on the museum's mezzanine level, with its selection of coffees, pastries, and sandwiches. The museum also houses a cafeteria and a restaurant (*see* Chapter 5), though prices are steep. If you can make it to the Tuileries, stop at **Angelina** (226 rue de Rivoli). Founded in 1903, this elegant salon de thé is famous for its "L'Africain"—a cup of hot chocolate so thick you'll need a fork to eat it (irresistible even in the summer). Non-chocoholics can select from a dizzying assortment of pastries and other goodies.

North of the Louvre

Stretching westward from the main entrance to the Louvre and the glass pyramid is an expanse of stately, formal gardens.

These are the **Tuileries Gardens** (*see* From the Arc de Triomphe
❻ to the Opéra, *below*). Leading to them is the **Arc du Carrousel,** a
small relation of the distant Arc de Triomphe and, like its big
brother, put up by Napoléon. To the north, in the Pavillon de
❼ Marsan, the northernmost wing of the Louvre, is the **Musée des
Arts Décoratifs,** which houses over 50,000 objects charting the
course of French furniture and applied arts through the centuries. The Musée de la Publicité, with its collection of 50,000 posters, stages temporary exhibits within the museum. *107 rue de
Rivoli. Admission: 23 frs. Open Wed.–Sat. 12:30–6, Sun.
12–6.*

Running the length of the Louvre's northern side is Napoléon's
❽ elegant, arcaded **rue de Rivoli,** a street whose generally dull
tourist shops add little to their surroundings. Cross it and
❾ you're in **place des Pyramides** and face-to-face with its gilded
statue of Joan of Arc on horseback. The square is a focal point
for city tour buses.

Walk up rue des Pyramides and take the first left, rue St-
❿ Honoré, to the Baroque church of **St-Roch.** The church was begun in 1653 but completed only in the 1730s, the decade of the
coolly classical facade. Classical playwright Corneille (1606–
1684) is buried here; a commemorative plaque honoring him is
located at the left of the entrance. It's worth having a look inside the church to see the bombastically baroque altarpiece in
the circular Lady Chapel at the far end.

Double back along rue St-Honoré to place du Palais-Royal. On
⓫ the far side of the square, opposite the Louvre, is the **Louvre
des Antiquaires,** a chic shopping mall housing upscale antiques
shops. It's a minimuseum in itself. Its stylish, glass-walled corridors deserve a browse whether you intend to buy or not.

Retrace your steps to place André-Malraux, with its exuberant
fountains. The Opéra building is visible down the avenue of the
same name, while, on one corner of the square, at rue de Riche-
⓬ lieu, is the **Comédie Française.** This theater is the time-honored
setting for performances of classical French drama, with trage-
dies by Racine and Corneille and comedies by Molière regularly
on the bill. The building itself dates from 1790, but the Comédie
Française company was created by that most theatrical of
French monarchs, Louis XIV, back in 1680. Those who understand French and who have a taste for the mannered, declama-
tory style of French acting—it's a far cry from method acting—
will appreciate an evening here. (*See* The Arts and Nightlife,
Chapter 7, for details on how to get tickets.)

To the right of the theater is the unobtrusive entrance to the
⓭ gardens of the **Palais-Royal.** The buildings of this former palace
—royal only in that all-powerful Cardinal Richelieu (1585–
1642) magnanimously bequeathed them to Louis XIII—date
from the 1630s. In his early days as king, Louis XIV preferred
the relative intimacy of the Palais-Royal to the intimidating
splendor of the Louvre. He soon decided, though, that his own
intimidating splendor warranted a more majestic setting;
hence, of course, that final word in un-intimacy, Versailles.

Today, the Palais-Royal is home to the French Ministry of Cul-
⓮ ture and is not open to the public. But don't miss the **Jardin du
Palais-Royal,** gardens bordered by arcades harboring discreet
boutiques and divided by rows of perfectly trimmed little trees.
They are a surprisingly little-known oasis in the gray heart of

the city. It's hard to imagine anywhere more delightful for doz-
ing in the afternoon sun. As you walk into the gardens, there's
not much chance that you'll miss the black-and-white striped
columns in the courtyard or the revolving silver spheres that
slither around in the two fountains at either end, the controversial work of architect Daniel Buren. Everyone will muse on the
days when this dignified spot was the haunt of prostitutes and
gamblers, a veritable sink of vice, in fact. It's hard to imagine
anywhere much more respectable these days. Walk up to the
end, away from the main palace, and peek into the opulent,
⑮ Belle Epoque, glass-lined interior of **Le Grand Véfour.** This is
more than just one of the swankiest restaurants in the city; it's
probably the most sumptuously appointed, too (*see* Chapter 5).

Around the corner from here, on rue de Richelieu, stands
⑯ France's national library, the **Bibliothèque Nationale.** It contains over 7 million printed volumes. A copy of every book and
periodical printed in France must, by law, be sent here. Visitors can admire Robert de Cotte's 18th-century courtyard and
peep into the 19th-century reading room. The library galleries
stage exhibits from time to time from the collections. *58 rue de
Richelieu. Open daily 10–8.*

From the library, walk southeast along rue des Petits-Champs
⑰ to the circular **place des Victoires.** It was laid out in 1685 by
Mansart, a leading proponent of 17th-century French classicism, in honor of the military victories of Louis XIV, that inde-
fatigible warrior whose near-continuous battles may have
brought much prestige to his country but came perilously close
to bringing it to bankruptcy, too. Louis is shown prancing on a
plunging steed in the center of the square; it's a copy, put up in
1822 to replace the original one destroyed in the Revolution.
You'll find some of the city's most upscale fashion shops here
and on the surrounding streets.

Head south down rue Croix des Petits-Champs. You'll pass the
undistinguished bulk of the Banque de France on your right.
The second street on the left leads to the circular, 18th-century
⑱ **Bourse du Commerce,** or Commercial Exchange. Alongside it is
a 100-foot-high fluted column, all that remains of a mansion
built here in 1572 for Catherine de Médicis. The column is said
to have been used as a platform for stargazing by Catherine's
astrologer, Ruggieri.

You don't need to scale Ruggieri's column to be able to spot the
⑲ bulky outline of the church of **St-Eustache,** away to the left.
Since the demolition of the 19th-century iron and glass market
halls at the beginning of the '70s, an act that has since come to
be seen as little short of vandalism, St-Eustache has re-
emerged as a dominant element on the central Paris skyline. It
is a huge church, the "cathedral" of Les Halles, built, as it
were, as the market people's Right Bank reply to Notre Dame
on the Ile de la Cité. St-Eustache dates from a couple of hundred years later than Notre Dame. With the exception of the
feeble west front, added between 1754 and 1788, construction
lasted from 1532 to 1637, spanning the twilight of Gothic and
the rise of the Renaissance. As a consequence, the church is a
curious architectural hybrid. Its exterior flying buttresses, for
example, are solidly Gothic. Its column orders, rounded
arches, and comparatively simple and thick window tracery are
unmistakably classical. Few buildings bear such eloquent witness to stylistic transition. St-Eustache also features occasion-

al organ concerts. *2 rue du Jour, tel. 46–27–89–21, for concert information. Open daily.*

Nothing now remains of either the market halls or the rumbustious atmosphere that led 19th-century novelist Emile Zola to dub Les Halles *le ventre de Paris* ("the belly of Paris"). Today, the vast site is part shopping mall and part garden. The latter, which starts by the provocative, king-size sculpture *Hand* in front of St-Eustache, is geared for children. They'll also love the bush shaped like a rhinoceros.

The once-grimy facades of the buildings facing Les Halles have been expensively spruced up to reflect the mood of the shiny **❷⓪** new **Forum des Halles,** the multilevel mall. Just how long the plastic, concrete, glass, and mock-marble of this gaudy mall will stay shiny is anyone's guess. Much of the complex is already showing signs of wear and tear, a state of affairs not much helped by the hordes of down-and-outs who invade it toward dusk. Nonetheless, the multitude of shops gathered at the Forum makes it somewhere no serious shopper will want to miss. The sweeping white staircase and glass reflections of the central courtyard have a certain photogenic appeal.

Leave by square des Innocents to the southeast; its 16th-century Renaissance fountain has recently been restored. As you make your way toward boulevard de Sébastopol, you can see the futuristic funnels of the Beaubourg jutting above the surrounding buildings (*see* The Marais and Ile St-Louis, *below*). Head right, toward the Seine. Just before you reach place du **❷①** Châtelet on the river, you'll see the **Tour St-Jacques** to your left. This richly worked, 170-foot stump, now used for meteorological purposes and not open to the public, is all that remains of a 16th-century church destroyed in 1797.

Time Out Just north of place du Châtelet, at 4 rue St-Denis, is **Le Trappiste.** Twenty different international beers are available on draft here, as well as more than 180 in bottles. Mussels and french fries are the traditional accompaniment, although various other snacks (hot dogs, sandwiches) are also available. There are tables upstairs and on the pavement.

The Ile de la Cité

From place du Châtelet, cross back over the Seine on the Pont au Change to the Ile de la Cité. To your right looms the impos-
❷② ing **Palais de Justice,** the Law Courts, built by Baron Haussmann in his characteristically weighty classical style about 1860. You can wander around the building, watching the bustle of the lawyers, or attend a court hearing. But the real interest here is the medieval part of the complex, spared by Haussmann in his otherwise wholesale destruction of the lesser medieval buildings of the Ile de la Cité. There are two buildings you'll want to see: the Conciergerie and the Sainte-Chapelle.

❷③ The **Conciergerie,** the northernmost part of the complex, was originally part of the royal palace on the island. Most people know it, however, as a prison, the grim place of confinement for Danton, Robespierre, and, most famously, Marie Antoinette during the French Revolution. From here, all three, and countless others who fell foul of the Revolutionary leaders, were taken off to place de la Concorde and the guillotine. The name of the building is derived from the governor, or *concierge*, of the palace, whose considerable income was swollen by the privilege he enjoyed of renting out shops and workshops. Inside, you'll see the guardroom, complete with hefty Gothic vaulting and intricately carved columns, and the Salle des Gens d'Armes, an even more striking example of Gothic monumentality. From there, a short corridor leads to the kitchen, with its four vast fireplaces. Those with a yen to throw a really memorable party can rent the room. The cells, including that in which Marie Antoinette was held, and the chapel, where objects connected with the ill-fated queen are displayed, complete the tour. *Admission: 25 frs adults, 16 frs students and senior citizens. Joint ticket with Sainte-Chapelle: 40 frs. Open daily 9:30–6:30, 10–4:30 in winter.*

The other perennial crowd puller in the Palais de Justice is the
㉔ Sainte-Chapelle, the Holy Chapel. It was built by the genial and pious Louis IX (1226–1270), whose good works ensured his subsequent canonization. He constructed it to house what he took to be the Crown of Thorns from Christ's crucifixion and fragments of the True Cross, all of which he had bought from the impoverished Emperor Baldwin of Constantinople at phenomenal expense. Architecturally, for all its delicate and ornate exterior decoration—notice the open latticework of the pencil-like *flèche*, or spire, on the roof—the design of the building is simplicity itself. In essence, it's no more than a thin, rectangular box, much taller than it is wide. But think of it first and foremost as an oversize reliquary, an ornate medieval casket designed to house holy relics.

The building is actually two chapels in one. The plainer, first-floor chapel, made gloomy by insensitive mid-19th-century restorations (which could do with restoration themselves), was for servants and lowly members of the court. The upper chapel, infinitely more spectacular, was for the king and more important members of the court. This is what you come to see. You reach it up a dark spiral staircase. Here, again, some clumsy 19th-century work has added a deadening touch, but the glory of the chapel—the stained glass—is spectacularly intact. The chapel is airy and diaphanous, the walls glowing and sparkling as light plays on the windows. Notice how the walls, in fact, consist of at least twice as much glass as masonry: The entire aim of the architects was to provide the maximum amount of window space. The Sainte-Chapelle is one of the supreme achievements of the Middle Ages and will be a highlight of your visit to Paris. Come early in the day to avoid the dutiful crowds that trudge around it. Better still, try to attend one of the regular, candle-lit concerts given here. *Tel. 43–54–30–09, for concert information. Admission: 25 frs adults, 14 frs students and senior citizens. Joint ticket with Conciergerie: 40 frs. Open daily 9:30–6:30; winter, daily 10–5.*

Take rue de Lutèce opposite the Palais de Justice down to place
㉕ Louis-Lépine and the bustling Marché aux Fleurs, the flower market. There's an astoundingly wide range of flowers on sale and, on Sundays, there are birds, too—everything from sparrows to swans. *Open daily 9–7.*

Notre Dame

Around the corner, looming above the large, traffic-free place du Parvis (*kilometre zéro* to the French, the spot from which all distances to and from the city are officially measured), is the most enduring symbol of Paris, its historic and geographic heart, the **Cathédrale Notre Dame.** The building was started in 1163, with an army of stonemasons, carpenters, and sculptors working on a site that had previously seen a Roman temple, an early Christian basilica, and a Romanesque church. The chancel and altar were consecrated in 1182, but the magnificent sculptures surrounding the main doors were not put into position until 1240. The north tower was finished 10 years later. Despite various changes in the 17th century, principally the removal of the rose windows, the cathedral remained substantially unaltered until the French Revolution. Then, the statues of the kings of Israel were hacked down by the mob, chiefly because they were thought to represent the despised royal line of France, and everything inside and out that was deemed "anti-Republican" was stripped away. An interesting postscript to this destruction occurred in 1977, when some of the heads of these statues were discovered salted away in a bank vault on boulevard Haussmann. They'd apparently been hidden there by an ardent royalist who owned the small mansion that now forms part of the bank. The restored heads are now on display in the Musée de Cluny (*see* The Left Bank, *below*). *Admission free.*

By the early 19th century, the excesses of the Revolution were over, and the cathedral went back to fulfilling its religious functions again. Napoléon crowned himself emperor here in May 1804. (David's heroic painting of this lavish ceremony can be seen in the Louvre.) Full-scale restoration started in the middle of the century, the most conspicuous result of which was the construction of the spire, the *flèche*, over the roof. It was then, too, that Haussmann demolished the warren of little buildings in front of the cathedral, creating the place du Parvis. The **Crypte Archéologique,** the archaeological museum under the square, contains remains unearthed during excavations here in the 1960s. Slides and models detail the history of the Ile de la Cité. The foundations of the 3rd-century Gallo-Roman rampart and of the 6th-century Merovingian church can also be seen. *Place du Parvis. Admission: 25 frs adults (40 frs including tower of Notre Dame), 14 frs age 18–24 and over 60, 6 frs age 7–17. Open daily 10–6:30, 10–5 in winter.*

Place du Parvis provides the perfect place from which to gaze at the facade, divided neatly into three levels. At the first-floor level are the three main entrances, or portals: the Portal of the Virgin on the left, the Portal of the Last Judgment in the center, and the Portal of Ste-Anne on the right. All three are surmounted by magnificent carvings—most of them 19th-century copies of the originals—of figures, foliage, and biblical scenes. Above this level are the restored statues of the kings of Israel, the Galerie des Rois. Above the gallery is the great rose window, and, above that, the Grand Galerie, at the base of the twin towers. Between them, you can glimpse the flèche. The south tower houses the great bell of Notre Dame, as tolled by Quasimodo, Victor Hugo's fictional hunchback. The interior of the cathedral, with its vast proportions, soaring nave, and gentle, multicolored light filtering through the stained-glass win-

76

Portal of the Last
Judgment, **1**
Portal to the Virgin, **2**
Portal of St. Anne, **3**
Le Brun, **4**
St. Stephen's Portal, **5**
South Rose Window, **6**
Our Lady of Paris, **7**
Le Sueur, **8**
North Rose Window, **9**
Cloister Portal, **10**

Cathédrale Notre Dame (Interior)

Ambulatory

Chancel

Transept

Nave

dows, inspires awe, despite the inevitable throngs of tourists. Visit early in the morning, when the cathedral is at its lightest and least crowded. You come first to the massive, 12th-century columns supporting the twin towers. Look down the nave to the transepts—the arms of the church—where, at the south (right) entrance to the chancel, you'll glimpse the haunting, 12th-century statue of Notre Dame de Paris, Our Lady of Paris. The chancel itself owes parts of its decoration to a vow taken by Louis XIII in 1638. Still without an heir after 23 years of marriage, he promised to dedicate the entire country to the Virgin Mary if his queen produced a son. When the longed-for event came to pass, Louis set about redecorating the chancel and choir.

On the south side of the chancel is the **Treasury,** with a collection of garments, reliquaries, and silver and gold plate. *Admission: 15 frs adults, 10 frs students and senior citizens, 5 frs children. Open daily 10–5:45.*

The 387-step climb to the top of the **towers** is worth the effort for the close-up view of the famous gargoyles—most of them added in the 19th century—and the expansive view over the city. *Entrance via north tower. Admission: 30 frs adults, 16 frs students and senior citizens. Open daily 10–4:30.*

On the subject of views, no visit to Notre Dame is complete ❷❽ without a walk behind the cathedral to **Square Jean XXIII,** located between the river and the building. It offers a breathtaking sight of the east end of the cathedral, ringed by flying buttresses, surmounted by the spire. From here, the building seems almost to float above the Seine like some vast, stone ship.

If your interest in the cathedral is not yet sated, duck into the ❷❾ **Musée Notre Dame.** It displays paintings, engravings, medallions, and other objects and documents, all of which trace the cathedral's history. *10 rue du Cloître-Notre-Dame. Admission: 10 frs, 6 frs students and senior citizens, 4 frs children under 14. Open Wed. and weekends only, 2:30–6.*

There's a final pilgrimage you may like to make on the Ile de la ❸⓿ Cité to the **Mémorial de la Déportation,** located at square de l'Ile-de-France, at the eastern tip of the island. Here, in what was once the city morgue, you'll find the modern crypt, dedicated to those French men and women who died in Nazi concentration camps. You may find a visit to the quiet garden above it a good place to rest and to muse on the mysterious dichotomy that enables the human race to construct buildings of infinite beauty and to treat its fellow men with infinite cruelty. *Admission free. Open daily 9–6, 9–dusk in winter.*

The Marais and Ile St-Louis

Numbers in the margin correspond to points of interest on the Marais and Ile St-Louis map.

This tour includes two of the oldest and most historic neighborhoods in Paris: the Marais—once a marshy area north of the Seine, today about the most sought-after residential and business district of the city—and the Ile St-Louis, the smaller of the two islands in the Seine. It also includes a side trip to the Bastille, site of the infamous prison stormed on July 14, 1789, an event that came to symbolize the beginning of the French Revolution. Largely in commemoration of the bicentennial of the Revolution in 1989, the Bastille area has been renovated.

Renovation is one of the key notes of this tour, especially around the Marais; the word *marais*, incidentally, means marsh or swamp. Well into the '70s, this was one of the city's poorest areas, filled with dilapidated tenement buildings and squalid courtyards. Today, most of the Marais's spectacular *hôtels particuliers*—loosely, "mansions," one-time residences of aristocratic families—have been restored and transformed into museums. The grubby streets of the Jewish quarter, around the rue des Rosiers, is about the only area to remain undeveloped. The area's regeneration was sparked by the building of the Beaubourg, arguably Europe's most vibrant—and architecturally whimsical—cultural center. The gracious architecture of the 17th and early 18th centuries, however, sets the tone for the rest of the Marais. Try to visit during the Festival du Marais, held every June and July, when concerts, theater, and ballet are performed.

The history of the Marais began when Charles V, king of France in the 14th century, moved the French court from the Ile de la Cité. However, it wasn't until Henri IV laid out the place Royale, today the place des Vosges, in the early 17th century, that the Marais became *the* place to live. Aristocratic dwellings began to dot the neighborhood, and their salons filled with the *beau monde*. But following the French Revolution, the Marais rapidly became one of the most deprived, dissolute areas in Paris. It was spared the attentions of Baron Haussmann, the man who rebuilt so much of Paris in the mid-19th century, so that, though crumbling, its ancient golden-hued buildings and squares remained intact.

Hôtel de Ville to Beaubourg

❶ Begin your tour at the **Hôtel de Ville,** the city hall, overlooking the Seine. The building is something of a symbol for the regeneration of the Marais, since much of the finance and direction for the restoration of the area has been provided by the Parisian municipal authorities. As the area has been successfully redeveloped, so the prestige of the mayor of Paris has grown with it. In fact, until 1977, Paris was the only city in France without a mayor; with the creation of the post and the election to it of Jacques Chirac, leader of the right-of-center Gaullist party, the position has become pivotal in both Parisian and French politics. It comes as no surprise, therefore, that Chirac has overseen a thorough-going restoration of the Hôtel de Ville, both inside and out. You can't go inside, but stand in the traffic-free square in front of it and ponder the vicissitudes that have plagued the Parisian municipal authorities down the years and the dramas that have been played out here. It was here, in 1357, that Etienne Marcel, cloth merchant and prominent city father, attempted to exploit the chaos of the Hundred Years War—the titanic struggle between France and England for control of France—by increasing the power of what he hoped would be an independent Paris. And it was just one year later that his supporters had him assassinated here, believing that his ambitions had outstripped their common interests.

There's a statue of Marcel in the little garden on the south side of the building overlooking the Seine. The square was also used for numerous public executions. Most victims were hanged, drawn, and quartered; the lucky ones were burned at the stake. It was also here, during the Revolution, that Robespierre, fanatical leader of the Terror, came to suffer the fate of his many victims when a furious mob sent him to the guillotine in 1794. Following the short-lived restoration of the Bourbon monarchy in 1830, the building became the seat of the French government, a role that came to a sudden end with the uprisings in 1848. In the Commune of 1871, the Hôtel de Ville was burned to the ground. Today's exuberant building, based closely on the Renaissance original, went up between 1874 and 1884. In 1944, following the liberation of Paris from Nazi rule, General de Gaulle took over the leadership of France here.

From the Hôtel de Ville, head north across rue de Rivoli and up rue du Temple. On your right, you'll pass one of the city's most
❷ popular department stores, the **Bazar de l'Hôtel de Ville,** or BHV, as it's known. The first street on your left, rue de la Verrerie, will take you down to rue St-Martin and the church
❸ of **St-Merri,** an ornate mid-16th-century structure. Its dark interior can be fun to explore, though it contains nothing of outstanding interest. You may find the upscale stores, restaurants, and galleries of rue St-Martin more diverting.

❹ The **Beaubourg/Pompidou Center** or, to give it its full name, the Centre National d'Art et de Culture Georges-Pompidou, is next. Georges Pompidou (1911–1974) was the president of France who inaugurated the project. If nothing else, the Beaubourg is an exuberant melting pot of culture, which casts its net far and wide: Anything goes here. The center hosts an innovative and challenging series of exhibits, in addition to housing the largest collection of modern art in the world. It boasts an avowedly open-door policy toward the public—witness the long hours—and a determination to bring in the crowds by whatever means possible. On the other hand, there's little getting away from the fact that the building itself has been the target of much unfavorable rhetoric. Unveiled in 1977, the Beaubourg is by far the most popular museum in the world, attracting upward of 8 million visitors a year; but it has begun to show its age in no uncertain terms. The much-vaunted, gaudily painted service pipes that snake up the exterior—painted the same colors that were used to identify them on the architects' plans—need continual repainting. The plastic tubing that encloses the exterior escalators is cracked and grimy. The skeletal supports in the interior are peeling and dirty. In essence, the massive solemnity of a building like the Louvre makes the brashness of the Beaubourg seem cheap, many now maintain. Does the Beaubourg display gross architectural bad manners, contemptuously ignoring the elegant proportions of the surrounding streets? Or is it a bold and potent architectural statement, feeling no need to apologize for its uncompromising nature?

❺ You'll approach the center across **plateau Beaubourg,** a substantial square that slopes gently down toward the main entrance. In summer, it's thronged with musicians, mime artists, dancers, fire-eaters, acrobats, and other performers. Probably the single most popular thing to do at the Beaubourg is to ride the escalator up to the roof, with the Parisian skyline unfolding

The Marais and Ile St-Louis

Bazar de l'Hôtel de Ville, **2**

Beaubourg/Pompidou Center, **4**

Hôtel Carnavalet, **15**

Hôtel d'Avaux, **7**

Hôtel de Beauvais, **21**

Hôtel de Clisson, **10**

Hôtel de Lauzun, **26**

Hôtel de Montmor, **8**

Hôtel de Sens, **23**

Hôtel de Sully/ Caisse Nationale des Monuments Historiques, **19**

Hôtel de Ville, **1**

Hôtel Peletier St-Fargeau, **16**

Ile St-Louis, **24**

Musée Cognacq-Jay, **14**

Musée de la Chasse et de la Nature, **9**

Musée de la Serrure/ Musée Bricard, **12**

Musée de l'Histoire de France, **11**

Musée Picasso, **13**

Place de la Bastille, **18**

Place des Vosges, **17**

Plateau Beaubourg, **5**

Quai de Bourbon, **27**

Quartier de l'Horloge, **6**

Rue St-Louis en l'Ile, **25**

St-Gervais-St-Protais, **22**

St-Merri, **3**

St-Paul-St-Louis, **20**

as you are carried through its clear plastic piping. There is a sizable restaurant and café on the roof. The major highlight inside is the modern art collection on the fourth floor. The emphasis is largely on French artists; American painters and sculptors are conspicuous by their absence. Movie buffs will want to take in the cinémathèque, a movie theater showing near-continuous programs of classic films from the world over. There are also magnificent reference facilities, among them a language laboratory, an extensive collection of tapes, videos, and slides, an industrial design center, and an acoustics and musical research center. The bookshop on the first floor stocks a wide range of art books, many in English, plus postcards and posters. *Beaubourg, plateau Beaubourg, tel. 42–77–12–33. Admission free. Admission to art museum: 28 frs, 32 frs for special exhibitions in the Grande Galerie. Open Wed.–Mon. noon–10 PM, weekends 10 AM–10 PM; closed Tues. Guided tours in English weekdays 3:30, weekends 11 during summer and Christmas seasons only.*

Time Out Don't leave the plateau without stopping for coffee at the **Café Beaubourg** on the corner of rue St-Merri. A staircase takes you up from the first floor to a *passerelle*, or footbridge, linking the two sides of a mezzanine. The severe high-tech design is lightened by the little glass-top tables, which are gradually being covered with artists' etchings.

You can leave plateau Beaubourg by its southwestern corner—to your right as you face the building—and head down little rue Ste-Croix de la Bretonnerie to visit the Marais's Jewish quarter; it represents an intriguing element of Parisian ethnic history but, especially since some relatively recent bomb attacks, is a rather cloistered quarter of the Marais.

You'll see the more obvious of the area's historical highlights if you take rue Rambuteau, which runs along the north side of the center (to your left as you face the building). The **Quartier de l'Horloge,** the Clock Quarter, opens off the plateau here. An entire city block has been rebuilt, and, though its shops and cafés make a brave attempt to bring it to life, it retains a resolutely artificial quality. The mechanical clock around the corner on rue Clairvaux will amuse kids, however. Saint George defends Time against a dragon, an eagle-beaked bird, or a monstrous crab (symbolizing earth, air, and water, respectively) every hour, on the hour. At noon, 6 PM, and 10 PM, he takes on all three at once. On the other side of the Quartier de l'Horloge, at 11 rue Brantôme, is **AS-ECO,** the only all-night supermarket in the city; note that it's closed on Sundays. However, it's more fun shopping in the little market at the beginning of rue Rambuteau.

Around the Marais

You are now poised to plunge into the elegant heart of the Marais. You won't be able to get into many of the historic homes here—the private hôtels particuliers—but this won't stop you from admiring their stately facades. And don't be afraid to push through the heavy formal doors—or *porte-cochères*—to glimpse the discreet courtyards that lurk behind them.

From the Clock Quarter, continue down rue Rambuteau and take the first left, up rue du Temple, to the **Hôtel d'Avaux** at no.

71, built in 1640. The immense entrance is decorated with the sculpted heads of what, in 17th-century France, passed for savages. A few doors up, at no. 79, is the **Hôtel de Montmor,** dating from the same period. It was once the scene of an influential literary salon—a part-social and part-literary group—that met here on an impromptu basis and included the philosopher Descartes (1596–1650) and the playwright Molière (1622–1673). Note the intricate ironwork on the second-floor balcony.

9 Head east on rue des Haudriettes to the little-known **Musée de la Chasse et de la Nature,** housed in one of the Marais's most stately mansions, the Hôtel de Guénégaud. The collections include a series of immense 17th- and 18th-century pictures of dead animals, artfully arranged, as well as a wide variety of guns and stuffed animals (you might want to pass this by if you are a vegetarian or an opponent of blood sports). *60 rue des Archives, tel. 42–72–86–43. Admission: 25 frs adults, 5 frs. children under 16. Open Wed.–Mon. 10–12:30 and 1:30–5:30.*

Next door, at 58 rue des Archives, two fairytale towers stand on either side of the Gothic entrance (1380) to the **Hôtel de Clisson.** In the mid-15th century this was the Paris base of the Duke of Bedford, regent of France after Henry V's demise, during the English occupation of Paris, a phase of the Hundred Years War that lasted from 1420 to 1435. At the end of the 17th century, it was bought by the glamorous princess of Soubise, a grande dame of Parisian literary society. She later moved into the neighboring Hôtel de Soubise, now the **Archives Nationales.** Its collections today form part of the **Musée de l'Histoire de France,** whose entrance is at the southern end of the Archives Nationales. There are thousands of intricate historical documents, many complete with impressive red seals. The highlights are the Edict of Nantes (1598), the wills of Louis XIV and Napoléon, and the Declaration of Human Rights. Louis XVI's diary is also in the collection, containing his sadly ignorant entry for July 14, 1789, the day the Bastille was stormed and, for all intents and purposes, the day the French Revolution can be said to have begun: *Rien* ("nothing"), he wrote. You can also visit the apartments of the prince and princess de Soubise; don't miss them if you have any interest in the lifestyles of 18th-century French aristocrats. *60 rue des Francs-Bourgeois, tel. 40–27–62–18. Admission: 12 frs adults, children under 18 free. Open Wed.–Mon. 1:45–5:45.*

Continue east on rue des Francs-Burgeois, turning left onto rue Vielle du Temple and passing the Hôtel de Rohan (on your left, on the corner), built for the archbishop of Strasbourg in 1705. Turn right onto rue de la Perle and walk down to the **Musée de la Serrure,** the Lock Museum. It's sometimes also called the **Musée Bricard,** a name you'll recognize on many French locks and keys. The sumptuous building in which the collections are housed is perhaps more interesting than the assembled locks and keys within; it was built in 1685 by Bruand, the architect of Les Invalides *(see* From Orsay to Trocadéro, *below).* But those with a taste for fine craftsmanship will appreciate the intricacy and ingenuity of many of the older locks. One represents an early security system—it would shoot anyone who tried to open it with the wrong key. Another was made in the 17th century by a master locksmith who was himself held under lock and key while he labored over it—the task took him four years. *1 rue de la Perle, tel. 42–77–79–62. Admission: 10* *frs. Open Mon.–Fri. 2–5; closed Sat., Sun., Aug., and last week of Dec.*

⑬ From here it is but a step to the Hôtel Salé, today the **Musée Picasso,** opened in the fall of 1985 and so far showing no signs of losing its immense popularity. Be prepared for long lines at any time of year. The building itself, put up between 1656 and 1660 for financier Aubert de Fontenay, quickly became known as the Hôtel Salé—*sal* meaning salt, and *salé* meaning salted—as a result of the enormous profits made by de Fontenay as the sole appointed collector of the salt tax. The building was restored by the French government at phenomenal expense as a permanent home for the pictures, sculptures, drawings, prints, ceramics, and assorted works of art given to the government by Picasso's heirs after the painter's death in 1973 in lieu of death duties. What's notable about the collection—other than the fact that it's the largest collection of works by Picasso in the world—is that these were works that Picasso himself owned; works, in other words, that he especially valued. There are pictures from every period of his life, adding up to a grand total of 230 paintings, 1,500 drawings, and nearly 1,700 prints, as well as works by Cézanne, Miró, Renoir, Braque, Degas, Matisse, and others. If you have any serious interest in Picasso, this is not a place you'd want to miss. The positively palatial surroundings of the Hôtel Salé add greatly to the pleasures of a visit. *5 rue de Thorigny, tel. 42–71–25–21. Admission: 26 frs. Open Thurs.–Mon. 9:30–6.*

Head back down rue de Thorigny and cross to rue Elzévir, op-
⑭ posite. Halfway down on the left is the **Musée Cognacq-Jay,** opened here in 1990 after being transferred from its original home on boulevard des Capucines near the Opéra. The museum is devoted to the arts of the 18th century and contains outstanding furniture, porcelain, and paintings (notably by Watteau, Boucher, and Tiepolo). *8 rue Elzévir, tel. 40–27–07–21. Admission: 12 frs, 6 frs students and children. Open Tues.–Sun. 10–5:30.*

Continue down rue Elzévir to **rue des Francs-Bourgeois.** Its name—Street of the Free Citizens—comes from the homes for the poor, or almshouses, built here in the 14th century, whose inhabitants were so impoverished that they were allowed to be "free" of taxes. In marked contrast to the street's earlier pover-
⑮ ty, the substantial **Hôtel Carnavalet** became the scene, in the late 17th century, of the most brilliant salon in Paris, presided over by Madame de Sévigné. She is best known for the hundreds of letters she wrote to her daughter during her life; they've become one of the most enduring chronicles of French high society in the 17th century, and the Carnavalet was her home for the last 20 years of her life. In 1880, the hotel was transformed into the **Musée Carnavalet,** or Musée Historique de la Ville de Paris. As part of the mammoth celebrations for the bicentennial of the French Revolution, in July 1989, the mu-
⑯ seum annexed the neighboring **Hôtel Peletier St-Fargeau.** Together the two museums chronicle the entire history of the city of Paris, with material dating from the city's origins until 1789 housed in the Hôtel Carnavalet, and objects from that time to the present in the Hôtel Peletier Saint-Fargeau. Parts of the older collections are quite interesting, albeit repetitive. There are large numbers of maps and plans, quantities of furniture, and a substantial assemblage of busts and portraits of Parisian

worthies down the ages. The sections on the Revolution, on the other hand, are extraordinary and include some riveting models of guillotines and a number of objects associated with the royal family's final days, including the chess set that the prisoners used to pass the time, and the king's razor. *23 rue de Sévigné, tel. 42–72–21–13. Admission: 40 frs adults, 30 frs students and senior citizens. Open Tues.–Sun. 10–5:30; closed Mon.*

⑰ Now walk a minute or two farther along rue des Francs-Bourgeois to **place des Vosges.** Place des Vosges, or place Royale as it was originally known, is the oldest square in Paris. Laid out by Henri IV at the beginning of the 17th century, it is the model on which all later city squares, that most French urban developments, are based. It stands on the site of a former royal palace, the Palais des Tournelles, which was abandoned by the French Queen, Italian-born Catherine de Médicis, when her husband, Henri II, was killed in a tournament here in 1559. The square achieves a harmony and a balance that make it deeply satisfying. The buildings have been softened by time, their pale pink stones crumbling slightly in the harsh Parisian air, their darker stone facings pitted with age. The combination of symmetrical town houses and the trim green square, bisected in the center by gravel paths and edged with plane trees, makes place des Vosges one of the more pleasant places to spend a hot summer's afternoon in the city. On these days, it will usually be filled with children playing in shafts of sunlight, with the roar of the traffic a distant hum.

Place des Vosges was always a highly desirable address, reaching a peak of glamour in the early years of Louis XIV's reign, when the nobility were falling over themselves for the privilege of living here. Notice the two larger buildings in the center of the north and south sides. The one on the south side was the king's pavilion; the one on the north was the queen's pavilion. The statue in the center is of Louis XIII. It's not the original; that was melted down in the Revolution, the same period when the square's name was changed in honor of the French district of the Vosges, the first area of the country to pay the new revolutionary taxes. You can tour the **Maison de Victor Hugo** at no. 6 (admission 12 frs, 6.50 frs students; open Tues.–Sun. 10–5:40), where the French author lived between 1832 and 1848. The collections here may appeal only to those with a specialized knowledge of the workaholic French writer.

Around the Bastille

⑱ From place des Vosges, follow rue de Pas de la Mule and turn right down boulevard Beaumarchais until you reach **place de la Bastille,** site of the infamous prison destroyed at the beginning of the French Revolution. Until 1988, there was little more to see at place de la Bastille than a huge traffic circle and the **Colonne de Juillet,** the July Column. As part of the countrywide celebrations for July 1989, the bicentennial of the French Revolution, an **opera house** (Opéra de la Bastille) was put up on the south side of the square. Designed by Argentinian-born Carlos Ott, it seats more than 3,000 and boasts five moving stages. This ambitious project has inspired substantial redevelopment on the surrounding streets, especially along rue de Lappe—once a haunt of Edith Piaf—and rue de la Roquette. What was formerly a humdrum neighborhood is rapidly becom-

ing one of the most sparkling and attractive in the city. Stream-
lined art galleries, funky jazz clubs, Spanish-style *tapas* bars—
very chic in Paris these days—and classy restaurants set the
tone. For a taste of the new Bastille-style nightlife, try **Balajo**
(9 rue de Lappe); it's the liveliest place here, with music (either
disco or live) nightly. Don't expect things to get too lively before 11 PM, however.

The Bastille, or, more properly, the Bastille St-Antoine, was a
massive building, protected by eight immense towers and a wide
moat (its ground plan is marked by paving stones set into the
modern square). It was built by Charles V in the late 14th century. He intended it not as a prison but as a fortress to guard the
eastern entrance to the city. By the reign of Louis XIII (1610–
1643), however, the Bastille was used almost exclusively to house
political prisoners. Voltaire, the Marquis de Sade, and the mysterious Man in the Iron Mask were all incarcerated here, along
with many other unfortunates. It was this obviously political
role—specifically, the fact that the prisoners were nearly always
held by order of the king—that led to the formation of the "furious mob" (in all probability no more than a largely unarmed rabble) to break into the prison on July 14, 1789, to kill the governor,
steal what firearms they could find, and set free the seven remaining prisoners.

Later in 1789, the prison was knocked down. A number of the
original stones were carved into facsimiles of the Bastille and sent
to each of the provinces as a memento of royal oppression. The key
to the prison was given by Lafayette to George Washington, and
it has remained at Mt. Vernon ever since. Nonetheless, the power
of legend being what it is, what soon became known as the
"storming of the Bastille" was elevated to the status of a pivotal
event in the course of the French Revolution, one that demonstrated decisively the newfound power of a long-suffering population. Thus it was that July 14 became the French national day, an
event celebrated with great nationalistic fervor throughout the
country. It's very much more than just a day off or an excuse for a
cookout. Needless to say, the place to be, especially in the evening, is place de la Bastille.

The July Column commemorates a more substantial political
event: the July uprising of 1830, which saw the overthrow of the
repressive Charles X, the Bourbon king about whom it was said
only too truthfully that "the Bourbons learnt nothing, and forgot
nothing." It's sometimes hard to imagine the turmoil that was a
feature of French political life from the Revolution of 1789 right
through the 19th century (and, arguably, well into the 20th). After the fall of Napoléon in 1815, the restoration of a boneheaded
monarchy, personified first by Louis XVIII, then by Charles X,
virtually guaranteed that further trouble was in store. Matters
came to a head in July 1830 with the Ordinances of St-Cloud, the
most contentious of which was to restrict the franchise—the
right to vote—to a handful of landowners. Charles was duly toppled in three days of fighting at the end of the month—the Three
Glorious Days—and a new, constitutionally elected monarch,
Louis-Philippe, took the throne. His reign was hardly more distinguished, despite attempts to curry favor among the populace.
Nor was it noticeably more liberal. Louis-Philippe did, nonetheless, have the July Column built as a memorial, stipulating that
500 of those killed in the fighting of 1830 were to be buried under
it. When, in 1848, Louis-Philippe himself was ousted, the names

of a handful of the Parisians killed in the fighting of 1848 were
then added to those already on the column. (Louis-Philippe and
his wife, disguised as Mr. and Mrs. William Smith, fled to Britain
and threw themselves on the mercy of the young Queen Victoria.)

Toward the Ile St-Louis

There's more of the Marais to be visited between place de la
Bastille and the Ile St-Louis, the last leg of this tour. Take wide
rue St-Antoine to the **Hôtel de Sully,** site of the **Caisse Nationale des Monuments Historiques,** the principal office for the administration of French historic monuments. Guided visits to
sites and buildings all across the city begin here, though all of
them are for French-speakers only. Still, it's worth stopping
here to look at the stately, 17th-century courtyard with its
richly carved windows and lavish ornamentation. The bookshop just inside the gate has a wide range of publications on
Paris, many of them in English (open daily 10–12:45 and
1:45–6). You can also wander around the gardens.

Those with a fondness for the Baroque should duck into the early 17th-century church of **St-Paul-St-Louis,** a few blocks west
on rue St-Antoine. Its abundant decoration, which would be
easier to appreciate if the church were cleaned, is typical of the
Baroque taste for opulent detail.

The **Hôtel de Beauvais,** located on rue François Miron, is a Ren-
aissance-era hôtel particulier dating from 1655. It was built for
one Pierre de Beauvais and financed largely by a series of discreet payments from the king, Louis XIV. These surprisingly
generous payments—the Sun King was normally parsimonious
toward courtiers—were de Beauvais's reward for having
turned a blind eye to the activities of his wife, Catherine-
Henriette Bellier, in educating the young monarch in matters
sexual. Louis, who came to the throne in 1643 at the age of 4,
was 14 at the time Catherine-Henriette gave him the benefit of
her wide experience; she was 40.

Continue down rue François Miron. Just before the Hôtel de
Ville is the site of one of the first churches in Paris, **St-Gervais-
St-Protais,** named after two Roman soldiers martyred by the
Emperor Nero in the 1st century AD. The original church—no
trace remains of it now—was built in the 7th century. The present church, a riot of Flamboyant-style decoration, went up
between 1494 and 1598, making it one of the last Gothic
constructions in the country. Some find this sort of late Gothic
architecture a poor, almost degraded, relation of the pure
styles of the 12th and 13th centuries. Does it carry off a certain
exuberance, or is it simply a mass of unnecessary decoration?
You'll want to decide for yourself. Pause before you go in, to
look at the facade, put up between 1616 and 1621. Where the
interior is late Gothic, the exterior is one of the earliest examples of classical, or Renaissance, style in France. It's also the
earliest example of French architects' use of the classical orders of decoration on the capitals (topmost sections) of the columns. Those on the first floor are plain and sturdy Doric; the
more elaborate Ionic is used on the second floor; while the most
ornate of all—Corinthian—is used on the third floor. The
church hosts occasional organ and choral concerts. *Tel. 47–26–
78–38 for concert information. Open Tues.–Sun. 6:30 AM–8
PM; closed Mon.*

Don't cross the Seine to Ile St-Louis yet: Take rue de l'Hôtel de
Ville to where it meets rue de Figuier. The painstakingly re-
㉓ stored **Hôtel de Sens** (1474) on the corner is one of a handful of
Parisian homes to have survived since the Middle Ages. With
its pointed corner towers, Gothic porch, and richly carved decorative details, it is a strange mixture, half defensive stronghold, half fairytale château. It was built at the end of the 15th
century for the archbishop of Sens. Later, its best-known occupants were Henri IV and his queen, Marguerite, philanderers
both. While Henri dallied with his mistresses—he is said to
have had 56—at a series of royal palaces, Marguérite entertained her almost equally large number of lovers here. Today
the building houses a fine arts library, the **Bibliothéque Forney**
(admission free; open Tues.–Fri. 1:30–8:30, Sat. 10–8:30).

The Ile St-Louis

㉔ Cross pont Marie to the **Ile St-Louis**, the smaller of the two islands in the heart of Paris, linked to the Ile de la Cité by pont
St-Louis. The contrast between the islands is striking, considering how close they are. Whereas the Ile de la Cité, the oldest
continuously inhabited part of the city, is steeped in history
and dotted with dignified, old buildings, the Ile St-Louis is a
discreet residential district, something of an extension of the
Marais. Once thought to be an unimportant backwater and an
area curiously out-of-sync with the rest of the city, Ile St-Louis
is now a highly desirable address; a little old-fashioned perhaps, certainly rather stuffy, but with its own touch of class.
There are no standouts here and no great sights, but for idle
strolling, window-shopping, or simply sitting on one of the little quays and drinking in the views while you watch the river
swirl by, the Ile St-Louis exudes a quintessentially Parisian
air. Come early in the day if you want to sample the full flavor of
this elegant haven.

The most striking feature of the island is its architectural uni-
ty, which stems from the efforts of a group of early 17th-cen-
tury property speculators. At that time, there were two islands
here, the Ile Notre Dame and Ile aux Vaches—the cows' island,
a reference to its use as grazing land. The speculators, led by an
energetic engineer named Christophe Marie (after whom the
pont Marie was named), bought the two islands, joined them
together, and divided the newly formed Ile St-Louis into building plots. Louis Le Vau (1612–1670), the leading Baroque architect in France, was commissioned to put up a series of
imposing town houses, and by 1664 the project was largely
complete.

There are three things you'll want to do here. One is to walk
㉕ along **rue St-Louis en l'Ile**, which runs the length of the island.
People still talk about its quaint, village-street feel, although
this village street is now lined with a high-powered array of designer boutiques and a constant throng of tourists patroling its
length.

Time Out **Berthillon** has become a byword for amazing ice cream. Cafés
all over Ile St-Louis sell its glamorous products, but the place
to come is still the little shop on rue St-Louis en l'Ile. Expect to
wait in line. *31 rue St-Louis en l'Ile. Closed Mon. and Tues.*

㉖ The second place to visit is the **Hôtel de Lauzun.** It was built in about 1650 for Charles Gruyn, who accumulated an immense fortune as a supplier of goods to the French army, but who landed in jail before the house was even completed. In the 19th century, the revolutionary critic and visionary poet Charles Baudelaire (1821–1867) had an apartment here, where he kept a personal cache of stuffed snakes and crocodiles. In 1848, the poet Théophile Gautier (1811–1872) moved in, making it the meeting place of the Club des Haschischines, the Hashish-Eaters' Club; novelist Alexander Dumas and painter Eugène Delacroix were both members. The club came to represent more than just a den of drug-takers and gossip, for these men believed passionately in the purity of art and the crucial role of the artist as sole interpreter of the chaos of life. Art for art's sake—the more exotic and refined the better—was their creed. Anything that helped the artist reach heightened states of perception was applauded by them. Now the building is used for receptions by the mayor of Paris. *17 quai d'Anjou, tel. 43–54–27–14. Admission: 22 frs. Open Easter–Oct., weekends only 10–5:30.*

The third and most popular attraction is a walk along the
㉗ quays. The most lively, **quai de Bourbon,** is at the western end, facing the Ile de la Cité. There are views of Notre Dame from here and of the Hôtel de Ville and church of St-Gervais-St-Protais on the Right Bank. It can be an almost eerie spot in the winter, when it becomes deserted. In the summer, rows of baking bodies attest to its enduring popularity as the city's favorite sunbathing spot.

Time Out The **Brasserie de l'Ile** remains the most noisy and bustling of the little island's eating spots. Food from the French Alsace region, on the German border, with beer to wash it down, is the draw. Scores of tourists can nearly always be found on the terrace, but good value is guaranteed. *55 quai de Bourbon, tel. 43–54–02–59. Closed Wed. and Thurs. lunch and Aug.*

From the Arc de Triomphe to the Opéra

Numbers in the margin correspond to points of interest on the Arc de Triomphe to the Opéra map.

This tour takes in grand, opulent Paris: the Paris of imposing vistas, long, arrow-straight streets, and plush hotels and jewelers. It begins at the Arc de Triomphe, standing foursquare at the top of the most famous street in the city, the Champs-Elysées. You'll want to explore both its commercial upper half and its verdant lower section. The hinterland of the Champs-Elysées, made up of the imposing streets leading off it, is equally stylish. You're within striking distance of the Seine here (and a ride on a Bateau Mouche) to the south, and the cheerful, crowded Faubourg St-Honoré to the north. This is not so much an area for museums as for window-shopping and monument-gazing. Dazzling vistas open up from place de la Concorde, place de la Madeleine, and L'Etoile. Fashion shops, jewelers, art galleries, and deluxe hotels proliferate. This is also where the French president resides in his "palace" (not a very Repub-

lican term, but then French presidents enjoy regal lifestyles)
just off the Champs-Elysées.

Local charm is not, however, a feature of this exclusive sector of
western Paris, occupying principally the 8th Arrondissement.
It's beautiful and rich—and a little impersonal. Frenchmen
moan that it's losing its character, and, as you notice the number of fast-food joints along the Champs-Elysées, you'll know
what they mean. In short: Visit during the day, and head elsewhere in search of Parisian *ambience* and an affordable meal in
the evening.

The Arc de Triomphe and Champs-Elysées

Place Charles de Gaulle is known by Parisians as **L'Etoile,** the
star—a reference to the streets that fan out from it. It is one of
Europe's most chaotic traffic circles, and short of a death-defy-
ing dash, your only way of getting to the Arc de Triomphe in
the middle is to take an underground passage from the
Champs-Elysées or avenue de la Grande Armée.

❶ The colossal, 164-foot **Arc de Triomphe** was planned by Napoléon—who believed himself to be the direct heir to the Roman
emperors—to celebrate his military successes. Unfortunately,
Napoléon's strategic and architectural visions were not entirely on the same plane, and the Arc de Triomphe proved something of a white elephant. When it was required for the
triumphal entry of his new empress, Marie-Louise, into Paris
in 1810, it was still only a few feet high. To save face, a dummy
arch of painted canvas was put up.

Empires come and go, and Napoléon's had been gone for over 20
years before the Arc de Triomphe was finally finished in 1836.
It boasts some magnificent sculpture by François Rude, such
as the *Departure of the Volunteers*, better known as *La Mar-
seillaise*, situated to the right of the arch when viewed from the
Champs-Elysées. After showing alarming signs of decay, the
structure received a thorough overhaul in 1989 and is now back
to its original neo-Napoléonic splendor. The view from the top
illustrates the star effect of Etoile's 12 radiating avenues and
enables you to admire the vista down the Champs-Elysées toward place de la Concorde and the distant Louvre. In the other
direction, you can see down avenue de la Grande Armée toward
La Tête Défense and its severe modern arch, surrounded by imposing glass and concrete towers. There is a small museum halfway up the arch devoted to its history. France's Unknown
Soldier is buried beneath the archway; the flame is rekindled
every evening at 6:30. *Pl. Charles-de-Gaulle. Admission: 31
frs adults, 17 frs students and senior citizens, 6 frs children.
Open daily 10–5:30, 10–5 in winter. Closed public holidays.*

The cosmopolitan pulse of Paris beats strongest on the grace-
fully sloping, 1¼-mile-long **Champs-Elysées.** It was originally
laid out in the 1660s by the landscape gardener Le Nôtre as a
garden sweeping away from the Tuileries, but you will see few
signs of these pastoral origins as you stroll past the cafés, restaurants, airline offices, car showrooms, movie theaters, and
chic arcades that occupy its upper half.

❷ Start off by stopping in at the main **Paris Tourist Office** at no.
127. It's at the Arc de Triomphe end of the Champs-Elysées, on
the right-hand side as you arrive from Etoile. It is an invalua-

ble source of information on accommodations, places to visit, and entertainment—both in Paris and in the surrounding Ile-de-France region. *Open daily 9–8, 9–9 on weekdays in summer, 9–6 on Sun. out of season.*

The Champs-Elysées occupies a central role in French national celebrations. It witnesses the finish of the Tour de France bicycle race on the last Sunday of July. It is also the site of vast ceremonies on July 14, France's national, or Bastille, day, and November 11, Armistice Day. Its trees are often decked with the French *tricolore* and foreign flags to mark visits from heads of state.

Three hundred yards down on the left, at 116b, is the famous ❸ **Lido** nightclub: Foot-stomping melodies in French and English and champagne-soaked, topless razzmatazz pack in the crowds ❹ every night. In contrast are the red-awninged **Prince de Galles** ❺ (Prince of Wales) and the blue-awninged **George V,** two of the city's top hotels on avenue George-V, a right-hand turn off Champs-Elysées. Continue down avenue George-V, and turn ❻ right down Pierre Ier-de-Serbie to the church of **St-Pierre de Chaillot** on avenue Marceau. The monumental frieze above the entrance, depicting scenes from the life of St. Peter, is the work of Henri Bouchard and dates from 1937.

Returning to avenue George-V, continue toward the slender ❼ spire of the **American Cathedral of the Holy Trinity,** built by G. S. Street between 1885 and 1888. *Open weekdays 9–12:30 and 2–5, Sat. 9–noon. Services: weekdays 9 AM, Sun. 9 AM and 11 AM; Sun. school and nursery. Guided tours Sun. and Wed. 12:30.*

❽ Continue down to the bottom of the avenue, passing the **Crazy Horse Saloon** at no. 12, one of Paris's most enduring and spectacular nightspots, to place de l'Alma and the Seine.

❾ The **pont de l'Alma** (Alma bridge) is best known for the chunky stone "Zouave" statue carved into one of the pillars. Zouaves were Algerian infantrymen recruited into the French army who were famous for their bravura and colorful uniforms. (The term came to be used for volunteers in the Union Army during the American Civil War.) There is nothing quite so glamorous, or colorful, about the Alma Zouave, however, whose hour of glory comes in times of watery distress: Parisians use him to judge the level of the Seine during heavy rains. As recently as the spring of 1988, the Zouave was submerged up to his chest, and the roads running along the riverbanks were under several feet of water.

❿ Just across the Alma bridge, on the left, is the entrance to **Les Egouts,** the Paris sewers (admission: 25 frs adults, 20 frs students and senior citizens; open Sat.–Wed. 11–5). Brave the unpleasant—though tolerable—smell and follow the underground passages and footbridges along the sewers' banks. Signs note the streets above you, and detailed panels and displays illuminate the history of waste disposal in Paris, which boasts the second largest sewer system in the world (after Chicago's). If you prefer a less malodorous tour of the city, stay on the Right Bank and head down the sloping side road to the ⓫ left of the bridge, for the embarkation point of the **Bateaux Mouches.** These popular motorboats set off every half hour, heading east to the Ile St-Louis and then back west, past the Eiffel Tower, as far as the Allée des Cygnes and its miniature

The Arc de Triomphe to the Opéra

American Cathedral of the Holy Trinity, **7**
Arc de Triomphe, **1**
Atelier de Gustave Moreau, **37**
Bateaux Mouches, **11**
Crazy Horse Saloon, **8**
Crillon, **26**
Eglise de la Madeleine, **20**

Fauchon, **22**
Galeries Lafayette, **33**
Gare St-Lazare, **38**
George V, **5**
Grand Palais, **16**
Hédiard, **23**
Jardin des Tuileries, **29**
Les Egouts, **10**

Lido, **3**
Maison de la Vigne et du Vin de France, **14**
Marks & Spencer, **35**
Maxim's, **24**
Musée Cernuschi, **44**
Musée de l'Orangerie, **28**
Musée du Jeu de Paume, **27**

Musée Jacquemart-André, **42**
Musée Jean-Jacques Henner, **46**
Musée Nissim de Camondo, **43**
Olympia, **31**
Opéra, **32**
Palais de la Découverte, **15**

Palais de l'Elysée, **18**
Parc Monceau, **45**
Paris Tourist Office, **2**
Petit Palais, **17**
Place de la
Concorde, **25**
Place Vendôme, **30**
Plaza Athénée, **13**
Pont de l'Alma, **9**

Prince de Galles, **4**
Printemps, **34**
St-Alexandre
Nevsky, **47**
St-Augustin, **40**
St. Michael's English
Church, **19**
St-Philippe du
Roule, **41**

St-Pierre de
Chaillot, **6**
Square Louis XVI, **39**
Théâtre des Champs-
Elysées, **12**
Ticket kiosk, **21**
Trinité, **36**

version of the Statue of Liberty. *Bateau Mouche* translates, misleadingly, as "fly boat"; but the name Mouche actually refers to a district of Lyon where the boats were originally manufactured.

12 Stylish avenue Montaigne leads from the Seine back toward the Champs-Elysées. The newly cleaned facade of the **Théâtre des Champs-Elysées** is a forerunner of the Art Deco style. The theater dates from 1913 and was the first major building in France to be constructed in reinforced concrete. *15 av. Montaigne.*

Time Out Although power brokers and fashion models make up half the clientele at the **Bar des Théâtres** (opposite the Théâtre des Champs-Elysées at 6 av. Montaigne), its blasé waiters refuse to bat an eyelid. This is a fine place for an aperitif or a swift, more affordable lunch than around the corner at the luxury restaurants on place de l'Alma.

13 A few buildings along is the **Plaza Athénée** hotel (the "Plaza"), a favorite hangout for the *beau monde* who frequent the neighboring haute couture houses. Around the corner on the rue **14** François-Ier is the **Maison de la Vigne et du Vin de France.** This is the classy central headquarters of the French wine industry and a useful source of information about wine regions. Bottles and maps are on display. *21 rue François-Ier, tel. 47–20–20–76. Admission free. Open weekdays 9–12:30 and 1:30–6.*

Double back on rue François-Ier as far as Place François-Ier, then turn left onto rue Jean-Goujon, which leads to avenue Franklin D. Roosevelt, another spacious boulevard between Champs-Elysées and the river. Halfway down it is the entrance **15** to the **Palais de la Découverte** (Palace of Discovery), whose scientific and technological exhibits include working models and a planetarium. *Av. Franklin-D-Roosevelt. Admission: 21 frs adults, 11 frs children under 18 (15 frs/10 frs extra for planetarium). Open Tues.–Sat. 9:30–6, Sun. 10–7.*

16 This "Palace of Discovery" occupies the rear half of the **Grand Palais.** With its curved glass roof, the Grand Palais is unmistakable when approached from either the Seine or the Champs-Elysées and forms an attractive duo with the **Petit Palais** on the other side of avenue Winston Churchill. Both these stone buildings, adorned with mosaics and sculpted friezes, seem robust and venerable. In fact, they were erected with indecent haste prior to the Paris World Fair of 1900. As with the Eiffel Tower, there was never any intention that they would be anything other than temporary additions to the city. But once they were up, no one seemed inclined to take them down. Together with the exuberant, lamp-lit Alexandre III bridge nearby, they recapture the opulence and frivolity of the Belle Epoque—the *fin de siècle* overripeness with which Paris is still so strongly associated. Today, the atmospheric iron and glass interior of the Grand Palais plays regular host to major exhibitions. Admire the view from the palaces across the Alexandre III bridge toward the Hôtel des Invalides. *Av. Winston Churchill. Admission varies according to exhibition. Usually open daily 10:30–6:30, and often until 10 PM Wed.*

17 The **Petit Palais** has a beautifully presented permanent collection of French painting and furniture, with splendid canvases by Courbet and Bouguereau. Temporary exhibits are often held here, too. The sprawling entrance gallery contains several enormous turn-of-the-century paintings on its walls and ceilings. *Av. Winston Churchill. Admission: 12 frs adults, 6 frs children. Open Tues.–Sun. 10–5:30.*

From the Rond-Point des Champs-Elysées, head down avenue de Marigny to rue du Faubourg St-Honoré, a prestigious address in the world of luxury fashion and art galleries. You'll soon spot plenty of both, but may be perplexed at the presence of crash barriers and stern policemen. Their mission: to protect **⑱** the French president in the **Palais de l'Elysée.** This "palace," where the head of state lives, works, and receives official visitors, was originally constructed as a private mansion in 1718. Although you catch a glimpse of the palace forecourt and facade through the Faubourg St-Honoré gateway, it is difficult to get much idea of the building's size or of the extensive gardens that stretch back to the Champs-Elysées. (Incidentally, when Parisians talk about "l'Elysée," they mean the President's palace; the Champs-Elysées is known simply as "les Champs," the fields.) The Elysée has known presidential occupants only since 1873; before then, Madame de Pompadour (Louis XV's influential mistress), Napoléon, Josephine, the Duke of Wellington, and Queen Victoria all stayed here. President Félix Faure died here in 1899 in the arms of his mistress. The French government—the Conseil des Ministres—attends to more public affairs when it meets here each Wednesday morning. *Not open to the public.*

Toward place de la Concorde

⑲ **St. Michael's English Church,** close to the British Embassy on rue du Faubourg St-Honoré, is a modern building whose ugliness is redeemed by the warmth of the welcome afforded to all visitors, English-speaking ones in particular. *5 rue d'Aguesseau, tel. 47–42–70–88. Services Thurs. 12:45 and Sun. 10:30 (with Sunday school) and 6:30; supervised nursery for younger children in the morning.*

Continue down rue du Faubourg St-Honoré to rue Royale. This classy street, lined with jewelry stores, links place de la **⑳** Concorde to the **Eglise de la Madeleine** (closed Sun. 1:30–3:30), a sturdy neo-Classical edifice that was nearly selected as Paris's first train station (the site of what is now the Gare St-Lazare, just up the road, was eventually chosen). With its rows of uncompromising columns, the Madeleine looks more like a Greek temple than a Christian church. Inside, the only natural light comes from three shallow domes. The walls are richly and harmoniously decorated, and gold glints through the murk. The church was designed in 1814 but not consecrated until 1842. The portico's majestic Corinthian colonnade supports a gigantic pediment with a sculptured frieze of the Last Judgment. From the top of the steps, you can admire the view down rue Royale across place de la Concorde to the Palais Bourbon. From the bottom of the steps, another view leads up boulevard Malesherbes to the dome of the church of St-Augustin.

Time Out | **L'Ecluse,** on the square to the west of the church, is a cozy wine bar that specializes in stylish snacks, such as foie gras and carpaccio, and offers a range of Bordeaux wines served by the glass. *15 pl. de la Madeleine. Open daily noon–2 AM.*

Alongside the Madeleine, between the church and L'Ecluse, is
㉑ a **ticket kiosk** (open Tues.–Sat. 12:30–8) selling tickets for
same-day theater performances at greatly reduced prices. Be-
㉒ ㉓ hind the church are **Fauchon** and **Hédiard,** two stylish delicates-
sens that are the ultimate in posh nosh. At the end of the rue
Royale, just before place de la Concorde, is the legendary
㉔ **Maxim's** restaurant. Unless you choose to eat here—an expensive and not always rewarding experience—you won't be able
to see the interior decor, a riot of crimson velvets and florid Art
Nouveau furniture.

There is a striking contrast between the sunless, locked-in feel
㉕ of the high-walled rue Royale and the broad, airy **place de la
Concorde.** This huge square is best approached from the
Champs-Elysées: The flower beds, chestnut trees, and sandy
sidewalks of the avenue's lower section are reminders of its
original leafy elegance. Place de la Concorde was built in the
1770s, but there was nothing in the way of peace or concord
about its early years. Between 1793 and 1795, it was the scene
of over a thousand deaths by guillotine; victims included Louis
XVI, Marie Antoinette, Danton, and Robespierre. The obelisk, a present from the viceroy of Egypt, was erected in 1833.
The handsome, symmetrical, 18th-century buildings facing the
㉖ square include the deluxe hotel **Crillon,** though there's nothing
so vulgar as a sign to identify it—just an inscribed marble
plaque above the doorway.

Facing one side of place de la Concorde are the **Tuileries Gardens.** Two smallish buildings stand sentinel here. To the left,
㉗ nearer rue de Rivoli, is the **Musée du Jeu de Paume,** fondly
known to many as the former home of the Impressionists (now
in the Musée d'Orsay). After extensive renovation, the Jeu de
Paume reopened in 1991 as a home to brash temporary exhibits
of contemporary art. *Admission: 30 frs adults, 20 frs students
and senior citizens. Open Tues. noon–9:30, Wed.–Fri. 12–7,
weekends 10–7.* The other, identical building, nearer the Seine,
㉘ is the recently restored **Musée de l'Orangerie,** containing some
early 20th-century paintings by Monet (including his vast,
eight-paneled *Water Lilies*), Renoir, and other Impressionists.
*Place de la Concorde. Admission: 26 frs adults, 14 frs students
and senior citizens. Open Wed.–Mon. 9:45–5:15; closed Tues.*

㉙ As gardens go, the **Jardin des Tuileries** is typically French: formal and neatly patterned, with statues, rows of trees, gravel
paths, and occasional patches of grass trying to look like lawns.
These may benefit from the overhaul ordered by Culture Minister Jack Lang for the early '90s. It is a charming place to stroll
and survey the surrounding cityscape. To the north is the disciplined, arcaded rue de Rivoli; to the south, the Seine and the
gold-hued Musée d'Orsay with its enormous clocks; to the west,
the Champs-Elysées and Arc de Triomphe; to the east, the Arc
du Carrousel and the Louvre, with its glass pyramid.

Place Vendôme and the Opéra

㉚ **Place Vendôme,** north of the Jardin des Tuileries, is one of the
world's most opulent squares. Mansart's rhythmic, perfectly
proportioned example of 17th-century urban architecture has
shone in all its golden-stoned splendor since being cleaned a few
years ago. Many other things shine here, too—in jewelers' display windows and on the dresses of guests of the top-ranking

Ritz hotel. Napoléon had the square's central column made from the melted bronze of 1,200 cannons captured at the battle of Austerlitz in 1805. That's him standing vigilantly at the top. Painter Gustave Courbet headed the Revolutionary hooligans who, in 1871, toppled the column and shattered it into thousands of metallic pieces.

Cross the square and take rue des Capucines on your left to boulevard des Capucines. The **Olympia** music hall is still going strong, though it has lost some of the luster it acquired as the stage for such great postwar singers as Edith Piaf and Jacques Brel.

Time Out There are few grander cafés in Paris than the **Café de la Paix,** on the corner of place de l'Opéra. This is a good place to people-watch, or just to slow down; but expect the prices to be as grand as the setting.

The **Opéra,** begun in 1862 by Charles Garnier at the behest of Napoléon III, was not completed until 1875, five years after the emperor's political demise. It is often said to typify the Second Empire style of architecture, which is to say that it is a pompous hodgepodge of styles, imbued with as much subtlety as a Wagnerian cymbal crash. After paying the entry fee, you can stroll around at leisure. The monumental foyer and staircase are boisterously impressive, a stage in their own right, where, on first nights, celebrities preen and prance. If the lavishly upholstered auditorium (ceiling painted by Marc Chagall in 1964) seems small, it is only because the stage is the largest in the world—over 11,000 square yards, with room for up to 450 performers. The **Musée de l'Opéra** (Opéra museum), containing a few paintings and theatrical mementos, is unremarkable. *Admission: 28 frs, 15 frs children. Open daily 10–4:30, but closed occasionally for rehearsals; call 47–42–57–50 to check.*

Around the Opéra

Behind the Opéra are the *grands magasins*, Paris's most renowned department stores. The nearer of the two, the **Galeries Lafayette,** is the most outstanding, if only because of its vast, shimmering, turn-of-the-century glass dome. The domes at the corners of **Printemps,** farther along boulevard Haussmann, to the left, can be best appreciated from the outside; there is a splendid view from the store's rooftop cafeteria. **Marks & Spencer,** across the road, provides a brave outpost for British goods, such as ginger biscuits, bacon rashers, and Cheddar cheese.

The **Trinité** church, several blocks north of the Opéra, is not an unworthy 19th-century effort at neo-Renaissance style. Its central tower is of dubious aesthetic merit but is a recognizable feature in the Paris skyline (especially since its cleaning in 1986). The church was built in the 1860s and is fronted by a pleasant garden.

The nearby **Atelier de Gustave Moreau** was the town house and studio of painter Gustave Moreau (1826–1898), doyen of the Symbolist movement that strove to convey ideas through images. Many of the ideas Moreau was trying to express remain obscure to the general public, however, even though the artist provided explanatory texts. But most onlookers will be content admiring his extravagant colors and flights of fantasy, which reveal the influence of Persian and Indian miniatures. Fantastic details cover every inch of his canvases, and his canvases cover every inch of wall space, making a trip to the museum one of the strangest artistic experiences in Paris. Go on a sunny day, if possible; the low lighting can strain the eyes even more than Moreau's paintings can. *14 rue de la Rochefoucauld. Admission: 17 frs adults, 10 frs children and senior citizens. Open Thurs.–Sun. 10–12:45 and 2–5:15, Mon. and Wed. 11–5:15.*

38 Rue St-Lazare leads from Trinité to the **Gare St-Lazare,** whose imposing 19th-century facade has been restored. In the days of steam and smoke, the station was an inspiration to several Impressionist painters, notably Monet. Note an eccentric sculpture to the right of the facade—a higgledy-piggledy accumulation of clocks.

39 The leafy, intimate **Square Louis XVI,** off boulevard Haussmann between St-Lazare and St-Augustin, is perhaps the nearest Paris gets to a verdant, London-style square—if you discount the bombastic mausoleum in the middle. The unkempt chapel marks the initial burial site of Louis XVI and Marie Antoinette after their turns at the guillotine on place de la Concorde. Two stone tablets are inscribed with the last missives of the doomed royals—touching pleas for their Revolutionary enemies to be forgiven. When compared to the pomp and glory of Napoléon's memorial at the Invalides, this tribute to royalty (France was ruled by kings until 1792 and again from 1815 to 1848) seems trite and cursory. *Open daily 10–noon and 2–6, 10–4 in winter.*

Before leaving the square, take a look at the gleaming 1930s-style facade of the bank at the lower corner of rue Pasquier. It has some amusing stone carvings halfway up, representing various exotic animals.

40 A mighty dome is the most striking feature of the innovative iron-and-stone church of **St-Augustin,** dexterously constructed in the 1860s within the confines of an awkward, V-shaped site. The use of metal girders obviated the need for exterior buttressing. The dome is bulky but well-proportioned and contains some grimy but competent frescoes by the popular 19th-century French artist William Bouguereau.

41 Rue La Boétie leads to another church, **St-Philippe du Roule,** built by Chalgrin between 1769 and 1784. Its austere classical portico dominates a busy square. The best thing inside this dimly lit church is the 19th-century fresco above the altar by Théodore Chassériau, featuring the Descent from the Cross.

42 Make your way back to boulevard Haussmann via avenue Myron T. Herrick. The **Musée Jacquemart-André** features Italian Renaissance and 18th-century art in a dazzlingly furnished, late 19th-century mansion. *158 blvd. Haussmann, tel. 42–89–04–91. Admission: 18 frs. Open Wed.–Sun. 1–6.*

43 Rue de Courcelles and a right on rue de Monceau will lead to place de Rio de Janeiro. Before venturing into the Parc Monceau at the far end of avenue Ruysdaël, continue along rue de Monceau to the **Musée Nissim de Camondo.** Inside, you will find the stylish interior of an aristocratic Parisian mansion in the style of Louis XVI, dating from the last days of the regal Ancien Régime. *63 rue de Monceau. Admission: 18 frs adults,*

12 frs students and senior citizens. Open Wed.–Sun. 10–noon
and 2–5.

④ Rue de Monceau and boulevard Malesherbes lead to the **Musée
Cernuschi,** whose collection of Chinese art ranges from neolith-
ic pottery (3rd century BC) to funeral statuary, painted 8th-
century silks, and contemporary paintings. *7 av. Velasquez.
Admission: 12 frs. Open Tues.–Sun. 10–5:40.*

④ The **Parc Monceau,** which can be entered from avenue Velasquez, was laid out as a private park in 1778 and retains some of
the fanciful elements then in vogue, including mock ruins and a
phony pyramid. In 1797, Garnerin, the world's first-recorded
parachutist, staged a landing in the park. The rotunda, known
as the Chartres Pavilion, was originally a tollhouse and has
well-worked iron gates.

Leave the Parc Monceau by these gates and follow rue Phals-
④ bourg and avenue de Villiers to the **Musée Jean-Jacques
Henner.** Henner (1829–1905), a nearly forgotten Alsatian artist, here receives a sumptuous tribute. His obsessive fondness
for milky-skinned, auburn-haired female nudes is displayed in
hundreds of drawings and paintings on the three floors of this
gracious museum. *43 av. de Villiers. Admission: 14 frs. Open
Tues.–Sun. 10–noon and 2–5.*

Boulevard de Courcelles, which runs along the north side of the
Parc Monceau, leads west to rue Pierre-le-Grand (Peter the
Great Street). At the far end of that street, at 12 rue Daru,
loom the unlikely gilt onion domes of the Russian Orthodox ca-
④ thedral of **St-Alexandre Nevsky,** erected in neo-Byzantine style
in 1860. Inside, the wall of icons that divides the church in two
creates an atmosphere seldom found in Roman Catholic or
Protestant churches.

From Orsay to Trocadéro

*Numbers in the margin correspond to points of interest on the
Orsay to Trocadéro map.*

The Left Bank has two faces: the cozy, ramshackle Latin Quarter (*see* The Left Bank, *below*) and the spacious, stately 7th Arrondissement. This tour covers the latter, then heads back
across the Seine for a look at the museums and attractions clustered around the place du Trocadéro. The latest addition to the
area is already the most popular: the Musée d'Orsay. Crowds
flock to this stylishly converted train station to see the Impressionists, but also discover important examples of other schools
of 19th- and early 20th-century art.

The atmosphere of the 7th Arrondissement is set by the National Assembly, down the river from Orsay, opposite place de
la Concorde. French deputies meet here to hammer out laws
and insult each other. They resume more civilized attitudes
when they return to the luxurious ministries that dot the nearby streets. The most famous is the Hôtel Matignon, official residence of the French prime minister.

The majestic scale of many of the area's buildings is totally in
character with the daddy of them all, the Invalides. Like the
Champ de Mars nearby, the esplanade in front of the Invalides
was once used as a parade ground for Napoléon's troops. In a
coffin beneath the Invalides dome, M. Bonaparte dreams on.

Musée d'Orsay

❶ The **Musée d'Orsay** opened in December 1986. It is devoted to the arts (mainly French) produced between 1848 and 1914, and its collections are intended to form a bridge between the classical collections of the Louvre and the modern collections of the Beaubourg. The building began in 1900 as a train station for routes between Paris and the southwest of France. By 1939, the Gare d'Orsay had become too small for mainline travel, and intercity trains were transferred to the Gare d'Austerlitz. Gare d'Orsay became a suburban terminus until, in the 1960s, it closed for good. After various temporary uses (a theater and auction house among them), the building was set for demolition. However, the destruction of the 19th-century Les Halles (market halls) across the Seine provoked a furor among conservationists, and in the late 1970s, President Giscard d'Estaing, with an eye firmly on establishing his place in the annals of French culture, ordered Orsay to be transformed into a museum. The architects Pierre Colboc, Renaud Bardou, and Jean-Paul Philippon were commissioned to remodel the building, while Gae Aulenti, known for her renovation of the Palazzo Grassi in Venice, was hired to redesign the interior.

Exhibits take up three floors, but the visitor's immediate impression is of a single, vast, stationlike hall. The use of an aggressively modern interior design in a building almost a century old has provoked much controversy, which you'll want to resolve for yourself.

The chief artistic attraction is the Impressionists, whose works are displayed on the top floor, next to the museum café. Renoir, Sisley, Pissarro, and Monet are all well represented. Highlights for many visitors are Monet's *Poppy Field* and Renoir's *Le Moulin de la Galette*. The latter differs from many Impressionist paintings in that Renoir worked from numerous studies and completed it in his studio rather than painting it in the open air. Nonetheless, its focus on the activities of a group of ordinary Parisians amusing themselves in the sun on a Montmartre afternoon is typical of the spontaneity, the sense of the fleeting moment captured, that are the very essence of Impressionism. Where Monet, the only one of the group to adhere faithfully to the tenets of Impressionism throughout his career, strove to catch the effects of light, Renoir was more interested in the human figure.

The Post-Impressionists—Cézanne, van Gogh, Gauguin, and Toulouse-Lautrec—are all also represented on this floor. Some may find the intense, almost classical serenity of Cézanne the dominant presence here; witness his magnificent Mont Sainte-Victoire series, in which he paints and repaints the same subject, in the process dissolving form until the step to abstract painting seems almost an inevitability. Others will be drawn by the vivid simplicity and passion of van Gogh, or by the bold, almost pagan rhythms of Gauguin.

On the first floor, you'll find the work of Manet and the delicate nuances of Degas. Pride of place, at least in art historical terms, goes to Manet's *Déjeuner sur l'Herbe*, the painting that scandalized Paris in 1863 at the Salon des Refusés, an exhibit organized by those artists refused permission to show their work at the Academy's official annual exhibit. The painting shows a nude woman and two clothed men picnicking in a park.

In the background, another naked girl bathes in a stream. Manet took the subject, poses and all, from a little-known Renaissance print in the Louvre. In that, of course, the clothed men wore contemporary 16th-century garb. In Manet's painting, the men also wear contemporary clothing, that of mid-19th-century France, complete with gray trousers and frock coats. What would otherwise have been thought a respectable "academic" painting thus became deeply shocking: two clothed men with two naked women! The loose, bold brushwork, a far cry from the polished styles of the Renaissance, added insult to artistic injury. Another reworking by Manet of a classical motif is his reclining nude, *Olympia*. Gazing boldly out from the canvas, she was more than respectable 19th-century Parisian proprieties could stand.

Those who prefer more correct academic paintings should look at Puvis de Chavannes's larger-than-life, classical canvases. The pale, limpid beauty of his figures is enjoying considerable attention after years of neglect. Those who are excited by more modern developments will make for the early 20th-century Fauves (meaning wild beasts, the name given them by an outraged critic in 1905)—particularly Matisse, Derain, and Vlaminck.

Sculpture at the Orsay means, first and foremost, Rodin (though there's more to enjoy at the Musée Rodin, *see below*). Two further highlights are the faithfully restored Belle Epoque restaurant and the model of the entire Opéra quarter, displayed beneath a glass floor.

The Musée d'Orsay, otherwise known as M.O., is already one of Paris's star attractions. Crowds are smaller at lunchtime and on Thursday evenings. *1 rue de Bellechasse. Admission: 31 frs adults, 16 frs students and senior citizens and on Sun. Open Tues.–Sat. 10–6, Thurs. 10–9:30, and Sun. 9–6.*

Time Out There is no better place to take a break than the **Musée d'Orsay café,** handily but discreetly situated behind one of the giant station clocks close to the Impressionist galleries on the top floor. From the rooftop terrace, there is a panoramic view across the Seine toward Montmartre and the Sacré-Coeur.

➋ Across from the Musée d'Orsay stands the **Musée de la Légion d'Honneur.** French and foreign decorations are displayed in this stylish mansion by the Seine (officially known as the Hôtel de Salm). The original building, constructed in 1786, burned during the Commune in 1871 and was rebuilt in 1878. *2 rue de Bellechasse. Admission: 10 frs. Open Tues.–Sun. 2–5.*

Toward the Invalides

➌ Continue along the left bank of the Seine to the 18th-century **Palais Bourbon** (directly across from place de la Concorde), home of the Assemblée Nationale (French Parliament). The colonnaded facade, commissioned by Napoléon, is a sparkling sight after a recent cleaning program (jeopardized at one stage by political squabbles as to whether cleaning should begin from the left or the right). There is a fine view from the steps across to place de la Concorde and the church of the Madeleine. *Not open to the public.*

Orsay to Trocadéro

Ecole Militaire, **7**
Eiffel Tower, **8**
Hôtel des Invalides, **6**
Hôtel Matignon, **4**
Musée d'Art
Moderne de la Ville
de Paris, **16**
Musée de la Légion
d'Honneur, **2**

Musée de la
Marine,**11**
Musée de l'Homme, **10**
Musée des Monuments
Français, **12**
Musée d'Orsay, **1**
Musée du Cinéma, **13**
Musée Guimet, **14**
Musée Rodin, **5**

Palais Bourbon, **3**
Palais de Chaillot, **9**
Palais Galliera, **15**

The quiet, distinguished 18th-century streets behind the Palais Bourbon are filled with embassies and ministries. The most famous, reached via rue de Bourgogne and rue de Varenne, is
❹ the **Hôtel Matignon,** residence of the French Prime Minister, and Left Bank counterpart to the President's Elysée Palace. "Matignon" was built in 1721 but has housed heads of government only since 1958. From 1888 to 1914, it was the embassy of the Austro-Hungarian Empire. *57 rue de Varenne. Neither house nor garden is open to the public.*

Another glorious town house along rue de Varenne is the
❺ Hôtel Biron, better known as the **Musée Rodin.** The splendid house, with its spacious vestibule, broad staircase, and light, airy rooms, retains much of its 18th-century atmosphere and makes a handsome setting for the sculpture of Auguste Rodin (1840–1917). You'll doubtless recognize the seated *Thinker (Le Penseur),* with his elbow resting on his knee, and the passionate *Kiss.* There is also an outstanding white marble bust of Austrian composer *Gustav Mahler,* as well as numerous examples of Rodin's obsession with hands and erotic subjects.

The second-floor rooms, which contain some fine paintings by Rodin's friend Eugène Carrière (1849–1906), afford views of the large garden behind the house. Don't go without visiting the garden: It is exceptional both for its rose bushes (over 2,000 of them, representing 100 varieties) and for its sculpture, including a powerful statue of the novelist Balzac and the despairing group of medieval city fathers known as the *Burghers of Calais. 77 rue de Varenne. Admission: 21 frs, 10 frs Sun. Open Easter–Oct., Tues.–Sun. 10–6; Nov.–Easter, Tues.–Sun. 10–5.*

❻ From the Rodin Museum, you can see the **Hôtel des Invalides,** along rue de Varenne. It was founded by Louis XIV in 1674 to house wounded (or "invalid") veterans. Although no more than a handful of old soldiers live at the Invalides today, the military link remains in the form of the **Musée de l'Armée**—one of the world's foremost military museums—with a vast collection of arms, armor, uniforms, banners, and military pictures down through the ages.

The **Musée des Plans-Reliefs,** housed on the fifth floor of the right-hand wing, contains a fascinating collection of scale models of French towns made to illustrate the fortifications planned by Vauban in the 17th century. (Vauban was a superb military engineer who worked under Louis XIV.) The largest and most impressive is Strasbourg, which takes up an entire room. Not all of Vauban's models are here, however. As part of a cultural decentralization program, France's socialist government of the early 1980s decided to pack the models (which had languished for years in dusty neglect) off to Lille in northern France. Only half the models had been shifted when a conservative government returned to office in 1986 and called for their return. Ex-Prime Minister Pierre Mauroy, the socialist mayor of Lille, refused, however, and the impasse seems set to continue.

The museums are not the only reason for visiting the Invalides. The building itself is an outstanding monumental ensemble in late-17th-century Baroque, designed by Bruand and Mansart. The main, cobbled courtyard is a fitting scene for the parades and ceremonies still occasionally held here. The most impressive dome in Paris towers over the **Eglise du Dôme** (church of the Dome). Before stopping here, however, visit the 17th-century **Eglise St-Louis des Invalides,** the Invalides's original church, and the site of the first performance of Berlioz's *Requiem* in 1837.

The Dôme church was built onto the end of Eglise St-Louis but was blocked off from it in 1793—no great pity perhaps, as the two buildings are vastly different in style and scale. It was designed by Mansart and built between 1677 and 1735. The remains of Napoléon are here, in a series of no fewer than six coffins, one inside the next, within a bombastic tomb of red porphyry, ringed by low reliefs and a dozen statues symbolizing Napoléon's campaigns. Among others commemorated in the church are French World War I hero Marshal Foch; Napoléon's brother Joseph, erstwhile king of Spain; and fortification-builder Vauban, whose heart was brought to the Invalides at Napoléon's behest. *Hôtel des Invalides. Admission: 32 frs adults, 20 frs children. Open daily 10–6; 10–5 in winter. A son-et-lumière (sound-and-light) show in English is held in the main courtyard on evenings throughout the summer.*

Time Out The 7th Arrondissement is one of the most expensive areas in Paris—so you may want to lunch at the **Invalides cafeteria,** situated to the west of the Dôme church, behind the souvenir shop. The decor may be uninspired, but the place is clean and boasts an imaginative and wide choice of hot and cold dishes.

Cross the pleasant lawns outside the Dôme church to place Vauban. Follow avenue de Tourville to the right, and turn left onto avenue de la Motte-Picquet.

The Eiffel Tower and the Trocadéro

A few minutes' walk will bring you face-to-face with the Eiffel Tower. Spare a thought for the **Ecole Militaire** on your left; it is 18th-century architecture at its most harmonious. It is still in use as a military academy and therefore not open to the public.

The pleasant expanse of the **Champ de Mars** makes an ideal approach to the **Eiffel Tower,** whose colossal bulk (it's far bigger and sturdier than pictures suggest) becomes evident the nearer you get. It was built by Gustave Eiffel for the World Exhibition of 1889, the centennial of the French Revolution, and was still in good shape to celebrate its own 100th birthday. Recent restoration hasn't made the elevators any faster (lines are inevitable), but the new nocturnal illumination is fantastic—every girder highlighted in glorious detail.

Such was Eiffel's engineering wizardry that even in the strongest winds his tower never sways more than 4½ inches. Today, it is Paris's best-known landmark and exudes a feeling of permanence. As you stand beneath its huge legs, you may have trouble believing that it nearly became 7,000 tons of scrap-iron when its concession expired in 1909. Only its potential use as a radio antenna saved the day; it now bristles with a forest of radio and television transmitters. If you're full of energy, stride up the stairs as far as the third deck. If you want to go to the top, you'll have to take the elevator. The view at 1,000 feet may

not beat that from the Tour Maine-Montparnasse (*see* The Left
Bank, *below*), but the setting makes it considerably more romantic. *Pont d'Iéna. Cost by elevator: 2nd floor, 17 frs; 3rd
floor, 34 frs; 4th floor, 51 frs. Cost by foot: 8 frs (2nd and 3rd
floors only). Open July–Aug., daily 9 AM–midnight; Sept.–
June, daily 9:30 AM–11 PM.*

Just across the Pont d'Iena from the Eiffel Tower, on the
heights of Trocadéro, is the muscular, sandy-colored **Palais de
Chaillot**—a cultural center built in the 1930s to replace a Moor-
ish-style building constructed for the World Exhibition of 1878.
The gardens between the Palais de Chaillot and the Seine contain an aquarium and some dramatic fountains. The terrace between the two wings of the palace offers a wonderful view of the
Eiffel Tower.

The Palais de Chaillot contains four large museums, two in each
wing. In the left wing (as you approach from the Seine) are the
Musée de l'Homme and the Musée de la Marine. The **Musée de
l'Homme,** on the second and third floors, is an earnest anthropological museum with primitive and prehistoric artifacts from
throughout the world. *Admission: 25 frs adults, 15 frs children. Open Wed.–Mon. 9:45–5.* The **Musée de la Marine,** on the
first floor, is a maritime museum with a salty collection of ship
models and seafaring paraphernalia, illustrating French naval
history right up to the age of the nuclear submarine. *Admission: 28 frs adults, 14 frs senior citizens, students, and children. Open Wed.–Mon. 10–6.*

The other wing is dominated by the **Musée des Monuments
Français,** without question the best introduction to French
medieval architecture. This extraordinary museum was
founded in 1879 by architect-restorer Viollet-le-Duc (the man
who more than anyone was responsible for the extensive renovation of Notre Dame). It pays tribute to French buildings,
mainly of the Romanesque and Gothic periods (roughly 1000–
1500), in the form of painstaking copies of statues, columns,
archways, and frescoes. It is easy to imagine yourself strolling
among ruins as you pass through the first-floor gallery. Substantial sections of a number of French churches and cathedrals
are represented here, notably Chartres and Vézelay. Mural
and ceiling paintings—copies of works in churches around the
country—dominate the other three floors. The value of these
paintings has become increasingly evident as many of the originals continue to deteriorate. On the ceiling of a circular room is
a reproduction of the painted dome of Cahors cathedral, giving
the visitor a more vivid sense of the skills of the original medieval painter than the cathedral itself. *Admission: 16 frs, 8 frs
on Sun. Open Wed.–Mon. 9:45–5:15.*

The **Musée du Cinéma,** located in the basement of this wing,
traces the history of motion pictures since the 1880s. *Admission: 22 frs. Open Wed.–Mon. Guided tours only, at 10, 11, 2, 3,
and 4.*

Time Out   The giant place du Trocadéro is so hideously expensive that
none of its many cafés can be recommended. But, if you have the
time, head left from the Palais de Chaillot (down rue Franklin)
to rue de Passy, a long, lively, narrow street full of shops and
restaurants. **Pastavino,** at 30 rue de Passy, has excellent pasta
and Italian wine in a room with gleaming modernistic decor.
Around the corner, at 4 rue Nicolo, the intimate **Au Régal** has

been serving up Russian specialties since 1934, abetted by a comradely welcome and ready supply of vodka.

The area around the Palais de Chaillot offers a feast for museum lovers. The **Musée Guimet** (down avenue du Président Wilson, at place d'Iéna) has three floors of Indo-Chinese and Far Eastern art, initially amassed by 19th-century collector Emile Guimet. Among the museum's bewildering variety of exhibits are stone buddhas, Chinese bronzes, ceramics, and painted screens. *6 pl. d'Iéna. Admission: 26 frs adults, 14 frs students and senior citizens. Open Wed.–Mon. 9:45–5:15.*

Some 200 yards down avenue Pierre-Ier-de-Serbie is the **Palais Galliera,** home of the small and some would say overpriced Museum of Fashion and Costume. This stylish, late-19th-century town house hosts revolving exhibits of costume, design, and accessories, usually based on a single theme. *10 av. Pierre-Ier-de-Serbie. Admission: 25 frs adults, 15 frs students and senior citizens. Open Tues.–Sun. 10–5:40.*

The **Musée d'Art Moderne de la Ville de Paris** has both temporary exhibits and a permanent collection of modern art, continuing where the Musée d'Orsay leaves off. Among the earliest works are Fauvist paintings by Vlaminck and Derain, followed by Picasso's early experiments in Cubism. No other Paris museum exudes such a feeling of space and light. Its vast, unobtrusive, white-walled galleries provide an ideal background for the bold statements of 20th-century art. Loudest and largest are the canvases of Robert Delaunay. Other highlights include works by Braque, Rouault, Gleizes, Da Silva, Gromaire, and Modigliani. There is also a large room devoted to Art Deco furniture and screens, where Jean Dunand's gilt and lacquered panels consume oceans of wall space. There is a pleasant, if expensive, museum café, and an excellent bookshop specializing in 19th- and 20th-century art and architecture, with many books in English. *11 av. du Président Wilson. Admission: 15 frs, half-price on Sun. for permanent exhibitions only. Open Tues.–Sun. 10–5:30, Wed. 10–8:30.*

The Left Bank

Numbers in the margin correspond to points of interest on the Left Bank map.

References to the Left Bank have never lost their power to evoke the most piquant of all images of Paris. Although the bohemian strain the area once nurtured has lost much of its vigor, people who choose it today as a place to live or work are, in effect, turning their backs on the formality and staidness of the Right Bank.

The Latin Quarter is the geographic and cerebral hub of the Left Bank, populated mainly by Sorbonne students and academics who fill the air of the cafés with their ideas—and their tobacco smoke. (The university began as a theological school in the Middle Ages and later became the headquarters of the University of Paris; in 1968, the student revolution here had an explosive effect on French politics, resulting in major reforms in the education system.) The name Latin Quarter comes from the university tradition of studying and speaking in Latin, a tradition that disappeared during the Revolution.

Most of the St-Germain cafés, where the likes of Sartre, Picasso, Hemingway, and de Beauvoir spent their days and nights, are patronized largely by tourists now, and anyone expecting to capture the feeling of this quarter when it was the epicenter of intellectual and artistic life in Paris will be disappointed. Yet the Left Bank is far from dead. It is a lively and colorful district, rich in history and character, with a wealth of bookshops, art stores, museums, and restaurants.

St-Michel to St-Germain

① **Place St-Michel** is a good starting point for exploring the rich slice of Parisian life, from its most ancient to its most modern, that the Left Bank offers. Leave your itineraries at home, and wander along the neighboring streets lined with restaurants, cafés, galleries, old bookshops, and all sorts of clothing stores, from tiny boutiques to haute couture showrooms.

If you follow quai des Grands Augustins and then quai de Conti west from St-Michel, you will be in full view of the Ile de la Cité and the Louvre, and you may catch a glimpse of the imposing dome of the Temple de l'Oratoire (built in 1621 and once one of the most important churches in France) across the Seine. The Hôtel des Monnaies (the mint), the Institut de France (home of the Académie Française), and the Ecole National des Beaux-Arts (Paris's fine-arts academy) together comprise a magnificent assembly of buildings on the river embankment that lies west of Paris's oldest bridge, the Pont Neuf.

② For a route crowded more with humanity and less with car and bus traffic, pick up the pedestrian rue St-André des Arts at the southwest corner of place St-Michel. **Studio St-André des Arts,** at no. 30, is one of Paris's most popular experimental cinemas.
③ Just before you reach the Carrefour de Buci crossroads at the end of the street, turn onto the **Cour du Commerce St-André.** Jean-Paul Marat printed his revolutionary newspaper, *L'Ami du Peuple*, at no. 8; and it was here that Dr. Guillotin conceived the idea for a new, "humane" method of execution that was used during the Revolution—it was rumored that he practiced it on sheep first—and that remained the means of executing convicted criminals in France until President Mitterrand abolished it in 1981.

④ Down a small passageway on the left stands one of the few remaining towers of the 12th-century fortress wall built by Philippe-Auguste. The passage leads you to the **Cour de Rohan,** a series of three cloistered courtyards that were part of the hôtel of the archbishops of Rouen, established in the 15th century; the name has been corrupted over the years to Rohan.

⑤ Rejoin the Cour du Commerce St-André and continue to the **Carrefour de Buci,** once a notorious Left Bank landmark. By the 18th century, it contained a gallows, an execution stake, and an iron collar for punishing troublemakers. In September 1792, the Revolutionary army used this daunting site to enroll its first volunteers, and many Royalists and priests lost their heads here during the bloody course of the Revolution. There's nothing sinister, however, about the Carrefour today. Brightly colored flowers spill onto the sidewalk at the **Grange à Buci**
⑥ flower shop, on the corner of rue Grégoire-de-Tours. **Rue de Buci** has one of the best markets in Paris. *Open Tues.–Sun. till 1 PM.*

Time Out If you happen to arrive when the market is closed, **La Vieille France** patisserie at 14 rue de Buci may help fill the gap.

Several interesting, smaller streets of some historical signifi-

❼ cance radiate from the Carrefour. **Rue de l'Ancienne-Comédie,** which cuts through to the busy place de l'Odéon, is so named because it was the first home of the now legendary French theater company, the Comédie Française. The street was named in 1770, the very year the Comédie left for the Tuileries palace. The company moved again later to the Odéon, before heading to its present home by the Palais-Royal (*see* The Historic Heart, *above*).

Across the street from the company's first home (no. 14) is the

❽ oldest café in Paris, **Le Procope.** Opened in 1686 by an Italian named Francesco Procopio (only three years before the Odéon itself opened), it has been a watering hole for many of Paris's most famous literary sons and daughters over the centuries; Diderot, Voltaire, Balzac, George Sand, Victor Hugo, and Oscar Wilde were some of its more famous and infamous regulars. Ben Franklin is said to have stopped in whenever business brought him to Paris. The fomenters of the French Revolution met at the Procope, too, so it is possible that old Ben may have crossed paths with the likes of Marat, Danton, Desmoulins, and Robespierre. Napoléon's hat, forgotten here, was encased in a glass dome. In 1988, Paris's second-largest restaurant group, Frères Blanc, bought the Procope (now really more of a restaurant), claiming to want to give it a "new lease on life and a new literary and cultural vocation."

Stretching north from the Carrefour de Buci toward the Seine

❾ is the **rue Dauphine,** the street that singer Juliet Greco put on the map when she opened the Tabou jazz club here in the '50s. It attracted a group of young intellectuals who were to become known as the Zazous, a St-Germain movement promoting the jazz culture, complete with all-night parties and free love. The cult author Boris Vian liked to play his trumpet through the night, an activity that did little to endear him to the club's neighbors. You may still find jazz played here, but the club is a shadow of its former self.

The next street that shoots out of the Carrefour (moving coun-

❿ terclockwise) is rue Mazarine. Here stands the **Hôtel des Monnaies,** the national mint. Louis XVI transferred the Royal Mint to this imposing mansion in the late 18th century. Although the mint was moved to Pessac, near Bordeaux, in 1973, weights and measures, medals, and limited-edition coins are still made here. In June 1988, an enlarged **Musée Monétaire** opened so that the vast collection of coins, documents, engravings, and paintings could be displayed. The workshops are on the second floor. On Tuesday and Friday afternoons you'll catch the coin and medal craftsmen at work; their ateliers overlook the Seine. *11 quai de Conti. Admission: 20 frs adults, 15 frs students and senior citizens. 15 frs Sun. Open Tues., Thurs.–Sun. 1–6, Wed. 1–9.*

⓫ Next door is the **Institut de France.** With its distinctive dome and commanding position over the quai at the foot of the Pont des Arts, it is not only one of France's most revered cultural institutions but also one of the Left Bank's most impressive waterside sights. The Tour de Nesle, which formed part of Philippe-Auguste's wall fortifications along the Seine, used to

The Left Bank

R. St-Honoré

1er

R. du Pont Neuf

Neuf

Conti

Pont St-Michel

Pont Neuf

Quai des Grands Augustins

R. St-André des Arts

Pl. St-Michel

Blvd. St-Germain

Blvd. Sébastopol

R. du Temple

R. des Archives

4e

R. des Francs-Bourgeois

R. de Turenne

Pont au Change

Hôtel de Ville

R. de Rivoli

R. Fr. Miron

R. St-Antoine

Pont du Palais

Ile de la Cité

Conciergerie

Notre Dame

Sq. R. Viviani

Quai de Montebello

Louis Philippe

Pont

R. St-Louis en l'Ile

Pont St-Louis

Pont Marie

Quai des Célestins

Ile St-Louis

Pont de la Tournelle

R. de l'Ave Maria

R. de l'Hôtel St-Paul

Blvd. Henri IV

Pont de Sully

Pl. Maubert

Blvd. St-Germain

R. St-Jacques

R. Bièvre

R. Monge

R. Galande

Lemoine

Pl. de la Sorbonne

R. des Ecoles

R. Cujas

R. Soufflot

Seine

Quai St-Bernard

R. du Cardinal-Lemoine

R. Rollin

5e

Pl. Monge

Pl. du Puits-de-l'Ermite

R. Daubenton

Jardin des Plantes

R. Buffon

Blvd. St-Michel

R. Gay Lussac

R. Thomond

R. Mouffetard

R. Claude Bernard

R. St-Jacques

Blvd. de Port Royal

Blvd. St-Marcel

Av. des Gobelins

13e

Blvd. de l'Hôpital

Gare d'Austerlitz

Arago

N

0   440 yards

0   400 meters

stand here, and, in its time, it had many royal occupants, including Henry V of England. The French novelist Alexandre Dumas (1824–1895) featured the stormy history of the Tour de Nesle—during which the lovers of a number of French queens were tossed from its windows—in a melodrama of the same name. In 1661, the wealthy Cardinal Mazarin left 2 million French pounds in his will for construction of a college here that would be dedicated to educating students from the provinces of Piedmont, Alsace, Artois, and Roussillon, all of which had been annexed to France during the years of his ministry. Mazarin's coat of arms is sculpted on the dome, and the public library in the east wing, which holds over 350,000 volumes, still bears his name. At the beginning of the 19th century, Napoléon stipulated that the Institut de France be transferred here from the Louvre. The **Académie Française,** the oldest of the five academies that comprise the Institut de France, was created by Cardinal Richelieu in 1635. Its first major task was to edit the French dictionary; today, among other functions, it is still charged with safeguarding the purity of the French language. Election to its ranks is the highest literary honor in the land, subject to approval by the French head of state, and there may only be 40 "immortal" members at any one time. The appointment of historian and authoress Marguerite Yourcenar to the Académie in 1986 broke the centuries-old tradition of the academy as a bastion of male-only linguistic and literary rule. The Institut also embraces the Académie des Beaux-Arts; the Académie des Sciences; the Académie des Inscriptions et Belles Lettres; and the Académie des Sciences Morales et Politiques. *Guided visits are reserved for cultural associations only.*

⓬ Just west along the waterfront, on quai Malaquais, stands the **Ecole Nationale des Beaux-Arts,** whose students can usually be seen painting and sketching on the nearby quais and bridges. The school—today the breeding ground for France's foremost painters, sculptors, and architects—was once the site of a convent, founded in 1608 by Marguerite de Valois, the first wife of Henri IV. During the Revolution, the convent was turned into a depot for works of art salvaged from the monuments that were under threat of destruction by impassioned mobs. Only the church and cloister remained, however, when the Beaux-Arts school was established in 1816. Allow yourself time to wander into the courtyard and galleries of the school to see the casts and copies of the statues that were once stored here, or stop in at one of the temporary exhibitions of professors' and students' works. *14 rue Bonaparte. Open daily 1–7.*

⓭ Tiny **rue Visconti,** running east–west off rue Bonaparte (across from the entrance to the Beaux-Arts), has a lot of history packed into its short length. In the 16th century, it was known as Paris's Little Geneva—named after Europe's foremost Protestant city—because of the Protestant ghetto that formed here. Racine, one of France's greatest playwrights and tragic poets, lived at no. 24 until his death in 1699. Balzac set up a printing shop at no. 17 in 1826, and the fiery Romantic artist Eugène Delacroix (1798–1863) worked here from 1836 to 1844.

Time Out The terrace at **La Palette** (43 rue de Seine) beckons as soon as you reach the rue de Seine, at the end of rue Visconti. This popular café has long been a favorite haunt of Beaux Arts students. One of them was allowed to paint an ungainly portrait of the *patron*, François, which presides with mock authority over the shaggy gathering of clients.

Swing right at the next corner onto the pretty rue Jacob, where both Wagner and Stendhal once lived. Follow rue Jacob across rue des Saints-Pères, where it changes to rue de l'Université. You are now in the Carré Rive Gauche, the Left Bank's concentrated quarter-mile of art dealers and galleries.

Return on rue Jacob until you are almost back to rue de Seine. Take the rue de Fürstemberg to the quiet place Fürstemberg, bedecked with white globe lamps and catalpa trees. Here is

⑭ Atelier Delacroix, Delacroix's former studio, containing only a paltry collection of sketches and drawings by the artist; the garden at the rear of the studio is almost as interesting. Nonetheless, those who feel the need to pay homage to France's foremost Romantic painter will want to make the pilgrimage. *Place Fürstemberg. Admission: 12 frs adults, 7 frs ages 18–25 and over 60, 7 frs on Sun. Open Wed.–Mon. 9:45–5:15.*

⑮ St-Germain-des-Prés, Paris's oldest church, began as a shelter for a relic of the True Cross brought back from Spain in AD 542. Behind it, rue de l'Abbaye runs alongside the former Abbey palace, dating from AD 990 and once part of a powerful Benedictine abbey. The chancel was enlarged and the church then consecrated by Pope Alexander III in 1163. Interesting interior details include the colorful 19th-century frescoes in the nave by Hippolyte Flandrin, a pupil of the classical painter Ingres, depicting vivid scenes from the Old Testament. The church stages superb organ concerts and recitals; programs are displayed outside and in the weekly periodicals *Officiel des Spectacles* and *Pariscope. Open weekdays 8–7:30; weekends 8–9.*

⑯ Across the cobbled place St-Germain-des-Prés stands the celebrated **Les Deux Magots** café, named after the grotesque Chinese figures, or *magots*, inside. It still thrives on its post–World War II reputation as one of the Left Bank's prime meeting places for the intelligentsia. Though the Deux Magots remains crowded day and night, these days, you're more likely to rub shoulders with tourists than with philosophers. Yet those in search of the mysterious glamour of the Left Bank can do no better than to station themselves at one of the sidewalk tables—or at a window table on a wintry day—to watch the passing parade.

⑰ In the postwar years, Jean-Paul Sartre and Simone de Beauvoir would meet "the family" two doors down at the **Café de Flore** on boulevard St-Germain. "The family" was de Beauvoir's name for their close-knit group, which included fellow-graduates from the prestigious École Normale Supérieure and writers from Gaston Gallimard's publishing house in the nearby rue Sébastien-Bottin. Today the Flore has become more of a gay hangout, but, along with the Deux Magots and the pricey

⑱ Brasserie Lipp across the street, where politicians and show-biz types come to wine and dine (after being "passed" by the doorman), it is a scenic spot that never lacks for action. In case you're in need of a sideshow, you'll also be able to see the street musicians—as likely to be playing Bolivian reed pipes or Scottish bagpipes as an old-style pump accordion—as well as acrobats and fire-eaters who perform in front of the church.

A large part of the area south of boulevard St-Germain, around rue de Grenelle and rue des Saints-Pères, has undergone enormous change but is still home to publishing houses, bookstores, and galleries.

For contrast, take rue du Vieux-Colombier through the Carrefour de La Croix Rouge to place St-Sulpice. This newly renovated square is ringed with cafés, and Yves St-Laurent's famous Rive Gauche store is at no. 6. Looming over the square ⑲ is the enormous 17th-century church of **St-Sulpice.** The 18th-century facade was never finished, and its unequal towers add a playful touch to an otherwise sober design. The interior is baldly impersonal, however, despite the magnificent Delacroix frescoes—notably Jacob wrestling with the angel—in the first chapel on your right. If you now pick up the long rue de Rennes and follow it south, you'll soon arrive in the heart of Montparnasse.

Montparnasse

With the growth of Paris as a business and tourist capital, commercialization seems to have filled any area where departing residents and businesses have created a vacuum. Nowhere else is this more true than in and around the vaulting, concrete space and starkly functionalist buildings that have come to rule Montparnasse. Seeing it now, it is difficult to believe that in the years after World War I, Montparnasse replaced Montmartre as *the* place in which Parisian artists came to live.

⑳ The opening of the 59-story **Tour Maine-Montparnasse** in 1973 forever changed the face of this painters' and poets' haunt. (The name Montparnasse itself came from some 17th-century students, who christened the area after Mount Parnassus, the home of Apollo, leader of the Muses.) The tower was part of a vast redevelopment plan that aimed to make the area one of Paris's premier business and shopping districts. Fifty-two floors of the tower are taken up by offices, while a vast commercial complex, including a Galeries Lafayette department store, spreads over the first floor. Although it is uninspiring by day, it becomes a neon-lit beacon for the area at night. As Europe's tallest high rise, it affords stupendous views of Paris; on a clear day, you can see for 30 miles. (There's a snack bar and cafeteria on the 56th floor; if you go to the top-floor bar for drinks, the ride up is free.) It also claims to have the fastest elevator in Europe! *Admission: 40 frs adults, 30 frs students and senior citizens, 22 frs children 5–14. Open daily 9:30 AM–10:30 PM, weekdays 10 AM–9:30 PM in winter.*

㉑ Immediately north of the tower is **place du 18 Juin 1940,** part of what was once the old Montparnasse train station and a significant spot in Parisian World War II history. It is named for the date of the radio speech Charles de Gaulle made, from London, urging the French to continue resisting the Germans after the fall of the country to Nazi Germany in May 1940. In August 1944, the German military governor, Dietrich von Choltitz, surrendered to the Allies here, ignoring Hitler's orders to destroy the city as he withdrew; the French General Philippe Leclerc subsequently used it as his headquarters.

Behind the older train station, Gare Montparnasse, you'll see the huge new train terminal that serves Chartres, Versailles, and the west of France. Since 1990, the high-speed *TGV*

Atlantique leaves here for Brittany (Rennes and Nantes) and the southwest (Bordeaux, via Tours, Poitiers, and Angoulême). South of this station is one of the oddest residential complexes to appear in this era of architectural experimentation. The
㉒ **Amphithéâtre,** built by Ricardo Boffil, is eye-catching but stark and lacking in human dimension.

㉓ The **Cimetière de Montparnasse** (Montparnasse cemetery) contains many of the quarter's most illustrious residents, buried only a stone's throw away from where they worked and played. It is not at all a picturesque cemetery (with the exception of the old windmill in the corner, which used to be a student tavern) but seeing the names of some of its inhabitants—Baudelaire, Maupassant, Saint-Saëns, and the industrialist André Citroën—may make the visit worthwhile. Nearby, at place Denfert-Rochereau, is the entrance to an extensive complex of
㉔ **catacombs** (*denfert* is a corruption of the word for hell, *enfer*). The catacombs are stocked with the bones of millions of skeletons that were moved here in 1785 from the area's charnel houses. *Admission: 16 frs adults, 10 frs students and senior citizens. Open Tues.–Fri. 2–4, weekends 9–11 and 2–4.*

Montparnasse's bohemian aura has dwindled to almost nothing, yet the area hops at night as *the* place in Paris to find movies of every description, many of them shown in their original language. Theaters and theater-cafés abound, too, especially
㉕ along seedy **rue de la Gaîté.** The Gaîté-Montparnasse, Le Théâtre Montparnasse, and Le Grand Edgar are among the most popular. Up boulevard du Montparnasse and across from the Vavin métro station are two of the better-known gathering
㉖ places of Montparnasse's heyday, the **Dôme** and **La Coupole** brasseries. La Coupole opened in 1927 as a bar/restaurant/dance hall and soon became a home away from home for some of the area's most famous residents, such as Apollinaire, Max Jacob, Cocteau, Satie, Stravinsky, and the ubiquitous Hemingway. It may not be quite the same mecca these days, but it still pulls in a classy crowd.

Across the boulevard, rue Vavin leads past two more celebrated Montparnasse cafés, the **Sélect** and the **Rotonde,** to the Jardin du Luxembourg. But stay on boulevard du Montparnasse for the intersection with boulevard St-Michel, where the
㉗ verdant **avenue de l'Observatoire** begins its long sweep up to the Luxembourg gardens. Here you'll find perhaps the most fa-
㉘ mous bastion of the Left Bank café culture, the **Closerie des Lilas.** Now a pricey bar/restaurant, the Closerie remains a staple on all literary tours of Paris not least because of the commemorative plaques fastened onto the bar, marking the places where renowned personages sat. Baudelaire, Verlaine, Hemingway, and Apollinaire are just a few of the names. Although the lilacs *(lilas)* have gone from the terrace, it is still a pretty place, opening onto the luxuriant green of the surrounding parkland, and as crowded in the summer as it ever was in the '30s.

㉙ The vista from the Closerie includes the **Paris Observatory** (to the right), built in 1667 by Louis XIV. Its four facades were built to align with the four cardinal points—north, south, east, and west—and its southern wall is the determining point for Paris's official latitude, 48° 50′11″N. French time was based on this Paris meridian until 1911, when the country decided to adopt the international Greenwich Meridian.

A tree-lined alley leads along the avenue de l'Observatoire to the gardens, but before the entrance, you'll pass Davioud's **Fontaine de l'Observatoire** (Observatory Fountain), built in 1873 and decked with four statues representing the four quarters of the globe. Look north from here and you'll have a captivating view of Montmartre and Sacré-Coeur, with the gardens in the foreground.

Palais du Luxembourg

30 From avenue de l'Observatoire walk up to the **Jardin du Luxembourg** (the Luxembourg Gardens), one of the city's few large parks. Its fountains, ponds, trim hedges, precisely planted rows of trees, and gravel walks are typical of the French fond-
31 ness for formal gardens. At the far end is the **Palais du Luxembourg,** gray and imposing, built, like the park, for Maria de' Medici, widow of Henri IV, at the beginning of the 17th century. Maria was born and raised in Florence's Pitti Palace, and, having languished in the Louvre after the death of her husband, she was eager to build herself a new palace, somewhere she could recapture something of the lively, carefree atmosphere of her childhood. In 1612, she bought the Paris mansion of the duke of Luxembourg, tore it down, and built her palace. It was not completed until 1627, and Maria was to live there for no more than five years. In 1632, Cardinal Richelieu had her expelled from France, and she saw out her declining years in Cologne, Germany, dying there almost penniless in 1642. The palace remained royal property until the Revolution, when the state took it over and used it as a prison. Danton, the painter David, and Thomas Paine were all detained here. Today, it is the site of the French Senate and is not open to the public.

32 The **Théâtre National de l'Odéon,** set at the north end of the Luxembourg Gardens, was established in 1792 to house the Comédiens Français troupe. The massive structure you see today replaced the original theater, which was destroyed by fire in 1807. Since World War II, it has specialized in 20th-century productions. It was the base for Jean-Louis Barrault's and Madeleine Renaud's theater company, the Théâtre de France, until they fell out of favor with the authorities for their alleged role in spurring on the student revolutionaries in May 1968. Today, the Théâtre de l'Odéon is the French home of the Theater of Europe and stages some excellent productions by major foreign companies.

The Sorbonne and the Latin Quarter

If you follow rue de Vaugirard (the longest street in Paris) one block east to boulevard St-Michel, you will soon be at the **place de la Sorbonne,** the hub of the Latin Quarter and nerve center of the student population that has always held such sway over Left Bank life. The square is dominated by the Eglise de la Sorbonne, whose outstanding exterior features are its cupola and 10 Corinthian columns. Inside is the white marble tomb of Cardinal Richelieu. (The church is open to the public only during exhibitions and cultural events.) The university buildings of La Sorbonne spread out around the church from rue Cujas down to the visitor's entrance on rue des Ecoles.

33 The **Sorbonne** is the oldest university in Paris—indeed, one of the oldest in Europe—and has for centuries been one of

France's principal institutions of higher learning. It is named after Robert de Sorbon, a medieval canon who founded a theological college here in 1253 for 16 students. By the 17th century, the church and university buildings were becoming dilapidated, so Cardinal Richelieu undertook to have them restored; the present-day Sorbonne campus is largely a result of that restoration. Despite changes in the neighborhood, the maze of amphitheaters, lecture rooms, and laboratories, and the surrounding courtyards and narrow streets, still have a hallowed air. For a glimpse of a more recent relic of Sorbonne history, look for Puvis de Chavannes's painting of the *Sacred Wood* in the main lecture hall, a major meeting point during the tumultuous student upheavals of 1968, and now a university landmark.

Behind the Sorbonne, bordering its eastern reach, is the rue St-Jacques. The street climbs toward the rue Soufflot, named ③④ to honor the man who built the vast, domed **Panthéon,** set atop place du Panthéon. One of Paris's most physically overwhelming sites—it was commissioned by Louis XV as a mark of gratitude for his recovery from a grave illness in 1744—the Panthéon is now a seldom-used church, with little of interest except for Puvis de Chavannes's monumental frescoes and the crypt, which holds the remains of Voltaire, Zola, and Rousseau. In 1789—the year the church was completed—its windows were blocked by order of the Revolutionary Constituent Assembly, and they have remained that way ever since, adding to its sepulchral gloom. The dome, which weighs about 10,000 tons, is best appreciated from a distance. *Admission: 25 frs, 14 frs ages 18–25, 6 frs children 7–17. Open daily 10–5:30.*

Diagonally across from the Panthéon on the corner of rue Clo- ③⑤ vis and rue Cujas stands the striking **St-Etienne-du-Mont.** This mainly 16th-century church's ornate facade combines Gothic, Baroque, and Renaissance elements. Inside, the fretted rood screen is the only one of its kind in Paris. Note the uneven-floored chapel behind the choir, which can be reached via a cloister containing some exquisite stained glass dating from the 17th century.

Up rue St-Jacques again and across from the Sorbonne are ③⑥ the **Lycée Louis-le-Grand** (Molière, Voltaire, and Robespierre studied here) and the elite **Collège de France,** whose grounds continue around the corner onto rue des Ecoles. In 1530, François I created this school as the College of Three Languages, which taught High Latin, Greek, and Hebrew, and any other subjects eschewed by academics at the Sorbonne. Diagonally across from the college, on the other side of rue des Ecoles, is the **square Paul-Painlevé;** behind it lies the entrance to the inimitable Hôtel et Musée de Cluny.

Built on the site of the city's enormous old Roman baths, the ③⑦ **Musée de Cluny** is housed in a 15th-century mansion that originally belonged to monks of Cluny Abbey in Burgundy. The remains of the baths that can still be seen are what survived a sacking by Barbarians in the 4th century. But the real reason people come to the Cluny is for its tapestry collection. The most famous series of all is the graceful *Lady and the Unicorn, or Dame à la Licorne,* woven in the 15th or 16th century, probably in the southern Netherlands. And if the tapestries themselves aren't enough at which to marvel, there is also an exhibition of decorative arts from the Middle Ages, a vaulted chapel, and a deep, cloistered courtyard with mullioned windows, set off by the *Boatmen's Pillar,* Paris's oldest sculpture, at its center. *Admission: 17 frs, 9 frs children and Sun. Open Wed.–Mon. 9:30–5:15.*

Above boulevard St-Germain, rue St-Jacques reaches toward the Seine, bringing you past the elegant proportions of the church of **St-Séverin.** Rebuilt in the 16th century and noted for its width and its Flamboyant Gothic style, the church dominates a close-knit Left Bank neighborhood filled with quiet squares and pedestrian streets. In the 11th century, it was the parish church for the entire Left Bank. Louis XIV's cousin, a capricious woman known simply as the Grande Mademoiselle, adopted St-Séverin when she tired of the St-Sulpice church; she then spent vast sums getting Le Brun to modernize the chancel. Note the splendidly deviant spiraling column in the forest of pillars behind the altar. *Open weekdays 11–5:30, Sat. 11–10.*

Running riot around the relative quiet of St-Séverin are streets filled with restaurants of every description, serving everything from souvlaki-to-go to five-course haute cuisine. There is definitely something for every budget here. Rue de la Huchette is the most heavily trafficked of the restaurant streets and especially good for its selection of cheaper Greek food houses and Tunisian patisseries. In the evening, many restaurants put out full window displays of the foods to be offered on that night's menu in order to induce people away from the umbrella-covered terraces of neighboring cafés.

Time Out   If you end up in this area in the evening and are in the mood for entertainment with your supper, duck into **Le Cloître** (19 rue St-Jacques). It's an old, heavily wood-beamed bar with a one- and sometimes two-woman revue in the *cave,* or cellar, performing songs of old Paris from the '20s, '30s, and '40s. For a quieter diversion, stop at **Polly Maggoo** (11 rue St-Jacques).

Cross to the other side of rue St-Jacques. In Square René Viviani, which surrounds the church of **St-Julien-le-Pauvre,** stands an acacia tree that is supposed to be the oldest tree in Paris (although it has a rival claim from another acacia at the Jardin des Plantes). This tree-filled square also gives you one of the more spectacular views of Notre Dame. The tiny church here was built at the same time as Notre Dame (1165–1220), on a site where a whole succession of chapels once stood. The church belongs to a Greek Orthodox order today, but was originally named for St. Julian, bishop of Le Mans, who was nicknamed "Le Pauvre" after he gave all his money away.

Behind the church, to the east, are the tiny, elegant streets of the recently renovated **Maubert** district, bordered by quai de Montebello and boulevard St-Germain. Rue de Bièvre, once filled with tanneries, is now guarded at both ends to protect President Mitterrand's private residence.

Between St-Julien-le-Pauvre and place Maubert, two tiny streets—**rue des Anglais** and **rue des Irlandais**—mark the presence of foreign students who have come to study at Paris's academic and theological institutions over the centuries. Very basic board was provided by the small college for Irish students studying to become priests; although it has now been taken over by Polish students, it is still sometimes possible to get accommodation here (for men) if you are one for staying in humble, monklike quarters.

Public meetings and demonstrations have been held in place Maubert ever since the Middle Ages. Nowadays, most gatherings are held inside or in front of the elegantly Art Deco **Palais de la Mutualité,** on the corner of the square, also a venue for jazz, pop, and rock concerts. On Tuesdays, Thursdays, and Saturdays, it is transformed into a colorful outdoor food market.

Head up rue Monge, turn right onto rue du Cardinal-Lemoine, and you'll find yourself at the minute **place de la Contrescarpe.** It doesn't start to swing until after dusk, when its cafés and bars fill up. During the day, the square looks almost provincial, as Parisians flock to the daily market on rue Mouffetard. There are restaurants and cafés of every description on rue Mouffetard, and if you get here at lunchtime, you may want to buy yourself the makings for an alfresco lunch and take it to the unconventional picnic spot provided by the nearby Gallo-Roman ruin of the **Arènes de Lutèce;** it begins on rue Monge, just past the end of rue Rollin. The ancient arena was discovered only in 1869 and has since been excavated and landscaped to reveal parts of the original Roman amphitheater. This site and the remains of the baths at the Cluny constitute the only extant evidence of the powerful Roman city of Lutetia that flourished here in the 3rd century. It is also one of the lesser-known delights of the Left Bank, so you are not likely to find it crowded.

The **Jardin des Plantes** is an enormous swath of greenery containing spacious botanical gardens and a number of natural history museums. It is stocked with plants dating back to the first collections here in the 17th century, and has been enhanced ever since by subsequent generations of devoted French botanists. It claims to shelter Paris's oldest tree, an *acacia robinia*, planted in 1636. There is also a small, old-fashioned zoo here; an alpine garden; an aquarium; a maze; and a number of hothouses. The **Musée Entomologique** is devoted to insects; the **Musée Paléontologique** exhibits fossils and prehistoric animals; the **Musée Minéralogique** houses a stupendous collection of rocks and minerals. *Admission: 12–25 frs. Museums open Wed.–Mon. 9–11:45 and 1–4:45, weekends 2–4:45.*

Time Out At the back of the gardens, in place du Puits-de-l'Hermite, you can drink a restorative cup of sweet mint tea in **La Mosquée,** a beautiful white mosque, complete with minaret. Once inside, you'll be convinced that you must be elsewhere than the Left Bank of Paris. The students from the nearby Jussieu and Censier universities pack themselves into the Moslem restaurant here, which serves copious quantities of couscous. The sunken garden and tiled patios are open to the public—the prayer rooms are not—and so are the *hammams*, or Turkish baths. *Baths open daily 11 AM–8 PM; Fri. and Sun. men only; Mon., Wed., Thurs., and Sat. women only. Admission: 15 frs, 65 frs for Turkish baths. Guided tours of mosque Sat.–Thurs. 10–noon and 2–5:30.*

In 1988, Paris's large Arab population gained another base: the huge **Institut du Monde Arabe,** which overlooks the Seine on quai St-Bernard, just beyond Université Jussieu. Jean Nouvel's harmonious mixture of Arabic and European styles was greeted with enthusiasm when the center first opened. Note on the building's south side the 240 shutter-like apertures that open and close to regulate light exposure. It contains a sound and image center, a wall of televisions, with Arab programming, a vast library, a documentation center, and fast glass elevators that will take you to the ninth floor for (yet another) memorable view over the Seine and Notre Dame. *23 quai St-Bernard. Admission free. Open Tues.–Sun. 10–6.*

Montmartre

Numbers in the margin correspond to points of interest on the Montmartre map.

On a dramatic rise above the city is Montmartre, site of the Sacré-Coeur basilica and home to a once-thriving artistic community, a heritage recalled today chiefly by the gangs of third-rate painters clustered in the area's most famous square, the place du Tertre. Despite their presence, and the fact that the fabled nightlife of old Montmartre has fizzled down to some glitzy nightclubs and porn shows, Montmartre still exudes a sense of history, a timeless quality infused with that hard-to-define Gallic charm.

The crown atop this urban peak, the Sacré-Coeur is something of an architectural oddity. Its silhouette, viewed from afar at dusk or sunrise, looks more like a mosque than a cathedral. The Sacré-Coeur has been called everything from ugly to sublime; try to see it from as many perspectives as you can before drawing your own conclusion.

Seeing Montmartre means negotiating a lot of steep streets and flights of steps. If the prospect of trudging up and down them is daunting, you can tour parts of Montmartre by public transportation, aboard the Promotrain or the Montmartrobus. The Promotrain offers daily 40-minute guided tours of Montmartre between 10 AM and midnight. The cost is 25 francs for adults, 15 francs for children under 12, and departures are from outside the Moulin Rouge on place Blanche. The Montmartrobus is a regular city bus that runs around Montmartre for the price of a métro ticket. It departs from place Pigalle. If you're visiting only Sacré-Coeur, take the funicular that runs up the hill to the church near Anvers métro station.

Exploring Montmartre

❶ Begin your tour at **place Blanche,** site of the Moulin Rouge. Place Blanche—White Square—takes its name from the clouds of chalky dust churned up by the windmills that once dotted Montmartre (or *La Butte,* meaning "mound" or "hillock"). They were set up here not just because the hill was a good place to catch the wind—at over 300 feet, it's the highest point in the city—but because Montmartre was covered with wheat fields and quarries right up to the end of the 19th century. The carts carrying away the wheat and crushed stone trundled across place Blanche, turning the square white as they passed. Today, only two of the original 20 windmills are intact. A number have been converted to other uses, none more famous than the

❷ **Moulin Rouge,** or Red Windmill, built in 1885 and turned into a dance hall in 1900. It was a genuinely wild place in its early days, immortalized by Toulouse-Lautrec in his boldly simple

Montmartre

Basilique du Sacré-Coeur, **17**
Bateau-Lavoir, **10**
Chapelle du Martyre, **9**
Cimetière de Montmartre, **4**

Cité Internationale des Arts, **12**
Espace Dali, **15**
La Mère Catherine, **14**
Lapin Agile, **20**
Marché St-Pierre, **23**
Moulin de la Galette, **5**

Moulin de Paris, **11**
Moulin Rouge, **2**
Musée d'Art Juif, **22**
Musée du Vieux Montmartre, **18**
Place Blanche, **1**
Place des Abbesses, **7**
Place du Tertre, **13**

Rue Lepic, **3**
St-Pierre de Montmartre, **16**
St-Vincent Cemetery, **21**
Studio 28, **6**
Théâtre Libre, **8**
Vineyard, **19**

posters and paintings. The place is still trading shamelessly on the notion of Paris as a city of sin: If you fancy a Vegas-style night out, with computerized light shows and troupes of bare-breasted girls sporting feather headdresses, this is the place to go *(see* The Arts and Nightlife, Chapter 7). The cancan, by the way—still a regular feature here—was considerably more raunchy when Lautrec was around.

❸ For a taste of something more authentically French, walk past the Moulin Rouge, up **rue Lepic,** site of one of the most colorful and tempting food markets in Paris (closed Mon.).

Time Out Stop in at the tiny **Lux Bar** (12 rue Lepic) for coffee and a sandwich. The wall behind the bar is covered with a 1910 mosaic showing place Blanche at the beginning of the century.

❹ Turn left onto rue des Abbesses and walk along to **Cimetière de Montmartre** (Montmartre cemetery). It's by no means as romantic or as large as the better known Père Lachaise cemetery in the east of the city, but it contains the graves of many prominent French men and women, including the 18th-century painters Greuze and Fragonard; Degas; and Adolphe Sax, inventor of the saxophone. The Russian ballet dancer Nijinsky is also buried here.

Walk back along rue des Abbesses. Rue Tholozé, the second street on the left, was once a path over the hill, the oldest in
❺ Montmartre. It leads to the **Moulin de la Galette,** one of the two remaining windmills in Montmartre, which has been unroman-
❻ tically rebuilt. To reach it, you pass **Studio 28.** This seems to be no more than a generic little movie theater, but when opened in 1928, it was the first purposely built *art et essai*, or experimental theater, in the world. Over the years, the movies of directors like Jean Cocteau, François Truffaut, and Orson Welles have often been shown here before their official premieres.

❼ Return to rue des Abbesses, turn left, and walk to **place des Abbesses.** The little square is typical of the kind of picturesque and slightly countrified style that has made Montmartre famous. The entrance to the métro station, a curving, sensuous mass of delicate iron, is one of a handful of original Art Nouveau stations left in Paris. The austere, red brick **church of St-Jean l'Evangéliste** (1904) is worth a look, too. It was one of the first concrete buildings in France; the brick had to be added later to soothe offended locals. The **café St-Jean,** next to it, is a popular local meeting place, crowded on weekends.

There are two competing attractions just off the square. Theater buffs should head down the tiny rue André-Antoine. At no.
❽ 37, you'll see what was originally the **Théâtre Libre,** or Free Theater, founded in 1887 by André Antoine and immensely influential in popularizing the work of iconoclastic young playwrights such as Ibsen and Strindberg. The other attraction is **rue Yvonne-le-Tac,** scene of a vital event in Montmartre's early history and linked to the disputed story of how this quarter got its name. Some say the name Montmartre comes from the Roman temple to Mercury that was once here, called the Mound of Mercury or *Mons Mercurii*. Others contend that it was an adaptation of *Mons Martyrum*, a name inspired by the burial here of Paris's first bishop, St-Denis. The popular version of his martyrdom is that he was beheaded by the Romans in AD 250, but arose to carry his severed head from rue Yvonne-le-Tac to a

place 4 miles to the north, an area now known as St-Denis. He is
commemorated by the 19th-century **Chapelle du Martyre** at no.
9, built over the spot where he is said to have been executed. It
was in the crypt of the original chapel here that St. Ignatius of
Loyola founded the Jesuit order in 1540, a decisive step in the
efforts of the Catholic Church to reassert its authority in the
face of the Protestant Reformation. A final twist on the name
controversy is that Montmartre briefly came to be known as
Mont-Marat during the French Revolution. Marat was a leading Revolutionary figure who was obliged to spend most of the
day in the tub, the result of a disfiguring and severe skin condition. It was in his bath that Charlotte Corday, a fanatical opponent of the Revolutionary government, stabbed him to death.

From rue Yvonne-le-Tac, retrace your steps through place des
Abbesses. Take rue Ravignan on the right, climbing to the
summit via place Emile-Goudeau, an enchanting little cobbled
square. Your goal is the **Bateau-Lavoir,** or Boat Wash House, at
its northern edge. Montmartre poet Max Jacob coined the
name for the old building on this site, which burned down in
1970. First of all, he said, it resembled a boat. Second, the warren of artists' studios within was always cluttered and paint-
splattered, and looked to be in perpetual need of a good hosing
down. The new building also contains art studios, but, if you
didn't know its history, you'd probably walk right past it; it is
the epitome of poured concrete drabness.

It was in the original Bateau-Lavoir that painters Picasso and
Braque, early this century, made their first bold stabs at the
concept of Cubism—a move that paved the way for abstract
painting. The poet Apollinaire, who also kept a Bateau-Lavoir
studio, helped Cubism gain acceptance with his book, *Les
Peintures du Cubisme* (1913), which set the seal on the movement's historical significance.

Continue up the hill to place Jean-Baptiste Clément. The Italian painter and sculptor Modigliani (1884–1920) had a studio
here at no. 7. Some have claimed he was the greatest Italian
artist of the 20th century, the man who fused the genius of the
Italian Renaissance with the modernity of Cézanne and Picasso. He claimed that he would drink himself to death—he eventually did—and chose the right part of town to do it in. This was
one of the wildest areas of Montmartre. Its bistros and cabarets have mostly gone now, though, and only the **Moulin de Paris** still reflects a glimmer of the old atmosphere. Look for the
octagonal tower at the north end of the square; it's all that's left
of Montmartre's first water tower, built around 1840 to boost
the area's feeble water supply.

Rue Norvins, formerly rue des Moulins, runs behind and parallel to the north end of the square. Turn left along it to reach
stylish avenue Junot, site of the **Cité Internationale des Arts**
(International Residence of the Arts), where the city authorities rent out studios to artists from all over the world. Retrace
your steps back to rue Norvins and continue east past the bars
and tourist shops, until you reach place du Tertre.

Place du Tertre *(tertre* means hillock) regains its village atmosphere only in the winter, when the somber buildings gather in
the grays of the Parisian light and the plane tree branches
sketch traceries against the sky. At any other time of year,
you'll have to fight your way through the crowds to the south-

ern end of the square and the breathtaking view over the city. The real drawback is the swarm of artists clamoring to dash off your portrait. If you're in the mood, however. . . . Most are licensed to be there, and, like taxi drivers, their prices are officially fixed. But there is no shortage of con men, sketch pads in hand, who will charge whatever they think they can get away with. If one produces a picture of you without having first asked, you're under no obligation to buy it, though that's not to say you won't have to argue your case. It's best just to walk away.

⓮ **La Mère Catherine,** the restaurant at the northern end of the square, has an honored place in French culinary history. It was a favorite with the Russian cossacks who occupied Paris in 1814 after Napoléon had been exiled to the island of Elba. Little did they know that when they banged on the tables and shouted *"bistro,"* the Russian word for "quick," they were inventing a new breed of French restaurant. For a restaurant catering almost entirely to the tourist trade, La Mère Catherine is surprisingly good, though prices are high for what's offered.

Time Out **Patachou,** opened in 1987, sounds the one classy note on place du Tertre (at n° 9). It offers exquisite, if expensive, cakes and teas.

⓯ Around the corner on rue Poulbot, the **Espace Dali** houses more than 300 works by Salvador Dali, who once kept a studio in the area. The museum's atmosphere is meant to approximate the surreal experience, with black walls, low lighting, and a new-agey musical score—punctuated by recordings of Dali's own voice. If you're interested in seeing some of Dali's less-familiar works, including a series of sculptures and bronzes, a visit will prove worthwhile. Those unmoved by this eccentric genius and showman may want to skip this stop in favor of strolling the place du Tertre. *11 rue Poulbot, tel. 42–64–40–10. Admission: 35 frs adults, 25 frs children. Open daily 10–7; until 8 in summer.*

It was in place du Tertre in March 1871 that one of the most destructively violent episodes in French history began, one that colored French political life for generations. Despite popular images of later-19th-century France—and Paris especially—as carefree and prosperous, for much of this period the country was desperately divided into two camps: an ever more vocal and militant underclass, motivated by resentment of what they considered an elitist government, and a reactionary and fearful bourgeoisie and ruling class. It was a conflict that went back at least as far as the French Revolution at the end of the 18th century, and one that twice flared into outbreaks of civil war and rebellion, in 1832 and 1848, as the country oscillated between republican and imperial forms of government. In 1870, France, under the leadership of an opportunistic but feeble Napoléon III (nephew of the great Napoléon), was drawn into a disastrous war with Bismarck's Prussia, which was rapidly growing into one of the most formidable military powers in Europe. (Soon after, Prussia was to dominate a newly united and aggressive Germany.) In September that year, Prussia invaded France, surrounded Paris, and laid siege to it. After four months of appalling suffering—during which time the Louvre became a munitions factory, the Gare de Lyon was converted into a cannon foundry, and the two elephants in the zoo, Castor and Pollux, were eaten by starving Parisians—the new government under French statesman Adolphe Thiers capitulated. Although mass starvation seemed imminent, fears that Thiers would restore an imperial rather than a republican government caused Parisians to refuse to surrender their arms to him. Thiers then ordered that the guns at Montmartre be captured by loyal government forces. Insurgents responded by shooting the two generals ordered to retake the guns. Almost immediately, barricades were thrown up across the city streets, and the fighting began in earnest. The antimonarchists formed the Commune, which for three heady months ruled Paris. In May, from his base at Versailles, Thiers ordered the city retaken. Estimates as to the numbers killed in the fighting vary greatly. Some say 4,000 Communards lost their lives; others claim 20,000. No one, however, doubts that upward of 10,000 Communards were executed by government troops after the collapse of the Commune.

In expiation for this bloodshed, the French government decided, in 1873 (after the downfall of Thiers), to build the basilica of the Sacré-Coeur. It was to be a sort of national guilt offering. Before visiting this landmark, walk to the church of **St-Pierre de Montmartre** at the east side of place du Tertre. It's one of the oldest churches in the city, built in the 12th century as the abbey church of a substantial Benedictine monastery. It's been remodeled on a number of occasions down through the years, and the 18th-century facade, built by Louis XIV, contrasts uncomfortably with the mostly medieval interior. Its setting is awkward, too: The bulk of the Sacré-Coeur looms directly behind it.

The **Basilique du Sacré-Coeur,** begun in 1873 and completed in 1910 (though not consecrated until 1919), symbolized the return of relative self-confidence to later-19th-century Paris after the turmoil of the Commune. Even so, the building was to some extent a reflection of political divisions within the country. It was largely financed by French Catholics fearful of an anticlerical backlash and determined to make a grand statement on behalf of the Church. Stylistically, the Sacré-Coeur borrows elements from Romanesque and Byzantine models, fusing them under its distinctive Oriental dome. Built on a grand scale, the effect is strangely disjointed and unsettling, rather as if the building had been designed by an architect of railway stations, with a pronounced taste for exoticism. (The architect, Abadie, died in 1884, long before the church was finished.) The gloomy, cavernous interior is worth visiting for its golden mosaics; climb to the top of the dome for the view over Paris.

More of Montmartre beckons north and west of the Sacré-Coeur. Take rue du Mont-Cenis down to rue Cortot, site of the **Musée du Vieux Montmartre.** Like the Bateau-Lavoir, the building that is now the museum sheltered an illustrious group of painters, writers, and assorted cabaret artists in its heyday toward the end of the 19th century. Foremost among them were Renoir—he painted the *Moulin de la Galette*, an archetypical Parisian scene of sun-drenched revels, while he lived here—and Maurice Utrillo, Montmartre painter par excellence. Utrillo was encouraged to paint by his mother, Suzanne Valadon, a regular model of Renoir's and a considerable painter in her own right. Utrillo's life was anything but happy, despite the considerable success his paintings enjoyed. He was an alcoholic continually in trouble with the police, and he spent most of his declining years in hospitals. Having taken the gray, crumbling streets of Montmartre as his subject matter, he discovered that he worked more effectively from postcards than from the streets themselves. For all that, his best works—almost all produced before 1916; he died in 1955—evoke the atmosphere of old Montmartre hauntingly. Look carefully at the pictures in the museum here and you can see the plaster and sand he mixed with his paints to help convey the decaying buildings of the area. Almost the best thing about the museum, however, is the

19 view over the tiny **vineyard** on neighboring rue des Saules, the only vineyard in Paris, which still produces a symbolic 125 gallons of wine every year. It's hardly vintage stuff, but there are predictably bacchanalian celebrations during the October harvest. *Musée du Vieux Montmartre, 12 rue Cortot. Admission: 25 frs adults, 15 frs students and senior citizens. Open Tues.–Sun. 11–5:30.*

There's an equally famous Montmartre landmark on the corner

20 of rue St-Vincent, just down the road: the **Lapin Agile.** It's a bar-cabaret and originally one of the raunchiest haunts in Montmartre. Today, it manages against all odds to preserve at least something of its earlier flavor, unlike the Moulin Rouge. It got its curious name—it means the Nimble Rabbit—when the owner, André Gill, hung a sign outside (you can see it now in the Musée du Vieux Montmartre) of a laughing rabbit jumping out of a saucepan clutching a wine bottle. In those days, the place was still tamely called La Campagne (The Countryside). Once the sign went up, locals rebaptized the place Lapin à Gill, which, translated, means rabbit, Gill-style. When in 1886 it was sold to cabaret singer Jules Jouy, he called it the Lapin Agile, which has the same pronunciation in French as Lapin à Gill. In 1903, the premises were bought by the most celebrated cabaret entrepreneur of them all, Aristide Bruand, portrayed by Toulouse-Lautrec in a series of famous posters.

21 Behind the Lapin Agile is the **St-Vincent Cemetery;** the entrance is off little rue Lucien-Gaulard. It's a tiny graveyard, but serious students of Montmartre might want to visit to see Utrillo's burial place.

Continue north on rue des Saules, across busy rue Caulain-

22 court, and you come to the **Musée d'Art Juif,** the Museum of Jewish Art. It contains devotional items, models of synagogues, and works by Pissarro and Marc Chagall. *42 rue des Saules. Admission: 20 frs adults, 15 frs students and children. Open Sun.–Thurs. 3–6.*

There are several routes you can take back over Montmartre's hill. Luxurious avenue Junot, from which you'll see the villa Léandre, one of Montmartre's most charming side streets, makes for a picturesque return from the area around the cemetery and the museum. Alternatively, you can turn east onto rue Lamarck, past several good restaurants, to circle around the quieter side of the Sacré-Coeur basilica. If you then take the little stairpath named after Utrillo down to rue Paul Albert,

23 you'll come upon the **Marché St-Pierre** (St. Pierre Market), the perfect place to rummage for old clothes and fabrics. Prices are low. *Open Tues.–Sun. 8–1.*

Take rue de Steinkerque, opposite the foot of the Sacré-Coeur gardens, then turn right onto boulevard de Rochechouart and continue down to **Place Pigalle** to complete your tour of the essential Montmartre. Despite the area's reputation as a tawdry red-light district, a number of trendy clubs have opened here. (*see* The Arts and Nightlife, ch. 7.) If you choose to visit at night, however, be aware that dubious characters and lewd sex shows still prevail.

On the Fringe

The Bois de Boulogne

Class and style have been associated with "Le Bois," as it is known, ever since it was landscaped into an upper-class playground by Baron Haussmann in the 1850s at the request of Napoléon III. This sprawling, 2,200-acre wood, crisscrossed by broad, leafy roads, lies just west of Paris, surrounded by the wealthy residential districts of Neuilly, Auteuil, and Passy. Here you will discover rowers, joggers, strollers, riders, lovers, hookers, *pétanque*-players, and picnickers. Horse races at Longchamp and Auteuil are high up the social calendar and recreate something of a Belle Epoque atmosphere. The French Open tennis tournament at the beautiful Roland Garros Stadium in late May is another occasion when Parisian style and elegance are on full display. The manifold attractions of these woods include cafés, restaurants, lakes, gardens, and waterfalls. Rowboats are available at the two largest lakes, the Lac Inférieur and Lac Supérieur. A cheap and frequent ferry crosses to the idyllic island in the middle of the Lac Inférieur.

Buses traverse the Bois de Boulogne during the day (service 244 from Porte Maillot), but the métro goes only to the fringe: Alight at Porte Dauphine (east), Les Sablons (north), or Porte d'Auteuil (south). Porte Dauphine is one of the few stations still to possess an original Art Nouveau iron-and-glass entrance canopy, designed by métro architect Hector Guimard. It stands at the bottom of avenue Foch, connecting the Bois to the Champs-Elysées. It used to be known as the avenue de l'Impératrice in honor of the Empress Eugénie (wife of Napoléon III) and is Paris's grandest boulevard—for both its sheer size (330 yards wide) and its high-priced real estate.

One of the best ways of getting around the Bois is by bicycle. Bikes can be rented on Wednesdays and on weekends from Le Relais du Bois restaurant, Route de Suresnes (tel. 45–27–54–65). The cost is 25 francs an hour or 90 francs a day.

A word of warning: The Bois becomes a distinctly adult playground after dark, when walking, and even driving, are not advisable; the Bois's night population can be dauntingly aggressive.

Besides being a charming place to stroll or picnic, the Bois de Boulogne boasts several individual attractions worth a visit in their own right:

Parc de Bagatelle. This is a beautiful floral park with irises, roses, tulips, and water lilies among the showpieces; it is at its freshest and most colorful between April and June. The velvet green lawns and majestic 18th-century buildings (often host to art exhibitions) are fronted by a terrace with views toward the Seine—an attractive sight at any time of year. *Entrance: Route de Sèvres à Neuilly, or off Allée de Longchamp (Bus 244 or Métro: Pont de Neuilly). Admission: 6 frs adults, 3 frs children to park, 35 frs adults, 25 frs children to château buildings. Open 8:30 AM–8 PM.*

Jardin d'Acclimatation. This delightful children's amusement park on the northern edge of the Bois de Boulogne has plenty to enchant adults as well. There are boat trips along an "enchanted river," a zoo with a refreshing mix of exotic and familiar animals, a miniature railway, a high-towered folly, and various fairground stalls to keep young and old entertained. The zoo and amusement park can be reached via the miniature railway—a surefire hit with children—that runs from Porte Maillot (Wed. and weekends from 1:30; 4 frs). Many of the attractions (though not the zoo, which is spread out through the park) have separate entry fees, notably the child-oriented **Musée en Herbe** (13 frs; 11 frs excluding garden; 20 frs with workshop). There are plenty of open-air cafés for a refreshing break. *Blvd. des Sablons (Métro: Les Sablons). Admission: 9 frs adults, 4 frs children. Open Sun.–Fri. 10–6, Sat. 2–6.*

Musée des Arts et Traditions Populaires. This museum, situated right alongside the Jardin d'Acclimatation in an ugly modern building, contains an impressive variety of artifacts related principally to preindustrial rural life. Many exhibits have buttons to press and knobs to twirl; however, there are no descriptions in English. The museum is a favorite destination for school field trips, so avoid weekday afternoons, except Wednesdays, when the children are not in school. *6 route du Mahatma-Gandhi (Métro: Les Sablons). Admission: 23 frs adults, 15 frs children and Sun. Open Wed.–Mon. 10–5:15.*

Pré Catalan. This pleasant, well-tended area in the heart of the Bois de Boulogne includes one of Paris's largest trees: a copper beech over 200 years old. The "Shakespeare Garden" contains flowers, herbs, and trees mentioned in Shakespearean plays. *Route de la Grande Cascade (Bus 244 or Métro: Porte Dauphine). Guided tours at 11, 1:30, 3, 5, and 5:30.*

The Bois de Vincennes

Situated to the southeast of Paris, sandwiched between the unexciting suburb of Charenton and the working-class district of Fontenay-sous-Bois, the Bois de Vincennes is often considered a poor man's Bois de Boulogne. Although the east of Paris has less to attract visitors than the west, the comparison is largely unfair. The Bois de Vincennes is no more difficult to get to (bus 46; métro to Porte Dorée) and has equally illustrious origins. It, too, was landscaped under Napoléon III—a park having been created here by Louis XV as early as 1731.

Also like the Bois de Boulogne, the Bois de Vincennes has several lakes, notably Lac Daumesnil, with two islands, and Lac des Minimes, with three. Rowboats can be hired at both. There is also a zoo, a cinder-track racecourse (Hippodrome de Vincennes), a castle, an extensive flower garden, and several cafés. The Foire du Trône, in spring, is one big fun fair. Bikes can be rented from Château de Vincennes métro station (tel. 47–66–55–92). The cost is 20 francs an hour or 80 francs a day.

Château de Vincennes. On the northern edge of the Bois is the historic Château de Vincennes, France's medieval Versailles, an imposing, high-walled castle surrounded by a dry moat and dominated by a 170-foot keep through which guided tours are offered. The sprawling castle grounds also contain a replica (1379–1552) of the Sainte-Chapelle on the Ile de la Cité, and two elegant, classical wings designed by Louis Le Vau in the mid-17th century (now used for naval/military administration, and closed to the public). *Av. de Paris, Vincennes (Métro: Château de Vincennes). Admission: 25 frs adults, 14 frs students and senior citizens. Open daily 10–6; 10–4 in winter. Guided tours of chapel every 45 minutes.*

Musée de l'Art Africain et des Arts Océaniques. This museum, housed in a building erected for the Colonial Exhibition of 1931, is devoted to African and Oceanic Art and features headdresses, bronzes, jewelry, masks, statues, and pottery from former French colonies in Africa and the South Seas. There is also a tropical aquarium. *293 av. Daumesnil (Métro: Porte Dorée). Admission: 23 frs adults, 15 frs children and on Sun. Open Wed.–Mon. 10–5:30, weekends 10–6.*

Parc Floral. The 70-acre Vincennes flower garden includes a lake and water garden and is renowned for its seasonal displays of blooms. The "exotarium" contains tropical fish and reptiles. *Route de la Pyramide, Vincennes (Métro: Château de Vincennes). Admission: 5 frs, children under 6 free. Open daily 9:30–8, 9:30–5 in winter.*

Zoo. Some 600 mammals and 200 species of bird can be seen at Vincennes Zoo, the largest in France. One of the most striking features is an artificial rock 236 feet high, inhabited by wild mountain sheep. *53 av. de St-Maurice (Métro: Porte Dorée). Admission: 35 frs adults, 20 frs children. Open Apr.–Oct., daily 9–6; Nov.–Mar., daily 9–5:30.*

La Défense

You may be pleasantly surprised by the absence of high-rise buildings and concrete towers in central Paris; one of the reasons for this is that French planners, with their usual desire to rationalize, ordained that modern high-rise development be relegated to the outskirts of the capital. Over the last 20 years, La Défense, just to the west of Paris, across the Seine from Neuilly, has been transformed into a futuristic showcase for state-of-the-art engineering and architectural design.

A few people actually live here amid all this glass and concrete, but most come here to work. The soaring high rises of La Défense are mainly taken up by offices—often the French headquarters of multinational companies—with no expense spared in the pursuit of visual ingenuity. Outlines, shadows, reflections, plays of light, and swirling underpasses make up a stimulating, but slightly terrifying, cityscape. At its heart is the giant arch of La Tête Défense, aligned with avenue de la Grande Armée, the Arc de Triomphe, the Champs-Elysées, and the Louvre. Tubular glass elevators whisk you to the top. *Métro or RER: La Défense. Admission: 30 frs. Open Sun.–Fri. 9–6, Sat. 9–7.*

Père Lachaise Cemetery

This largest, most interesting, and most prestigious of Paris cemeteries dates back to the start of the 19th century. Situated on the eastern fringe of Paris, it is a veritable necropolis whose tombs compete in grandiosity, originality, and often, alas, dilapidation. Cobbled avenues, steep slopes, and lush vegetation contribute to a powerful atmosphere. The cemetery was the site of the Paris Commune's final battle on May 28, 1871, when the rebel troops were rounded up, lined against the **Mur des Federes** (Federalist's Wall; now in the southeast corner of the cemetery), and shot. Named after the Jesuit father—Louis XIV's confessor—who led the reconstruction of the Jesuit Rest House completed here in 1682, the cemetery houses the tombs of the French author Colette; the composer Chopin; the playwright Molière; the writers Honoré Balzac, Marcel Proust, Paul Eluard, and Oscar Wilde; the popular French actress Simone Signoret and her husband, singer-actor Yves Montand; and Edith Piaf. Perhaps the most noticeable shrine is to rock star Jim Morrison: Lyrics scribbled on tombstones will lead you to the gravesite, where dozens of hippie faithfuls sit in silent homage to the songwriter. Get hold of a map at the entrance—and remember that Père Lachaise is an easy place to get lost in. *Rue des Rondeaux (Métro: Gambetta, Père Lachaise). Open daily 8–6, 8–dusk in winter.*

St-Denis

Although today St-Denis is a pretty seedy, downmarket northern suburb, its history—exemplified by its huge green-roof cathedral—is illustrious. The **Basilique de St-Denis** can be reached by métro from Paris and is worth visiting for several reasons. It was here, under dynamic prelate Abbé Suger, that Gothic architecture (typified by pointed arches and rib vaults) arguably made its first appearance. Suger's writings also show the medieval fascination with the bright, shiny colors that appear in stained glass. The kings of France soon chose St-Denis as their final resting place, and their richly sculpted tombs—along with what remains of Suger's church—can be seen in the choir area at the east end of the church. The vast 13th-century nave is a brilliant example of structural logic. Its elements—columns, capitals, and vaults—are a model of architectural harmony. The facade retains the rounded arches of the Romanesque style that preceded Gothic and is set off by a small rose window, reputedly the earliest in France. There was originally a left tower, with spire, as well as a right one; there is currently talk of reconstructing it. *Métro: St-Denis–Basilique. Admission to choir: 24 frs adults, 13 frs students and senior citizens. Open daily 10–7, 10–5 in winter.*

La Villette

The so-called **Cité des Sciences et de l'Industrie** is housed in the vast **Parc de la Villette,** created in the mid-1980s on the site of a former *abattoir* (slaughterhouse) in the unfashionable outskirts of northeast Paris. The sprawling complex includes a science and industry museum; planetarium; curved-screen cinema; an "inventorium," or children's play area; a concert hall (the Zénith—a major rock venue); and the huge iron-and-glass Grande Halle, used for concerts and exhibitions.

The **museum** tries to do for science and industry what the look-alike Pompidou Center does for modern art. It is a brave attempt to make technology seem fun and easy. The visual displays are bright and thought-provoking, while dozens of "try-it-yourself" contraptions make the visitor feel more participant than onlooker. It's fascinating stuff and, perhaps, a forerunner of the museums of tomorrow—despite the huge, echoing main hall that is unpleasantly like a high-tech factory, and the lines (especially during school holidays), which can be absurdly long. *Métro: Porte de la Villette. Admission: 45 frs adults, 35 frs children (planetarium 15 frs extra). Open Tues.–Sun. 10–6.*

The **Géode** cinema, facing the museum building across the unruffled sheen of a broad moat, looks like a huge silver golf ball: It's actually made of polished steel. Thanks to its enormous, 180-degree-curved screen, it has swiftly become a cult movie venue. As its capacity is limited, we suggest you materialize in the morning or early afternoon to be sure of a same-day ticket. *Admission: 50 frs (joint ticket with museum 85 frs adults, 75 frs children). Screenings Tues.–Sun. 10–9.*

The futuristic outlines of the Géode and Science Museum shimmer in the canals that crisscross the Parc de la Villette, principally the barge-bearing Canal de l'Ourcq on its way from Paris to St-Denis. The whole area is ambitiously landscaped—there are sweeping lawns, a children's playground, canopied walkways, and weird, brightly painted pavilions—and is at last beginning to take shape, although a massive musical academy by the Porte de Pantin entrance will need several years of additional construction before completion.

The former slaughterhouse—the **Grande Halle**—is a magnificent structure that provides an intelligent link with the site's historic past: Its transformation into an exhibition-cum-concert center has been carried out as ingeniously as that of the former Gare (now Musée) d'Orsay. It is an intriguing sight at night, too, when strips of red neon along the roof and facade flicker on and off like a beating heart.

Sightseeing Checklists

Historic Buildings and Sites

Arc de Triomphe. Napoléon's triumphal arch forms part of the most imposing architectural vista in Europe, and dominates the circling traffic below it. Métro or RER: Etoile. (*See* From the Arc de Triomphe to the Opéra.)

Arènes de Lutèce. One of the two remaining vestiges of Gallo-Roman Paris (Cluny is the other; *see* Museums and Galleries, *below*). The arena, designed as a theater and circus, was almost totally destroyed by the barbarians in AD 280; you can still see part of the stage and tiered seating. Métro: Monge. (*See* The Left Bank.)

Bourse. The Paris Stock Exchange, a serene, colonnaded 19th-century building, is a far cry from Wall Street. Take your passport if you want to tour it. *Métro: Bourse.*

Bourse du Commerce. Paris's Commercial Exchange, an attractive, 18th-century circular building, now stands in contrast to the ultramodern Forum des Halles. Métro: Louvre, Les Halles; RER: Châtelet-Les Halles. (*See* The Historic Heart.)

Château de Vincennes. Known as the medieval Versailles, the château on the northern edge of the Bois de Vincennes is a majestic ensemble. Before you enter, walk around the outside for the best views of the fortified towers. Métro: Château de Vincennes. (*See* On the Fringe.)

Conciergerie. The fairy-tale towers of the Conciergerie disguise the fact that this was the grim prison that housed Marie Antoinette, Robespierre, and Danton during the French Revolution. The view of the building from quai de la Mégisserie across the Seine, especially at night, is memorable. Métro: Cité. (*See* The Historic Heart.)

Ecole Militaire. Still used as a military academy, the Ecole Militaire, overlooking the Champ de Mars and the Eiffel Tower, is not open to visitors, but you can admire its harmonious, 18th-century architecture from the Champ de Mars. Métro: Ecole Militaire. (*See* From Orsay to Trocadéro.)

Ecole Nationale des Beaux-Arts. The National Fine Arts College, founded at the beginning of the 17th century, occupies three large mansions on the Left Bank quayside. The school regularly stages temporary exhibits. Métro: St-Germain-des-Prés. (*See* The Left Bank.)

Eiffel Tower. The most famous landmark in Paris, built to celebrate the centennial of the French Revolution in 1889. Métro: Bir Hakeim; RER: Champ-de-Mars. (*See* From Orsay to Trocadéro.)

Hôtel de Lauzun. This is the only *hôtel particulier* on Ile St-Louis open to visitors. With its magnificent painted ceilings, tapestries, and gilded carvings, it provides a rich taste of aristocratic life in 17th-century Paris. Métro: Pont Marie. (*See* The Marais and Ile St-Louis.)

Hôtel de Sens. This is one of the few private mansions in Paris to have survived from the Middle Ages. Originally the home of the archbishops of Sens, it now houses a fine- and applied-arts library, the **Bibliothèque Forney,** and stages some excellent temporary exhibits. Métro: Pont Marie. (*See* The Marais and Ile St-Louis.)

Hôtel des Invalides. Built in the 17th century to house war veterans or "invalids," the Invalides now houses two museums, the **Musée de l'Armée** and the **Musée des Plans-Reliefs.** (*See* Museums and Galleries, *below.*) Son-et-lumière concerts are held in the main courtyard on summer evenings. Métro: Latour-Maubourg, Varenne. (*See* From Orsay to Trocadéro.)

Hôtel de Sully. This superb 17th-century mansion houses the **Caisse Nationale des Monuments Historiques,** which organizes some excellent guided tours and conferences on historical monuments throughout the city. Métro: St-Paul. (*See* The Marais and Ile St-Louis.)

Hôtel de Ville. The Paris city hall has been splendidly cleaned and its vast square transformed into an elegant pedestrian area. Métro: Hôtel de Ville. (*See* The Marais and Ile St-Louis.)

Hôtel Matignon. The French prime minister's residence is obviously not open to visitors, but the courtyard of this elegant mansion, built in 1721, is worth a discreet peek. Métro: Varenne. (*See* From Orsay to Trocadéro.)

Institut de France. You will see the distinctive cupola of the French Institute standing out against the Left Bank skyline over the river from the Louvre. The Institute is home to the

Académie Française and four other, lesser-known academies. Métro: Pont Neuf. (*See* The Left Bank.)

Opéra. The Paris Opéra, with its monumental foyer and staircase, is a pastiche of architectural styles. Don't miss Marc Chagall's famous painted ceiling. Métro: Opéra; RER: Auber. (*See* From the Arc de Triomphe to the Opéra.)

Opéra de la Bastille. Argentinian architect Carlos Ott's gigantic new Paris opera, which has transformed place de la Bastille, opened on July 14, 1989, the bicentennial of the French Revolution. Métro: Bastille. (*See* The Marais and Ile St-Louis.)

Palais Bourbon. This 18th-century palace on the Left Bank, opposite place de la Concorde, is home to the French Parliament (Assemblée Nationale). Its colonnaded facade offers a superb view over the Seine. Métro: Assemblée Nationale. (*See* From Orsay to Trocadéro.)

Palais de l'Elysée. You can catch a glimpse of the French president's official residence, a sumptuous, early 18th-century mansion, from rue du Faubourg St-Honoré. Métro: Champs-Elysées–Clemenceau. (*See* From the Arc de Triomphe to the Opéra.)

Palais-Royal. Louis XIV lived in this palace, built by Cardinal Richelieu in the 1630s, before his move to Versailles. Today it houses the French Culture Ministry. Be sure to see the courtyard and the gardens. Métro: Palais-Royal. (*See* The Historic Heart.)

Panthéon. The Panthéon's huge dome, perched on the Montagne Ste-Geneviève, dominates the Sorbonne area. Built in the late 18th century, it houses the remains of many of the country's greatest men. Métro: Cardinal-Lemoine; RER: Luxembourg. (*See* The Left Bank.)

Place de la Bastille. This is the site of the infamous Bastille prison, destroyed on July 14, 1789. It's marked now by the July Column, commemorating the 1830 and 1848 uprisings. Métro: Bastille. (*See* The Marais and Ile St-Louis.)

Place de la Concorde. This huge square, built in the 1770s, was the gruesome scene of numerous deaths at the guillotine. The obelisk, bang in the center of the vast square, was salvaged from the ruins of the Egyptian Temple of Luxor; the viceroy of Egypt gave it to Charles X in 1829. Métro: Concorde. (*See* From the Arc de Triomphe to the Opéra.)

Place des Vosges. The oldest and most harmonious square in Paris, built by Henri IV at the beginning of the 17th century. Métro: St-Paul, Chemin-Vert. (*See* The Marais and Ile St-Louis.)

Place du Tertre. Once Montmartre's main village square, place du Tertre is best known for its artists and caricaturists. You will capture the former village atmosphere at its best in the morning; hordes of visitors and tourists transform it in the afternoon and evening. Métro: Abbesses. (*See* Montmartre.)

Place Vendôme. The most imposing square in the city was laid out by Mansart in the 17th century. Napoléon stands on the summit of the mighty central column. Métro: Opéra, Tuileries. (*See* From the Arc de Triomphe to the Opéra.)

Sorbonne. France's oldest university, founded in 1253 by Robert de Sorbon, was rebuilt and enlarged by Cardinal Richelieu in the 17th century and now forms a sprawling ensemble stretching from rue des Ecoles to rue Cujas in the heart of the Latin Quarter. Métro: Cluny-Sorbonne; RER: Luxembourg. (*See* The Left Bank.)

Théâtre National de l'Odéon (National Theater). The colonnaded Odéon theater looks out over the Luxembourg Gardens on one side and down to the busy place de l'Odéon on the other. This early 19th-century building is now the French base of the Theater of Europe. Métro: Odéon. (*See* The Left Bank.)

Museums and Galleries

Paris has a plethora of museums. Most are closed once a week, usually Monday or Tuesday. Admission prices vary. A few museums are free; most offer reductions for children, students, and senior citizens. Paris also boasts a wealth of art galleries, often housing temporary exhibits that aim to sell the works displayed but that the general public is welcome to visit. These galleries are too numerous for us to list; they are mainly situated in the Carré Rive Gauche on the Left Bank between St-Germain-des-Prés and the Musée d'Orsay or on the Right Bank off and along the Faubourg St-Honoré north of the Champs-Elysées. Among the most famous are **Galerie Schmit** (396 rue St-Honoré), **Galerie Malingue** (26 avenue Matignon), and **Galerie Gismondi** (20 rue Royale). **Hôtel Drouot** (9 rue Drouot), the Paris auction house east of Opéra, is a "living museum," with thousands of different objects on display each day.

Atelier de Gustave Moreau. Town house–cum–studio of Symbolist painter Gustave Moreau (1826–1898); those with a taste for the wilder shores of late-19th-century Romanticism will love it. Métro: Trinité. (*See* From the Arc de Triomphe to the Opéra.)

Atelier Delacroix. The small and carefully preserved studio of Romantic painter Eugène Delacroix is delightfully located on the quiet and leafy rue Fürstemberg. Métro: St-Germain-des-Prés. (*See* The Left Bank.)

Cité des Sciences et de l'Industrie de la Villette. Children adore this extensive and imaginatively laid out museum; it's very much a hands-on sort of place. Métro: Porte de la Villette. (*See* On the Fringe.)

Espace Dali. Dozens of Dali paintings and sculptures housed in a surrealistic atmosphere. Métro: Lamarck-Caulaincourt. (*See* Montmartre.)

Grand Palais. What was intended as no more than a temporary exhibit space back in the early years of the century has become a permanent part of the art scene in Paris; it houses major exhibits. Métro: Champs-Elysées–Clemenceau. (*See* From the Arc de Triomphe to the Opéra.)

Institut du Monde Arabe. A new addition to the Left Bank, opposite the east end of Ile St-Louis, it does for Arab culture what the Beaubourg does for modern art. Métro: Cardinal-Lemoine, Jussieu. (*See* The Left Bank.)

Maison de Balzac. This was the Paris home of France's great 19th-century novelist. It contains a wide range of exhibits charting his tempestuous life. *47 rue Raynouard (Métro: La Muette). Admission: 15 frs adults, 10 frs students and senior citizens. Open Tues.–Sun. 10–5:40.*

Maison de la Vigne et du Vin de France. Those who think that only the absence of vineyards stops Paris from being perfect will feel the need to stop in here. Métro: Franklin-Roosevelt. (*See* From the Arc de Triomphe to the Opéra.)

Maison de Victor Hugo. The elegant Paris home of prolific 19th-century French author Victor Hugo is filled with mementos of

We can wire money to every major city in Europe almost as fast as you can say, "Zut alors! J'ai perdu mes valises".

How fast? We can send money in 10 minutes or less, to 13,500 locations in over 68 countries worldwide. That's faster than any other international money transfer service. And when you're *sans* luggage, every minute counts.

MoneyGram from American Express® is available throughout Europe. For more information please contact your local American Express Travel Service Office or call: 44-71-839-7541 in England; 33-1-47777000 in France; or 49-69-21050 in Germany. In the U.S. call 1-800-MONEYGRAM.

MoneyGram

INTERNATIONAL MONEY TRANSFERS.

519 M.P.H.

190 M.P.H.

75 M.P.H.

0 M.P.H.

WE LET YOU SEE EUROPE AT YOUR OWN PACE.

Regardless of your personal speed limits, Rail Europe offers everything to get you over, around and through anywhere you want in Europe. For more information, call your travel agent or **1-800-4-EURAIL.**

OFFICIAL DISTRIBUTOR
Rail Europe
OF THE EURAIL PASS

his varied life. Métro: St-Paul. (*See* The Marais and Ile St-Louis.)

Les Martyres de Paris. A one-of-a-kind museum of horror that showcases the history of torture and suffering in Paris. Complete with wax figures and amplified screams and moans. *Nouveau Forum des Halles, Porte du Louvre. (Métro: Châtelet/Les Halles.) Admission: 40 frs adults, 29 frs children. Open daily 10:30–6:30.*

Musée Bourdelle. Antoine Bourdelle (1861–1929) was a French artist whose sculpture reveals the influence of Auguste Rodin, with whom he worked. Bourdelle's bust of Rodin is here, along with other works displayed in Bourdelle's house, garden, and studio. There is a notable series of portraits of Beethoven. *16 rue Antoine-Bourdelle (Métro: Falguière). Admission: 20 frs adults, 15 frs children and students. Open Tues.–Sun. 10–5:30.*

Musée Bricard/Musée de la Serrure. The art of locks and lockmakers down the years. Métro: St-Paul-le-Marais. *(See* The Marais and Ile St-Louis.)

Musée Carnavalet. Maps, plans, furniture, and portraits reveal the history of Paris. Métro: St-Paul-le-Marais. *(See* The Marais and Ile St-Louis.)

Musée Cognacq-Jay. This lavish, 18th-century town house is home to one of the finest small collections of art and artifacts in the city. (*See* The Marais and Ile St-Louis.)

Musée Dapper. Pre-colonial African art is beautifully displayed in a tranquil four-story hôtel particulier. *50 av. Victor Hugo (Métro: Victor Hugo). Admission: 15 fr adults, 7 fr children; free Wed. Open daily 11–7.*

Musée d'Art Juif. Paris's small Jewish museum contains devotional items, synagogue models, and a few works by Pissarro and Chagall. Métro: Lamarck-Caulaincourt. (*See* Montmartre.)

Musée d'Art Moderne de la Ville de Paris. A collection of 20th-century pictures and sculpture. Métro: Iéna. (*See* From Orsay to Trocadéro.)

Musée de Cluny. The atmospheric medieval former headquarters of the abbots of Cluny is now one of the most fascinating museums in the city, filled with Roman and medieval works of art. Métro: Cluny–Sorbonne. *(See* The Left Bank.)

Musée de la Chasse et de la Nature. Some may find the assembled paintings, guns, and traps here unpleasant; others will enjoy them. Métro: Rambuteau. *(See* The Marais and Ile St-Louis.)

Musée de la Femme et Collection d'Automates. A curious mixture of feminine artifacts and automata. The clockwork collection bursts into life every afternoon at 3 (guided tours only). *12 rue du Centre, Neuilly (Métro: Pont de Neuilly). Admission: 12 frs adults, 6 frs children and senior citizens. Open Wed.–Mon. 2:30–5.*

Musée de la Holographie. The Museum of Holography has a suitably modern setting in the Forum des Halles. *15 Grand Balcon, Forum des Halles (Métro/RER: Les Halles). Admission: 30 frs adults, 25 frs students and senior citizens. Open Mon.–Sat. 10–7, Sun. 1–7.*

Musée de la Légion d'Honneur. The headquarters of the most prestigious civilian awards in France. Métro: Solférino; RER: Musée d'Orsay. *(See* From Orsay to Trocadéro.)

Musée de la Marine. Those with salt in their veins will not want to miss this extensive maritime museum in the Palais de Chaillot. Métro: Trocadéro. *(See* From Orsay to Trocadéro.)

Musée de la Musique Mécanique. A pleasantly rustic museum, stuck down a dead end near the Pompidou Center, featuring mechanical musical instruments (hourly tours with working demonstrations). *Impasse Berthaud (Métro: Rambuteau). Admission: 30 frs adults, 15 frs children under 12. Open weekends 2–7.*

Musée de la Poste. This museum of postal history, spread over five floors, includes displays of international and French stamps (since 1849), postmen's uniforms and postboxes, sorting and stamp-printing machines, and the balloon used to send mail out of Paris during the Prussian siege of 1870. *34 blvd. de Vaugirard (Métro: Falguière). Admission: 25 frs adults, 12.50 frs students and senior citizens, children under 6 free. Open Mon.–Sat. 10–6.*

Musée de l'Armée. The glorious and sometimes not-so-glorious history of the French army is traced in this imposing museum in Les Invalides. Métro: Latour-Maubourg, Varenne. (*See* From Orsay to Trocadéro.)

Musée de l'Art Africain et des Arts Océaniques. Artifacts from Africa and the South Seas are intriguingly displayed in this sizable museum. Métro: Porte-Dorée. (*See* On the Fringe.)

Musée de l'Art Naïf Max Fourny. Varied exhibitions of naive paintings; many people love it. *2 rue Ronsard (Métro: Anvers). Admission: 22 frs adults, 16 frs students and senior citizens. Open Tues.–Sun. 10–6.*

Musée de l'Histoire de France. It contains everything from Marie Antoinette's last letter to the sumptuous apartments of 18th-century French aristocrats. The museum includes the **Archives Nationales,** with thousands of documents charting French history back to the 10th century. (*See* The Marais and Ile St-Louis.)

Musée de l'Homme. This is the city's principal anthropological museum, housed in the Palais de Chaillot. Métro: Trocadéro. *(See* From Orsay to Trocadéro.)

Musée de l'Opéra. The Opéra museum contains paintings and operatic mementos of the lavish Paris opera house. Métro: Opéra. *(See* From the Arc de Triomphe to the Opéra.)

Musée de l'Orangerie. Twentieth-century French paintings are housed in this elegant neoclassical pavilion at the west end of the Tuileries Gardens. Métro: Concorde. *(See* From the Arc de Triomphe to the Opéra.)

Musée de l'Ordre de la Libération. The Order of Liberation was created by General de Gaulle after the fall of France in 1940 to honor those who made outstanding contributions to the Allied victory in World War II. (Churchill and Eisenhower figure among the rare foreign recipients.) Some 200 display cabinets evoke various episodes of the war: De Gaulle's Free France organization, the Resistance, the Deportation, and the 1944 Liberation. *51 bis blvd. de Latour-Maubourg (Métro: Latour-Maubourg). Admission: 5 frs. Open Mon.–Sat. 2–5.*

Musée des Arts Décoratifs. French decorative arts down the centuries are covered in this quiet museum in the Louvre complex. Métro: Palais-Royal. (*See* The Historic Heart.)

Musée des Arts et Traditions Populaires. Preindustrial objects from all the regions of France. Métro: Les Sablons. *(See* On the Fringe.)

Musée des Monuments Français. If you have any interest in French medieval architecture, make a point of seeing this excellent museum; it's one of the most imaginative and instructive in the city. Métro: Trocadéro. *(See* From Orsay to Trocadéro.)

Musée des Plans-Reliefs. Plans and models of French-fortified towns and cities in the 17th century make for a museum that is substantially more interesting than many visitors realize. It's located in the Hôtel des Invalides. Métro: Latour-Maubourg, Varenne. *(See* From Orsay to Trocadéro.)

Musée d'Orsay. One of the Big Three museums in Paris, rivaling the Louvre and the Beaubourg (Pompidou Center) for the extent of its collection. It covers art in France from 1848 to 1914. For many, the Impressionists are the major draw. Métro: Solférino; RER: Musée d'Orsay. *(See* From Orsay to Trocadéro.)

Musée du Cinéma. This is one of a number of museums near Trocadéro at the Palais de Chaillot; it charts the history of movies in colorful and vibrant detail. Métro: Trocadéro. *(See* From Orsay to Trocadéro.)

Musée du Jeu de Paume. The former home of the Impressionists reopened in 1991 with a redesigned, shiny white interior featuring temporary exhibits of brash contemporary art. Métro: Concord. (*See* From the Arc de Triomphe to the Opéra.)

Musée du Louvre. This is the world's biggest museum, legendary home of the *Mona Lisa,* now reorganized and boasting the controversial glass pyramid entrance. Few people will want to come to Paris and skip the Louvre. Métro: Palais-Royal. *(See* The Historic Heart.)

Musée du Rock. A multimedia rock 'n roll hall of fame, with wax figures depicting everyone from Buddy Holly to Madonna. *Nouveau Forum des Halles. Porte du Louvre (Métro: Châtelet-Les-Halles), tel. 40–28–08–96. Admission: 43 frs adults, 32 frs students and children. Open daily 10:30–6:30.*

Musée du Sport. A sports museum housed at the French national stadium in southwest Paris, featuring posters, trophies, equipment, and other sporting paraphernalia. *Parc des Princes, 24 rue du Commandant-Guilbaud (Métro: Porte de St-Cloud). Admission: 20 frs adults, 10 frs children and senior citizens. Open Sun.–Tues., Thurs., and Fri. 9:30–12:30 and 2–5.*

Musée du Vieux Montmartre. The history of rowdy and picturesque Montmartre is traced in this likable little museum. Métro: Lamarck-Caulaincourt. *(See* Montmartre.)

Musée du Vin (Wine Museum). This museum is pretty, petite, and a gourmet's treat. Devoted to the vine and traditional wine-making artifacts, it is housed in the cellars of a former 13th-century abbey. The premises double as a medieval wine bar: A selection of wines is served by the glass, along with excellent cheese and meat platters. *Caveau des Echansons, rue des Eaux (Métro: Passy). Admission and wine-tasting: 26 frs. Open daily noon–6.*

Musée Grévin. This waxworks museum, founded in 1882, ranks with London's Madame Tussaud's. Dozens of wax renderings of historical and contemporary celebrities are on display. *10 blvd. Montmartre (Métro: Rue Montmartre). Admission: 48 frs adults, 34 frs children under 14. Open daily 1–7, during school holidays 10–7.*

Musée Guimet. Indo-Chinese and Far Eastern art are housed in this elegant museum. Métro: Iéna. *(See* From Orsay to Trocadéro.)

Musée Jacquemart-André. A sumptuous, 19th-century town house is the setting for this little-known museum that contains a rich collection of Renaissance and 18th-century art. Métro: St-Phillipe-du-Roule. (*See* From the Arc de Triomphe to the Opéra.)

Musée Marmottan. Paris's "other" Impressionist museum (after the Musée d'Orsay), the Marmottan contains more than 100 works by Claude Monet. There are also fine Impressionist works by other artists like Pissarro, Renoir, and Sisley. The first and second floors boast some magnificent medieval illuminated manuscripts and the original furnishings of a sumptuous early 19th-century Empire mansion. Marmottan is one of the most underestimated museums in Paris. *2 rue Louis-Boilly (Métro: La Muette). Admission: 30 frs adults, 15 frs children and senior citizens. Open Tues.–Sun. 10–5:30.*

Musée National d'Art Moderne. The largest collection of modern art in the world is housed in the brash and vibrant **Beaubourg.** Métro: Rambuteau. (*See* The Marais and Ile St-Louis.)

Musée National de la Céramique, in St-Cloud park, displays hundreds of Sèvres porcelain creations, together with the manufacturing premises. *Pl. de la Manufacture, Sèvres (Métro: Pont de Sevres). Admission: 23 frs, 15 frs on Sun. Open Wed.–Mon. 10–5:15.*

Musée National des Techniques. The former church and priory of St-Martin des Champs were confiscated during the Revolution and used first as an educational institution, then as an arms factory before becoming, in 1799, the Conservatoire des Arts et Métiers. Today, the 11th- to 13th-century church, with its fine belfry and skillfully restored east end, forms part of the Musée National des Techniques, an industrial museum with a varied collection of models (locomotives, vehicles, and agricultural machinery), astronomical instruments, looms, and glass, together with displays on printing, photography, and the history of television. The splendid 13th-century refectory, a large hall supported by central columns, is now used as a library. *270 rue St-Martin (Métro: Arts et Métiers). Admission: 20 frs, 10 frs on Sun. Open Tues.–Sun. 10–5:15.*

Musée Notre Dame. A small museum charting the turbulent history of the most venerable building in Paris. Métro: Cité. (*See* The Historic Heart.)

Musée Picasso. The elegant Hôtel Salé provides the setting for the largest collection of Picassos in existence. Métro: St-Sébastien. (*See* The Marais and Ile St-Louis.)

Musée Rodin. This is probably the best single-artist museum in Paris. An elegant town house is filled with sculptures, plans, and drawings by the prolific 19th-century sculptor. Métro: Varenne. (*See* From Orsay to Trocadéro.)

Musée Zadkine. Russian-born sculptor Ossip Zadkine (1890–1967) trained in London before setting up in Paris in 1909. The works on exhibit here, in Zadkine's former house and studio, reveal the influences of Rodin, African art, and Cubism. *100 bis rue d'Assas (Métro: Vavin). Admission: 12 frs adults, 6.50 frs students and senior citizens, Sun. free. Open Tues.–Sun. 10–5:40.*

Nouveau Musée Grévin (Les Halles). This branch of the Musée Grévin (*see above*) is situated in the Forum des Halles and boasts waxwork scenes from Belle Epoque Paris. *Grand Balcon, Forum des Halles (Métro/RER: Les Halles). Admission: 38 frs adults, 28 frs children under 14. Open Mon.–Sat. 10:30–7:30, Sun. 1–7.*

Palais de la Découverte. Substantial science museum, complete

with planetarium, adjoining the Grand Palais. Métro: Champs-
Elysées–Clemenceau. (*See* From the Arc de Triomphe to the
Opéra.)
Petit Palais. This is the smaller twin of the Grand Palais (*see
above*), housing a collection of 19th-century French paintings
and furniture. Métro: Champs-Elysées–Clemenceau. (*See*
From the Arc de Triomphe to the Opéra.)

Churches

Paris boasts numerous historic churches. Those of outstanding
interest are detailed in the Exploring sections above and are
also listed here, along with some others that are well worth a
visit if you are in the neighborhood. Most are open 9–noon and
2–5, but there are no set hours. Some stage daily services at
lunchtime. Quiet and appropriate dress are expected.

Paris is rich in churches of two architectural styles: late Gothic
(the Flamboyant style of the 14th and 15th centuries, with its
intricate stone tracery) and 17th-century Baroque (columns,
rounded arches, and smaller windows inspired by classical an-
tiquity and the Italian Renaissance). Another feature is the
phenomenal number of wall paintings, to be found mainly in
side chapels and dating, for the most part, from the first half of
the 19th century.

American Cathedral of the Holy Trinity. A neo-Gothic structure
built between 1885 and 1888. Métro: Alma-Marceau. (*See* From
the Arc de Triomphe to the Opéra.)
American Church in Paris. Another neo-Gothic church, this one
built rather later (1927–1931), on the Left Bank. *65 quai
d'Orsay (Métro: Alma-Marceau), tel. 47–05–07–99.*
Basilique de St-Denis. Built between 1136 and 1286, this is in
some ways the most important Gothic church in the Paris region, the first in which the guiding principles of Gothic architecture were fully developed. Today, it's in a seedy northern
suburb. Métro: St-Denis–Basilique. (*See* On the Fringe.)
Basilique du Sacré-Coeur. Many find this monumental white
church in Montmartre the ugliest major church in the city. It is,
however, a major and highly visible landmark. Métro: Anvers.
(*See* Montmartre.)
Cathédrale Notre Dame. If you visit only one church in Paris, it
should be Notre Dame, the most historic and dominant church
in the city. Métro: Cité. (*See* The Historic Heart.)
Eglise de la Madeleine. The stern neoclassical exterior of the
Madeleine belies the richly harmonious, if dimly lit, interior.
Métro: Madeleine. (*See* From the Arc de Triomphe to the Op-
éra.)
Eglise du Dôme. Under the dome of this magnificently com-
manding Baroque church, part of Les Invalides, Napoléon
rests in imperial splendor. Métro: St-François-Xavier. (*See*
From Orsay to Trocadéro.)
Eglise St-Louis des Invalides. The Baroque church at Les
Invalides. Métro: Latour-Maubourg. (*See* From Orsay to
Trocadéro.)
Mosquée de Paris. Not far from the Jardin des Plantes, you can
plunge into a Moslem atmosphere beneath the arcades and min-
aret of an authentic mosque (built 1922–1925) decorated in the
style of Moorish Spain. *Pl. du Puits de l'Ermite (Métro:
Monge). Open Sat.–Thurs. 9–noon and 2–5.* (*See* The Left
Bank.)

Notre-Dame de l'Assomption. This 1670 church, with its huge dome and solemn interior, was the scene of Lafayette's funeral in 1834. It is now used as the chapel of the Polish community. *Rue Cambon (Métro: Concorde).*

Notre-Dame des Blancs Manteaux. The Blancs Manteaux were white-robed 13th-century mendicant monks, whose monastery once stood on this spot. For the last 100 years, this late 17th-century church has boasted an imposing 18th-century facade that belonged to a now-destroyed church on the Ile de la Cité. Unfortunately, the narrow streets of the Marais leave little room to step back and admire it. The inside boasts some fine woodwork and a Flemish-style Rococo pulpit whose marquetry panels are inlaid with pewter and ivory. *Rue des Blancs-Manteaux (Métro: Rambuteau).*

Notre-Dame de Bonne Nouvelle. This wide, soberly neoclassical church is tucked away off the Grands Boulevards near Strasbourg-St-Denis. The church is unusual in that it faces north-south instead of east-west. The previous church on the spot (the second) was ransacked during the Revolution, and the current one, built 1823–1829 after the restoration of the French monarchy, was ransacked by Communard hooligans in May 1871. The highlight of the interior is the semicircular apse behind the altar, featuring some fine 17th-century paintings beneath a three-dimensional, 19th-century grisaille composition by Abel de Pujol. A wide variety of pictures, statues, and works of religious art can be found in the side chapels and in the church museum (ask at the sacristy to the left of the altar). *Rue de la Lune (Métro: Bonne-Nouvelle).*

Notre-Dame de Lorette. This little-known church below Montmartre was built from 1823 to 1836 in the neoclassical style popular at the time. Of principal interest is the vast array of religious wall paintings; they are of varying quality but have been successfully restored. *Rue de Châteaudun (Métro: Notre-Dame-de-Lorette).*

Notre-Dame des Victoires. You'll want to visit this 17th-century church, built from 1666 to 1740, to see the 30,000 ex voto tablets that adorn its walls. *Place des Petits-Pères (Métro: Sentier, Bourse).*

St-Alexandre Nevsky. The onion domes of the Russian Orthodox cathedral of Paris are among the city's most distinctive landmarks. Métro: Courcelles. *(See* From the Arc de Triomphe to the Opéra.)

Sainte-Chapelle. Built by Louis IX (1226–1270) to house what he believed to be the Crown of Thorns from Christ's crucifixion and fragments of the True Cross, the Ste-Chapelle is one of the supreme architectural achievements of the Middle Ages. Metro: Cité. *(See* The Historic Heart.)

Ste-Clotilde. This neo-Gothic church (1846–1858) is chiefly of note for its imposing twin towers, visible from across the Seine. French classical composer César Franck was the organist here from 1858 to 1890. *Rue Las-Cases (Métro: Solférino).*

Ste-Croix-St-Jean. This much-restored church, erected in 1624, is now used as the Armenian Cathedral of Paris. Its chancel contains some splendid 18th-century gilded paneling. The exterior underwent extensive cleaning and restoration in 1988. *Rue du Perche (Métro: Rambuteau).*

St-Denis du St-Sacrement. This severely neoclassical edifice (close to the Picasso Museum in the Marais) dates from the 1830s. It is a formidable example of architectural discipline, oozing restraint and monumental dignity (or banality, according to taste). The grisaille frieze and gilt fresco above the semicircular apse have clout if not subtlety; the Delacroix *Deposition* (1844), in the front right-hand chapel as you enter, has both. *Rue de Turenne (Métro: St-Sébastien).*

Ste-Elisabeth. This studied essay (1628–1646) in Baroque has a pleasantly unpretentious feel to it; there's no soaring bombast here. There are brightly restored wall paintings and a wide, semicircular apse around the choir, with stupendous carved 17th-century wood paneling featuring biblical scenes (transferred from an abbey at Arras in northern France). *Rue du Temple (Métro: Temple).*

St-Etienne du Mont. This church (1492–1632) in the shadow of the Panthéon has two major claims to fame: its mishmash facade and its curly, carved rood screen (1525–1535), separating nave and chancel, the only one of its kind in Paris. Métro: Cardinal Lemoine. (*See* The Left Bank.)

St-Eustache. The "Cathedral of the Right Bank" was built between 1532 and 1637 and offers a considerable contrast to the brash modernity of the neighboring Forum des Halles. Métro or RER: Les Halles. (*See* The Historic Heart.)

St-Germain-des-Prés. Graceful St-Germain-des-Prés, in the heart of the Left Bank, is the oldest church in the city; its classical facade disguises its late-Romanesque interior. Métro: St-Germain-des-Prés. (*See* The Left Bank.)

St-Germain l'Auxerrois. Built from the 13th to the 16th centuries, this rich, late-Gothic church opposite the east end of the Louvre was once the royal church in Paris. Métro: Louvre. (*See* The Historic Heart.)

St-Gervais-St-Protais. Built from 1494 to 1657, this church stands on the site of what was the oldest church in the city. Métro: Hôtel de Ville. (*See* The Marais and Ile St-Louis.)

St-Jean l'Evangéliste. Church of St-Jean is an innovative 1904 essay in concrete, which has since been clad in reassuring red brick. Métro: Abbesses. (*See* Montmartre.)

St-Louis-en-l'Ile. Built from 1664 to 1726, this is the only church on the Ile St-Louis. (*Métro: Pont-Marie.*)

St-Louis de la Salpêtrière. This is the church of the Salpêtrière Hospital next to the Gare d'Austerlitz, an unmistakable sight with its lantern-topped octagonal dome. The church, built 1670–1677 according to the designs of Libéral Bruant, is shaped like a Greek cross. *Blvd. de l'Hôpital (Métro: Gare d'Austerlitz).*

St-Médard. The nave and facade, with its large late-Gothic window, date from the late 15th century. The 17th-century choir is in the contrasting classical style. A picturesque churchyard lines rue Censier. *Square St-Médard (Métro: Censier-Daubenton).*

St. Michael's English Church. Modern building, with a friendly welcome. Métro: Madeleine. (*See* The Arc de Triomphe to the Opéra.)

St-Nicolas des Champs. Here's another Parisian example of Gothic colliding with Renaissance: The round-arched, fluted Doric capitals in the chancel date from 1560 to 1587, a full century later than the pointed-arched nave (1420–1480). There is a majestic mid-17th-century organ and a fine *Assumption of the Virgin* (1629) above the high altar by Simon Vouet. The south door (1576) in rue au Maire is gloriously carved and surrounded by a small but unexpectedly well-tended lawn complete with rosebushes. *Rue St-Martin (Métro: Arts et Métiers).*

St-Nicolas du Chardonnet. The first church on the site was apparently built in a field of thistles *(chardons* in French), and over recent years, St-Nicolas has been a thorn in the side of the Catholic Church by refusing to abandon Latin mass. Stubborn priests are not, however, the most visible attraction of this pleasant Baroque edifice (1656–1709) on the bustling Left Bank. There is a Corot study for the *Baptism of Christ* in the first chapel on the right and a *Crucifixion* by Brueghel the Younger in the sacristy. *Rue St-Victor (Métro: Maubert-Mutualité).*

Ste-Odile. The colossal, dark-brick tower of this modern church (built 1938–1946) surges into the northern Paris skyline like a stumpy rocket, reminiscent of something out of Soviet Russia. The inside, however, smacks more of Scandinavian architecture, with its harmony, simple lines, and decorative restraint. As modern stained glass goes, the stuff here is first-rate. *Av. Stéphane-Mallarmé (Métro: Porte de Champerret).*

St-Pierre de Montmartre. Much-restored little church dating from the 12th century and now overshadowed by Sacré-Coeur. Métro: Anvers. *(See* Montmartre.)

St-Roch. A dynamically Baroque church, built between 1635 and 1740, in the swanky heart of the Right Bank. Métro: Tuileries. *(See* The Historic Heart.)

St-Sulpice. Built from 1646 to 1780, this is the "Cathedral of the Left Bank." Métro: St-Sulpice. *(See* The Left Bank.)

St-Vincent de Paul. With its pair of square towers, this early 19th-century church (1824–1844) stands out in the midst of the undistinguished streets surrounding the Gare du Nord. The facade is lent drama by a pedimented portico and the majestic flight of steps leading up from a cheerful square. Inside, the outstanding feature is the glittering gold fresco high up the nave walls by Hippolyte Flandrin, depicting an endless procession of religious figures. *Place Franz-Liszt (Métro: Poissonnière).*

Temple de l'Oratoire. Built from 1616 to 1630 by Le Mercier as mother church for the Carmelite Congregation of the Oratory, although the Jesuit-style facade dates from the 18th century and the main portal from 1845. During the Revolution, the church became an arms depot, a storehouse, and then, from 1811, a Protestant church. *Rue de l'Oratoire (Métro: Louvre).*

Temple Ste-Marie. This building, constructed 1632–1634 by François Mansart as the chapel of the Convent of the Visitation, is now a Protestant church. The dome above the distinctive nave rotunda is one of the earliest in Paris and is said to have influenced Christopher Wren when planning St. Paul's Cathedral in London. *Rue St-Antoine (Métro: Bastille).*

Parks and Gardens

Bois de Boulogne. These 2,200 acres of woodland and lakes on Paris's western outskirts are crisscrossed by broad, leafy roads and are full of amenities, including a children's amusement park. Métros: Porte Dauphine (east), Les Sablons (north), and Porte d'Auteuil (south). *(See* On the Fringe.)

Bois de Vincennes. Another vast area of woodland, on the southeast outskirts of Paris, with a sprawling castle, a zoo, and a floral park. Métro: Château de Vincennes (north), Porte Dorée (south). *(See* On the Fringe.)

Buttes-Chaumont. In the 1860s Haussmann transformed this former steep-sloped quarry into an immensely picturesque park with lake, waterfalls, and oft-painted belvedere—and a charming restaurant. Métro: Buttes-Chaumont, Botzaris. (*See* Off the Beaten Track.)

Champ de Mars. This long, formal garden, landscaped at the start of the century, lies between the Eiffel Tower and Ecole Militaire. It was previously used as a parade ground and site of the World Exhibitions of 1867, 1889 (date of the construction of the Eiffel Tower), and 1900. Métro: Bir-Hakeim; RER: Champ-de-Mars. (*See* From Orsay to Trocadéro.)

Jardin des Halles. This brand-new urban park near the church of St-Eustache is geared mainly for children—there's an old-fashioned carousel—but it's also a pleasant place to stroll in this busy new center. Watch out for rhino-shaped bushes. (*Métro and RER: Les Halles.*)

Jardin des Plantes. Paris's botanical gardens house a zoo, an alpine garden, greenhouses, an aquarium, a maze, various museums, and a *robinia* tree planted in 1636. Métro: Monge, Jussieu. (*See* The Left Bank.)

Jardin des Tuileries. Le Nôtre's masterpiece, with its understated elegance, fountains, and statues, runs from the Louvre to place de la Concorde. It's ideal for a stroll or a drink in an open-air café in the heart of Paris. Métro: Tuileries. (*See* From the Arc de Triomphe to the Opéra.)

Jardin du Luxembourg. These formal gardens are in the heart of Paris, with fountains, statues, and tree-lined alleys. They are built around the Palais du Luxembourg, home to the French Senate. Métro: Odéon, Cluny-Sorbonne; RER: Luxembourg. (*See* The Left Bank.)

Jardin du Palais-Royal. A delightful, little-known oasis in the center of Paris, bordered by arcades. Come here to see Daniel Buren's controversial black-and-white striped columns in the courtyard. Métro: Palais-Royal. (*See* The Historic Heart.)

Jardins Albert-Kahn. On the Paris side of the Seine, across from Parc de St-Cloud (*see below*), these gardens add a surprising note of oriental greenery to the undistinguished suburb of Boulogne. (*Métro: Boulogne–Pont de St-Cloud.*) *Admission: 10 frs adults, 5 frs children.*

Moorish Gardens (Mosquée de Paris). The patio and arcades under the minaret of the Paris mosque make the setting a mecca for garden and mint-tea lovers. *Pl. du Puits de l'Ermite (Métro: Monge). Tours Sat.–Thurs. 2–5; closed Fri.*

Parc Andre-Citroën. In the 15th arrondissement, this innovative park, still being built at press time on the site of the former car factory, features 35 acres of sensational river views, poetic gardens, and—to the delight of children—a computer-programmed "dancing fountain." (*Métro: Javel or Balard.*)

Parc de Bagatelle. A beautiful floral park famous for its rose gardens on the west side of Bois de Boulogne. Métro: Pont de Neuilly. (*See* On the Fringe.)

Parc Monceau. An 18th-century park in the chic 17th Arrondissement, with lake, rotunda, and mock ruins. Métro: Monceau. (*See* From the Arc de Triomphe to the Opéra.)

Parc Montsouris. Very pretty, English-style gardens in the south of the city, with cascades, a lake, and a meteorological observatory disguised as a Tunisian Palace. (*Métro: Glacière; RER: Cité Universitaire.*)

Parc de St-Cloud. This tumbling, wooded park on a hill to the southwest of Paris offers some superb views of the city. (*Métro: Boulogne–Pont de St-Cloud.*)

Parc de la Villette. A vast new park now surrounds the glimmering science-and-industry museum complex, with a children's play area, the Inventorium. It's a pleasant place for a stroll near the Canal de l'Ourcq, in the once-unfashionable 19th Arrondissement in the northeast of Paris. Métro: Porte de Pantin, Porte de la Villette. *(See* On the Fringe.)

Serres d'Auteuil. A bewildering variety of plants and flowers are grown in these greenhouses for use in Paris's municipal parks and in displays at official occasions. Tropical and exotic plants sweat it out in the mighty hothouses, while the surrounding gardens' leafy paths and well-tended lawns offer cooler places to admire floral virtuosity. *3 av. de la Porte d'Auteuil (Métro: Porte d'Auteuil). Admission: 5 frs. Open daily 10–5:30.*

Cemeteries

This is not such a macabre listing as it sounds. The cemeteries of Paris are remarkable for their statues, elaborate monuments, tombs of the famous, and melancholy disrepair. They are usually open from 7:30 to 6 in summer and from 8 to 5:30 in winter.

Cimetière de Montmartre. Situated on the west side of the Montmartre hill, this cemetery, built in 1795, houses the tombs of the writer Stendhal, the composer Berlioz, the painter Degas, and the famous French film director François Truffaut. Métro: Place de Clichy. *(See* Montmartre.)

Cimetière de Montparnasse. High walls encircle the Montparnasse cemetery, a haven of peace in one of Paris's busiest shopping and business areas. You can visit the tombs of Jean-Paul Sartre, Baudelaire, Bartholdi—who designed the Statue of Liberty—and André Citroën. Métro: Raspail, Edgar Quinet. *(See* The Left Bank.)

Cimitière de Picpus. This convent cemetery marks the spot where thousands were guillotined in 1794. The grave of General Lafayette is also here. Métro: Nation, Picpus. *(See* Off the Beaten Track.)

Cimetière du Père Lachaise. This cemetery—the largest in Paris—is also the most attractive. Métro: Gambetta, Père Lachaise. *(See* On the Fringe.)

What to See and Do with Children

Aquariums A spell of fish-gazing is a soothing, mesmerizing experience for young and old alike. There are two principal aquariums in Paris, plus the exciting new marine center dreamt up by the famous ocean explorer Captain Cousteau.

Aquarium Tropical, *293 av. Daumesnil, 12e. Admission: 20 frs, 10 frs on Sun. Open Wed.–Mon. 10–noon and 1:30–5:30. Métro: Porte Dorée.*

Centre de la Mer et des Eaux, *195 rue St-Jacques, 5e. Admission: 25 frs adults, 15 frs children. Open Tues.–Fri. 10–12:30 and 1:15–5:30, weekends 10–5:30. RER: Luxembourg.*

Boating Rowboats can be rented at the **Lac Inférieur** in the Bois de Boulogne and at **Lac des Minimes** and **Lac Daumesnil** in the Bois de Vincennes.

Boat Trips An hour on the Seine on a Bateau Mouche or Vedette is good fun and a great way to get to know the capital. The cost is 30–40 francs for adults, 15–20 francs for children under 10. Departures every half-hour from:

Eiffel Tower, *7e. Métro: Bir-Hakeim.*
Pont de l'Alma, *8e. Métro: Alma-Marceau.*
Square du Vert Galant, *1er. Métro: Pont-Neuf.*

Circus There's no need to know French to enjoy a circus. Tickets range from 40 to 180 francs. There are evening and weekend matinee performances. Check for details with:

Cirque d'Hiver, *110 rue Amelot, 11e, tel. 47–00–12–25. Métro: Filles-du-Calvaire.*
Cirque Grüss, *145 quai de la Gare, 13e, tel. 45–86–00–52. Métro: quai de la Gare.*
Cirque Bormann–Moreno, *Jardin d'Acclimatation, 16e, tel. 45–01–88–91. Métro: Les Sablons.*

Eiffel Tower Climb, and then ride the elevator to the top level of the Eiffel Tower for a breathtaking view of Paris and beyond.

Ice Cream An ice cream is an ice cream, but the city's best (with a choice of some 30 flavors) is sold at **Berthillon's** on the Ile St-Louis. *31 rue St-Louis-en-l'Ile; closed Mon. and Tues. 4e. Métro: Pont-Marie.*

Ice Skating The only ice rink in Paris is near the Buttes-Chamont park to the northeast. *30 rue Edouard-Pailleron, 19e, tel. 42–08–72–26. Admission: 25 frs adults, 20 frs children under 16 (skate hire 15 frs). Open weekdays 4:30–6:15, Wed. and Sun. 10–6, Sat. 10–5 and 8:30–midnight. Métro: Bolivar.*

Jardin d'Acclimatation This charming children's play-park in the Bois de Boulogne boasts a miniature train, boat rides, a zoo, and a game area, plus fairground stalls and cafés. *Admission: 9 frs adults, 4 frs children. Open daily 10–6. Métro: Les Sablons.*

Parc Floral de Paris This is the east Paris equivalent of the Jardin d'Acclimatation, situated in the Bois de Vincennes near the château. It features a miniature train, a game area, and miniature golf. *Route de la Pyramide, Vincennes. Admission: 5 frs, children under 6 free. Open daily 9:30–8 (to 5 in winter). Métro: Château de Vincennes.*

Movies There is no shortage of English movies in Paris, some (often cartoons) geared for children. Consult *Pariscope* or *L'Officiel des Spectacles* for details.

Museums **Musée de la Femme et Collection d'Automates.** The collection of automata and clockwork dolls bursts into life each afternoon; it's well worth making the short trip to Neuilly, especially since the Jardin d'Acclimatation and Bois de Boulogne *(see above)* are close at hand. *12 rue du Centre, Neuilly. Admission: 12 frs adults, 6 frs children. Open Wed.–Mon. 2:30–5; guided tours at 3. Métro: Pont de Neuilly.*
Musée Grévin. A visit to a waxwork museum is a good way to spend a rainy afternoon. The long-established boulevard Montmartre museum concentrates on imitations of the famous, the newer one in Halles on recapturing the Belle Epoque. *10 blvd. Montmartre, 9e. Admission: 48 frs adults, 34 frs children under 14. Open 1–7, 10–6 during school holidays. Métro: Rue Montmartre.* **Nouveau Musée Grévin.** *Forum des Halles, 1er.*

Admission: 38 frs adults, 28 frs children under 14. Métro: Les Halles. Open Mon.–Sat. 10:30–7:30, Sun. 1–7.

Parks Paris is not renowned as an open-space city. Its major parks (Bois de Boulogne and Bois de Vincennes) are on the outskirts, but there is room to stroll and play at:

Arènes de Lutèce, *5e. Métro: Monge.*
Champs de Mars, *7e. Métro: Ecole Militaire.*
Jardin des Halles, *1er. Métro: Les Halles.*
Jardin des Plantes, *5e. Métro: Jussieu.*
Jardin des Tuileries, *1er. Métro: Tuileries.*
Jardin du Luxembourg, *6e. RER: Luxembourg.*
Jardin du Ranelagh, *16e. Métro: La Muette.*
Parc de la Villette, *19e. Métro: Porte de la Villette.*
Parc de Montsouris, *14e. RER: Cité Universitaire.*
Parc des Buttes-Chaumont, *19e. Métro: Buttes-Chaumont.*
Parc Monceau, *8e. Métro: Monceau.*

Puppet Shows On most Wednesday, Saturday, and Sunday afternoons, the Guignol, the French equivalent of Punch and Judy, can be seen going through their ritualistic battles at the following spots throughout Paris:

Champs de Mars, *av. du Gén.-Margueritte, 7e. Métro: Ecole Militaire.*
Chaussée de l'Etang, *St-Mandé (Bois de Vincennes). Métro: St-Mandé-Tourelle.*
Jardin des Tuileries, *1er. Métro: Concorde.*
Jardin du Luxembourg, *6e. Métro: Vavin. RER-B: Luxembourg.*
Jardin du Ranelagh, *av. Ingres, 16e. Métro: La Muette.*
Parc des Buttes-Chaumont, *av. Simon-Bolivar, 19e. Métro: Buttes-Chaumont.*
Parc Montsouris, *av. Reille, 14e. Métro: Porte d'Orléans. RER-B: Cité Universitaire.*
Parc de St-Cloud, *Métro: Boulogne–Pont de St-Cloud.*
Rond-Point des Champs-Elysées, *8e. Métro: Champs-Elysée–Clemenceau.*

Roller Skating Paris's unofficial outdoor roller-skating venue is the concourse between the two wings of the Palais de Chaillot at Trocadéro. Or try: **La Main Jaune,** *rue du Caporal-Peugeot, 17e, tel. 47–63–26–47. (Métro: Porte de Champerret.) Admission: 40 frs (skate hire 10 frs). Open Wed. and weekends 2:30–7.*

Zoos Monkeys, deer, birds, and farm animals star at the **Jardin d'Acclimatation** (*see above*), while the **Ménagerie** in the Jardin des Plantes also boasts elephants, lions, and tigers. *57 rue Cuvier, 5e. Admission: 25 frs adults, 13 frs children. Open daily 9–6 (9–5 in winter). Métro: Jussieu, Monge.*

Paris's biggest zoo is in the **Bois de Vincennes,** which in addition to wild beasts includes a museum, films, and exhibitions. *53 av. de St-Maurice, 12e. Admission: 35 frs adults, 20 frs children. Open daily 9–6 (9–5 in winter). Métro: Porte Dorée.*

Off the Beaten Track

Académie de la Bière

Beer and *moules-frites* (mussels cooked in white wine and served with french fries) is more a Belgian than a French specialty, yet it's readily available in Paris, as if to underline the gastronomic as well as linguistic ties between the two neighbors. A good place to sample this satisfying combination is the friendly, unpretentious Académie de la Bière, near Montparnasse, the nearest Paris comes to the atmosphere of a British pub, with a cozy, wood-benched interior and pavement terrace for lazy summer evenings. There is a choice of 200 beers from numerous countries (several on draft), plus various snacks. *88 bis blvd. de Port-Royal, 5e, tel. 43–54–66–65. Open evenings 6 PM–2 AM; closed Sun. RER: Port-Royal.*

Bercy

There are few more striking contrasts between old and new in Paris than in Bercy, which is tucked away on the Right Bank of the Seine, south of the Gare de Lyon, in the 12th arrondissement. In a few years' time, there probably won't be any of the industrial past left to compete with the schemes of rapacious city planners. Given the pace of transformation, there's little point checking the neighborhood map as you step out of Bercy métro station and come face-to-face with the mighty glass wall of the new **French Finance Ministry,** arching over the quayside highway. To your left, the ingeniously sloping, green-walled **Palais Omnisports** looms like a moss-covered pyramid, approached on all sides by gleaming white steps.

Walk around to the left of the stadium—those green walls are actually upholstered in some of the best-cut grass in Paris—as far as a newly planted garden, with seats, trees, lawn, and rosebushes. Alongside once stood **Le Grand Bercy,** former home to the vintners and wine distributors of Les Entrepôts des Vins; its crumbling cobbles used to clatter with crates filled with bottles of Alsace, Burgundy, and Bordeaux. Across rue de Dijon, a quarter of a mile east of the Palais Omnisports, you will stumble across **Le Petit Bercy,** where remnants of the now-scattered Paris wine distribution business still linger. Trucks trundle along the broad avenues, while the premises still in activity exude a sense of tidy affluence—a couple of them (follow the signs) sell wine to intrepid explorers at remarkably cheap prices. *Métro: Bercy.*

Buttes-Chaumont

This is an immensely picturesque park in the downbeat 19th arrondissement of northeast Paris. It boasts a lake, waterfall, and cliff-top folly or "belvedere." Until town planner Baron Haussmann got his hands on it in the 1860s, the area was a garbage dump and quarry—hence the steep slopes. *Rue Botzaris. Métro: Buttes-Chaumont, Botzaris.*

Canal St-Martin

Place de la République is the gateway to east Paris, a largely residential area often underestimated by tourists. One of its highlights is the Canal St-Martin, which starts just south of the Bastille but really comes into its own during the mile-long stretch north of République, across the 10th arrondissement. With its quiet banks, locks, and footbridges, the Canal St-Martin has an unexpected flavor of Amsterdam—and is much-loved by novelists and film directors. (Simenon's famous inspector Maigret solved many a mystery along its deceptively sleepy banks.) Major development has transformed the northern end of the canal, around the place de Stalingrad and its 18th-century rotunda, and there are boat trips along the once-industrial Bassin de la Villette to the nearby Parc de la Villette. *Métro: Jacques-Bonsergent, Colonel-Fabien, or Jaurès.*

Hôtel Drouot

Hidden away in a grid of narrow streets not far from the Opéra is Paris's central auction house, offering everything from stamps and toy soldiers to Renoirs and 18th-century commodes. Open six days a week, the Drouot's 16 salesrooms make for fascinating browsing and there's no obligation to bid. The mix of fur-coated ladies with money to burn, penniless art lovers desperate to unearth an unidentified masterpiece, and scruffy dealers trying to look anonymous makes up Drouot's unusually rich social fabric. *Entrance at the corner of rue Rossini and rue Drouot. Viewings Mon.–Sat. 11–noon and 2–6, with auctions starting at 2. Métro: Richelieu-Drouot.*

Les Catacombes

The catacombs consist of an extensive underground labyrinth built by the Romans, tunneling under much of the Left Bank and into the near suburbs. They were subsequently used to store bones from disused graveyards; then, during World War II, they became the headquarters of the French Resistance. You are well advised to take a flashlight with you. *1 pl. Denfert-Rochereau. Admission: 16 frs, 10 frs students and senior citizens. Open Tues.–Fri. 2–4, weekends 9–11 and 2–4. Guided tours on Wed. at 2:45; 20 frs extra. Métro and RER: Denfert-Rochereau.*

The Métro

Many visitors spend considerable time on the cheap and practical métro system without realizing it is a considerable attraction in its own right. For a start, it is not strictly a "subway" or "underground," inasmuch as it ventures out of its tunnels at several points to offer a delightful rooftop tour of the city. Part of **Line 2** (Dauphine–Nation) is above ground, yielding views of the Sacré-Coeur and the Canal St-Martin. Nearly all of **Line 6** (Nation–Etoile) is above ground and gives terrific views of the Invalides and Eiffel Tower. There is a charming glimpse of Notre Dame, Ile de la Cité, and Ile St-Louis as **Line 5** crosses the Seine between quai de la Rapée and Gare d'Austerlitz, continuing past the fine 17th-century Hôpital de la Salpêtrière.

A number of métro stations are attractions in themselves—the **Louvre** and **Varenne** stations are well-known for their muse-umlike feeling, **Cluny-Sorbonne** and **Pasteur** for their imaginative use of mosaics. The entrance canopies to **Porte Dauphine** and **Abbesses** stations are the best remaining examples of the florid, interlacing Art Nouveau ironwork created by Hector Guimard at the start of the century.

Nation Quarter

The towering, early 19th-century statue-topped columns on the majestic **place de la Nation** stand sentinel at the Gates of Paris, the eastern sector's equivalent of the Arc de Triomphe; the bustling but unpretentious Cours de Vincennes provides a down-to-earth echo of the Champs-Elysées. Place de la Nation (originally known as place du Trône, but Throne Square was far too monarchical a title to survive the Revolution) was the scene of over 1,300 executions at the guillotine in 1794. Most of these unfortunates were buried around the corner (via rue Fabre d'Eglantine) in the **Cimetière de Picpus**, a peaceful convent cemetery containing the grave of General Lafayette, identified by its U.S. flag. *35 rue Picpus. Open Tues.–Sun. 2–6, 2–4 in winter; closed Mon. Métro: Nation, Picpus.*

4 Shopping

*By Corinne
LaBalme*

*Corinne LaBalme
is a Paris-based
freelance writer
and a contributing
editor for United
Airlines'*
Hemispheres.

Window-shopping is one of Paris's great spectator sports. Tastefully displayed wares—luscious cream-filled éclairs, lacy lingerie, rare artwork, gleaming copper pots—entice the eye and awaken the imagination. And shopping is one of the city's greatest pastimes, a chance to mix with Parisians and feel the heartbeat of the country. Who can understand the magic of French cuisine until they've explored a French open-air produce market on a weekend morning? Or resist the thrill of seeing a Chanel evening gown displayed in its own glossy Paris boutique—where even the doorknobs are shaped like Chanel Number 5 crystal perfume stoppers?

Happily, the shopping opportunities in Paris are endless and geared to every taste. You can price emerald earrings at Cartier, spend an afternoon browsing through bookstalls along the Seine, buy silk-lined gloves at Dior, tour the high-gloss department stores, or haggle over prices in the sprawling flea markets on the outskirts of town. For many, perfume and designer clothing are perhaps the most coveted Parisian souvenirs. However, even on haute couture's home turf, bargains are surprisingly elusive. Foreign visitors, subject to the slings and arrows of international exchange rates, are advised to know prices in their own country before arrival. A Pierre Cardin tie or a Lalique bottle of *L'Air du Temps* may possibly be cheaper at the mall back home . . . although it won't be as much fun to buy.

Bargain hunters should watch for the word *soldes* (sale). Sales are generally held in July and January, but the relatively meager mark-downs (10–15%) may disappoint international visitors. There are exceptions, however; the January 1993 sales, for instance, saw markdowns of 30%–50%. If you are in town at sale times, it's certainly worth your while to check prices. Outside of sales, there are other good deals to be had, particularly in some of the discount shops, often located on the edge of town. Some of these are listed below.

You'll be spending most of your time in Paris sightseeing rather than shopping. Keep in mind that Paris's museums have some gloriously chic gift shops. Some of the best are in the Louvre (books, posters, reproduction statues, and jewelry), the Musée des Arts de la Mode (designer scarves and accessories), and the Musée des Arts Décoratifs (unusual craft items and reproductions of historic china, toys, linens, and glassware from the museum collections). Museum-quality art and antiques are also in ready supply here, and reputable dealers handle the necessary paperwork and shipping.

Paris is highly cosmopolitan, with numerous outlets for Burberry raincoats, Benetton sweaters, and Levi's jeans. We've concentrated our listings on characteristically French products.

Credit Cards Even stores that will accept currency other than francs will generally give you a lower rate of exchange than in banks or exchange offices. You're better off using credit cards, which are more widely used in France than in the U.S. Even the corner newstand or flea market salesperson is likely to honor plastic. VISA is the most common and preferred card, followed closely by MasterCard/EuroCard. American Express, Diners Club, and Access are accepted in the larger international stores.

Right Bank Shopping

A la Mère de
Famille, **53**

Agatha, **22**

Agnès b., **69**

Annick Goutal, **40**

Arts-Céramiques, **56**

Au Bain Marie, **30**

Au Nain Bleu, **37**

Au Printemps, **49**

Baby Dior, **15**

Baccarat, **54**

Bazar de l'Hôtel
de Ville, **72**

Bouchara, **50**

Brummel, **49**

Cartier, **42, 45**

Catherine Baril, **10**

Chanel, **14, 38**

Chantal Thomass, **63**

Charvet, **43**

Christian Dior, **17**

Christian
Lacroix, **16, 24**

Christofle, **46**

Fauchon, **35**

FNAC, **70**

Forum des Halles, **70**

Galerie du Claridge, **3**

Galerie du Lido, **2**

Galerie du Rond-
Point, **21**

Galerie Véro-
Dodat, **67**

Galerie Vivienne, **58**

Galeries Lafayette, **51**

Geneviève Lethu, **78**

Givenchy Boutique, **6**

Guerlain, **4**

Hédiard, **32**

Hermès, **27**

Inès de la
Fressange, **12**
Isabel Canovas, **13**
Jadis et
Gourmande, **23, 26**
Jean-Paul Gaultier, **57**
Jean Pierre
de Castro, **75**
Kenzo, **66**
La Bagagerie, **28, 34**
La Maison du
Chocolate, **1, 7**

La Samaritaine, **71**
La Tisanière, **55**
Lalique, **31**
Lanvin, **29, 39**
Laurent
Mercadel, **33, 62**
Le Monde
du Bagage, **59**
Lolita bis, **74**
Lolita Lempicka, **73**
Louis Vuitton, **19**

Louvre des
Antiquaires, **68**
Marché St-Pierre, **52**
Marks and Spencer, **48**
Mendès, **61**
Michel Swiss, **44, 47**
Natalys, **77**
Nina Ricci, **8**
Porthault, **11**
Réciproque, **9**

Rodin, **20**
Romeo Gigli, **79**
Sonia Rykiel, **25**
Stéphane
Kélian, **36, 65**
Suzette Idier, **76**
Thierry
Mugler, **18, 64**
Victoire, **60**
Virgin Megastore, **5**
W.H. Smith, **41**

Left Bank Shopping

Duty-Free Shopping Visitors from outside the European Community, aged 15 and over, whose stay in France and/or the EC is less than six months can benefit from VAT (Value Added Tax) reimbursements, known in France as TVA or *détaxe*. To qualify, non-EC residents must spend at least 2,000F in a single store. Refunds vary from 13% to 18.6% and are mailed to you by check or credited to the purchaser's charge card. The major department stores have simplified the process with special détaxe desks where the *bordereaux* (export sales invoices) are prepared. Most high-profile shops with international clients have détaxe forms, but stores are not required to do this paperwork. If the discount is extremely important to you, ask if it is available before making your purchase. Invoices and bordereaux forms must be presented to French customs upon leaving the country. The items purchased should also be available for inspection.

Mailing Purchases Home Smaller shops are reluctant to mail purchases overseas, in case the goods get lost. Mailing goods oneself is possible—all French post offices sell self-sealing mailing boxes—but postage is costly. Remember that if you are claiming a Value Added Tax deduction (*see above*), you should have the goods with you when you leave the country.

Shopping Areas

Avenue Montaigne The names atop the showcase windows lining this gracious boulevard are the honor roll of haute couture: Chanel, Dior, Nina Ricci, Christian Lacroix, Emanuel Ungaro, Céline, Valentino, Per Spook, Escada, Thierry Mugler, Hanae Mori. Here you'll also find Louis Vuitton, accessorists S. T. Dupont and Isabel Canovas, and the lively new boutique run by former Chanel super-model Inès de la Fressange. Yves St-Laurent's salon is located nearby, at 5 av. Marceau.

Left Bank Browsing through the antiques shops, bookstores, and art galleries of St-Germain-des-Prés, Paris's intellectual core, is window-shopping at its most varied. High fashion arrived here in the '70s, when YSL opened Rive Gauche boutiques for men and women on the place Saint-Sulpice. The area around rue de Grenelle and rue Saint-Pères is known for intimate designer boutiques (Sonia Rykiel, Claude Montana) and shoe shops (Maud Frizon, Charles Jourdan, Stéphane Kélian, and Carel).

Le Marais The elegant mansions and tiny kosher food stores that characterized the low-lying area between the Beaubourg and place des Vosges were overtaken by New Wave fashion and trendy gift shops in the 1980's. Avant-garde designers Azzedine Alaia, Lolita Lempicka, Issey Miyake, and Romeo Gigli have boutiques within a few blocks of the stately Picasso and Carnavalet museums. Shopping for off-beat decorative household items is also excellent here.

Les Halles The narrow pedestrian streets on the former site of Paris's wholesale food market are lined with fast-food joints, sex shops, jeans outlets, and garish souvenir stands. Street artists claim the plaza in front of the Pompidou Center, and prostitutes rule the nearby rue St-Dénis. In the middle of the action, the **Forum des Halles**—a multilevel underground shopping mall—caters to a noisy teenage clientele.

Opéra to Madeleine Three major department stores—Au Printemps, Galeries Lafayette, and the British Marks and Spencer (*see* Department
Stores, *below*)—are clustered behind Paris's ornate 19th-cen-
tury Opera house. The place de la Madeleine is home to two luxurious food stores, Fauchon and Hédiard, plus a 75-shop mall,
Les Trois Quartiers. Lalique and Baccarat Crystal also have
opulent showrooms near the Madeleine Church.

Montparnasse The bohemian mecca for artists and writers in the '20s and '30s,
Montparnasse is better known for bars and restaurants than
shops. A recently built commercial center near the train station
boasts a Galeries Lafayette outlet but is too charmless to attract many tourists. The rue d'Alésia on the southern fringe of
Montparnasse is known for discount clothing shops.

Place des Victories Françoise Chassagnac, the canny retailer who "discovered"
Azzedine Alaia and Angelo Tarlazzi, put this graceful, circular
plaza near the Palais-Royal on the fashion map when she
opened her Victoire boutique in 1967. Kenzo, Thierry Mugler,
and Cacharel soon followed. Avant-garde boutiques like
Chantal Thomass, Jean-Charles de Castelbajac, and En At-
tendant les Barbares have since fanned into the sidestreets,
while Jean-Paul Gaultier (Madonna's favorite dresser) has his
shop in the nearby Galerie Vivienne arcade.

Place Vendôme and Here's where Holly Golightly would eat breakfast. The magnif-
the Rue de la Paix icent 17th-century place Vendôme, and the rue de la Paix leading north from Vendôme, have attracted the world's most
elegant jewelers: Cartier, Boucheron, Buccellati, Van Cleef
and Arpel, Répossi, Mellerio, Mauboussin, and Mikimoto. This
super-posh pedestrian square was repaved with silver-gray
granite in 1992, and shines brighter than ever.

Rue du Faubourg The presence of the Elysée Palace and the official residences of
St-Honoré the American and British ambassadors mean this chic shopping
and residential street is well patrolled by the police. The Paris
branch of Sotheby's and renowned antiques galleries such as
Didier Aaron and Odermatt-Cazeau add artistic flavor. Boutiques include Hermès, Lanvin, Karl Lagerfeld, Reveillon
Furs, Louis Feraud, and Christian Lacroix.

Trocadéro–Victor This aristocratic and conservative neighborhood in the 16th ar-
Hugo rondissement attracts predictably classic retailers, most of
whom are centered around the place Victor Hugo. Bargain
hunters know that the secondhand shops in this wealthy area
offer exceptionally fine goods. **Réciproque** (123 rue de la
Pompe) is one of the biggest and best, with three storefronts of
nearly new designer fashions and gifts for both men and
women.

Champs-Elysées Cafés and movie theaters keep the once-chic Champs-Elysées
active 24 hours a day, but the invasion of exchange banks, car
showrooms, and fast-food chains has lowered the tone. Four
glitzy 20th-century arcade malls (Galérie du Lido, Le Rond-
Point, Le Claridge, and Elysées 26) capture most of the retail
action.

Department Stores

Paris's top department stores offer both convenience and chic.
Some are open until 10 PM one weekday evening, and all six major
stores listed below have multilingual guides, international welcome desks, détaxe offices, and restaurants.

Opéra area **Au Printemps** (64 blvd. Haussmann, 9e, tel. 42–82–50–00) is a glittery three-store complex that includes "La Maison," for housewares and furniture; "La Mode," for ladies and children; and "Brummel," a six-floor emporium devoted to menswear. Flo Prestige, the celebrated Parisian brasserie chain, caters the in-house restaurants. *Open Mon.–Sat. 9:30–7.*

Galeries Lafayette (40 blvd. Haussmann, 9e, tel. 42–82–34–56) is equally elegant, and it spices up its Parisian aura with periodic exhibits featuring crafts from exotic countries. Be sure and look up while in the main store: The glorious Belle Epoque stained-glass dome is a Parisian landmark. Stylish private-label fashions (Briefing and Jodphur) offer good value, and the elegant floor-wide gourmet shop includes several sophisticated snack/wine bars. *Open Mon.–Sat. 9:30–6:45. Another branch is at Centre Commercial Montparnasse, 15e, tel. 45–38–52–87.*

Marks & Spencer (35 blvd. Haussmann, 9e, tel. 47–42–42–91) is a British store chiefly noted for its moderately priced sportswear and its excellent English grocery and take-out food service. *Open Mon.–Sat. 9:30–7, Tues. 10–7.*

Louvre–Pont Neuf area **La Samaritaine** (19 rue de la Monnaie, 1er, tel. 40–41–20–20), a sprawling four-store complex, is rapidly shedding its fusty, grandmotherly image. Especially good for kitchen supplies, housewares, and furniture, it's famous for its rooftop snackbar that offers a marvelous view of Notre Dame. *Open Mon.–Sat. 9:30–7, Thurs. 9:30–10.*

Hôtel de Ville/Marais area **Bazar de l'Hôtel de Ville** (52–64 rue de Rivoli, 4e, tel. 42–74–90–00), affectionately called BHV, houses an enormous basement hardware store that sells everything from doorknobs to cement mixers! The fashion offerings are minimal, but BHV is noteworthy for quality household goods, home decor materials, and office supplies. *Open Mon.–Sat. 9:30–7, Wed. 9:30–10.*

Left Bank **Au Bon Marché** (22 rue de Sèvres, 7e, tel. 44–39–80–00), founded in 1852, is chiefly known for linens, table settings, and high-quality furniture. La Grande Epicerie, a grocery store and deli here, is a gourmet's delight, and the sleek restaurant was designed by jet-set decorator Andrée Putman. The basement is a treasure trove for books, records, and arty gifts. *Open Mon.–Fri. 9:30–6:30, Sat. 9:30–7.*

Budget Most Parisians dash into their neighborhood **Monoprix** or **Prisunic** stores—with branches throughout the city—at least once a week. These handy shops stock inexpensive cosmetics, toothpaste, groceries, toys, typing paper, bathmats—a little of everything. Clothing often represents good value: Noted designers like Elisabeth de Senneville occasionally create special low-price lines for these stores.

Tati stores are known for bargain-basement prices, although goods are not always top quality. One of the largest is at 140 rue de Rennes, 6e.

Specialty Shops

Antiques Antiques shops and art gallery enclaves are scattered throughout the city. For a full day's browsing, try:

Louvre des Antiquaires (2 pl. du Palais-Royal, 1er), is an elegant multifloor complex where 250 of Paris's leading dealers showcase their rarest objects.

Carré **Rive Gauche** is a compact Left Bank district, bordered by the quai Voltaire and the rue de l'Université, whose narrow sidestreets shelter dozens of fine arts and antiques galleries.

Bags and Luggage **La Bagagerie** (41 rue du Four, 6e, tel. 45–48–85–88; also 11 rue Fbg. St-Honoré, 8e, tel. 47–42–79–13, and 12 rue Tronchet, 8e, tel. 42–65–03–40) features brightly colored bags and belts with youthful style and moderate prices.
Hermès (24 rue Fbg. St-Honoré, 8e, tel. 40–17–47–17) was established as a saddlery in 1837 but since went on to scarves and more: Its most famous leather creation is the eternally chic Kelly bag, created for Grace Kelly. Prices are astronomical.
Louis Vuitton (78 av. Marceau, 8e, tel. 47–20–47–00; also 54 av. Montaigne, 8e, tel. 45–62–90–43) sells the world's best-known, monogram-patterned luxury luggage and accessories.
Le Monde du Bagage (4 rue des Petits Champs, 2e, tel. 42–86–90–45) features crushable-but-chic, leather-trimmed canvas carry-alls and knapsacks.

English-Language An eternal Parisian pastime is strolling by the open-air book-
Books stalls along the Seine.

W.H. Smith (248 rue de Rivoli, 1er, tel. 44–77–88–89) carries an excellent range of travel and language books, cookbooks, and fiction for adults and children. **Brentano's** (37 av. de l'Opéra, 2e, tel. 42–61–52–50) is another well-stocked general bookstore.
Village Voice (6 rue Princesse, 6e, tel. 46–33–36–47), known for its selection of contemporary authors, hosts regular literary readings.
Shakespeare and Company (5 rue de la Brulerie, 5e, no phone) is a sentimental Left Bank favorite, specializing in expatriate literature.
Tea and Tattered Pages (24 rue Mayet, 6e, tel. 40–65–94–35) sells cheap, secondhand English tomes.

Clothing **Chanel** (42 av. Montaigne, 8e, tel. 47–23–74–12, and 29 rue
(Women's) Cambon, 1er) has undergone a radical transformation under
Classic Chic Karl Lagerfeld, who has added leather 'n' chains to classic suits and accessories.
Christian Dior (30 av. Montaigne, 8e, tel. 40–73–54–44) is a pearl gray palace selling ladies' and menswear, perfumes, jewelry, lingerie, furs, leather goods, porcelain, and gifts.
Givenchy Boutique (8 av. Georges V, 8e, tel. 47–20–81–31) presents slightly more affordable versions of the designer's elegant ready-to-wear.
Nina Ricci (39 av. Montaigne, 8e, tel. 47–23–78–88) clothes are supremely ladylike, and the lingerie is luxuriantly romantic.

Trendsetters **Christian Lacroix** (26 av. Montaigne, 8e, tel. 47–20–68–95, and 73 rue du Fbg. St-Honoré, 8e) turns haute couture into a Provençal carnival with daring cuts and candy-coated colors.
Jean-Paul Gaultier (6 rue Vivienne, 2e, tel. 42–86–05–05), Madonna's clothier, specializes in outrageously attention-getting garments for men and women.
Lolita Lempicka (13 bis rue Pavée, 4e, tel. 42–74–50–48) serves up sharp suits and whimsical silk dresses. Lolita bis, a lower-priced junior line, is sold in a shop across the street.
Romeo Gigli (46 rue de Sévigné, 4e, tel. 48–04–57–05) offers the oversized Renaissance-style clothing for men and women that has bestowed cult status upon this Milan-based designer.
Thierry Mugler (10 pl. des Victoires, 2e, tel. 42–60–06–37, and

49 av. Montaigne, 8e, tel. 47–23–37–62), with kinky lace-up dresses and sexy cat-suits, keeps fans coming back for more—menswear is next door at no. 8.

Victoire (12 pl. des Victoires, 2e, tel. 42–61–09–02) is a discreet boutique that taps into new trends.

Chic and Casual **Agnès b.** (3 and 6 rue du Jour, 1er, tel. 45–08–49–89) has knit-wear separates that are wardrobe basics for young Parisians.

Inès de la Fressange (14 av. Montaigne, 8e, tel. 47–23–08–94), the former Chanel super-model creates casual looks based on evergreen V-neck sweaters and slim, velvet jeans.

Sonia Rykiel (175 blvd. St-Germain, 6e, tel. 49–54–60–60 and 79 rue Fbg. St-Honoré, 8e, tel. 42–65–20–81) singlehandedly made cotton velour into a recognized fashion statement.

Suzette Idier (9 rue de Birague, 4e, tel. 42–77–72–52) runs an intimate, pocket-sized boutique chockful of superb "little black dresses," elegant daywear, and all the latest Paris accessories.

Clothing (Men's) **Brummel** (Au Printemps department store, 64 blvd. Haussmann, 9e, tel. 42–82–50–00) is Paris's menswear fashion leader: six floors of suits, sportswear, underwear, coats, ties, and accessories in all price ranges.

Charvet (28 pl. Vendôme, 1er, tel. 42–60–30–70) is the Parisian equivalent of a London tailor or New York's Brooks Brothers: a conservative, aristocratic institution famed for made-to-measure shirts and exquisite ties and accessories.

Dominique Morlotti (25 rue St-Sulpice, 6e, tel. 43–54–89–89) offers an easy-going approach to menswear. Moderately priced designer separates have that debonair Parisian flair.

Kenzo (3 pl. des Victoires, 2e, tel. 40–39–72–03, and 17 blvd. Raspail, 7e, tel. 45–49–33–75) brings exhuberant color and fantasy to his menswear collections. Move on if you're looking for a classic three-piece suit.

Lanvin (2 rue Cambon, 1er, tel. 42–60–38–83, and 15 rue Fbg. St-Honoré, 8e) offers elegant tailoring plus fine sportswear. The branch for women is at 15 rue Fbg. St-Honoré.

Clothing (Children) Top Paris designers now offer mini-couture: **Baby Dior** (28 av. Montaigne, 8e, tel. 40–73–55–14) features velvet suits and ballgowns for little princes and princesses; **Sonia Rykiel Enfant** (4 rue de Grenelle, 6e, tel. 49–54–61–10) has sturdy but sophisticated fashions in washable velour and waxed cotton for infants and toddlers; and **Kenzo Bébé** (3 pl. des Victoires, 1er, tel. 40–39–72–87) has colorful kilts and jackets.

Natalys (32 rue St-Antoine, 4e, tel. 48–87–77–42, and 92 av. des Champs-Elysées, 8e, tel. 43–59–17–65) is a major French chain selling clothing, toys, furniture, and accessories for newborns and grade-school children.

Clothing (Resale) **Réciproque** (95, 101, and 123 rue de la Pompe, 16e, tel. 47–04–30–28 [women's] and 47–27–93–52 [menswear]) is Paris's most exclusive swap shop. Anyone hoping to sell designer cast-offs here must make an appointment weeks in advance (no appointment is necessary to buy). There's not much in the way of service or space, but savings are significant: 4,200 frs for a brocade Nina Ricci dinner suit, 300 frs for Camille Unglick shoes. Closed Mondays and from the end of July through August.

Catherine Baril (14–16–25 rue de la Tour, 16e, tel. 45–20–95–21), smaller than Réciproque and even more exclusive, has one-of-a-kind haute couture in addition to designer ready-to-wear.

Clothing (Discount)
Rue d'Alésia This street in the 14th arrondissement is lined with stock shops selling last season's items at a discount. Be forewarned: Dressing rooms are not always provided.

SR Store (64 rue d'Alésia, 14e, tel. 43–95–06–13) slices 50% off last year's prices for Sonia Rykiel fashions for men, women, and children, and still manages to hold 20–30% sales in January and July.

Cacharel Stock (114 rue d'Alésia, 14e, tel. 45–42–53–04) offers impressive savings for men's, women's, and children's clothing (plus even bigger markdown sales racks on the second floor).

Chipie Stock (82 rue d'Alésia, 14e, tel. 45–42–07–52) has jeans and sweaters for the whole family.

Dorothée bis Stock (74 rue d'Alésia, 14e, tel. 45–42–17–11) practices multiple markdowns on selected gowns and sportswear.

Central Paris **Mendès** (65 rue Montmartre, 2e, tel. 42–36–83–32), the manufacturer of Yves St-Laurent's Rive Gauche and Variations lines for women, sells last season's clothes at half price.

Fabrics **Rodin** (36 av. Champs-Elysées, 8e, tel. 43–59–58–82) and **Bouchara** (54 blvd. Haussmann, 9e, tel. 42–80–66–95) sell top-quality apparel and upholstery fabrics.

Discount **Marché Saint Pierre** (2 rue Charles Nodier, 18e, tel. 46–06–92–25), a raucous, four-floor warehouse in Montmartre, supplied designers like Kenzo in its salad days. It offers cheap end-of-bolt specials, upholstery, and wall fabrics.

Food
Bread **Poilâne** (8 rue du Cherche-Midi, 6e, tel. 45–48–42–59) produces the most famous bread in the world. The chewy sourdough loaves are sold in hundreds of Paris restaurants and shops and are airmailed to U.S. and Tokyo restaurants every day.

Candy and Chocolate **A la Mère de Famille** (35 rue du Fbg. Montmarte, 9e, tel. 47–70–83–69) is an enchanting shop specializing in old-fashioned bonbons, sugar candy, and more.

Jadis et Gourmande (49 bis av. Franklin Roosevelt, 8e, tel. 42–25–06–04; 27 rue Boissy d'Anglas, 8e, tel. 42–65–23–23; and 88 blvd. de Port-Royal, 5e, tel. 43–26–17–75) personalizes chocolate bars with names and initials.

La Maison du Chocolat (52 rue François 1er, 8e, tel. 47–23–38–25) is heaven for cocoa purists. Take home chocolates, ice cream, and other treats, or meet a friend in the tearoom for sinfully rich hot chocolate and chocolate-mousse *frappés* (cold drinks). Take-out only at 8 rue de la Madeleine, 9e, tel. 47–42–86–52 and 225 rue Fbg. St-Honoré, 8e, tel. 42–27–39–44.

Gourmet Shops **Fauchon** (26–28–30 pl. de la Madeleine, 8e, tel. 47–42–60–11) and **Hédiard** (21 pl. de la Madeleine, 8e, tel. 42–66–44–36) sell prestigious house brands of paté, mustard, honey, jellies, and private label champagne, plus sumptuous produce from around the world. The **Galeries Lafayette Gourmet shop** (40 blvd. Haussmann, 9e, tel. 42–82–34–56) is equally chic, with its gold shopping carts and bistro-style snackbars for caviar and smoked salmon, but less intimidating. The Grande Epicerie, on the ground floor of **Au Bon Marché** (22 rue de Sèvres, 7e, tel. 44–39–80–00), has an excellent array of fine French foodstuffs.

Jewelry Most of the big names are based near the place Vendôme. Designer costume and semiprecious jewelry is sold in most of the av. Montaigne and rue du Faubourg St-Honoré boutiques.

Cartier (7 and 23 pl. Vendôme, 1er, tel. 42–61–55–55) has two less formal "Les Must" boutiques, which carry lighters, pens, watches, key-chains, and other gift items.

Costume **Agatha** (97 rue de Rennes, 6e, tel. 45–48–81–30; 45 rue Bonaparte, 6e, tel. 46–33–20–00; and 12–14 av. Champs-Elysées, 8e, tel. 43–59–68–68) has trendy but moderately priced seasonal collections.

Isabel Canovas (16 av. Montaigne, 8e, tel. 47–20–10–80) offers faux bijoux, that, while not cheap, are prized by fashion mavens for their wittiness and glamor.

Linens **Porthault** (18 av. Montaigne, 8e, tel. 47–20–75–25) makes hand-embroidered table linens, luxurious old world-style sheets, and the most sumptuous layettes in town.

Lingerie **Chantal Thomass** (1 rue Vivienne, 1er, tel. 40–15–02–36) sets the right mood for her trademark black-lace hosiery, satin corsets, and feather-trimmed negligees in this plush, pink velvet boutique that resembles a Victorian bordello.

Natari (7 pl. Vendôme, 1er, tel. 42–96–22–94) seduces all, with selections for every pocketbook. Movie-star lingerie and peignoir sets come in pure silk or washable synthetic versions.

Music/Records **FNAC** (Forum des Halles, 1er, tel. 40–41–40–00; 26 av. Ternes, 17e, tel. 44–09–18–00; and 136 rue de Rennes, 6e, tel. 49–54–30–00) is a high-profile French chain selling music; photo, TV, and audio equipment; and books.

Virgin Megastore (52–60 av. des Champs-Elysées, 8e, tel. 40–74–06–48) has acres of CD's and tapes—everything from classic to rap—plus a book division.

Perfumes **Annick Goutal** (14 rue de Castiglione, 1er, tel. 42–60–52–82) is a gilt-and-ivory cream puff selling this exclusive signature perfume line.

Guerlain (68 av. des Champs Elysées, 8e, tel. 47–89–71–84, and 47 rue Bonaparte, 6e, tel. 43–26–71–19) boutiques are the only authorized Paris outlets for legendary perfumes like Shalimar, Jicky, Vol de Nuit, Mitsouko, and Chamade.

Discount **Michel Swiss** (16 rue de la Paix, 2nd fl., 2e, tel. 42–61–61–11, and 24 av. de l'Opéra, 1er, tel. 47–03–49–11) offers large savings on perfumes and fashion accessories. Service is not helpful; know what you want before flagging a salesperson.

Scarves **Hermès** (24 rue Fbg. St-Honoré, 8e, tel. 40–17–47–17) clocks a scarf sale every 20 seconds before the Christmas holidays! The all-silk *carrés*—truly fashion icons—are legendary for their brilliant colors and intricate designs, which change yearly.

Souleiado (78 rue de Seine, 6e, tel. 43–54–62–25, and 83 av. Paul Doumer, 16e, tel. 42–24–99–34) uses traditional Provençal patterns for cotton scarves, quilted bags, and linens.

Shoes **Laurent Mercadel** (31 rue Tronchet, 8e, tel. 42–66–01–28, and 3 pl. des Victoires, 1er, tel. 45–08–84–44) offers classic styles updated with unusual accents.

Stéphane Kélian (23 blvd. de la Madeleine, 1er, tel. 42–96–01–84, and 6 pl. des Victoires, 2e, tel. 42–61–55–60) creates chic, high-style shoes that are also comfortable for men and women.

Stationery **Marie Papier** (26 rue Vavin, 6e, tel. 43–26–46–44) sells an extraordinary variety of colored writing paper and notebooks.

Tablewares **Au Bain Marie** (8 rue Boissy d'Anglas, 8e, tel. 42–66–59–74) is
China and Crystal an enchanted kingdom for amateur and professional cooks.

Come here for crockery, porcelain, and a world-class collection of cookbooks.

Lalique (11 rue Royale, 8e, tel. 42–66–52–40) crystal vases and statuettes are prized for their sinuous, romantic forms and delicate design.

Geneviève Lethu (28 rue St-Antoine, 4e, tel. 42–74–21–25) is a homey, casual shop selling tea services, potpourri mixtures, and table linens for your real or imagined country house.

Discount The **rue de Paradis** in the 10th arrondissement is lined with china and crystal showrooms. Shoppers with style numbers, pocket calculators, and comparison prices from home often profit from serious savings on fine Limoges porcelain.

La Tisanière (21 rue de Paradis, 10e, tel. 47–70–22–80) sells china "seconds."

Arts-Céramiques (15 rue de Paradis, 10e, tel. 48–24–83–70) has special promotional sales in its back room.

NOTE: Although there aren't any bargains at the **Baccarat Crystal showroom** (30 bis rue de Paradis, 10e, tel. 47–70–64–30), this elegant, red-carpeted spot with a fascinating in-house museum is well worth a visit.

Silver **Christofle** (24 rue de la Paix, 2e, tel. 42–65–62–43, and 9 rue Royale, 8e, tel. 49–33–43–00), founded in 1830, presents the finest French silver services in sumptuous velvet display cases.

Jean-Pierre de Castro (17 rue des Francs-Bourgeois, 4e, tel. 42–72–04–00) is a dusty second-hand shop selling old-fashioned silver settings by the kilo-weight. The inexpensive bracelets made of Victorian silver spoons and forks make marvelous gifts.

Toys **Au Nain Bleu** (406–410 rue St-Honoré, 8e, tel. 42–60–39–01) is a high-price wonderland, with elaborate dollhouses, miniature sports cars, and enchanting hand-carved rocking horses.

Le Monde en Marche (34 rue Dauphine, 6e, tel. 43–26–66–53) specializes in unusual, old-fashioned wooden toys.

Drugstores

The **Pharmacie les Champs-Elysées** (84 av. des Champs-Elysées, 8e, tel. 45–62–02–41) is open 24 hours a day, 365 days a year.

Pharmacie Les Petits Champs (21 rue des Petits Champs, 1e, tel. 42–96–97–20; open daily 8–8).

Drugstore Saint-Germain (149 blvd. Saint-Germain, 6e, tel. 42–22–80–00; open daily 9 AM–2 AM).

Pharmacie Européene de la Place Clichy (6 pl. Clichy, 9e, tel. 48–74–65–18; open daily 8 AM–1 AM).

Shopping Arcades

The various shopping arcades, or *passages*, scattered around Paris offer a pleasant shopping alternative, especially those dating back to the 19th century, most of which have been splendidly restored. Their arching glass roofs, mosaic or marble flooring, and brass lamps, are now set off to full advantage.

Most arcades are conveniently located in the central 1st and 2nd arrondissements on the Right Bank. Our favorite is **Galerie Vivienne** (4 rue des Petits-Champs, 2e) between the Stock Exchange (Bourse) and the Palais-Royal. It has a range of interesting shops and an excellent tearoom and is home to **Cave Legrand,** a quality wine shop. **Galerie Véro-Dodat** (19 rue Jean-Jacques Rousseau, 1er) has painted ceilings and slender copper pillars. You'll find an arcade called **Passage des Pavillons** at 6 rue de Beaujolais, 1er, near the Palais-Royal gardens; and **Passage des Princes** at 97 rue de Richelieu, 2e. **Passage des Panoramas** (11 blvd. Montmartre, 2e) is the oldest of them all, opened in 1800. Across the Grands Boulevards is **Passage Jouffroy** (12 blvd. Montmartre, 9e), with shops selling toys, perfumes, original cosmetics, and dried flowers: Try **Pain d'Epices** (no. 29) and **Au Bonheur des Dames** (no. 39).

Markets

Food Markets   Paris's open-air food markets are among the city's most colorful attractions. Every *quartier* (district) has one, although many are open only a few days each week. Sunday morning, till 1 PM, is usually a good time to go; Monday is the day these markets are likely to be closed. The local markets usually concentrate on food, but they always have a few brightly colored flower stalls. The variety of cheeses is always astounding.

Many of the better-known markets are located in areas you'd visit for sightseeing; our favorites are on **rue de Buci,** 6e (open daily); **rue Mouffetard,** 5e; and **rue Lepic** in Montmartre (the latter two best on weekends). The **Marché d'Aligre** (open Sat., Sun., and Mon. mornings) is a bit farther out, beyond the Bastille on rue d'Aligre in the 12th arrondissement, but you won't see many tourists in this less-affluent area of town, and Parisians from all over the city know it and love it. The prices come tumbling down as the morning draws to a close.

Flower and Bird Markets   Paris's main flower market is located right in the heart of the city on Ile de la Cité, between Notre Dame and the Palais de Justice. It's open every day except Sunday, when a bird market takes its place, and Monday, when it's closed. Birds and a host of other animals are also sold in the shops and stalls on the quai de la Mégisserie on the Right Bank of the Seine. Other colorful flower markets are held beside the Madeleine church, 8er, on place des Ternes, 17e, down the road from the Arc de Triomphe. Both are open daily except Monday.

The Stamp Market   Philatelists should head for Paris's unique stamp market on avenue Marigny and avenue Gabriel, overlooking the gardens at the bottom of the Champs-Elysées. *Open Thurs., Sat., Sun., and public holidays.*

Flea Markets   The **Marché aux Puces** on Paris's northern boundary (Métro: Porte de Clignancourt) still attracts the crowds, but its once unbeatable prices are now a feature of the past. This century-old labyrinth of alleyways packed with antiques dealers' booths and junk stalls now spreads for over a square mile. But be warned—if there's one place in Paris where you need to know how to barter, this is it! For lunch, stop for mussels and fries in one of the rough-and-ready cafés. *Open Sat., Sun., and Mon.*

There are other, less-impressive flea markets on the southern and eastern slopes of the city—at **porte de Montreuil** and **porte de Vanves**—but they have a depressing amount of real junk and are best avoided, except by obsessive bargain hunters.

5 Dining

By Robert Noah

Robert Noah is the founder of Paris en Cuisine, *a company that offers food-related tours in Paris and elsewhere in France, and the editor of its English-language newsletter on French food.*

Whether your dream meal in Paris is savoring truffle-studded foie gras from Limoges china, or breaking the crust of a steaming cassoulet in a thick crockery bowl, you can find it here. Despite rumblings about lowered standards and increasingly bland fare, Paris remains one of the world's great food capitals. For most visitors, the prospect of eating here is exciting; for many, it's the main reason for a trip.

It's not unusual to hear of mediocre food, haughty service, and outrageous prices in Paris restaurants. It's certainly possible to have a bad meal here. Yet the city's restaurants exist principally for the demanding Parisians themselves, for whom every meal is—if not a way of life—certainly an event worthy of their undivided attention. Most restaurants that cannot attain the high standard of their French patrons will not last long. If you want to dine well, therefore, look for restaurants where the French go, and avoid places that cater to tourists. Keep in mind, however, that world-famous restaurants are bound to be frequented by foreigners as well as Parisians, and that a Midwestern accent at the next table is not always a bad sign.

In making the selections for this guide, we have tried to include restaurants with a variety of styles and price levels, from formal dining rooms serving haute cuisine to cheery wine bars offering open-faced sandwiches and not much more. More than half are in the 1st—8th arrondissements, within easy reach of hotels and sights; many others are in the 14th and 16th arrondissements, also popular visitor areas. In addition, we have included a number of restaurants with excellent food, atmosphere, and service that are off the beaten tourist path. In this we follow the lead of the French, for whom a good meal is worth a trip. Because space is at a premium, our selection is limited to places with primarily French rather than ethnic dishes.

Restaurant Types   What's the difference between a bistro and a brasserie? Can you order food at a café? Do you go to a restaurant for just a snack? The following definitions should help.

A **restaurant** traditionally serves a three-course (first, main, and dessert) meal at both lunch and dinner. Although this category includes the most formal, three-star establishments, it also applies to humble neighborhood spots. Don't expect to grab a quick snack. In general, restaurants are what you choose when you want a complete meal and when you have the time to linger over it. Wine is typically drunk with restaurant meals. Hours are fairly consistent; *see* Mealtimes, *below.*

Many say **bistros** served the world's first fast food. After the fall of Napoléon, the Russian soldiers who occupied Paris were known to bang on zinc-topped café bars, crying "bistrot"— "hurry" in Russian. In the past, bistros were simple places with minimum decor and service. Although many nowadays are quite upscale, with beautiful interiors and chic clientele, most remain cozy establishments serving straightforward, frequently gutsy cooking, with plenty of variety meats and long-simmered dishes such as *pot-au-feu* and veal *blanquette.*

Brasseries—ideal places for quick, one-dish meals—originated when Alsatians fleeing German occupiers after the Franco-Prussian War came to Paris and opened restaurants serving specialties from home. Pork-based dishes, *choucroute* (sauerkraut and sausages), and beer (brasserie also means brewery) were—and still are—mainstays here. The typical brasserie is convivial and keeps late hours. Some are open 24 hours a day—a good thing to know, since many restaurants stop serving at 10:30 PM.

Like bistros and brasseries, **cafés** come in confusing variety. Usually informal neighborhood hangouts, cafés may also be veritable showplaces attracting chic, well-heeled crowds. At most cafés, regulars congregate at the bar, where coffee and drinks are cheaper than at tables. At lunch, tables are set and a limited menu is served. Sandwiches, usually with *jambon* (ham) or *fromage* (cheese, often Gruyere or Camembert), or *mixte* (ham and cheese) are served throughout the day. Cafés are for lingering, for people-watching, and for daydreaming.

Wine bars, or *bistrots à vins*, are a newer phenomenon. These informal places serve very limited menus, often no more than open-faced sandwiches (*tartines*) and selections of cheeses and cold cuts (*charcuterie*). Owners concentrate on their wine lists, which often include less well known, regional selections, many of them available by the glass. Like today's bistros and brasseries, some wine bars are very fancy indeed, with costly wine lists and full menus. Most remain friendly and unassuming, good places for sampling wines you might otherwise never try.

If you're not very hungry or want to eat at an odd hour, consider one of Paris's many **charcuteries.** Today's charcuterie is virtually a restaurant (though without waiter service), and the pâtés and meat products that once filled the shelves have moved over to make room for prepared salads, quiches, breads, and desserts. Choose what appeals to you most and take it to one of the city's green spaces for your own *déjeuner sur l'herbe.* Or you can put together your picnic by visiting a number of shops, including **boulangeries** (bakeries), **pâtisseries** (pastry shops), and **fromageries** (cheese shops).

Mealtimes Generally, Paris restaurants are open from noon to about 2, and from 7:30 or 8 to 10 or 10:30. Brasseries have longer hours and often serve all day and late into the evening; some are open 24 hours. The iconoclastic wine bars do as they want, frequently serving hot food only through lunch and cold assortments of *charcuterie* and cheese until a late afternoon or early evening close.

We have included days closed in all our listings, including yearly vacations when known. Assume a restaurant is open seven days a week, year-round, unless otherwise indicated. Surprisingly, many prestigous restaurants close on Saturday as well as Sunday. July and August are the most common months for annual closings, but Paris in August is no longer the wasteland it used to be, and many restaurants now close for a few weeks in winter instead. The past couple of years have been hard for many Paris restaurants, and management may hesitate to announce vacation dates too far in advance or suddenly decide not to close after all. We suggest you call ahead to confirm that the establishment of your choice will be open when you plan to visit.

Because most restaurants are open for only a few set hours for lunch and dinner, and because meals are much longer affairs here than they are in the United States, we strongly advise you to make reservations. Most wine bars do not take reservations; reservations are also unnecessary for brasserie and café meals

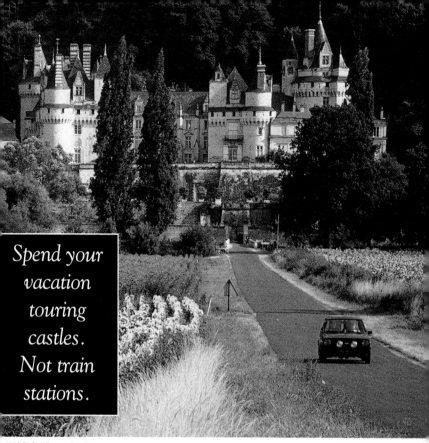

Spend your
vacation
touring
castles.
Not train
stations.

Vacation Cars. Vacation Prices. Wherever your destination in Europe, there is sure to be one of more than 1,000 Budget locations nearby. Budget offers considerable values on a wide variety of quality cars, and if you book before you leave the U.S., you'll save even more with a special rate package from the Budget World Travel Plan.℠ For information and reservations, contact your travel consultant or call Budget in the U.S. at **800-472-3325.** Or, while traveling abroad, call a Budget reservation center.

THE SMART MONEY IS ON BUDGET.®

We feature Ford and other fine cars.   *A system of corporate and licensee owned locations.*

MCI brings Europe and America closer together.

Call the U.S. for less with MCI CALL USA.®

It's easy and affordable to call home when you use MCI CALL USA!

- Less expensive than calling through hotel operators
- Available from over 80 countries and locations worldwide
- You're connected to English-speaking MCI® Operators
- Even call 800 numbers in the U.S.†

†Regular MCI CALL USA rates apply to 800 number calls.

Call the U.S. for less from these European locations.

Dial the toll-free access number for the country you're calling from. Give the U.S. MCI Operator the number you're calling and the method of payment: MCI Card, U.S. local phone company card or collect. Your call will be completed!

Austria	022-903-012	Hungary	00*-800-01411	Poland	0*-01-04-800-222
Belgium	078-11-00-12	Ireland	1-800-551-001	Portugal	05-017-1234
Czech/Slovak	00-42-000112	Italy	172-1022	San Marino	172-1022
Denmark	8001-0022	Liechtenstein	155-0222	Spain	900-99-0014
Finland	9800-102-80	Luxembourg	0800-0112	Sweden	020-795-922
France	19*-00-19	Monaco	19*-00-19	Switzerland	155-0222
Germany	0130-0012	Netherlands	06*-022-91-22	United Kingdom	0800-89-0222
Greece	00-800-1211	Norway	050-12912	Vatican City	172-1022

* Wait for 2nd dial tone.
Collect calls not accepted on MCI CALL USA calls to 800 numbers.
Some public phones may require deposit of coin or phone card for dial tone.

Call 1-800-444-3333 in the U.S. to apply for your MCI Card® now!

at odd hours. In the reviews below, we have indicated where reservations are advised or required (and when booking weeks or months in advance is necessary), and where reservations are not accepted. If you want nonsmoking, make this clear when you reserve. Though the law requires all restaurants to provide a nonsmoking area, this is sometimes limited to a very few tables.

Menus All establishments must post their menus outside, so study them carefully before deciding to enter. Most restaurants offer two basic types of menu: à la carte and fixed price (*prix fixe*, or *un menu*). The prix-fixe menu will usually offer the best value, though choices are limited. Most menus begin with a first-course section, often subdivided into cold and hot starters, followed by fish and poultry, then meat; it's rare today that anyone orders something from all three. However, outside of brasseries, wine bars, and other simple places, it's inappropriate to order just one dish, as you'll understand when you see the waiter's expression. In recent years, the *menu dégustation* has become popular; consisting of numerous small courses, it allows for a wide sampling of the chef's offerings. In general, consider the season when ordering. Daily specials are usually based on what's freshest in the market that day.

Following are a number of menu items that appear frequently on French menus and throughout the reviews that follow. *See also* our Menu Guide at the end of the book for additional guidance.

bavarois—usually, a dessert of whipped cream, custard, and gelatin; it can also be savory, made with vegetables or fish.
blanquette—a stew—often veal—with a white-sauce base.
bouef à la Bourguignonne—a beef stew cooked in red wine, with onions, mushrooms, and bacon.
boeuf à la ficelle—pieces of beef tied with string and simmered in stock.
bouef à la mode—a refined beef stew.
boudin blanc—sausage made with white meat.
boudin noir—sausage made with pig's blood.
brandade—creamy cod purée, sometimes incorporating potato purée and garlic.
charcuterie—a selection of cold, pork-based products such as sausages, pâtés, and terrines.
choucroute—hearty dish of sauerkraut, usually accompanied by sausage, pork, and sometimes duck; also called *choucroute garnie*.
clafoutis—a hearty, flan-like tart with a base of seasonal fruit.
confit—meat (often duck), cooked in fat and preserved.
coq au vin—a classic preparation of chicken cooked in red wine and garnished with pearl onions, mushrooms, and bacon.
daube—beef stew.
fondant—traditionally, a shiny glaze used to decorate cakes and other desserts. Today, the word has a number of meanings, including flourless cake.
fricassée—any of several kinds of stews and braised dishes.
langoustine—a type of crustacean, similar to crawfish but smaller.
mille-feuille—a classic dessert composed of alternate layers of puff pastry and pastry cream (Napoléon in English).
navarin—a kind of stew, frequently made with lamb.

pastilla—originally a flaky pastry used in Moroccan cuisine. Today's French chefs use it to encase a variety of foods.

profiterole—a small cream puff with a savory or sweet filling (often ice cream).

quenelle—a dumpling, usually of fish or poultry.

ragoût—a kind of stew.

rillettes—potted, minced meat, often pork or goose.

sabayon—traditionally, an egg-and-wine-based dessert; also a savory preparation based on an egg-and-wine mixture.

Wine The wine that suits your meal is the wine you like. The traditional rule of white with fish and red with meat no longer applies. If the restaurant has a *sommelier*, let him help you. Most sommeliers are knowledgeable about their lists, and will suggest what is appropriate after you've made your tastes and budget known. In addition to the wine list, informal restaurants will have a *vin de la maison* (house wine) that is less expensive. Simpler spots will have wines *en carafe* or *en pichet*. Except for wine bars and brasseries, most restaurants do not sell wine by the glass. If you'd like something before the meal, consider ordering your wine for the meal ahead of time, or sample a typical French *apéritif*.

Dress Code Perhaps surprisingly, casual dress is acceptable at all but the fanciest restaurants. Use your judgment, of course, and remember that casual to the French does not mean without style. When in doubt, leave the sloppier blue jeans behind. In the reviews below, we have indicated where a jacket and tie are advised or required, and where casual attire is appropriate.

Prices Although prices are high, a trend toward cheaper, more informal eateries continues. We have made an effort to include a number of lower-priced establishments below. All prices include tax and tip (*service compris* or *prix nets*). No additional tip is expected, though pocket change left on the table in simple places, or an additional 5% of the bill in better restaurants, is appreciated.

The following credit card abbreviations are used: AE, American Express; DC, Diners Club; MC, MasterCard; and V, Visa.

Highly recommended restaurants are indicated by a ★.

Category	Cost*
Very Expensive	over 550 frs
Expensive	300 frs–550 frs
Moderate	175 frs–300 frs
Inexpensive	under 175 frs

* *per person, including tax and service but not drinks*

1st Arrondissement (Louvre)
See Right Bank Dining map

Very Expensive **Le Grand Véfour.** This sumptuously decorated restaurant is perhaps the prettiest in Paris, and its 18th-century origins make it one of the oldest. Chef Guy Martin impresses with his unique blend of sophisticated yet rustic dishes, including langoustines with calves' ear and cabbage ravioli with truffle cream. Luminaries from Napoléon to Colette have frequented this intimate address under the arcades of the Palais-Royal; you can request to be seated at their preferred table. *17 rue Beaujolais, Métro: Palais-Royal, tel. 42–96–56–27. Reservations 1 week in advance essential. Jacket and tie required. AE, DC, MC, V. Closed Sat. lunch, Sun., and Aug.*

Expensive **Le Carré des Feuillants.** Star chef Alain Dutournier pays homage to the cuisine of his native Southwest France here. Many of the restaurant's ingredients are delivered from there, including poultry, beef, and game in season. The decor, with its mix of homey and elegant, includes gorgeous Venetian glass, handsome *faux-bois* painted walls, and fanciful *trompe-l'oeil* ceilings. The Carré has one of the finest wine lists in Paris, and a special wine-and-food menu lets you sample a variety. The visible kitchen adds to the conviviality of this friendly restaurant. *14 rue Castiglione, Métro: Tuileries, tel. 42–86–82–82. Reservations advised. Dress: casual but elegant. AE, DC, MC, V. Closed Sat. lunch, Sun., and Aug.*

Pierre. M. and Mme. Dez are always on hand to greet you in their long, two-dining-room address, a classic Parisian restaurant next to the Comédie Française. The many habitués return for the house specialties and want no contemporary gastronomic foolishness. Try the foie gras, pike *quenelles, beef à la ficelle,* and *tarte Tatin.* Dinner starts at 7 PM to accommodate Comédie Française theatergoers. *10 rue de Richelieu, Métro: Palais-Royal, tel. 42–96–09–17. Reservations advised. Dress: casual but elegant. DC, MC, V. Closed Sat., Sun., and Aug.*

Moderate **Au Pied de Cochon.** This landmark brasserie in the former Les Halles district has been popular since its founding in 1946. Recent renovation has given it an Italian look incongruous to its classic French menu of shellfish, onion soup, steaks and, of course, the eponymous pig's feet. It's open 24 hours a day, and the terrace is a good spot for people-watching in fine weather. *6 rue Coquillière, Métro: Les Halles, tel. 42–36–11–75. Reservations advised. Dress: casual. AE, DC, MC, V.*

Gaya. Come here for seafood in all its guises, from marinated anchovies to fish soup, to grilled sole—much of it with a Mediterranean accent. The colorful Portuguese azulejos on the ground floor are delightful; upstairs is less attractive. *17 rue Duphot, Métro: Madeleine, tel. 42–60–43–03. Reservations advised. Dress: casual. AE, DC, MC, V. Closed Sun. and Mon.*

Le Grand Louvre. The austere metal-and-wood decor is in keeping with this restaurant's location under the pyramid of the Louvre. Cuisine from the southwest of France predominates and includes foie gras with raisins, pigeon terrine with walnuts, and prune ice cream with Armagnac. After dinner, the hushed, illuminated pyramid will seem to belong to you alone. *Louvre, Métro: Palais-Royal, tel. 40–20–53–41. Reservations advised. Dress: casual. AE, DC, MC, V. Closed Tues.*

★ **Le Petit Bourbon.** This charming restaurant offers two fixed-price menus, one in the Inexpensive category. On both, first and main courses such as mushroom terrine with shellfish sauce, stuffed rabbit medallions, and chocolate soup transcend the ordinary. The intimate dining room has exposed stone walls, cream colors, and pretty paintings of the Midi region. *15 rue du Roule, Métro: Louvre, tel. 40–26–08–93. Reservations advised. Dress: casual. MC, V. Closed Sun., Mon.*

Right Bank Dining

A. Beauvilliers, **35**
A La Cloche
des Halles, **45**
A La Courtille, **54**
Amphyclès, **14**
Apicius, **15**
Astier, **58**
Au Couchon d'Or, **52**
Au Petit Colombier, **11**
Au Pied de Cochon, **47**

Au Pressoir, **72**
Au Trou Gascon, **74**
Augusta, **17**
Aux Négotiants, **36**
Baracane, **67**
Benoît, **61**
Berry's, **20**
Bistrot de l'Etoile
Lauriston, **9**
Bistrot des Deux
Théâtres, **34**

Bofinger, **68**
Brasserie Flo, **51**
Café Drouant, **33**
Chartier, **38**
Chez Fernand, **55**
Chez Géraud, **1**
Chez Jenny, **57**
Chez Philippe/
Pyrénées-
Cévennes, **56**
Drouant, **33**

Gaya, **30**
Guy Savoy, **19**
Jacques Mélac, **69**
Jamin/Robuchon, **7**
Julien, **50**
La Butte Chaillot, **6**
La Ferme
St. Hubert, **29**
La Fermette
Marbeuf, **23**
La Niçoise, **13**

Left Bank Dining

Au Petit Marguéry, **28**
Au Pied de Fouet, **13**
Au Sauvignon, **17**
Aux Charpentiers, **20**
Aux Fins
Gourmets, **10**
Campagne et
Provence, **22**
Chez Pento, **27**

Chez René, **24**
Contre-Allée, **29**
Duquesnoy, **3**
Entre-Siècle, **6**
Jules Verne, **2**
La Cagouille, **16**
La Coupole, **14**
La Rôtisserie
d'En Face, **21**

La Tour d'Argent, **23**
L'Armoise, **1**
L'Arpège, **12**
Le Barrail, **7**
Le Bistrot
du Dôme, **15**
Le Clos Morillons, **9**
Le Pavillon
Montsouris, **30**

Le Petit Navire, **26**
Le Petit Zinc, **19**
Le Télégraphe, **11**
Lipp, **18**
Moissonnier, **25**
Morot-Gaudry, **5**
Pierre Vedal, **8**
Thoumieux, **4**

173

Pharamond. A Halles landmark since its founding in 1870. No one would dare touch the polychrome tiles and mosaics, mirrors, and handsome woodwork, or the classic bistro menu with Norman specialties such as scallops in cider, grilled meats, *tripes à la mode de Caen,* and souffléed potatoes. *24 rue de la Grande Truanderie, Métro: Les Halles, tel. 42–33–06–72. Reservations advised. Dress: casual. AE, DC, MC, V. Closed Sun., Mon. lunch, and mid-July–mid-Aug.*

Willi's Wine Bar. This English-owned wine bar, a renowned haunt for Anglophiles as well as a chic French crowd, is a Paris phenomenon. The simple, frequently original menu changes to reflect the market's offerings and might include chicken liver terrine, sea trout with lemon butter, or guinea hen with herb vinaigrette; crème brûlée is the favorite dessert. The wine list includes more than 250 listings with an emphasis on Rhônes. *13 rue des Petits-Champs, Métro: Bourse, tel. 42–61–05–09. Reservations advised. Dress: casual. MC, V. Closed Sun.*

Inexpensive **A La Cloche des Halles.** Get here by 12:30 PM if you want to lunch at this small and popular wine bar in the Les Halles neighborhood. Forgive the tacky decor and enjoy quiche (the only hot dish) and the assortments of high-quality cheeses and charcuterie. Wines, served by the glass or bottle, include some good Beaujolais. The simple menu is served until closing at 10 PM. *28 rue Coquillière, Métro: Les Halles, tel. 42–36–93–89. No reservations. Dress: casual. No credit cards. Closed Sun.*

Le Rubis. This humble, neighborhood wine bar enjoys tremendous popularity with everyone from executives to laborers. One or two hearty plats du jour, such as *petit salé* (salted, slow-cooked pork ribs) with lentils and boudin noir plus omelettes, cheeses, and charcuterie assortments, make up the menu here. There's an eclectic selection of adequate wines by the glass or bottle. *10 rue du Marché St. Honoré, Métro: Tuileries, tel. 42–61–03–34. No reservations. Dress: casual. No credit cards. Closed Sat. eve., Sun., and mid-Aug.*

La Taverne Henri IV. This informal wine bar near the Pont Neuf, on the tip of the Ile de la Cîté, is an excellent choice for a quick lunch or snack. No full meals are served, but a selection of open-faced sandwiches on Poilâne bread (from the celebrated bakery), cheese and charcuterie plates, and varied wines by the glass or bottle make for a satisfying meal. *13 pl. du Pont Neuf, Métro: Pont Neuf, tel. 43–54–27–90. No reservations. Dress: casual. No credit cards. Closed Sat., Sun., and Aug.*

2nd Arrondissement (Stock Exchange)
See Right Bank Dining map

Very Expensive **Drouant.** A costly renovation recently restored the luster to this Paris landmark, founded in 1880. Amid stylish Art Deco decor, diners enjoy the creations of celebrated chef Louis Grondard, whose menu might include charlotte of langoutines with eggplant, and poached fillet of veal. *Pl. Gaillon, Métro: Opéra, tel. 42–65–15–16. Reservations advised. Jacket and tie required. AE, DC, MC, V. Closed Sun.*

Moderate **Café Drouant.** The Café across the hall from Drouant (*see above*) shares its illustrious history and 1930's decor, but the limited menu is one-third the price (à la carte at noon, prix-fixe at dinner). The Café serves until midnight, and its proximity to the Opéra makes it a good choice for after the ballet. *Pl. de Gaillon, Métro: Opéra, tel. 42–65–15–16. Reservations advised. Dress: casual. AE, DC, MC, V.*

Le Grand Colbert. This very pretty brasserie, owned by the Bibliothèque Nationale, is airy and light, with its frosted glass and many mirrors. The large menu, which includes oysters, herring fillets with potatoes, snails, and grilled meats, has something for every taste. Waiters in their black and whites with long aprons complete the picture of a classic brasserie. It's open until 1 AM. *2 rue Vivienne, Métro: Bourse, tel. 42–86–87–88. Reservations advised. Dress: casual. AE, DC, MC, V.*

Le Vaudeville. Like the other six Parisian brasseries of Jean-Paul Bucher, the Vaudeville has history and a good-looking clientele (many of them from the stock exchange across the street), and represents an excellent value, thanks to its assortment of fixed-price menus. Shellfish, house smoked salmon, and desserts are particularly fine. You can enjoy the handsome 1930's decor and joyful din until 2 AM daily. *29 rue Vivienne, Métro: Bourse, tel. 40–20–04–62. Reservations advised. Dress: casual. AE, DC, MC, V. Closed Christmas eve.*

3rd Arrondissement (Le Marais/Beaubourg)
See Right Bank Dining map

Inexpensive
★

Chez Jenny. Order the filling choucroute Jenny and a carafe of Alsatian wine, then sit back and watch the bustle at this large Alsatian brasserie decorated with museum-quality marquetry and woodwork. Waitresses in regional costume wend their way through many salons on two levels, serving forth hearty fare. Though the clientele is not the chic crowd of some other brasseries, everyone's having just as much fun. *39 blvd. du Temple, Métro: République, tel. 42–74–75–75. Reservations advised. Dress: casual. AE, DC, MC, V.*

4th Arrondissement (Le Marais/Ile St-Louis)
See Right Bank Dining map

Very Expensive
★

L'Ambroisie. You must reserve a month in advance for a meal in this tiny, romantic restaurant on the patrician place des Vosges. Chef-owner Bernard Pacaud's refined, oft-imitated cuisine featuring such dishes as mousse of red bell peppers and braised oxtail is served in a jewel-like Italianate setting of flowers, tapestries, and subdued lighting. *9 pl. des Vosges, Métro: St. Paul, tel. 42–78–51–45. MC, V. Reservations one month in advance essential. Dress: casual but elegant. Closed Sun., Mon., Aug., and mid-Feb.*

Expensive
★

Benoît. Founded in 1912, Benoît retains the feel of a classic bistro—with its frosted glass, lace curtains, polished brass, and a warm welcome—despite its high prices. Try the layered beef tongue–foie gras Lucullus, marinated salmon, cassoulet, or game in season. Patrons debate the merits of the front or back room, but conviviality reigns in both. *20 rue St. Martin, Métro: Châtelet, tel. 42–72–25–76. Reservations required. Dress: casual. No credit cards. Closed Sat., Sun., Aug.*

Miravile. This latest Miravile—the third for successful young owners Gilles and Muriel Epié—has vaguely California decor and a Provençal-inspired menu. Mr. Epié's celery *remoulade* with foie gras, and chocolate mille-feuille exemplify his full-flavored style. The restaurant is popular with staff members from the adjacent Hôtel de Ville (city hall). *72 quai de l'Hôtel de Ville, Métro: Pont-Marie, tel. 42–74–72–22. Reservations advised. Dress: casual. MC, V. Closed Sat. lunch, Sun.*

Moderate **Bofinger.** Founded in 1864, this may be Paris's oldest brasserie. It's also one of the prettiest, with its authentic Belle Epoque decor, white linen tablecloths, black leather banquettes, and beautiful stained-glass dome (ask to be seated on the main floor). The menu offers excellent shellfish and choucroute (including a lighter version with fish), and there's a large selection of Alsatian beers. Only steps from the place de la Bastille, and open until 1 AM, Bofinger makes a good postopera rendezvous. *5 rue de la Bastille, Métro: Bastille, tel. 42–27–87–82. Reservations advised. Dress: casual. AE, DC, MC, V.*

Le Grizzli. It's said this turn-of-the-century bistro was one of the last to have dancing bears as entertainment—thus the name. Today's owner gets many of his ingredients—especially the wonderful ham and cheeses—from his native Auvergne. Several dishes are cooked on hot slate, including salmon and lamb. There's an interesting selection of wines from Southwest France. Prices here are at the low end of our Moderate range. *7 rue St. Martin, Métro: Chatelet, tel. 48–87–77–56. Reservations advised. Dress: casual. MC, V. Closed Sun., Mon. lunch.*

Le Maraîcher. With its exposed stone walls and wood beams, this intimate little restaurant on a quiet street in the Marais is very *vieux Paris*. The young owner worked at the renowned Lucas-Carton, which may account for the table settings and service, which are surprisingly refined considering the reasonable prices. Freshness and seasonality are hallmarks of such dishes as sweetbreads with ginger, rabbit medallions with cabbage, and fresh fig crêpes. *5 rue Beautreillis, Métro: Sully-Morland, tel. 42–71–42–49. Reservations advised. Dress: casual. MC, V. Closed Sat. lunch, Sun., late July-early Aug.*

Le Vieux Bistrot. Forgive the corny name and touristy location next to Notre Dame. This really *is* generations old, and its menu is full of bistro classics such as blanquette of veal, beef fillet with marrow, and giant éclairs. Decor is nondescript, but the frequently fancy crowd doesn't seem to notice. *14 rue du Cloître-Notre-Dame, Métro: Hôtel de Ville, tel. 43–54–18–95. Reservations advised. Dress: casual. MC, V.*

Inexpensive **Baracane.** This is one of the best values in the Marais district.
★ The owner oversees the menu, full of the robust specialties of his native Southwest France, including rabbit confit, braised oxtail with foie gras, and pear poached in wine and cassis. A reasonable dinner menu and cheaper menu at lunch keep the Baracane solidly in the Inexpensive range. *38 rue des Tournelles, Métro: Bastille, tel. 42–71–43–33. Reservations advised. Dress: casual. MC, V. Closed Sat. lunch, Sun.*

Trumilou. Popular with students, artist types, and others on a budget, the Trumilou serves unremarkable bistro cuisine such as leg of lamb, and apple tart. But the homely non-decor is somehow homey, and the friendly staff remains friendly despite the crowd. The location facing the Seine and the Ile St-Louis is especially pleasant in nice weather, when you can sit on a narrow terrace under the trees. *84 quai de l'Hôtel de Ville, Métro: Pont-Marie, tel. 42–77–63–98. Reservations accepted. Dress: casual. MC, V. Closed Mon.*

5th Arrondissement (Latin Quarter)
See Left Bank Dining map

Very Expensive **La Tour d'Argent.** Dining at this temple to haute cuisine is a
★ theatrical and unique event—from apéritifs in the ground-floor
bar to dinner in the top-floor dining room, with its breath-tak-
ing view of Notre Dame. In recent years elegant owner Claude
Terrail has hired a series of young chefs, and today's menu is a
mix of Tour classics and contemporary creations. Venerable favorites such as *caneton* Tour d'Argent (pressed duck), quenelles André Terrail, and filets de sole Cardinal have been
lightened, and new dishes added, including scallop salad with
truffles and double-thick lamb chops with carrots. The wine
list is one of the greatest in the world. *15 quai de la Tournelle,
Métro: Cardinal Lemoine, tel. 43–54–23–31. Reservations required at least one week in advance. Jacket and tie required at
dinner, advised at lunch. AE, DC, MC, V. Closed Mon.*

Moderate **Campagne et Provence.** The talented young owners of the
Miravile (*see* 4th Arrondissement, *above*) also run this small establishment on the quai across from Notre Dame. Fresh, colorful, Provençal-inspired cuisine includes vegetables stuffed
with cod brandade and ratatouille omelettes. The list of reasonably priced regional wines helps keep prices down—almost in
the Inexpensive range. *25 quai de la Tournelle, Métro:
Maubert-Mutualité, tel. 43–54–05–17. Reservations advised.
Dress: casual. MC, V. Closed Sat. lunch, Sun.*

Chez Pento. Few Paris locations are more touristy than that of
this simple neighborhood restaurant near the Panthéon. But it
offers quality and good value, with one remarkable prix-fixe
menu priced well under 200F. The limited choices here include
both classic bistro fare such as *petit salé* of duck with lentils and
steak of the day, and more original dishes, such as guinea hen
marinated in lime. The bistro setting includes modern posters,
moleskin banquettes, and bare tabletops. *9 rue Cujas, Métro:
St-Michel, tel. 43–26–81–54. Reservations advised. Dress: casual. V. Closed Sat. lunch, Sun.*

Moissonnier. Mr. and Mme. Moissonnier are always present to
greet their faithful habitués. The Lyonnais cuisine includes
saladiers Lyonnais (assorted cold salads), pike quenelles, eggs
in a *meurette* (red wine) sauce, and, to drink, a variety of
Beaujolais. With its homey decor, this is the perfect place to experience a typical French Sunday lunch. Ask to be seated in the
ground-floor dining room. *28 rue des Fossés-St-Bernard,
Métro: Cardinal Lemoine, tel. 43–29–87–65. Reservations advised. Dress: casual. MC, V. Closed Sun. eve., Mon., Aug.*

Le Petit Navire. Attentive Mme. Cousty takes care of the series
of intimate dining rooms in this charming neighborhood restaurant, while her husband prepares mostly fish dishes with the
taste of the Mediterranean: *tapenade* (anchovy and black olive
spread), fish soup, and sea bass grilled with fennel. Careful ordering will put your meal in the Inexpensive range. *14 rue des
Fossés-St-Bernard, Métro: Cardinal-Lemoine, tel. 43–54–22–
52. Reservations advised. Dress: casual. AE, DC, MC, V.
Closed Sun., Mon., mid-Aug., mid-Feb., and Christmas week.*

Inexpensive **Chez René.** This reliable address at the eastern end of the blvd.
St-Germain has satisfied three generations of Parisians, who
count on finding Burgundian dishes such as boeuf à la

Bourguignonne and coq au vin, and the wines of the Maconnais and Beaujolais. The dining rooms are cozy. *14 blvd. St-Germain, Métro: Cardinal Lemoine, tel. 43–54–30–23. Reservations advised. Dress: casual. MC, V. Closed Sat., Sun., Aug.*

6th Arrondissement (Luxembourg)
See Left Bank Dining map

Moderate **Lipp.** At this classic Left Bank brasserie, politicians, entertainers, rubber-necking tourists, and everyone else vie for tables, especially in the ground-floor dining room. Food is classic brasserie-style too: herring in cream, choucroute, and mille-feuille. The pretty decor is straight from the 1920's, and the ceramics are landmarked. *151 blvd. St-Germain, Métro: St-Germain-des-Prés, tel. 45–48–53–91. No reservations; expect lines. Dress: jacket and tie required. AE, DC, MC, V. Closed mid-July–mid-Aug.*

Le Petit Zinc. It's hard to believe the extravagant *fin-de-siècle*-style decor is new. The kitchen does a creditable job with shellfish, veal liver, and duck confit. Careful ordering will keep your meal in our Inexpensive range. Le Muniche, next door, has the same owners and lively atmosphere. *11 rue St. Benoît, Métro: St-Germain-des-Prés, tel. 46–33–51–66. Reservations strongly advised. Dress: casual. AE, DC, MC, V.*

La Rôtisserie d'En Face. A long rotisserie is part of the attractive country-elegant decor at this bistro created by renowned chef Jacques Cagna. The cuisine includes roast chicken with mashed potatoes, grilled salmon with spinach, and chocolate éclairs. The menu is fixed-price only, and it's cheaper at lunch. Dinner is two set seatings only. *2 rue Christine, Métro: Odéon, tel. 43–26–40–98. MC, V. Closed Sat. lunch, Sun.*

Inexpensive **Aux Charpentiers.** This old, large neighborhood bistro in St-Germain-des-Prés is eternally popular with students, locals, and tourists. Enjoy the homemade preparations of foie gras, cod *aïoli* (garlic mayonnaise) with vegetables, boeuf à la mode, and chocolate mousse—and the boisterous atmosphere. *10 rue Mabillon, Métro: Mabillon, tel. 43–26–30–05. Reservations advised. Dress: casual. AE, DC, MC, V. Closed Sun.*

7th Arrondissment (Invalides)
See Left Bank Dining map

Very Expensive ★ **L'Arpège.** This small, striking restaurant one block from the Rodin Museum is currently one of the most talked-about of Paris's restaurants. It features the cuisine of young chef-owner Alain Passard, whose menu is both original (lobster/turnip starter in a sweet-sour vinaigrette, stuffed sweet tomato) and classic (beef Burgundy, pressed duck). With its curving, hand-crafted wood panels and wrought-iron window frames, the decor is unusually minimalist. Service, although young and energetic, sometimes falls behind. *84 rue de Varenne, Métro: Varenne, tel. 45–51–47–33. Reservations advised. Dress: casual but elegant. AE, DC, MC, V. Closed Sat., Sun. lunch, Aug.*

★ **Duquesnoy.** This pretty, pastel dining room is one of the most enjoyable restaurants in Paris. Mr. Duquesnoy's cuisine is original without pretense or excess, with dishes such as truffle and potato ravioli, cabbage, and baby *babas au rhum*. An excellent wine list, professional service (overseen by the charming Mme. Duquesnoy), and a discreet atmosphere complete the picture. *6 av. Bosquet, Métro: Ecole Militaire, tel. 47–05–96–78. Reservations advised. Dress: casual but elegant. AE, MC, V. Closed Sat. lunch, Sun., Aug.*

Jules Verne. Distinctive all-black decor, stylish service, and a top chef—not to mention a location at 400 feet, on the second level of the Eiffel Tower—have made the Jules Verne one of the hardest dinner reservations to get in Paris. Asparagus and foie gras aspic, sole fillet with crab sauce, and veal medallions with bell pepper sauce are examples of Chef Bariteau's colorful, flavorful cuisine. The restaurant is open daily, and a lunch table is easier to snag. *Eiffel Tower, Métro: Bir-Hakeim, tel. 45–55–61–44. Reservations 2 months in advance for dinner at window table. Jacket and tie required. AE, DC, MC, V.*

Moderate   **Le Télégraphe.** This cavernous restaurant near the Musée d'Orsay was once a residence for female postal workers. Today's occupants are youngish, fashionable inhabitants of the wealthy neighborhood, who like the reasonable fixed-price menu (à la carte is more). Although the cuisine is fine (cassoulette of oysters, *sauté* of beef, chocolate surprise), people come here for the atmosphere. *41 rue de Lille, Métro: Bac, tel. 40–15–06–65. Reservations advised. Dress: casual. AE, V.*

Inexpensive   **Aux Fins Gourmets.** What would the far western end of the blvd. St-Germain be without this comforting bistro? Solid country dishes prevail: *pipérade* (mixture of eggs, peppers, onions, tomatoes, and garlic), duck confit, and cassoulet. Pastries come from the excellent shop Peltier. In warm weather, dinner or lunch on the sidewalk terrace, under the shady plane trees, is a delight. *213 blvd. St-Germain, Métro: Bac, tel. 42–22–06–57. Reservations advised. Dress: casual. No credit cards. Closed Sun., Mon. lunch, Aug.*

Au Pied de Fouet. As much a home as a restaurant for some people, the very simple Au Pied de Fouet has no decor to mention and serves plain homecooked food (lentil salad, veal blanquette, tarts) with absolutely no pretense. It's noisy, always crowded, and very inexpensive. *45 rue de Babylone, Métro: Vaneau, tel. 47–05–12–27. No reservations. Dress: casual. No credit cards. Closed Sat. eve., Sun., Aug., Christmas week, and Easter.*

★   **Au Sauvignon.** A young, modish, intellectual crowd fills this tiny wine bar, where you'll find the usual limited menu of *tartines*, or open-faced sandwiches, on the famous Poilâne loaf, topped with good-quality charcuterie, cheese, or both. The colorful murals will amuse you, but it's even more fun to people-watch from one of the tables set on the narrow sidewalk. *80 rue des Saints Pères, Métro: Sèvres-Babylone, tel. 45–48–04–69. No reservations. Dress: casual. No credit cards. Closed Sat. eve., Sun., Aug., Christmas week, and Easter.*

Thoumieux. Virtually everything at this third-generation restaurant is made on the premises, including foie gras, rillettes, duck confit, cassoulet, and the homey desserts. The red velour banquettes, mellow yellow walls, and bustling waiters in long, white aprons are delightfully Parisian. *79 rue St. Dominique, Métro: Invalides, tel. 47–05–49–75. Reservations advised. Dress: casual. MC, V.*

8th Arrondissement (Champs-Elysées)
See Right Bank Dining map

Very Expensive **Les Ambassadeurs.** This dining room in the opulent Crillon is one of the finest hotel restaurants in Paris. Respected chef Christian Constant is a master at giving even the humblest ingredients sophistication, as exemplified by his *petit salé* of cod, his rabbit with marjoram, and his pork with spider crab. Some find the all-marble dining room, with its crystal chandeliers, mirrors, and heavy blue draperies, to be stiff and inhospitable. But no one can fault the view onto the place de la Concorde, the distinguished service, or the memorable wine list. Lunch is more affordable, though still expensive; there's also a good brunch. *Pl. de la Concorde, Métro: Concorde, tel. 44–71–16–16. Jacket and tie required at dinner. Reservations advised. AE, DC, MC, V.*

Lucas-Carton. Chef Alain Senderens continues to create a provocative blend of nouvelle and classic cuisine, including foie gras wrapped in cabbage, a very spicy duck Apicius, and pastilla of rabbit and veal kidney with chorizo cream. The beautiful dining rooms glow with Belle Epoque splendor, and the crowd is international and one of the dressiest in Paris. *9 pl. de la Madeleine, Métro: Madeleine, tel. 42–65–22–90. Reservations at least 3 weeks in advance essential. Jacket and tie required at dinner. MC, V. Closed Sat. lunch, Sun., Christmas week, and Aug.*

★ **Taillevent.** Many say it's the best restaurant in Paris. Within the wood-paneled main dining rooms of this mid-19th-century mansion you will find exceptional service that is never overbearing, a stellar wine list, and the tempered classic cuisine of young chef Philippe Legendre. Among his signature dishes are celery turnover with morels and truffles and lamb with cabbage. Pastry chef Gilles Bajolle is one of the finest in Paris. Try his *nougatine glacée aux poires* (thin layers of nougatine and pear sherbet) or tarte Tatin with quince. Book months ahead. *15 rue Lamennais, Métro: Charles de Gaulle/Etoile, tel. 45–63–39–94. Reservations essential. Jacket and tie required. MC, V. Closed weekends, Aug.*

Expensive **Le Carré des Champs-Elysées.** This luxury brasserie sits below the landmark restaurant Ledoyen in the gardens of the Champs-Elysées, near the place de la Concorde. The varied menu of chef Jean-François Lemercier has something for everyone: salmon carpaccio with parmesan, grilled fish, pigeon salad with mushrooms. The handsome, curved dining room is a pleasure year-round, and the terrace is a special treat in warm weather. *Carré des Champs-Elysées, Métro: Champs-Elysées-Clemenceau, tel. 47–42–23–23. Reservations advised. Dress: casual but elegant. AE, DC, MC, V. Closed Sun.*

Moderate **L'Espace.** Pierre Cardin's L'Espace has unappealing decor but excellent prices. Bypass the à la carte menu in favor of the savory and dessert buffets, which are huge and varied. Eating on the big terrace in the gardens of the Champs-Elysées is delightful in nice weather. *1–3 av. Gabriel, Métro: Concorde, tel. 42–66–17–30. Reservations advised. Dress: casual. AE, DC, MC, V. Closed Sat. lunch and Sun. dinner.*

★ **La Fermette Marbeuf.** It's a favorite haunt of French TV and movie stars, who like the spectacular Belle Epoque mosaics, tiles, and stained glass (discovered by accident when the restaurant was being redecorated), and appreciate the solid, updated classic cuisine. Try *gâteau* of chicken livers and sweetbreads, lamb navarin stew with vegetables, and bitter chocolate fondant. Prices here are exceptional, considering the quality of the food, the surroundings, and the neighborhood. The Fermette becomes animated late, around 9. *5 rue Marbeuf, Métro: Franklin Roosevelt, tel. 47–20–63–53. Reservations advised. Dress: casual but elegant. AE, DC, MC, V.*

Savy. This 60-year-old restaurant still wears an honest, homey face, despite its rarified avenue Montaigne location. Expect 1950's decor and substantial cuisine, with specialties of central France such as stuffed cabbage, roast lamb shoulder, and prune tart. *23 rue Bayard, Métro: Champs-Elysées-Clemenceau, tel. 47–23–46–98. MC, V. Reservations advised. Dress: casual. Closed weekends and Aug.*

Sébillon. The original Sébillon has nurtured chic residents of the fashionable suburb of Neuilly for generations, and this elegant, polished new branch off the Champs-Elysées should do as well. The menu is similar, with lobster salad, lots of shellfish, and—its great specialty—roast leg of lamb sliced at table and served in unlimited quantity. Service is notably friendly. *66 rue Pierre Charron, Métro: Franklin Roosevelt, tel. 43–59–28–15. Reservations advised. Dress: casual chic. AE, DC, MC, V.*

Inexpensive Berry's. This tiny annex next door to the more expensive Le Grenadin, near the Parc Monceau, is a bargain. Talented chef-owner Patrick Cirotte prepares dishes of his native Berry region (e.g., veal simmered in red wine) and serves local wines, including fine Sancerres. Decor is lean and modern, the atmosphere young and upbeat. It's open until 1 AM. *46 rue de Naples, Métro: Villiers, tel. 40–75–01–56. Reservations advised. Dress: casual. AE, MC, V. Closed Sun.*

La Ferme St. Hubert. Reserve ahead for lunch, as this unpretentious spot serving primarily cheese dishes is mobbed then. The owner has a cheese shop next door—one of the best in the city—and from its shelves come the main ingredients for fondue, raclette, and the best *croque Hubert* (toasted cheese sandwich) in Paris. The house wines are decent, and the location is convenient to the fancy food shop, Fauchon, on the place de la Madeleine. *21 rue Vignon, Métro: Madeleine, tel. 47–42–79–20. Reservations essential at lunch, advised at dinner. Dress: casual. AE, DC, MC, V. Closed Mon. dinner and Sun.*

9th Arrondissement (Opéra)
See Right Bank Dining map

Expensive La Table d'Anvers. One of the best restaurants near Montmar-
★   tre, it serves an interesting menu, with Italian and Provençal touches in dishes like gnocchi of langoustines and *girolles* (wild mushrooms), saddle of rabbit with polenta, and *croustillant* of asparagus with crab. The Table's desserts, such as strawberry tart with rhubarb, are among the best in Paris; serious sweet-tooths can indulge in an all-dessert menu, which includes a single token fish dish. *2 pl. d'Anvers, Métro: Anvers, tel. 48–78–35–21. Reservations advised. Dress: casual but elegant. AE, MC, V. Closed Sat. lunch, Sun., mid-Aug.*

Inexpensive **Bistrot des Deux Théâtres.** Quality is high and prices are low in this well-run restaurant in the Pigalle/Clichy area. The prix-fixe menu includes apéritif, first and main courses, a cheese or dessert course, half a bottle of wine, and coffee. The food is far from banal; try salad of foie gras and the apple tart flambéed with Calvados. *18 rue Blanche, Métro: Trinité, tel. 45-26-41-43. Reservations advised. Dress: casual. MC, V.*

Chartier. This cavernous turn-of-the-century restaurant enjoys a huge following among the budget-minded, including students, solitary bachelors, and tourists. You may find yourself sharing a table with strangers as you study the long, old-fashioned menu of such favorites as hard-boiled eggs with mayonnaise, pâté, and roast veal with spinach. *7 rue du Faubourg-Montmartre, Métro: rue Montmartre, tel. 47-70-86-29. No reservations. Dress: casual. No credit cards.*

10th Arrondissement (République)
See Right Bank Dining map

Moderate **Brasserie Flo.** This, the first of brasserie king Jean-Paul Bucher's seven Paris addresses, is hard to find down its passageway near the Gare de l'Est, but worth the effort. The rich wood- and stained-glass interior is typically Alsatian, the service enthusiastic, and the brasserie standards such as shellfish, steak tartare, and choucroute tasty. Order one of the carafes of Alsatian wine. It's open until 1:30 AM, with a special night-owl menu from 11 PM. *7 cour des Petites Ecuries, Métro: Château d'Eau, tel. 47-70-13-59. Reservations advised. Dress: casual but elegant. AE, DC, MC, V. Closed Christmas eve.*

Julien. Another Bucher brasserie (*see above*), this one is a kind of poor man's Maxim's, with dazzling Belle Epoque decor. The menu offers brasserie fare, with smoked salmon, foie gras, cassoulet, and good sherbets. The crowd is ebullient and lots of fun. There's service until 1:30 AM, with a special night-owl menu from 11 PM. *16 rue du Faubourg St. Denis, Métro: Strasbourg-St.-Denis, tel. 47-70-12-06. Reservations advised. Dress: casual but elegant. AE, DC, MC, V. Closed Christmas eve.*

11th Arrondissement (Bastille)
See Right Bank Dining map

Moderate **Chez Fernand.** The chef-owner of this neighborhood spot near the place de la République is more concerned with his Normandy-inspired cuisine than with his restaurant's inconsequential decor. Mackerel rillettes, skate with Camembert, and duck are examples of his varied style. Also try the selection of Camemberts. The owner's smaller Fernandises, next door, is even less expensive. *17 rue Fontaine-au-Roi, Métro: République, tel. 43-57-46-25. Reservations advised. Dress: casual. MC, V. Closed Sun., Mon., Aug.*

★ **Chez Philippe/Pyrénées-Cévennes.** Old-timers still refer to this comfortable bistro by its original name—Pyrénées-Cévennes—while others know it as Chez Philippe. The eclectic menu combines the cooking of Burgundy, central France—even Spain—in such dishes as snails in garlic butter, cassoulet, and paella. An attentive staff bustles amid cozy surroundings, with beamed ceiling and polished copper. *106 rue de la Folie-*

Méricourt, Métro: République, tel. 43–57–33–78. Reservations advised. Dress casual. MC, V. Closed weekends, Aug.

Inexpensive **Astier.** You'll find remarkable value at this pleasant restaurant, where the prix-fixe menu (there's no à la carte) includes first and main courses, cheese (excellent), and dessert. Among high-quality dishes, try mussel soup with saffron, fricassée of beef cheeks, and plum clafoutis. Service can be rushed, but the enthusiastic crowd does not seem to mind. Study the excellent wine list, which has some surprising buys. *44 rue Jean-Pierre Timbaud, Métro: République, tel. 43–57–16–35. Reservations advised. Dress: casual. MC, V. Closed weekends, Aug.*

★ **Jacques Mélac.** There's robust cuisine to match the noisy camaraderie at this popular wine bar–restaurant, owned by mustachioed Jacques Mélac. Charcuterie, a salad of preserved duck gizzards, braised beef, and cheeses from central France make good choices here. Mr. Mélac has his own miniature vineyard out the front door and hosts a jolly party at harvest time. *42 rue Léon Frot, Métro: Charonne, tel. 43–70–59–27. Reservations advised. Dress: casual. MC, V. Closed weekends Aug.; dinner Tues–Fri. to 8:30 only.*

Le Passage. The friendly Passage is located in the rather obscure Passage de la Bonne Graine, not far from the place de la Bastille. Though it bills itself as a wine bar, it has a full menu, including five styles of *andouillettes* (chitterling sausage), sometimes a succulent, hot duck and cabbage *terrine*, and giant chocolate éclairs. The wine list is excellent. *18 Passage de la Bonne Graine (enter by 108 ave. Ledru-Rollin), Métro: Ledru-Rollin, tel. 47–00–73–30. Reservations advised. Dress: casual. AE, DC, MC, V. Closed Sat. lunch, Sun.*

Le Villaret. The owner of this newcomer once ran the excellent Astier (*see above*), and his experience shows. Menu choices are often interesting, always well prepared. Try salmon tart, hot foie gras salad, duck confit, and seasonal fruit clafoutis. Decor, with exposed stone and half-timbering, combines traditional and modern styles. The restaurant does not serve lunch, but makes up for that by serving dinner until 1 AM. *13 rue Ternaux, Métro: Parmentier, tel. 43–57–89–76. Reservations advised. Dress: casual. MC, V. Closed lunch, Sun.*

12th Arrondissement (Gare de Lyon)
See Right Bank Dining map

Expensive **Au Pressoir.** This excellent restaurant in the eastern part of Paris deserves more attention than it receives. Chef-owner Séguin's menu is original, with exciting choices such as fricassée of lobster with morels, pigeon with eggplant blinis, and chocolate soup with brioche. The wine list is tops, and service is friendly and professional. *257 av. Daumesnil, Métro: Michel Bizot, tel. 43–44–38–21. Reservations advised. Dress: casual. MC, V. Closed weekends, mid-Feb.*

★ **Au Trou Gascon.** The success of this Belle Epoque establishment off the place Daumesnil enabled owner Alain Dutournier to open the now-renowned Carré des Feuillants in the 1st arrondissement (*see above*). He's still the owner here, too, and continues to serve his personal version of the cuisine of Gascony, a region of outstanding ham, foie gras, lamb, and poultry. His white chocolate mousse is now a classic. *40 rue Taine,*

Métro: Daumesnil, tel. 43–44–34–26. Reservations advised. Dress: casual. AE, DC, MC, V. Closed weekends, Christmas week, Aug.

L'Oulette. Chef-owner Baudis once ran his restaurant from a smaller location in the 4th, but success encouraged him to open this larger, fancier spot, with lean, modern decor. Although something indefinable was lost in the move, the cuisine of Baudis's native Southwest France is as good as ever. Recommended dishes include *émincé* (thin slices) of duck with coriander and fresh figs, fresh cod with celeriac and walnuts, and *pain d'épices* (spice cake). The restaurant, in the rebuilt Bercy district, a bit hard to find. *15 pl. Lachambeaudie, Métro: Dugommier, tel. 40–02–02–12. Reservations advised. Dress: casual. MC, V. Closed Sat. lunch, Sun., Aug.*

Le Train Bleu. This historic brasserie in the Gare de Lyon was recently restored, and its gorgeous 19th-century frescos are more impressive than ever. Well-known chef Michel Comby heads the kitchen, and turns out excellent brasserie fare, such as herring in cream and hot sausage. If you come to the station to catch a train, consider stopping here, even if just for a drink. *Gare de Lyon, Métro: Gare de Lyon, tel. 43–43–09–06. Reservations advised. Dress: casual. AE, DC, MC, V.*

13th Arrondissement (Les Gobelins)
See Left Bank Dining map

Expensive **Au Petit Marguéry.** Both staff and diners seem to be having a good time in this warm, convivial bistro run by three brothers. The menu goes beyond the usual bistro classics to include such dishes as cold lobster and caviar consommé, cod fillet with spices, and excellent lamb of the Pyrénées. Prices are at the low end of this category. *9 blvd. de Port Royal, Métro: Les Gobelins, tel. 43–31–58–59. Reservations advised. Dress: casual. AE, DC, MC, V. Closed Sun., Mon., Christmas week, Aug.*

14th Arrondissement (Montparnasse)
See Left Bank Dining map

Expensive **La Cagouille.** This is one of the best fish restaurants in Paris.
★ Bear-like Gérard Allemandou moved his intimate and very successful *bistro à poissons* to this vast, modern space on the somewhat sterile place Brancusi several years ago. But his style remains the same: Few sauces or adornments mask the fresh, clean flavors of fish, from elegant sole and turbot to more pedestrian sardines and mackerel. Besides his excellent wine list, La Cagouille has the finest collection of Cognacs in the city. There's a large terrace for warm-weather dining. *10–12 pl. Brancusi, Métro: Gaité, tel. 43–22–09–01. Reservations advised. Dress: casual but elegant. AE, MC, V.*

Moderate **Contre-Allée.** This large, simply decorated restaurant is popular with a Left Bank crowd of students and professor-types. The interesting menu includes original choices, such as squid salad with mussels, and roast cod with parmesan. Homemade fresh pasta accompanies many dishes. A sidewalk terrace enlivens shady Denfert-Rochereau. The restaurant serves until 11:30 PM. *83 av. Denfert-Rochereau, Métro: Denfert-*

Rochereau, tel. 43–54–99–86. Reservations advised. Dress: casual. AE, DC, MC, V. Closed Sat. lunch.

La Coupole. This world-renowned, cavernous address in Montparnasse practically defines the term brasserie. Everyone from Left Bank intellectuals (Jean-Paul Sartre and Simone de Beauvoir were regulars) to bourgeois grandmothers come here. New owner Jean-Paul Bucher (of the Flo group of brasseries) had the sense to leave well enough alone when he restored it, simply polishing and cleaning the famous murals. Expect the usual brasserie menu, including perhaps the largest shellfish presentation in Paris, choucroute, and a big choice of desserts. The buffet breakfast from 7:30 to 10:30 daily is an excellent value. *102 blvd. du Montparnasse, Métro: Vavin, tel. 43–20–14–20. Reservations advised. Dress: casual. AE, DC, MC, V.*

★ **Le Pavillon Montsouris.** This bucolic building on the edge of Parc Montsouris was recently restored, and the pretty pastel interior and large terrace facing the park make for a charming spot on a sunny day. A multichoice, prix-fixe menu is a real bargain, and dishes prepared by the bright, young chef here are fresh and interesting. Try mussel soup with langoustines, *hachis Parmentier* (a kind of rich man's shepherd's pie) with foie gras and duck, and mango clafoutis. Service can slow down during peak times; go when you have time for a leisurely meal. *20 rue Gazan, Métro: RER Cité-Universitaire, tel. 45–88–38–52. Reservations advised. Dress: casual. DC, MC, V.*

Inexpensive **Le Bistrot du Dôme.** This cheery yellow fish bistro in Montparnasse belongs to the fancy and expensive Dôme, and benefits from that elegant brasserie's excellent sources of fish. The many seafood dishes are always very fresh and simply presented. Decor includes colorful tiles and pretty Italian glass light fixtures. Jovial service and a limited but affordable wine list add to the enjoyment. *1 rue Delambre, Métro: Vavin, tel. 43–35–32–00. Reservations advised. Dress: casual. MC, V.*

15th Arrondissement (Front de Seine)
See Left Bank Dining map

Expensive **Entre-Siècle.** Chef Olivier Simon is from northern France and is a true believer in that region's cooking. The flavorful, original cuisine here makes frequent use of beer, such as in eel *au vert* (in a spinach and sorrel sauce), trout in a beer aspic—even beer-based sabayon. Overseeing the dining room is Madame Simon, who will help you design a menu of regional specialties. About a dozen carefully chosen beers are offered, along with a wine selection. Prix-fixe menus are a good value at both lunch and dinner. *29 av. de Lowendal, Métro: Ségur, tel. 47–83–51–22. Reservations advised. Dress: casual but elegant. AE, MC, V. Closed Sat. lunch, Sun., Aug.*

Pierre Vedel. Burly Pierre Vedel's very Parisian bistro attracts entertainers and other fashionable patrons. Mr. Vedel's menu changes according to what looks good in the market, but generally includes Mediterranean-inspired dishes such as brandade, poached eggs with tomato sauce, *osso bucco* (braised veal shanks) with lemon, and peach soup with mint. *19 rue Duranton, Métro: Boucicaut, tel. 45–58–43–17. Reservations advised. Dress: casual chic. MC, V. Closed weekends.*

★ **Morot-Gaudry.** Located on top of a building near the Ecole Militaire, this popular address offers the luxury of well-spaced tables and an unusual outlook over Paris. Chef-owner Jean-Pierre Morot-Gaudry prepares a personalized cuisine that's a combination of classic and modern. Recommended are scallops with Jerusalem artichokes, veal blanquette, and chocolate mille-feuille with wild raspberries. The menu marries a different wine with each dish; the prix-fixe menu at lunch puts Morot-Gaudry in our Moderate range. *6 rue de la Cavalerie, Métro: Motte-Picquet, tel. 47–34–62–92. Reservations advised. Dress: casual. AE, MC, V. Closed weekends.*

Moderate **Le Barrail.** A favorite with staff from nearby *Le Monde*, this good neighborhood spot offers hospitable service in an unassuming setting. Impeccable ingredients go into such dishes as mushroom terrine, lobster with pepper risotto, and the increasingly hard-to-find potatoes *Dauphine* (potatoes mashed with pâté à choux and deep-fried) Ordering the prix-fixe menu here will put your meal in the Inexpensive range. *17 rue Falguière, Métro: Pasteur, tel. 43–22–42–61. Reservations advised. Dress: casual. AE, MC, V. Closed weekends, early Aug.*

Le Clos Morillons. The chef here has made many trips to the Far East, and his cuisine incorporates such oriental flavorings as sesame and ginger. But the menu is unmistakably French, with its delicious terrine of potato with foie gras, roast guinea fowl, and the all-chocolate dessert (several kinds of chocolate desserts on one plate). Added pluses are the professional service in the quiet dining room, an interesting wine list emphasizing Loire wines, and fixed-price menus at lunch and dinner that put the Clos in the low-Moderate and Inexpensive ranges. *50 rue Morillons, Métro: Convention, tel. 48–28–04–37. Reservations advised. Dress: casual. MC, V. Closed Sat. lunch, Sun.*

Inexpensive **L'Armoise.** There's excellent value-for-money in this quiet neighborhood restaurant near the Front de Seine development. Chef-owner Georges Outhier prepares one of the best veal livers in Paris, along with such treats as a delicious duck breast with honey and sea trout with spice butter. Madame Outhier is an attentive hostess in the salmon-pink dining rooms. *67 rue des Entrepreneurs, Métro: Charles Michel, tel. 45–79–03–31. Reservations advised. Dress: casual. MC, V. Closed Sat. lunch, Sun. mid-Feb., Aug.*

16th Arrondissement (Trocadéro/Bois de Boulogne)
See Right Bank Dining map

Very Expensive **Port Alma.** The charming welcome of Mme. Canal and the nau-
★ tical-blue and pastel decor of this very pretty restaurant will have you feeling festive from the start. Mr. Canal, the chef, is from Southwest France near Spain, and his cuisine is bursting with full, sunny flavors. Try turbot with thyme, sea bass in a salt crust with fennel gratin, or *bouillabaisse* (ordered ahead). Look forward to attentive, polite service, too. *10 av. de New York, Métro: Alma-Marceau, tel. 47–23–75–11. Reservations advised. Dress: casual. AE, DC, MC, V. Closed Sun., Aug.*

Le Pré Catalan. Dining beneath the chestnut trees on the terrace of this fanciful palace restaurant in the Bois de Boulogne is a Belle Epoque fantasy. Chef Roland Durand has brought new life to the cuisine of this venerable establishment, with elegant dishes such as risotto with langoustines, sweetbreads with morels and asparagus tips, and chocolate pastilla. The lunch menu is more reasonably priced. *Bois de Boulogne, rte. de Surèsnes, Métro: Porte Dauphine, tel. 45-24-55-58. Reservations essential. Jacket and tie advised. AE, DC, MC, V. Closed Sun. eve., Mon., mid-Feb.*

★ **Jamin/Robuchon.** Surely it's the hardest reservation to obtain in France. Chef-owner Joël Robuchon, though under 50, has already attained cult status, and his influence on cooks around the globe is great. Under his inspired vision, everything from John Dory with ginger and cream of cauliflower with caviar to saddle of lamb in a salt crust and even pig's head become visual and gustatory revelations. Antoine Hernandez, chef-sommelier, is a gentle guide through the impressive wine list, and service in general is attentive and professional. The pretty, pastel dining room is less impressive than the cuisine; the restaurant is due to move into its own *hôtel particulier* in the future. *32 rue de Longchamp, Métro: Trocadéro, tel. 47-27-12-27. Reservations essential. Jacket required, jacket and tie advised. MC, V. Closed weekends, July.*

★ **Le Vivarois.** Chef-owner Claude Peyrot is one of the most inspired and creative of contemporary French chefs, though his cooking can be uneven. He is a master with fish and puff pastry, his *bavarois* of red bell pepper (a creamy, molded concoction) is oft-imitated, and his original dishes shine: scallops with sesame and ginger, *rissolette* of lamb's feet with artichokes and basil, and chocolate soufflé with chicory ice cream. Service is not always up to par. *192 av. Victor Hugo, Métro: Rue de la Pompe, tel. 47-04-04-31. Reservations advised. Dress: casual. AE, DC, MC, V. Closed weekends, Aug.*

Expensive **Le Relais du Parc.** Facing an interior garden in a luxury hotel in
★ Paris's posh 16th arrondissement is the long-awaited second restaurant of Joël Robuchon of Jamin fame (*see above*). The menu is a mix of original, sparkling creations such as *croustillant* of salmon and lacy fried potatoes, and substantial, traditional fare such as the skate with cabbage and the succulent beef tail with carrots. The warm *tarte fine* of apples is fabulous. Prices are lower and service less formal than at Jamin, but this is still a most elegant restaurant. Though larger and easier to book than the original, plan at least a month ahead for dinner. *55 av. Raymond Poincaré, Métro: Trocadéro, tel. 44-05-66-10. Reservations essential. Dress: casual. AE, MC, V.*

Moderate **La Butte Chaillot.** This, the latest of star-chef Guy Savoy's fashionable bistros, is the largest and most impressive: A dramatic iron staircase connects two levels, decorated in turquoise and earth colors. Dining here is part theater, as the *à la mode* clientele will attest, but it's not all show: The very good food includes tasty raviolis of Royans (tiny cheese pillows), roast chicken with mashed potatoes, and stuffed veal breast with rosemary. A wide sidewalk terrace fronts tree-shaded av. Kléber. *112 av. Kléber, Métro: Trocadéro, tel. 47-27-88-88. Reservations advised. Dress: casual chic. AE, MC, V.*

Bistrot de l'Etoile Lauriston. Another bistro from Guy Savoy (*see above*), this attractive, subdued establishment features the intelligent yet homey cuisine of Chef William Ledeuil. His full-flavored dishes include stuffed, gratinéed zucchini, raviolis with *pistou* and lamb sautéed with rosemary. An upscale crowd includes many Americans. *19 rue Lauriston, Métro: Charles de*

Gaulle, tel. 40–67–11–16. Reservations advised. Dress: casual. AE, MC, V. Closed Sun.

Chez Géraud. Cherubic, jolly Géraud Rongier runs this fairly new bistro in the chic Passy district. Dishes such as salad of preserved duck gizzards, roast pigeon with Port sauce, and bitter chocolate cake exemplify the robust cuisine here. Rongier's knowledge of wine is vast, and his eclectic wine list has everything from great chateaux to little-known regional bottles. Notice the pretty tile mural at the back of the dining room. *31 rue Vital, Métro: Passy, tel. 45–20–33–00. Reservations advised. Dress: casual. MC, V. Closed weekends, Aug.*

Inexpensive **L'Auberge du Bonheur.** Food is not the reason to come to this informal spot behind the Grande Cascade restaurant in the Bois de Boulogne. Instead, come in warm weather to dine on the huge gravel terrace, surrounded by chestnut and plane trees, wisteria, and bamboo. Order simply: Salads and grilled meats are best. *Allée Longchamp, Métro: Porte Dauphine, tel. 42–24–10–17. Reservations advised. Dress: casual. MC, V. Open daily Apr.–Oct.; lunch only Sun.–Fri. Nov.–Mar.*

17th Arrondissement (Monceau/Clichy)
See Right Bank Dining map

Very Expensive **Amphyclès.** Young chef-owner Philippe Groult had already
★ made a name for himself before opening this much-anticipated restaurant a few years ago. Since then Groult, trained under Joël Robuchon (*see above*), has not disappointed, and his exciting menu includes cauliflower soup with caviar, herb salad, and duck with coriander and orange. Service is excellent, and Amphyclès is one of the few grand Parisian restaurants that still proffers desserts from a pastry trolley. *78 av. des Ternes, Métro: Porte Maillot, tel. 40–68–01–01. Reservations advised. Dress: casual. AE, DC, MC, V. Closed Sun., July.*

Apicius. Chef-owner Jean-Pierre Vigato excels at mixing the humble with the rarified, as he does here in dishes from duck *tourte* (pie) and pig's foot to roasted sweetbreads and Bresse chicken cooked in salt. A good-looking crowd occupies the airy, flower-filled dining rooms. *122 av. de Villiers, Métro: Pereire, tel. 43–80–19–66. Reservations advised. Dress: casual but elegant. AE, MC, V. Closed weekends and Aug.*

Guy Savoy. Guy Savoy is one of a handful of top chefs in Paris today, and his four bistros have not managed to distract him too much from his handsome green, luxury restaurant near the Arc de Triomphe. Savoy's oysters in aspic, sea bass with spices, and pigeon with lentils reveal the magnitude of his talent. His *mille-feuille* is a contemporary classic. *18 rue Troyon, Métro: Ternes, tel. 43–80–40–61. Reservations advised. Dress: casual. AE, V. Closed Sat. lunch (and dinner in summer), Sun.*

Expensive **Augusta.** In this fine fish restaurant in a prosperous corner of the 17th, the menu combines fish classics with chef Lionel Maître's original creations. Sample mussels with garlic butter, bouillabaisse with potatoes, or langoustines with vanilla. At least one meat dish is always offered. The comfortable dining room invites lingering. *98 rue de Toqueville, Métro: Malesherbes, tel. 47–63–39–97. Reservations advised. Dress: casual but elegant. MC, V. Closed Sat. lunch, Sun., Aug.*

Le Graindorge. Chef-owner Bernard Broux, formerly at the immensely popular Trou Gascon (*see* 12th Arrondissement, *above*), recently opened his own establishment. Here he prepares an original mix of the cuisines of Southwest France and of his native Flanders. Try his succulent eel terrine in a delicious herb aspic, pork cheeks with juniper, and caramelized brioche *galette* (pancake). Mme. Broux oversees the pleasant dining rooms, and can help you choose one of the fine beers offered here. *15 rue de l'Arc-de-Triomphe, Métro: Charles De Gaulle/ Etoile, tel. 47–54–00–28. Reservations advised. Dress: casual but neat. AE, MC, V. Closed Sat. lunch, Sun.*

Moderate **La Niçoise.** Posters of Nice adorn the simple upstairs dining room, and Mediterranean flavors emerge from the kitchen at this enjoyable Niçoise oasis. Try ricotta ravioli with basil, or *petits farcis Niçois* (stuffed vegetables). Moderately priced Provençal wines help keep prices down. *4 rue Pierre Demours, Métro: Ternes, tel. 45–74–42–41. Reservations advised. Dress: casual. AE, DC, MC, V. Closed Sat. lunch, Sun.*

Au Petit Colombier. It's a perennial favorite among Parisians, who come to eat comforting *cuisine bourgeoise* in the warm dining rooms, accented with wood and bright copper. Menu standards include *gâteau* of pike, milk-fed lamb chop *en cocotte*, and *coq au vin*. Service is friendly and unpretentious. It's open for Sunday dinner. *42 rue des Acacias, Métro: Ternes, tel. 43–80–28–54. Reservations advised. Dress: casual. AE, MC, V. Closed Sat., Sun. lunch, mid-Aug.*

La Rôtisserie d'Armaillé. Admire the handsome oak paneling, cranberry and green upholstery, and the very Parisian crowd at star-chef Jacques Cagna's third restaurant. The prix-fixe menu has many tempting choices, among them *tagliatelles* (flat noodles) with shellfish, *pastilla* of guinea hen, and a terrific chocolate cake. Wines are a little pricey. *6 rue d'Armaillé, Métro: Argentine, tel. 42–27–19–20. Reservations advised. Dress: casual. AE, DC, MC, V. Closed Sat. lunch, Sun.*

La Table de Pierre. The Louis XVI–style setting is somewhat surprising in this, one of the best Basque restaurants in Paris. Such dishes as peppers stuffed with cod brandade, *émincé* (thin slices) of squid, duck confit, and *gâteau Basque* are full of the colors and flavors of the *Pays Basque*. Owner Pierre Darrieumerlou is an agreeable host. *116 blvd. Pereire, Métro: Pereire, tel. 43–80–88–68. Reservations advised. Dress: casual. MC, V. Closed Sat. lunch, Aug.*

Inexpensive **L'Huitrier.** Come here if you share the Parisians' craving for oysters. Owner Alain Bunel will describe the different kinds available, and you can follow these with any of several fish specials offered daily. The excellent cheeses are from the outstanding shop of Roger Alléosse. Blond wood and cream colors prevail. *16 rue Saussier-Leroy, Métro: Ternes, tel. 40–54–83–44. Reservations advised. Dress: casual. MC, V.*

18th Arrondissement (Montmartre)
See Right Bank Dining map

Very Expensive **A. Beauvilliers.** Pickwickian owner Edouard Carlier is a born party-giver, and his flower-filled restaurant is one of the most festive in Paris. The three dining rooms are filled with his personal collection of paintings and valuable *bibelots*, and a tiny, vine-covered terrace makes for delightful summer dining. Chefs here come and go, but Mr. Carlier maintains quality, serving both original creations and reinterpreted classics. Recommended are the red mullet *en escabèche* (in a peppery marinade) and foie gras, lobster, and sweetbread *tourte*. The mouth-puckering lemon tart is not to be missed. One drawback: Service can be distant if you are not known. *52 rue Lamarck, Métro: Lamarck-Caulaincourt, tel. 42-54-54-42. Reservations essential. Jacket and tie advised. AE, MC, V. Closed Sun., Mon. lunch, and Sept.*

Inexpensive **Aux Négotiants.** This wine bar in Montmartre has zero decor, but gives a warm welcome to its mix of neighborhood regulars and well-heeled clientele. One or two hot plates are offered daily; otherwise, enjoy the terrines, cheeses, and other simple choices, served with affordable wines by the glass or bottle. *27 rue Lambert, Métro: Château Rouge, tel. 46-06-15-11. No reservations. Dress: casual. No credit cards. Closed weekends; dinner served Tues., Thurs., and Fri. only.*

19th Arrondissement (La Villette)
See Right Bank Dining map

Expensive **Au Cochon d'Or.** This old-fashioned restaurant on the outskirts of northeast Paris serves meat and plenty of it—fitting for its location near a former Paris slaughterhouse. Everything bespeaks sturdy tradition here, from the overblown decor to the rich, filling cuisine—pepper steak, souffléed potatoes, and crêpes flambéed in Calvados. The faithful serving staff and the crowd of regulars heighten the mood of old-time Paris. The restaurant is convenient to the Parc de la Villette and the Cité des Sciences et de l'Industrie. *192 av. Jean Jaurès, Métro: Porte de Pantin, tel. 42-45-46-46. Reservations advised. Dress: casual. AE, DC, MC, V.*

Le Pavillon Puebla. This turn-of-the-century building in the spectacular Parc des Buttes-Chaumont is a bit hard to find, but feels wonderfully removed from the bustle of the city. Chef Vergès prepares an original, flavorful cuisine, including oyster ravioli with curry, lamb tournedos with truffle juice, and *gâteau* of crêpes and apples. Mme. Vergès oversees the elegant dining rooms and large terrace. *Parc Buttes-Chaumont (entrance rue Botzaris), Métro: Buttes-Chaumont, tel. 42-08-92-62. Reservations advised. Dress: casual but elegant. MC, V. Closed Sun., Mon., mid-Aug.*

20th Arrondissement (Père Lachaise)
See Right Bank Dining map

Inexpensive **A La Courtille.** This large wine bar–restaurant with a trendy following has a spectacular view of Paris over the new Parc de Belleville. (Notice the black and white photos of the quaint old Belleville neighborhood before the wrecking ball.) The kitchen prepares modernized versions of bistro classics and fresh, light creations such as marinated salmon with dill, roast cod with zucchini, and veal liver. An excellent wine list offers many choices by the glass. There's a large terrace, and service until 11 PM. *1 rue des Envierges, Métro: Pyrénées, tel. 46-36-51-59. Reservations advised. Dress: casual chic. MC, V.*

6 Lodging

Updated by
David Downie

Winding staircases, geranium pots in the windows, a concierge who seems to have stepped from a 19th-century novel—all of these still exist in abundance in Paris hotels. So do palatial rooms with marble baths, Belle Epoque lobbies, and a polished staff at your beck and call. In Paris, unlike some international cities, there are wonderful hotels for every taste and budget. The Paris Tourist Office's annual lodging guide lists well over 1,000 member hotels in the city's 20 arrondissements. The true count, though, is closer to 2,000—some 80,000 rooms in all.

Our criteria when selecting the hotels reviewed below, were quality, location, and—where possible—character. Few chain hotels are listed, since they usually lack the charm and authenticity found in typical Parisian lodgings. Similarly, we do not list many hotels in outlying arrondissements (the 10th to the 15th, the 18th to the 20th) because these are far from the sites most visitors want to see. Generally, there are more Right Bank hotels offering luxury—or at any rate formality—than there are on the Left Bank, where hotels tend to be smaller but often loaded with character. The Right Bank's 1st, 2nd, and 8th arrondissements are still the most sought-after for lodging, and prices here reflect this. Less-expensive alternatives on the Right Bank are the fashionable Marais quarter (3rd and 4th arrondissements), where hotels have mushroomed in recent years, and the 11th and 12th, near the Opéra Bastille.

Once upon a time, obvious high and low seasons existed in Paris. Nowadays, the city is as likely to be overrun in November or February as in summer. The French in general and the Parisians in particular take their vacations in July and August, so most of the trade fairs and conventions that fill hotels the rest of the year come to a halt at this time, freeing up rooms for tourists. The French Tourist Office publishes a calendar showing peak periods.

Despite the huge choice of hotels here, you should always reserve well in advance, especially if you're determined to stay in a specific hotel. You can do this by telephoning ahead, then writing or faxing for confirmation. If you are asked to send a deposit, make sure you discuss refund policies before mailing your check or money order. Always ask for some form of written confirmation of your reservation, detailing the duration of your stay, the price, location and type of your room (single or double, twin beds or double), and bathroom (*see below*).

As part of a general upgrade of the city's hotels in recent years, dozens of well-worn, inexpensive Paris lodgings have disappeared, replaced by good-value establishments in the lower-to-middle price ranges. Despite widespread improvement, however, many Paris hotels still have idiosyncracies—some charming, others less so. Rooms are not always perfectly square, floors not always perfectly flat. The standard French double bed is slightly smaller than its American counterpart. In many smaller hotels, you'll find a long bolster (*traversin*) instead of pillows (*oreillers*). (If you prefer pillows, request them when you are shown the room.) Air-conditioning is uncommon in all but the most luxurious hotels. (Paris's hot-weather season doesn't last long.)

The most enduring example of quirkiness is French plumbing, which sometimes looks like avant-garde sculpture. Shared toilets or bathrooms down the hall, though increasingly rare, are still found in many modest establishments. Never assume that what is billed as a bathroom (*salle de bain*) will necessarily contain a tub. Some rooms have toilets (what the French call *wc* or *cabinet de toilet*), some have *bidets* only—but no tub or shower. Others have a shower but no toilet, and still others have only washstands. Our reviews indicate the number of rooms with full bath facilities including tub (*baignoire*) or shower (*douche*), and number of rooms with shared baths. Make sure you know what you are getting when you book.

Almost all Paris hotels charge extra for breakfast, with prices ranging from 30 francs to over 100 francs per person in luxury establishments. Hotels generally assume you will be having breakfast there, and will add the breakfast charge to your bill automatically. If you don't want to have breakfast at the hotel, say so when you check in. For anything more than the standard Continental breakfast of *cafe au lait* (coffee with hot milk) and *baguette* (bread) or croissants, the price will be higher. Some hotels have especially pleasant breakfast areas, and we have noted this where applicable. Luxury hotels often have restaurants, but finding a restaurant is rarely a problem in Paris.

You'll notice that the French government grades hotels from four-star deluxe to one star, and that the stars appear on a shield on the hotel's facade. Theoretically, the ratings depend on amenities and price. They can be misleading, however, since many hotels prefer to be understarred for tax reasons. Many two- and three-star establishments offer excellent price-to-quality ratios. We list hotels by price, but often a hotel in a certain price category will have a few rooms that are less expensive; it's worthwhile to ask. Rates must be posted in all rooms, and all extra charges clearly shown.

Unless otherwise stated, the hotels reviewed below have elevators, and rooms have TVs and telephones. Additional facilities, such as restaurants and health clubs, are listed at the end of each review.

The following credit card abbreviations are used: AE, American Express; DC, Diners Club; MC, MasterCard; and V, Visa.

Highly recommended lodgings are indicated by a star ★.

Category	Cost*
Very Expensive	over 1,200 frs
Expensive	750 frs–1,200 frs
Moderate	450 frs–750 frs
Inexpensive	under 450 frs

* *All prices are for a standard double room, including tax and service.*

1st Arrondissement (Louvre)
See Right Bank Lodging map

Very Expensive
★

Inter-Continental. An aura of elegant luxury reigns throughout this exquisite late-19th-century hotel, one of the largest of the city's top hotels. It was designed by the architect of the Paris Opéra, Garnier. Three of its gilt and stuccoed public rooms are official historic monuments. Spacious guest rooms overlook

Left Bank Lodging

Acacias
St-Germain, **15**

Aramis-
St-Germain, **14**

Champ de Mars, **3**

Collège de France, **28**

Duc de Saint-Simon, **6**

Elysa Luxembourg, **25**

Esméralda, **29**

Grands Ecoles, **23**

Hôtel d'Angleterre, **9**

Istria, **18**

Jardin des Plantes, **22**

Kensington, **1**

L'Abbaye
St-Germain, **13**

Lenox, **16**

L'Hôtel, **10**

Marronniers, **11**

Midi, **19**

Oriental, **27**

Pantheon, **24**

Parc Montsouris, **20**

Pavillon, **2**

Relais Christine, **12**

Résidence les
Gobelins, **21**

Royal, **17**

Saints-Pères, **8**

Solférino, **5**

Sorbonne, **26**

Université, **7**

Varenne, **4**

Louvre

1er M

R. de Rivoli

Blvd. Sébastopol

R. Beaubourg

4e

R. de Rivoli

Pont Royal

Pont du Carrousel

Pont des Arts

Pont Neuf

R. du Change

Pont d'Arcade

Quai des Célestins

7

9

10

R. Jacob

R. Mazarine

11

12

R. St-André des Arts

Ile de la Cité

Notre Dame

Ile St-Louis

R. des Sts-Pères

Blvd. St-Germain

Pl. St-Michel

Quai de Montebello

Pont de la Tournelle

Pont de Sully

8

R. du Four

29

R. de Rennes

Pl. St. Sulpice

R. St-Jacques

28

Pl. Maubert

Quai St-Bernard

13

Pl. de l'Odéon

26

R. des Ecoles

R. Monge

27

R. de Vaugirard

R. Cujas

Pl. du Panthéon

5e

R. Guynemer

24

23

Pl. de la Contrescarpe

22

Jardin des Plantes

R. d'Assas

Jardin du Luxembourg

25

Blvd. St-Michel

R. Gay Lussac

R. Mouffetard

Pl. Monge

R. Monge

Montparnasse

6e

18

R. Claude Bernard

Blvd. Raspail

14e

19

20

21

Blvd. St-Marcel

quiet inner courtyards. In summer, breakfast on the patio is a delicious experience. Service is impeccable. *3 rue de Castiglione, 75001, Métro: Concorde, tel. 44–77–11–11, fax 44–77–14–60. 380 rooms with bath, 70 suites with bath. English spoken. Facilities: 2 restaurants, bar, patio. AE, DC, MC, V.*

★ **Meurice.** Once part of the Grand Metropolitan chain, the Meurice, one of the finest hotels in the city, is now owned by the Italian CIGA chain. The sumptuous Versailles-style first-floor salons have all been renovated, and the bedrooms are adorned with Persian carpets. Most bathrooms are done in pink marble. The hotel's fabled restaurant opens on to the hotel garden. You'll have to book well in advance if you want one of the few double rooms or one of the suites overlooking the Tuileries Gardens, but you won't be disappointed by the opulence and plushness of the others. *228 rue de Rivoli, 75001, Métro: Tuileries, tel. 42–60–38–60, fax 49–27–94–97. 148 rooms with bath, 40 suites with bath. English spoken. Facilities: restaurant. AE, DC, MC, V.*

★ **Ritz.** Surrounded by the city's finest jewelers, the Ritz is the crowning gem on the newly sparkling place Vendôme. Festooned with gilt and ormolu, dripping with crystal chandeliers and tapestries, and swathed in heavy silk, this 96-year-old monument to the hotelier's art is the epitome of fin-de-siècle Paris. Yet despite the elaborate neo-Rococo decoration ornamenting every surface, and an air of aristocratic privilege that might prove overwhelming to some, the atmosphere is unexpectedly intimate. The suites are legendary for their enormity and opulence, but every room is uniquely decorated with antiques and reproductions of furniture copied from museum collections. Worth seeking out is the fabulous lower-level swimming pool, with cove ceilings, bucolic frescoes, and towering columns and piers. The Espadon is one of Paris's finest restaurants. There's warm-weather seating in the charming adjacent garden. *15 pl. Vendôme, 75001, Métro: Madeleine, tel. 42–60–38–30, fax 42–86–00–91. 142 rooms and 45 suites, all with bath. English spoken. Facilities: 2 restaurants, 2 bars, indoor pool, health club, shopping gallery, cooking school, beauty salon. AE, DC, MC, V.*

Expensive **Normandy.** The Belle Epoque decor, warm welcome, and central location near the Palais-Royal and theaters make this hotel a fine choice. The comfortable rooms are individually decorated. Some are much smaller than others, and a handful of the least expensive have shower only. A wonderful wood-paneled bar with roaring fireplace is frequented by hotel guests and well-heeled theatergoers. *7 rue de l'Echelle, 75001, Métro: Pyramides, tel. 42–60–30–21, fax 42–60–45–81. 116 rooms with bath, 6 with shower, 7 suites with bath. English spoken. Facilities: restaurant (closed weekends), bar. AE, DC, MC, V.*

★ **Régina.** Set in the handsome place des Pyramides, this Art Nouveau gem stuffed with fine antiques is pleasantly old-fashioned. Request a room overlooking the Louvre and the Tuileries Gardens. *2 pl. des Pyramides, 75001, Métro: Tuileries, tel. 42–60–31–10, fax 40–15–95–16. 120 rooms and 10 suites, all with bath. English spoken. Facilities: restaurant (closed August), bar. AE, DC, MC, V.*

Moderate **Britannique.** A friendly, family-owned hotel in a restored 19th-century building, the Britannique has a handsome winding staircase and nicely decorated, soundproofed rooms. Ask for a

American Express offers Travelers Cheques built for two.

American Express® Cheques *for Two*. The first Travelers Cheques that allow either of you to use them because both of you have signed them. And only one of you needs to be present to purchase them.

Cheques *for Two* are accepted anywhere regular American Express Travelers Cheques are, which is just about everywhere. So stop by your bank, AAA* or any American Express Travel Service Office and ask for Cheques *for Two*.

AMERICAN EXPRESS **Travelers Cheques** ®

room on one of the top three floors. *20 av. Victoria, 75001, Métro: Chatelet, tel. 42–33–74–59, fax 42–33–82–65. 25 rooms with bath, 15 with shower. English spoken. AE, DC, V.*

Londres Stockholm. An appealing combination of character and comfort singles out this small hotel. The lobby has exposed oak beams, statues in niches, and rustic-looking stone walls. The freshly repainted, rough-cast white walls in the rooms are off-set by deep red carpeting. There's no restaurant or bar, but limited room service is available. *13 rue St-Roch, 75001, Métro: Pyramides, tel. 42–60–15–62, fax 42–60–16–00. 29 rooms with bath, 2 with shower. English spoken. AE, MC, V.*

Tamise. Just off the rue de Rivoli and Tuileries Gardens, this small hotel was once a private town house. Modestly luxurious, it boasts many English antiques in its charming rooms. *4 rue Alger, 75001, Métro: Tuileries, tel: 42–60–51–54, fax 42–86–89–97. 15 rooms with bath, 4 with shower. English spoken. DC, V.*

Inexpensive **Lille.** You won't find a less expensive base for exploring the Louvre than this hotel, located a short distance from the Cour Carrée. The facade got a face-lift a few years ago, but the some-what shabby interior and minimal plumbing down long corri-dors was not upgraded. Hence the rock-bottom prices. Still, the Lille is a slice of Old Paris. There's no elevator, and not all rooms have TVs or phones. *8 rue du Pélican, 75001, Métro: Palais-Royal, tel. 42–33–33–42. 5 rooms with shower, 8 with shared bath. Some English spoken. No credit cards.*

2nd Arrondissement (Stock Exchange)
See Right Bank Lodging map

Very Expensive **Westminster.** This former private mansion was built in the mid-19th century on what was then the most elegant street between the Opéra and place Vendôme. Tastefully renovated several years ago, the hotel has preserved its gracious turn-of-the-cen-tury atmosphere, with marble fireplaces, chandeliers, and par-quet floors. Air-conditioning has been added, and the large bathrooms are clad with gray marble. The pleasant piano bar is a popular rendezvous. The hotel's restaurant serves excellent classic French cuisine. *13 rue de la Paix, 75002, Métro: Opéra, tel. 42–61–57–46, fax 42–60–30–66. 102 rooms and 20 suites, all with bath. English spoken. Facilities: parking lot (on pl. Vendôme), restaurant, tearoom, bar. AE, DC, V.*

Expensive **★** **Gaillon-Opéra.** The oak beams, stone walls, and marble tiles of the Gaillon-Opéra single it out as one of the most charming ho-tels in the Opéra neighborhood. The plants throughout and a flower-filled patio also delight. There's a small bar but no res-taurant. *9 rue Gaillon, 75002, Métro: Opéra, tel. 47–42–47–74, fax 47–42–01–23. 26 rooms and 1 suite, all with bath. English spoken. Facilities: bar. AE, DC, MC, V.*

Moderate **Choiseul-Opéra.** The historic, classical facade of the Choiseul-Opéra, located between the Opéra and place Vendôme, belies the strictly functional interior. The entrance hall, salon, and bar were remodeled in 1992, and many rooms were freshened up. Service is relaxed but efficient, and the staff are happy to try out their English on guests. There's no restaurant or bar. *1 rue Daunou, 75002, Métro: Opéra, tel. 42–61–70–41, fax 42–86–91–96. 30 rooms with bath, 15 with shower, 2 suites with bath. English spoken. AE, DC, MC, V.*

3rd Arrondissement (Le Marais/Beaubourg)
See Right Bank Lodging map

Very Expensive
★ **Pavillon de la Reine.** The best hotel in the Marais, it's set around two flower-filled courtyards behind the historic Queen's Pavilion on the 17th-century place des Vosges. Although this cozy mansion looks old, it was actually reconstructed from scratch in 1986 following original plans and using period timbers, rough-hewn paving stones, Louis XIII fireplaces, and antiques. Ask for a duplex with French windows overlooking the first courtyard (there are no rooms overlooking the place des Vosges). Breakfast is served in a vaulted cellar. *28 pl. des Vosges, 75003, Métro: Chemin Vert, tel. 42–77–96–40, fax 42–77–63–06. 31 rooms with bath, 24 suites with bath. English spoken. Facilities: cellar dining room, parking. AE, DC, MC, V.*

Moderate **Hôtel du Marais.** On the edge of the Marais, this small hotel in a restored old building is near the Bastille Opéra and the Picasso Museum. For extremely reasonable (borderline inexpensive) rates you get amenities generally reserved for more expensive hotels, such as minibars and color TVs in rooms. Some rooms have exposed beams; all are functional, soundproofed, and clean. *2 bis rue des Commines, 75003, Métro: Filles-du-Calvaire, tel. 48–87–78–27, fax 48–87–09–01. 12 rooms with bath, 27 with shower. Some English spoken. Facilities: minibar in rooms. AE, DC, MC, V.*

4th Arrondissement (Le Marais/Ile St-Louis)
See Right Bank Lodging map

Expensive **Bretonnerie.** This small, three-star hotel is located on a tiny street in the Marais, a few minutes' walk from the Beaubourg. The snug rooms are decorated in Louis XIII style, but vary considerably in size from spacious to cramped. Some boast antiques, beamed ceilings, and marble-clad bathrooms. There's a bar and breakfast room in the vaulted cellar. The smallest rooms are moderately priced. *22 rue Ste-Croix-de-la-Bretonnerie, 75004, Métro: Hôtel de Ville, tel. 48–87–77–63, fax 42–77–26–78. 30 rooms with bath, 1 with shower, 1 suite with bath. English spoken. Facilities: bar and breakfast room. MC, V. Closed late-July to late-August.*

★ **Deux-Iles.** This converted 17th-century mansion on the Ile St-Louis has long won plaudits for charm and comfort. Flowers and plants are scattered around the stunning hall. The fabric-hung rooms, though small, have exposed beams and are fresh and airy. Ask for a room overlooking the little garden courtyard. There's no restaurant, but drinks are served in the cellar bar until 1 AM. The lounge is dominated by a fine chimneypiece and doubles as a second bar. If the hotel is full, go to the Lutèce *(see below)* down the road; it belongs to the same owners. *59 rue St-Louis-en-l'Ile, 75004, Métro: Pont-Marie, tel. 43–26–13–35, fax 43–29–60–25. 8 rooms with bath, 9 with shower. English spoken. Facilities: bar (closed Sun.). No credit cards.*

Lutèce. You'll find the same friendly reception, fabric-hung rooms, and clean, whitewashed stone walls here as at the neighboring Deux-Iles *(see above)*. Try for rooms on the top floor; they offer terrific views over rooftops to the dome of the Panthéon. There's no restaurant, but guests are welcome at the bar of the Deux-Iles. *65 rue St-Louis-en-l'Ile, 75004, Métro:*

Pont-Marie, tel. 43–26–23–52, fax 43–29–60–25. 13 rooms with bath, 10 with shower. English spoken. No credit cards.

St-Louis. The St-Louis is another of the Ile St-Louis's converted 17th-century town houses. Antique furniture and oil paintings decorate the public areas. The bedrooms are elegantly simple, with exposed beams and stone walls. Blue-gray or light brown tiles adorn bathrooms. Breakfast is served in the atmospheric cellar. *75 rue St-Louis-en-l'Ile, 75004, Métro: Pont-Marie, tel. 46–34–04–80, fax 46–34–02–13. 15 rooms with bath, 6 with shower. English spoken. No credit cards.*

Moderate **Axial Beaubourg.** Opened in 1990, this three-star hotel in a 17th-century building is one of the better deals going in the Marais. There are beamed ceilings in the lobby and in the six first-floor rooms; decor is functional. The clientele is a mix of Europeans and Americans. The Beaubourg and Picasso Museums are a five-minute walk away. *11 rue du Temple, 75004, Métro: Hôtel de Ville, tel. 42–72–72–22, fax 42–72–03–53. 34 rooms with bath, 5 with shower. English spoken. AE, V.*

★ **Place des Vosges.** A loyal American clientele swears by this small, historic hotel located on a charming street just off the exquisite square of the same name. Oak-beamed ceilings and rough-hewn stone in public areas and some of the guest rooms add to the atmosphere. Ask for the top-floor room, the hotel's largest, with a view of Marais rooftops. Some rooms, the size of walk-in closets, are inexpensive. There's a welcoming little breakfast room. *12 rue de Birague, 75004, Métro: Bastille, tel. 42–72–60–46, fax 42–72–02–64. 5 rooms with bath, 11 with shower. English spoken. AE, DC, V.*

Hôtel du 7e Art. The decor of this small Marais two-star hotel is 1940s–60s Hollywood movies, complete with posters and photographs (the name means "Seventh Art," what the French call filmmaking). Rooms have brown carpets and beige walls; they're small and sparsely furnished, but clean and quiet. The clientele tends to be young, and Americans are made to feel welcome. Breakfast and snacks are served in handsome ground-floor or cellar rooms with stone walls, and there's also a pleasant bar. No elevator. *20 rue St-Paul, 75004, Métro: St-Paul, tel. 42–77–04–03, fax 42–77–69–10. 6 rooms with bath, 15 with shower, 2 suites with bath. English spoken. Facilities: bar. AE, DC, MC, V.*

★ **Vieux Marais.** As its name implies, this charming, two-star hotel lies in the heart of the Marais. The rooms and bathrooms are simply decorated in light, refreshing colors and are impeccably clean. Try to get a room overlooking the courtyard. Breakfast is served in a pretty lounge, and a second lounge with a TV is located in the cellar. The staff is exceptionally courteous. *8 rue de Plâtre, 75004, Métro: Hôtel de Ville, tel. 42–78–47–22, fax 42–78–34–32. 22 rooms with bath, 8 with shower. English spoken. Facilities: TV lounge. MC, V.*

Inexpensive **Castex.** This family-run, two-star hotel in a 19th-century build-
★ ing is a real find. It was remodeled from top to bottom in 1989, and rooms are squeaky clean. The decor is strictly functional, but the extremely friendly owners and rock-bottom prices mean the Castex is often fully booked months ahead. There's a large American clientele. The eight least expensive rooms, two per floor, share toilets on the immaculate, well-lit landings. There's no elevator, and TV is in the lobby only. *5 rue Castex, 75004, Métro: Bastille, tel. 42–72–31–52, fax 42–72–57–91. 4 rooms with bath, 23 with shower. English spoken. MC, V.*

5th Arrondissement (Latin Quarter)
See Left Bank Lodging map

Expensive **Elysa Luxembourg.** The Elysa is what the French call an *hôtel*
★ *de charme*. Though the building is not large, most rooms are
surprisingly spacious, and all are exquisitely maintained and
refurbished yearly. Cream-colored furniture is set against pale
blue or pink fabrics. You'll find a minibar in every room and a
breakfast lounge serving Continental or buffet breakfasts. The
Elysa is one of the rare hotels in the city with a sauna. Rooms
with shower are moderately priced. *6 rue Gay Lussac, 75005,
Métro: Luxembourg, tel. 43–25–31–74, fax 46–34–56–27. 25
rooms with bath, 5 with shower. English spoken. Facilities:
sauna. AE, DC, MC, V.*

Moderate **Collège de France.** The Collège de France offers peace and
quiet in the heart of the Latin Quarter. Rooms are simply decorated in pale greens and light browns. The prettiest three—often booked months ahead—have oak beams and are up on the
sixth floor under the eaves. *7 rue Thénard, 75005, Métro:
Maubert-Mutualité, tel. 43–26–78–36, fax 46–34–58–29. 23
rooms with bath, 6 with shower. Some English spoken. AE.*

★ **Esméralda.** Lovers of small, charming Parisian hotels will want
to stay at this simple lodging, where the rooms are a little dusty
but positively exude timeworn Gallic charm. Esméralda is set in
a fine 17th-century building opposite Notre Dame (request a
room with a view), near Square Viviani. All the rooms are
small—some are midget-size. Many have copies of 17th-centu-
ry furniture. Those with showers on the landing are inexpensive. *4 rue St-Julien-le-Pauvre, 75005, Métro: St-Michel, tel.
43–54–19–20, fax 40–51–00–68. 16 rooms with bath, 3 with
shower on the landing. Some English spoken. No credit cards.*

★ **Grands Ecoles.** Recently upgraded from no stars to two, this
delightful hotel in three small old buildings is set far off the
street in a beautiful garden. There are parquet floors, antiques, and a piano in the breakfast area. Most rooms have
beige carpets and flowery wallpaper. You won't find a quieter,
more charming hotel for the price. There's a faithful American
clientele, including some backpackers. The rooms with bathroom facilities on the well-lit landings are inexpensive. *75 rue
du Cardinal Lemoine, 75005, Métro: Cardinal Lemoine, tel.
43–26–79–23, fax 43–25–28–15. 29 rooms with bath, 10 with
shower, 9 with shared bath. English spoken. V.*

Jardin des Plantes. Across the street from the lovely Jardin des
Plantes botanical gardens on the edge of the Latin Quarter,
this pleasant two-star hotel offers botanical-theme decor and
very reasonable prices. There's a fifth-floor terrace where you
can breakfast or sunbathe in summer, and a sauna and ironing
room in the cellar. *5 rue Linné, 75005, Métro: Monge, tel. 47–
07–06–20, fax 47–07–62–74. 29 rooms with bath, 4 with shower. English spoken. Facilities: sauna, bar-tearoom, terrace.
AE, DC, MC, V.*

★ **Pantheon.** In a handsome 18th-century building facing the Pantheon, this excellent three-star hotel has prices that range from
moderate to expensive. Some of the charming rooms have exposed beams, balconies, and stunning views; a vaulted breakfast room and impressive lobby are additional attractions. The
desk staff is very helpful. *19 pl. du Pantheon, 75005, Métro: St-
Michel, tel. 43–54–32–95, fax 43–26–64–65. 32 rooms with
bath. English spoken. AE, DC, V.*

Sorbonne. This pretty, early 18th-century hotel, located right by the Sorbonne, was transformed in 1988 when its handsome stone facade was cleaned. Fresh flowers adorn each room, and great clusters of geraniums hang from the windows. Try for a room overlooking the little garden. *6 rue Victor-Cousin, 75005, Métro: Luxembourg, tel. 43–54–58–08, fax 40–51–05–18. 11 rooms with bath, 26 with shower. English spoken. MC, V.*

Inexpensive **Oriental.** This no-frills one-star in an old building has clean rooms, and is located near the Arènes de Lutèce. Plumbing is minimal, some of it down corridors. *2 rue Arras, 75005, Métro: Jussieu, tel. 43–54–38–12, fax 40–51–86–78. 2 rooms with bath, 25 with shower, 5 with shared bath. Some English spoken. AE, MC, V.*

6th Arrondissement (Luxembourg)
See Left Bank Lodging map

Very Expensive **L'Hôtel.** The cream of French society has signed the guest book of this classic Left Bank hotel. Oscar Wilde died in room 16 ("I am dying beyond my means," he wrote). The stunning marble-clad hall boasts an extraordinary eliptical staircase. Each room or suite—some pleasantly timeworn—is individually and tastefully decorated. The hotel has a fine restaurant, Le Belier, whose decor includes a fountain and a live tree. The bar, open until 1 AM, is popular with a well-heeled international crowd. *13 rue des Beaux-Arts, 75006, Métro: St-Germain-des-Prés, tel. 43–25–27–22, fax 43–25–64–81. 16 rooms with bath, 8 with shower, 3 suites with bath. English spoken. Facilities: restaurant, bar. AE, DC, MC, V.*

★ **Relais Christine.** The Relais Christine is one of the most appealing of the Left Bank hotels, impeccably luxurious yet oozing charm. The hotel is located on a quiet street between the Seine and the boulevard St-Germain and occupies some precious 16th-century cloisters. The best rooms look out over the central lawn. All are spacious and comfortable, particularly the duplexes on the upper floors. Air-conditioning and double-glazed windows add to their appeal. There's no restaurant, and only guests may use the bar. *3 rue Christine, 75006, Métro: St-Michel, tel. 43–26–71–80, fax 43–26–89–38. 34 rooms and 17 suites, all with bath. English spoken. Facilities: parking, bar. AE, DC, MC, V.*

Expensive **Hôtel d'Angleterre.** Some claim the Hôtel d'Angleterre is the
★ ultimate Left Bank hotel—a little small and shabby, but elegant and perfectly managed. The 18th-century building was originally the British ambassador's residence; later, Hemingway made it his Paris home. Room sizes and rates vary greatly, though all rooms are individually decorated. Some are imposingly formal, others are homey and plain. Ask for one overlooking the courtyard. *44 rue Jacob, 75006, Métro: St-Germain-des-Prés, tel. 42–60–34–72, fax 42–60–16–93. 26 rooms and 3 suites, all with bath. English spoken. Facilities: bar, patio. AE, DC, MC, V.*

★ **L'Abbaye St-Germain.** This delightful hotel is a former 18th-century convent near St-Sulpice, in the heart of the Left Bank. The first-floor rooms open onto flower-filled gardens. Some rooms on the top floor have oak beams and alcoves. The entrance hall is sturdily authentic, with stone vaults. All bathrooms are decorated with colored marble. The bar is for guests only. *10 rue Cassette, 75006, Métro: St-Sulpice, tel. 45–44–38–*

11, fax 45–48–07–86. 42 rooms and 4 suites, all with bath. English spoken. Facilities: bar. MC, V.

★ **Saints-Pères.** The Saints-Pères is an old favorite, offering peace and quiet in the heart of St-Germain. Several rooms in this 17th-century town house are decorated in authentic period style. Try to reserve the striking frescoed room (*chambre à la fresque*); it has a painted 17th-century ceiling. Most rooms look out over the hotel garden, where breakfast and tea are served. There's no restaurant, but the cane-and-bamboo bar is an ever-popular rendezvous. Rooms with shower are moderately priced. *65 rue des Saints-Pères, 75006, Métro: Sèvres, tel. 45–44–50–00, fax 45–44–90–83. 30 rooms with bath, 4 with shower, 3 suites with bath. English spoken. Facilities: bar. MC, V.*

Acacias St-Germain. This three-star hotel in a 19th-century building near Montparnasse was completely remodeled in 1992. It offers spotlessly clean rooms decorated in summery fabrics and colors, and a small, flower-filled patio. Check into the remarkable low-season and weekend discounts. *151 bis rue de Rennes, 75006, Métro: Montparnasse, tel. 45–48–97–38, fax 45–44–63–57. 24 rooms with bath, 17 with shower. English spoken. Facilities: 24-hour room service, parking. AE, DC, V.*

Moderate **Aramis-St-Germain.** Despite its location on busy rue de Rennes, the Aramis-St-Germain, opened only in 1985, has proved a hit. All windows are double-glazed (keeping out street noise), and rooms are individually decorated with wallpapers and fabrics. Several have Jacuzzis. There's no restaurant. Harvey's Piano Bar on the first floor is popular. *124 rue de Rennes, 75006, Métro: Rennes, tel. 45–48–03–75, fax 45–44–99–29. 36 rooms with bath, 6 with shower. English spoken. Facilities: bar, parking. AE, DC, MC, V.*

★ **Marronniers.** There are few better places in Paris than the Marronniers for great value and atmosphere. Located on appealing rue Jacob, the hotel is reached through a small courtyard. All rooms are light and full of character. Those on the attic floor have sloping ceilings, uneven floors, and terrific views over the church of St-Germain-des-Prés. The vaulted cellars have been converted into two atmospheric lounges. Prices can creep into the expensive range. *21 rue Jacob, 75006, Métro: St-Germain-des-Prés, tel. 43–25–30–60, fax 40–46–83–56. 17 rooms with bath, 20 with shower. English spoken. Facilities: bar. No credit cards.*

7th Arrondissement (Invalides)
See Left Bank Lodging map

Very Expensive **Duc de Saint-Simon.** Set back from a peaceful little street leading to boulevard St-Germain, the Saint-Simon is a favorite with American visitors. Parts of the building date back to the 17th century, others date from the 18th. Try for one of the rooms with a terrace; they look over the courtyard and neighboring gardens. There's a pleasant bar and a cellar lounge for breakfast. The regular doubles are significantly less expensive than the suites. *14 rue St-Simon, 75007, Métro: Bac, tel. 45–48–35–66, fax 45–48–68–25. 29 rooms and 5 suites, all with bath. English spoken. Facilities: bar. No credit cards.*

Expensive **Université.** This appealingly converted 17th-century town
★ house is located between boulevard St-Germain and the Seine. Rooms have their original fireplaces and are decorated with English and French antiques. Ask for one of the two rooms

with a terrace on the sixth floor. Though there's no restaurant, you can rent the vaulted cellar for parties. Drinks and snacks are served all day in the bar or, in good weather, in the court-yard. Rooms with shower are moderately priced. *22 rue de l'Université, 75007, Métro: Bac, tel. 42–61–09–39, fax 42–60–40–84. 20 rooms with bath, 7 with shower. English spoken. Facilities: bar. No credit cards.*

Moderate **Kensington.** Perhaps the main reason for wanting to stay in this small two-star hotel is the superb view of the Eiffel Tower from the two top floors. Rooms are tiny and uninspiring with white Formica, but they are freshly decorated and always impeccably clean; all have double-glazed windows. There's no restaurant, but limited room service is available. Rooms with shower are inexpensive. *79 av. de la Bourdonnais, 75007, Métro: Ecole-Militaire, tel. 47–05–74–00, fax 47–05–25–81. 12 rooms with bath, 14 with shower. English spoken. AE, DC, MC, V.*

★ **Pavillon.** The entrance to the family-run Pavillon lies behind a garden at the end of an alley off rue St-Dominique, guarantee-ing peace and quiet. Although some rooms in this former 19th-century convent are tiny, all have been redecorated and feature Laura Ashley wallpaper and old prints. Breakfast is served in the little courtyard in summer. There's no elevator, but the ho-tel is only two stories high. *54 rue St-Dominique, 75007, Métro: Invalides, tel. 45–51–42–87, fax 45–51–32–79. 3 rooms with bath, 15 with shower. English spoken. AE, MC, V.*

Solférino. Located across the street from the Musée d'Orsay, the Solférino is a charming little hotel with a variety of rooms, many of them inexpensive (those with shower only and shared bath). The rooms' decor is light and summery, and the break-fast room–lounge is lit by a skylight. *91 rue de Lille, 75007, Métro: Musée d'Orsay, tel. 47–05–85–54, fax 45–55–51–16. 22 rooms with bath, 5 with shower, 5 with shower and shared wc. English spoken. MC, V. Closed Christmas–New Year's.*

Varenne. The Varenne stands in a flower-filled courtyard set back from the street; windows of rooms facing the road are dou-ble-glazed to reduce noise. Decor is contemporary—and at times basic—with oak furniture and colorful curtains and wall-paper. *44 rue de Bourgogne, 75007, Métro: Varenne, tel. 45–51–45–55, fax 45–51–86–63. 14 rooms with bath, 10 with show-er. English spoken. AE, V.*

Inexpensive **Champ de Mars.** This simple, clean two-star hotel has one-star prices. Don't expect luxury or atmosphere, just a very good deal, in a nice neighborhood near the Eiffel Tower and Invalides. *7 rue Champ de Mars, 75007, Métro: Ecole Militaire, tel. 45–51–52–30. 19 rooms with bath, 6 with shower. Some English spoken. MC, V. Closed two weeks in mid-Aug.*

8th Arrondissement (Champs-Elysées)
See Right Bank Lodging map

Very Expensive **Crillon.** In a city filled with world-class hotels, only the Crillon
★ can provide a front-row seat to history, set as it is in two 18th-century town houses on the place de la Concorde, site of the French Revolution's infamous guillotine. Marie-Antoinette, who met her end there, took singing lessons at the Hôtel de Crillon, where one of the original *grand appartments*, now sumptuous salons protected by the French National Historic Landmark Commission, has been named for the Queen. Guests must pay dearly for a balcony overlooking the great square,

with seemingly all of Paris at their feet; only the suites have them. Lesser mortals still get magnificent digs, individually decorated with Rococo and Directoire antiques, crystal and gilt wall sconces, and gold fittings. Most double rooms have separate sitting rooms, and the bathrooms, stocked with wonderful Annick Goutal toiletries, are clad in marble. The sheer quantity of the marble downstairs—in the lobby, the adjacent lounge, and especially the grand, top-rated Les Ambassadeurs restaurant is staggering. The staff anticipates your every need. *10 pl. de la Concorde, 75008, Métro: Concorde, tel. 44–71–15–00, fax 44–71–15–02. 120 rooms and 43 suites, all with bath. English spoken. Facilities: 2 restaurants, 2 bars, shop. AE, DC, MC, V.*

George V. Some say the George V lacks the "this-could-only-be-Paris" atmosphere of other superdeluxe Parisian hotels. Its style is more international. But there's no lack of authentic period furniture, or, indeed, of excellent, highly trained staff. Most rooms are impeccably decorated and imposing, though the penthouse suites are the only ones to enjoy a commanding view over the city. There are two restaurants; the better is Les Princes, where, in summer, you can eat on the leafy patio. *31 av. George V, 75008, Métro: George V, tel. 47–23–54–00, fax 47–20–40–00. 298 rooms and 53 suites, all with bath. English spoken. Facilities: 2 restaurants, bars, shopping mall, hairdresser. AE, DC, MC, V.*

★ **Lancaster.** The phrase "small is beautiful" sums up the appeal of the Lancaster. This charming, old-fashioned hotel—behind a now-gleaming facade—offers all the same services as its bigger and better-known sisters, but with the atmosphere of a luxurious private home. All rooms are individually decorated with Louis XV and Louis XVI furniture. Bathrooms vary, but most are clad with marble. A fountain, statues, and flowers fill the pretty garden. *7 rue de Berri, 75008, Métro: George V, tel. 43–59–90–43, fax 42–89–22–71. 58 rooms and 8 suites, all with bath. English spoken. Facilities: restaurant, 2 private dining rooms. AE, DC, MC, V.*

★ **Le Bristol.** Luxury and discretion are the Bristol's trump cards. The understated facade on rue du Faubourg St-Honoré might mislead the unknowing, but the Bristol ranks among Paris's top four hotels. The air-conditioned and spaciously elegant rooms all have authentic Louis XV and Louis XVI furniture. Moreover, the management has filled public areas with Old Master paintings, sculptures, sumptuous carpets, and tapestries. The marble bathrooms are simply magnificent. Nonguests can take tea in the vast garden or dine in the summer restaurant; later, you can listen to the pianist in the bar, open till 1 AM. There's an enclosed pool on the roof, complete with solarium and sauna for guests only. The service throughout is impeccable. *112 rue du Fbg. St-Honoré, 75008, Métro: St-Philippe du Roule, tel. 42–66–91–45, fax 42–66–68–68. 155 rooms and 45 suites, all with bath. English spoken. Facilities: restaurant, bar, pool, sauna, solarium, parking. AE, DC, MC, V.*

Plaza-Athénée. With its distinctive turn-of-the-century facade, accented with wrought iron and red awnings, the Plaza is a favorite among those visiting the haute-couture houses on avenue Montaigne. Eighteenth-century decor predominates in the vast air-conditioned rooms and suites. The bar is a long-standing rendezvous and is always busy. The Regence restaurant serves haute cuisine in correspondingly imposing surroundings. The art deco Relais restaurant is an upscale grill room. *25* *av. Montaigne, 75008, Métro: F.D. Roosevelt, tel. 47–23–78–33, fax 47–20–20–70. 215 rooms and 42 suites, all with bath. English spoken. Facilities: 2 restaurants, bars, tearoom. AE, DC, MC, V. Relais restaurant closed in Aug.*

Résidence Maxim's de Paris. Fashion king Pierre Cardin has transformed this hotel at the foot of the Champs-Elysées into a sumptuous museum of a hotel. Every suite—there are only four regular double rooms—is decorated in an entirely different style, unified only by opulent luxury. There are 17th-century rooms, Chinese rooms, Art Nouveau rooms, English country manor rooms, and more. *42 av. Gabriel, 75008, Métro: Champs-Elysées-Clemenceau, tel. 45–61–96–33, fax 42–89–06–07. 39 suites, 4 double rooms, all with bath. English spoken. Facilities: restaurant, bar, gym, sauna. AE, DC, MC, V. Caviarteria restaurant closed weekends.*

Expensive   **Bradford.** The turn-of-the-century, family-run Bradford has an appealing, old-fashioned feel. An old wooden elevator carries you from the flower-filled lobby to the spacious, comfortable rooms, some equipped with Louis XVI-style furniture, brass beds, and fireplaces. Not all rooms have TV. Some rooms with shower qualify as moderate. *10 rue St-Philippe-du-Roule, 75008, Métro: St-Philippe-du-Roule, tel. 45–63–20–20, fax 45–63–20–07. 36 rooms with bath, 12 with shower, 2 suites with bath. English spoken. Facilities: bar. AE, DC, MC, V.*

Alison. Conveniently located near the place de la Madeleine on a pleasant side street, the Alison is a small, friendly hotel in a 19th-century building. The rooms are decorated in simple, modern style. *21 rue de Surène, 75008, Métro: Madeleine, tel. 42–65–54–00, fax 42–65–08–17. 24 rooms with bath, 11 with shower. English spoken. Facilities: bar. AE, DC, V.*

Moderate   **Ceramic.** These are the lowest rates you'll pay this close to the Arc de Triomphe—just a few hundred yards away. The hotel has a handsome Belle Epoque tiled facade and a crystal chandelier in the reception area. The rooms haven't been remodeled in some time but are still comfortable. Those facing the street (among them 412, 422, 442) boast bay windows and intricate plaster moldings. Those facing the courtyard are quieter but less appealing. *34 av. de Wagram, 75008, Métro: Etoile, tel. 42–27–20–30, fax 46–22–95–83. 27 rooms with bath, 26 with shower. English spoken. MC, V.*

Inexpensive   **Argenson.** This friendly, family-run hotel provides what may
★   well be the best value in the swanky 8th arrondissement. Some of the city's greatest sights are just a 10-minute walk away. Old furniture, molded ceilings, and skillful flower arrangements add to the charm. An ongoing room-by-room renovation means new bathrooms in many. The best rooms have full bath, but they are moderately priced; reserve well in advance for one of these. The smallest rooms have shared baths and are inexpensive. *15 rue d'Argenson, 75008, Métro: Miromesnil, tel. 42–65–16–87. 5 rooms with bath, 19 with shower, 3 with shared bath. Some English spoken. DC, MC, V.*

9th Arrondissement (Opéra)
See Right Bank Lodging map

Very Expensive   **Grand Hotel Inter-Continental.** It's Paris's biggest luxury hotel, with endless hallways and a facade that seems as long as the Louvre. And after four years of thorough restoration this

19th-century gem sparkles like new. The grand salon, with its Art Deco dome, is a registered landmark. All rooms and suites have been luxuriously redecorated in Art Nouveau style. The famed Café de la Paix is one of the city's great people-watching spots. *2 rue Scribe, 75009, Métro: Opéra, tel. 40–07–32–32, fax 42–66–12–51. 470 rooms, 23 suites, all with bath. English spoken. Facilities: 3 restaurants, 2 bars, secretarial services, travel agency, shops, parking. AE, DC, MC, V.*

Moderate **Hôtel du Pré.** Located near the pretty square Montholon, slightly off the beaten track, this three-star hotel was thoroughly remodeled in the 1980s. Its reasonable prices, charming and sunny public areas, comfortable rooms done in summery colors, and large bathrooms make it a very good deal. The owners also run the equally good Relais du Pré and Résidence du Pré on the same street (at numbers 16 and 15). *10 rue Pierre-Sémard, 75009, Métro: Poissonière, tel. 42–81–37–11, fax 40–23–98–28. 22 rooms with bath, 19 with shower. English spoken. Facilities: bar. AE, V.*

Inexpensive **Riboutté-Lafayette.** This small, cozy two-star hotel in a 19th-century building near the busy rue La Fayette is family-run and filled with charming bric-a-brac and old furniture. The clean, sunny rooms are decorated in pastel colors, and those on the top floor have sloping ceilings. *5 rue Riboutté, 75009, Métro: Cadet, tel. 47–70–62–36, fax 48–00–91–50. 15 rooms with bath, 9 with shower. English spoken. V.*

11th Arrondissement (Bastille)
See Right Bank Lodging map

Moderate **Méridional.** This three-star hotel in a 19th-century building is a five-minute walk from either the Bastille or the Marais. It's located on a handsome but busy tree-lined boulevard. Though the lobby is a bit garish, the comfortable, quiet rooms are simply decorated in earth tones. The hotel was entirely remodeled in 1991. Prices are lower in winter. *36 blvd. Richard Lenoir, 75011, Métro: Bréguet-Sabin, tel. 48–05–75–00, fax 43–57–42–85. 26 rooms with bath, 10 with shower. English spoken. AE, DC, V.*

Inexpensive **Garden-Hotel.** Set on a pretty garden square in a quiet residential neighborhood just 10 minutes from Père-Lachaise cemetery, this family-run, two-star hotel has little character but is spotlessly clean. Rooms in front have lovely views; all units have double-glazed windows and are soberly decorated with brown carpets and beige walls. Note that bathtubs are half-size in rooms with baths. The breakfast room decor leaves much to be desired. *1 rue du Général-Blaise, 75011, Métro: Saint-Ambroise or Voltaire, tel. 47–00–57–93, fax 47–00–45–29. 3 rooms with bath, 39 with shower. No English spoken. No credit cards.*

★ **Résidence Alhambra.** This hotel is on the edge of the historical Marais quarter and is conveniently close to five Métro lines. The Alhambra's gleaming white exterior and flower-filled window boxes provide a bright spot in an otherwise drab neighborhood. The smallish guest rooms are painted in fresh pastel shades and have marble-topped breakfast tables. The lobby is filled with plants and leather armchairs. Most rooms have color TV, unusual for hotels in this price range. The reception area and breakfast room were remodeled in 1992. *13 rue de Malte,*

75011, Métro: République, tel. 47–00–35–52, fax 43–57–98–75. 10 rooms with bath, 48 with shower. English spoken. MC, V.

12th Arrondissement (Gare de Lyon)
See Right Bank Lodging map

Moderate **Modern Hôtel-Lyon.** This three-star, family-run hotel, conveniently located between the Bastille and the Gare de Lyon, changed ownership in 1992. As a result, rooms have been remodeled and redecorated in light colors, and many bathrooms are being upgraded. The new owners are as friendly and helpful as their predecessors. *3 rue Parrot, 75012, Métro: Gare de Lyon, tel. 43–43–41–52, fax 43–43–81–16. 36 rooms with bath, 12 with shower. English spoken. Facilities: bar. AE, MC, V.*

Paris-Lyon Palace. Located near the Gare de Lyon, this attractive three-star hotel has modern, strictly functional rooms, but the large, plant-filled lobby is decorated in an appealing art deco style. There's no restaurant, but the bar is open from lunch till 1 AM. Service is notably warm. *11 rue de Lyon, 75012, Métro: Gare de Lyon, tel. 43–07–29–49, fax 46–28–91–55. 64 rooms with bath, 64 with shower. English spoken. Facilities: bar. AE, DC, MC, V.*

Inexpensive **Jules-César.** The address may be unfashionable, but the Bastille, Jardin des Plantes, and Ile St-Louis are just a short walk away, and the Gare de Lyon is just around the corner. The hotel, built in 1914, has been restored: The lobby is rather glitzy, but the guest rooms are more subdued. Rooms facing the street are larger than those in the back and have a somewhat better view. The largest is room 17, which can accommodate a third bed. *52 av. Ledru-Rollin, 75012, Métro: Gare de Lyon, tel. 43–43–15–88, fax 43–43–53–60. 4 rooms with bath, 44 with shower. English spoken. MC, V.*

13th Arrondissement (Les Gobelins)
(See Left Bank Lodging map)

Inexpensive **Résidence les Gobelins.** Located five minutes from the Latin Quarter, this simple, small two-star hotel on a quiet street offers pleasant rooms in warm, coordinated colors. The breakfast room faces a small flower-filled garden. There's cable TV in every room. *9 rue des Gobelins, 75013, Métro: Gobelins, tel. 47–07–26–90, fax 43–31–44–05. 18 rooms with bath, 14 with shower. English spoken. AE, DC, MC, V.*

14th Arrondissement (Montparnasse)
See Left Bank Lodging map

Moderate **Istria.** This small, charming two-star hotel was once a Montparnasse artists' hangout. Totally rebuilt in 1988 around a flower-filled courtyard on a quiet street, it is now a family-run establishment with simple, clean, and comfortable rooms decorated in soft, summery colors. *29 rue Campagne-Première, 75014, Métro: Raspail, tel. 43–20–91–82, fax 43–22–48–45. 4 rooms with bath, 22 with shower. English spoken. AE, MC, V.*

Lenox. You'll want to stay in this new hotel mainly to take advantage of its location in the heart of Montparnasse; it's just around the corner from the famous Dôme and Coupole brasseries, and close to the Luxembourg Gardens. Try for one of the south-facing rooms; they are noticeably lighter and fresher than the others. Room decor varies considerably. The best rooms have original fireplaces, old mirrors, and exposed beams; others are decorated in functional modern styles. All have gleaming white-tile bathrooms. There's no restaurant, but snacks are served in the bar, and room service is available. *15 rue Delambre, 75014, Métro: Edgar-Quinet, tel. 43–35–34–50, fax 43–20–46–64. 36 rooms with bath, 10 with shower, 6 suites with bath. English spoken. Facilities: bar. AE, DC, MC, V.*

★ **Royal.** This small hotel, set in a late-19th-century building on attractive boulevard Raspail, has won much praise, especially from American guests. The mood throughout is stylish yet simple, with salmon-pink rooms and a wood-paneled, marble-floored lobby filled with plants. You can sit in the small conservatory, where drinks are served; there's no bar or restaurant. This hotel is borderline expensive, but worth it. *212 blvd. Raspail, 75014, Métro: Raspail, tel. 43–20–69–20, fax 42–79–95–23. 33 rooms with bath, 15 with shower. English spoken. AE, MC, V.*

Inexpensive **Midi.** This hotel is close to both Montparnasse and the Latin Quarter, and there are Métro and RER stations nearby. Don't be put off by the nondescript facade and reception area; most of the rooms are adequately furnished, and those facing the street are both large and quiet. Request room 32, if possible, and avoid the cheapest rooms, which are quite dingy and unattractive. *4 av. Réné-Coty, 75014, Métro: Denfert-Rochereau, tel. 43–27–23–25, fax 43–21–24–58. 20 rooms with bath, 21 with shower, 9 with shared bath. Some English spoken. No credit cards.*

Parc Montsouris. This modest two-star hotel in an early 1900s building is on a charming and quiet residential street next to the lovely Parc Montsouris; it's a five-minute walk to the RER station. Remodeled throughout in 1991, its smallish rooms are decorated with pastel colors and modern furniture. Some rooms with shower are very inexpensive. *4 rue du Parc-Montsouris, 75014, Métro: RER Cité-Universitaire, tel. 45–89–09–72, fax 45–80–92–72. 18 rooms with bath, 17 with shower, 7 suites with bath. English spoken. AE, MC, V.*

16th Arrondissement (Trocadéro/Bois de Boulogne)
See Right Bank Lodging map

Expensive **Kléber.** Located just a short walk from Etoile and Trocadéro, the little Kléber benefits greatly from the calm and greenery of nearby place des Etats-Unis. Decor is strictly modern throughout, but the thick blue carpets, set against beige walls, create a warm atmosphere. The hotel is impeccably clean. Though there's no restaurant, there's a comfortable first-floor lounge and bar. Rooms on the 2nd and 5th floors have balconies. Those with shower are moderate. *7 rue de Belloy, 75016, Métro: Etoile, tel. 47–23–80–22, fax 49–52–07–20. 11 rooms and 1 suite with bath, 10 rooms with shower. English spoken. Facilities: bar, parking. AE, DC, MC, V.*

Moderate **Keppler.** Ideally located on the edge of the 8th and 16th arrondissements near the Champs-Elysées, this small two-star hotel in a 19th-century building boasts many three-star features (room service, small bar) at extremely reasonable prices. The spacious and airy rooms are simply decorated with modern furnishings. Some rooms with shower are inexpensive. *12 rue*

Keppler, 75016, Métro: Kléber, tel. 47–20–65–05, fax 47–23–02–29. 31 rooms with bath, 18 with shower. English spoken. Facilities: bar. AE, MC, V.

Queen's Hotel. One of only a handful of hotels located in the desirable residential district around rue la Fontaine, Queen's is within walking distance of the Seine and the Bois de Boulogne. The hotel is small and functional, but standards of comfort and service are high. Flowers on the facade add an appealing touch. Most rooms with shower are inexpensive. *4 rue Bastien-Lepage, 75016, Métro: Michel-Ange-Auteuil, tel. 42–88–89–85, fax 40–50–67–52. 7 rooms with bath, 15 with shower. English spoken. MC, V.*

17th Arrondissement (Monceau/Clichy)
See Right Bank Lodging map

Expensive **Etoile-Pereire.** Pianist Ferrucio Pardi, owner and manager
★ here, has created a unique small hotel, set behind a quiet, leafy courtyard in a chic residential district. Renovated in 1986, rooms and duplexes are decorated in soothing pastels—pinks, grays, and apricots—with Laura Ashley curtains and chair covers, and prints on the walls. There's no restaurant, but a copious breakfast is available—with 23 different jams and jellies. The bar is always busy in the evening. For a lively, personally run hotel, few places beat this likable spot. *146 blvd. Pereire, 75017, Métro: Pereire, tel. 42–67–60–00, fax 42–67–02–90. 18 rooms with bath, 3 with shower; 4 duplexes and 1 suite, all with bath. English spoken. Facilities: bar. AE, DC, MC, V.*

★ **Regent's Garden.** The large number of repeat visitors is a safe indication that this is a special place. Located near the Arc de Triomphe, the hotel was built in the mid-19th century by Napoleon III for his doctor. Inside, it is every bit as you would imagine, with marble fireplaces, mirrors, gilt furniture, and stucco work. But the real attraction is the garden—a room overlooking it is something to be treasured. The levels of service match the spectacular architecture and decor. *6 rue Pierre-Demours, 75017, Métro: Wagram, tel. 45–74–07–30, fax 40–55–01–42. 39 rooms with bath, 1 with shower. English spoken. AE, DC, MC, V.*

Moderate **Palma.** This prim and proper two-star hotel located between
★ the Arc de Triomphe and Porte Maillot is run by the friendly and efficient Couderc family. Small and charming, it is one of the best modest hotel deals in the city. Ask for a top-floor room with a view. All rooms have cable TV with CNN. Those with a shower are borderline inexpensive. Breakfast is included in the price. *46 rue Brunel, 75017, Métro: Argentine, tel. 45–74–74–51, fax 45–74–40–90. 15 rooms with bath, 22 with shower. English spoken. MC, V.*

Inexpensive **Ouest.** Although this unpretentious hotel overlooks the railroad near Pont-Cardinet station, you can be sure of a quiet night's sleep, since all the rooms are soundproofed. Some are lighter and more spacious than others, so be sure to make your preference known. The area may not have much to interest tourists, but Montmartre, Parc Monceau, and the Grands Magasins are all within easy reach. *165 rue de Rome, 75017, Métro: Rome, tel. 42–27–50–29, fax 42–27–27–40. 17 rooms with bath, 31 with shower. English spoken. Facilities: parking, bar. MC, V.*

18th Arrondissement (Montmartre)
See Right Bank Lodging map

Moderate **Regyn's Montmartre.** Despite small rooms (all recently renovated), this small, owner-run hotel on Montmartre's place des Abbesses is rapidly gaining an enviable reputation for simple, comfortable accommodations. A predominantly young clientele and a correspondingly relaxed atmosphere have made this an attractive choice for some. Try for one of the rooms on the upper floors, with great views over the city. *18 pl. des Abbesses, 75018, Métro: Abbesses, tel. 42–54–45–21, fax 42–54–45–21. 14 rooms with bath, 8 with shower. English spoken. MC, V.*

Inexpensive **Timhotel Montmartre.** The reason for listing what is only one of eight Timhotels in Paris is simply the location of the Montmartre member of the chain—right in the leafy little square where Picasso lived at the turn of the century. Rooms are basic and functional, though the Montmartre theme is continued by the Toulouse-Lautrec posters. *11 rue Ravignan, 75018, Métro: Abbesses, tel. 42–55–74–79, fax 42–55–71–01. 6 rooms with bath, 57 with shower. English spoken. AE, DC, MC, V.*

Utrillo. Newly renovated, the Utrillo is on a quiet side street at the foot of Montmartre. The decor is appealing, with prints in every room and a marble-topped breakfast table. Because the color white is emphasized throughout, the hotel seems light, clean, and more spacious than it actually is. *7 rue Aristide-Bruant, 75018, Métro: Blanche, tel. 42–58–13–44, fax 42–23–93–88. 5 rooms with bath, 25 with shower. English spoken. Facilities: sauna. AE, DC, MC, V.*

19th Arrondissement (La Villette)
See Right Bank Lodging map

Inexpensive **Le Laumière.** Though it's located some ways from downtown, the low rates of this family-run, two-star hotel, close to the tumbling Buttes-Chaumont park, are hard to resist. Most rooms are functional only, but some of the larger ones overlook the garden. The staff is exceptionally helpful. Shared baths (both showers and w.c.) are on well-lit landings. *4 rue Petit, 75019, Métro: Laumière, tel. 42–06–10–77, fax 42–06–72–50. 18 rooms with bath, 28 with shower, 8 with shared bath. English spoken. AE, DC, MC, V.*

Apartment Rentals

If you want to do your own cooking or need a base large enough for a family, consider a furnished rental. Among companies that rent apartments in Paris are **French Experience** (370 Lexington Ave., New York, NY 10017, tel. 212/986–1115, fax 212/986–3808) and **Chez Vous** (220 Redwood Hwy., Suite 129, Mill Valley, CA 94941, tel. 415/331–2535, fax 415/331–5296).

7 The Arts and Nightlife

The Arts

Parisians consider their city a bastion of art and culture, and indeed it is. But surprisingly, much of the theater, opera, music, and ballet here is not on a par with what you'll find in London, New York, or Milan. Mime and contemporary dance performances are often better bets, and they pose no language problems.

The music season usually runs from September to June. Theaters stay open during the summer, but many productions are at summer festivals elsewhere in France. The weekly magazines *Pariscope, L'Officiel des Spectacles*, and *7 à Paris* are published every Wednesday and give detailed entertainment listings. The best place to buy tickets is at the venue itself. Otherwise, try your hotel or a travel agency such as **Paris-Vision** (214 rue de Rivoli). Tickets for some events can be bought at the **FNAC** stores—especially Alpha-FNAC (1–5 rue Pierre Lescot, 1e, Forum des Halles, third level down). **Virgin Megastore** (52 av. des Champs Elysées) sells theater and concert tickets. Half-price tickets for many same-day theater performances are available at the **Kiosque Théâtre** across from 15 place de la Madeleine; expect a line. There's another branch at Châtelet RER station (closed Sun.).

Theater A number of theaters line the Grands Boulevards between Opéra and République, but there is no Paris equivalent to Broadway or the West End. Shows are mostly in French. **Le Mogador** (25 rue de Mogador, 9e, tel. 42–85–45–30) is one of Paris's most sumptuous theaters. Classical drama is performed at the distinguished **Comédie Française** (Palais-Royal, 1er, tel. 40–15–00–15). You can reserve seats in person about two weeks in advance, or turn up an hour beforehand and wait in line for returned tickets.

The intimate **Gymnase** (38 blvd. de Bonne-Nouvelle, 10e, tel. 42–46–79–79) and the homely **Renaissance** (20 blvd. St-Martin, 10e, tel. 42–08–18–50), once home to Belle Epoque star Sarah Bernhardt, rub shoulders along the Grands Boulevards. The rue de la Gaîté near Montparnasse, lined with some of the raunchier Paris theaters since the 19th century, is still home to the stylish, old-fashioned **Gaîté-Montparnasse** (26 rue de la Gaîté, 14e, tel. 43–22–16–18).

The avant-garde is well represented by a number of small, offbeat theaters in the Marais and Bastille neighborhoods, or go a little farther north to Peter Brooks's **Bouffes du Nord** (37, bis blvd. de la Chapelle, 10e, tel. 46–07–34–50), offering wonderful experimental productions.

Ionesco admirers should visit the tiny Left Bank **Théâtre de la Huchette** (23 rue de la Huchette, 5e, tel. 43–26–38–99), where the playwright's short modern plays make a deliberate mess of the French language. In the Latin Quarter, the popular and inexpensive **Nouveau Théâtre Mouffetard** (73 rue Mouffetard, 5e, tel. 43–31–11–99) is great fun.

Many Paris theaters are worthy of a visit based solely on architectural merit and ambience, such as the elegantly restored **Théâtre des Champs-Elysées** (15 av. Montaigne, 8e, tel. 49–52–50–00), a plush Art Deco temple that hosts concerts and ballet as well as plays.

A particularly Parisian form of theater is *Café-Théâtre*—a mixture of satirical sketches and variety show riddled with slapstick humor and viewed in a café setting. It's fun if you have a good grasp of French. We suggest either the **Café de la Gare** (41 rue du Temple, 4e, tel. 42–78–52–51) or Montmartre's pricier **Chez Michou** (80 rue des Martyrs, 18e, tel. 46–06–16–04).

Concerts Before the new Opéra de la Bastille opened, the **Salle Pleyel** (252 rue du Fbg. St-Honoré, 8e, tel. 45–63–07–96), near the Arc de Triomphe, was Paris's principal home of classical music. The Paris Symphony Orchestra and other leading international orchestras still play here regularly. Paris isn't as richly endowed as New York or London when it comes to orchestral music, but the city compensates with a never-ending stream of inexpensive lunchtime and evening concerts in churches. The candlelit concerts held in the Sainte-Chapelle are outstanding—make reservations well in advance. Notre Dame is another church where you can combine sightseeing with good listening. Others that offer concerts are St-Eustache, near Les Halles; St-Germain-des-Prés, on the Left Bank; St-Louis-en-l'Ile; St-Roch, north of the Louvre; and the lovely St-Louis des Invalides.

Both the **Musée du Louvre** (34 quai du Louvre, 1e, tel. 40–20–51–51) and the **Musée d'Orsay** (1 rue de Bellechasse, 7e, tel. 45–49–48–14) hold concerts, often at lunchtime.

Opera The **Opéra** itself, or **Opéra Garnier** (pl. de l'Opéra, 9e, tel. 47–42–53–71) has alas conceded its role as Paris's main opera house to the **Opéra Bastille** (pl. de la Bastille, tel. 40–01–16–16). The old Opéra now devotes itself to classical dance; French ballet superstar Patrick Dupont is the reigning artistic director. The Opéra Bastille, meanwhile, has had its share of start-up and management problems, and many feel it is not living up to its promise of grand opera at affordable prices. In the lofty old hall of the **Opéra Comique** (5 rue Favart, 2e, tel. 42–90–12–20), you'll hear often excellent comic operas and lightweight musical entertainments. The **Théâtre Musical de Paris,** better known as the Théâtre du Châtelet (2 pl. du Châtelet, 1er, tel. 40–28–28–28) offers opera and ballet for a wider audience, at more reasonable prices.

Dance Apart from the traditional ballets sometimes on the bill at the Opéra (*see above*), the highlights of the Paris dance year are the visits of major foreign troupes, usually to the **Palais des Congrès** at Porte Maillot (tel. 40–68–22–22) or the **Palais des Sports** at the Porte de Versailles (tel. 48–28–40–48).

Movies Parisians are far more addicted to the cinema as an art form than are Londoners or New Yorkers. There are hundreds of movie theaters in the city, and a number of them, especially in principal tourist areas such as the Champs-Elysées and the boulevard des Italiens near the Opéra, run English films. Check the *Officiel du Spectacle* or *Pariscope* for a movie of your choice. Look for the initials "v.o.," which mean *version originale;* i.e., not subtitled or dubbed. Cinema admission runs from 40 francs to 55 francs; there are reduced rates on Wednesdays and, in some cinemas, for morning shows. Most ushers and usherettes expect a franc or two tip.

Real movie buffs should visit the **Pompidou Center,** with lots of classics and obscure films. The **Musée du Cinéma** at the Palais de Chaillot houses a fabulous collection of posters, costumes, set designs, and props from all over the world. The **Cinémathéque Française** at Trocadéro has a reference library and photograph collection as well as an outstanding collection of films. The **Vidéothéque de Paris,** in the Forum des Halles, is a public archive of films and videos on the city of Paris.

The Champs-Elysées bristles with cinemas, among them the **Pathé Marignan-Concorde** (No. 27), **Gaumont Ambassade** (No. 50), **Gaumont Champs-Elysées** (No. 66), **Publicis** (No. 129), and the **George V** (No. 146). Big-screen fanatics should try the **Max Linder Panorama** (24 blvd. Poissonière, 9e), the **Kinopanorama** (60 av. de la Motte-Piquet, 15e), or the **Grand Rex** (1 blvd. Poissonière, 2e), which sometimes doubles as a rock venue.

On the Left Bank, the Action chain of cinemas, including the **Action Ecoles** (23 rue des Ecoles, 5e), **Action Rive Gauche** (5 rue des Ecoles, 5e), and **Action Christine** (4 rue Christine, 6e), show offbeat films and reruns; so do the **Studio Galande** (42 rue Galande, 5e), the **Saint-André-des-Arts** (30 rue Saint-André-des-Arts, 6e), and the **Lucernaire Forum** (53 rue Nôtre-Dame-des-Champs, 6e). The Chinese-style **Pagoda** (57 rue de Babylone, 7e) is a national monument, and well worth a visit.

Nightlife

The French are definitely nightbirds, though these days that means smart, elegant *bars de nuit* rather than frenetic discos. The **Champs-Elysées,** that ubiquitous cabaret land, is making a comeback, though the clientele remains predominantly foreign. The tawdry **Pigalle** and down-at-the-heels **Bastille** areas are trendy these days, and the **Left Bank** boasts a bit of everything. During the week, people are usually home after closing hours at 2 AM, but weekends mean late-night partying.

Cabaret Paris's nightclubs are household names, shunned by wordly Parisians and beloved of foreign tourists, who flock to the shows. Prices can range from 350 francs (simple admission plus one drink) to more than 1,000 francs (dinner plus show). For 600 francs, you can get a good seat plus half a bottle of champagne.

The **Crazy Horse** (12 av. George V, 8e, tel. 47–23–32–32) is one of the best known clubs for pretty girls and dance routines, lots of humor, and lots less clothes. The **Moulin Rouge** (pl. Blanche, 18e, tel. 46–06–00–19), that old favorite in Montmartre, mingles the can-can and crocodiles in an extravagant spectacle. The **Lido** (116 bis av. des Champs-Elysées, 8e, tel. 40–76–56–10) stars the famous Bluebell Girls and tries to win you over through sheer exuberance. The legendary **Folies Bergères** (32 rue Richer, 9e, tel. 42–46–77–11), expected to reopen by the end of 1993, is still renowned for its glitter.

Other leading haunts include the **Milliardaire** (68 rue Pierre-Charron, 8e, tel. 42–25–25–17), with lots of leather and lace; the lively, crowded, and trendy **Paradis Latin** (28 rue du Cardinal-Lemoine, 5e, tel. 43–29–07–07); the **Nouvelle Eve** (25 rue Fontaine, 9e, tel. 48–78–37–96), which has a postwar music-hall flavor, with songs, dance, and magicians; and the **Eléphant Bleu** (49 rue de Ponthieu, 8e, tel. 43–59–58–64), a cabaret-cum-restaurant with an exotic (usually oriental) touch to most of its shows.

Bars and Nightclubs   The more upscale Paris nightclubs tend to be both expensive (1,000 francs for a bottle of gin or whiskey) and private—in other words, you'll usually need to know someone who's a member in order to get through the door. It helps to be famous to get into **Les Bains** (7 rue du Bourg-l'Abbé, 3e). **Keur Samba** (73 rue La Boétie, 8e) has a jungle setting. The Pigalle area in Montmartre is becoming the place to be nowadays, despite its reputation as a seedy red-light district. Among hot places here are: **Moloko** (26 rue Fontaine, 9e), a smoky late-night bar for all ages; **la Poste** (34 rue Duperré, 9e), with dinner and dancing; **Lili la Tigresse** (98 rue Blanche, 9e), a sexy bar with a trendy crowd; and—not to be missed—the brasserie **Pigalle** (22 blvd. de Clichy, 18e), whose '50s frescoes and ceramics have been classified as a national treasure.

Literary types will head for **Harry's Bar** (5 rue Daunou, 2e), a cozy, wood-paneled hangout for Americans that's haunted by the ghosts of Ernest Hemingway and F. Scott Fitzgerald. Also highly popular among the nostalgic set are the many hotel bars in the city, including at the **Ritz** (15 pl. Vendôme, 1er), the **Lutètia** (45 blvd. Raspail, 6e), the **Bristol** (112 rue du Fbg. St-Honoré, 8e), the **Normandy** (7 rue de l'Echelle, 1er), and the **Bélier** at **l'Hôtel** (13 rue des Beaux Arts, 6e).

Other popular spots are **Le Rosebud** (11 bis rue Delambre, 14e) a cult spot for the Jeunesse Dorée (young and fashionable) of the Left Bank; **La Casbah** (18 rue de la Forge Royale, 11e), a bit of Casablanca in the Bastille area; and **le Forum** (4 blvd. Malsherbes, 8e), an archtypical French cocktail bar with one of the best selection of drinks in Paris.

Other fun places for an evening out include: **Caveau des Oubliettes.** Listen to Edith Piaf songs in a medieval cellar that was once the dungeons of a prison. It's complete with minstrels, troubadours, and serving wenches—and tourists love it. *11 rue St-Julien-le-Pauvre, 5e. Admission: 130 frs. Open 9 PM–2 AM. Closed Sun.*

Au Lapin Agile. It considers itself the "doyen of cabarets," and Picasso once paid for a meal with one of his paintings. The setting in Montmartre is touristy but picturesque. *22 rue des Saules, 18e. Admission: 110 frs. Open 9 PM–2 AM. Closed Mon.*

La Rôtisserie de l'Abbaye. French, English, and American songs are accompanied by the guitar in a medieval setting. You can dine here, too. *22 rue Jacob, 6e. Admission: 200–350 frs. Open evenings only.*

Madame Arthur. A wacky, burlesque transvestite-and-drag show that's not for the faint-hearted. *75 bis rue des Martyrs, 19e. Admission: 280 frs, including show. Open evenings only.*

L'Ane Rouge. A mixed Parisian and foreign crowd frequent this typical French cabaret. The emphasis is on laughs, and entertainment includes singers, magicians, comedians, and ventriloquists. *3 rue Laugier, 17e. Admission starts at 200 frs including show. Open 8 PM–midnight.*

Jazz Clubs   The French take jazz seriously, and Paris is one of the great jazz cities of the world, with plenty of variety, including some fine, distinctive local coloring. (You're in Europe now, so why insist on American performers?) For nightly schedules, consult the specialty magazines *Jazz Hot* or *Jazz Magazine*. Remember that nothing gets going till 10 or 11 PM, and that entry prices can vary widely from about 35 francs to over 100 francs.

Start on the Left Bank at the **Caveau de la Huchette** (5 rue de la Huchette, 5e), a smoke-filled shrine to the Dixieland beat. **Le Petit Journal** (71 blvd. St-Michel, 5e), opposite the Luxembourg gardens, serves up good food and traditional jazz. **Le Bilboquet** (13 rue Saint-Benoît, 6e) plays mainstream jazz in a faded Belle Epoque decor. Nearby, the **Montana** (28 rue Saint-Benoît, 6e) is a well-known spot for jazz lovers. **La Villa** (29 rue Jacob, 6e), a newcomer on the jazz scene, has been attracting serious musicians.

Elsewhere in the city, **Au Duc des Lombards** (42 rue des Lombards, 1er) is an ill-lit, romantic venue. **Le Petit Opportun** (15 rue des Lavandières-Ste-Opportun, 1er) is a converted bistro that sometimes features top-flight American soloists with French backup. The **Slow Club** (130 rue de Rivoli, 1er) plays swing and Dixieland jazz. **New Morning** (7 rue des Petites Ecuries, 10e) is a premier spot for visiting musicians and French bands. The **Lionel Hampton jazz club** at the Meridien Hotel near Porte Maillot (81 blvd. Gouvion-St-Cyr, 17e) also boasts top jazz artists.

Rock Clubs Unlike French jazz, French rock is not generally considered to be on par with its American and British cousins. Most places charge from 80 to 100 francs for entrance and get going around 11 PM. Leading English and American groups usually play at the large **Bercy** or **Zenith** halls in eastern Paris; check posters and papers for details. To hear live rock in a more intimate setting, try the **Dancing Gibus Club** (18 rue du Fbg. du Temple, 11e), a place of long standing. The **Locomotive** (90 blvd. de Clichy, 18e) claims to offer rock's cutting edge, and **Le Bataclan** (50 blvd. Voltaire, 11e) features mostly French punk rock bands. **Le Sunset** (60 rue des Lombards, 1er) is a small, whitewashed cellar with first-rate live music and a clientele that's there to listen. The legendary **Olympia** (28 blvd. des Capucines, 9e, tel. 47–42–25–49), once favored by Jacques Brel and Edith Piaf, still hosts leading French singers.

Discos Discos aren't as hot as they once were here; you'll find more Parisians seeking moody little cocktail bars these days. Still, stalwarts continue to seek the beat. A Paris disco's life is often short and sweet, so don't be surprised if some of those listed here have closed their doors or changed their names. The **Balajo** (9 rue de Lappe, 11e), is a Bastille institution that thumps to sounds old and new. On the same street, the **Chapelle des Lombards** (19 rue de Lappe, 11e) goes for an Afro-Cuban beat. Those with a penchant for Latin rhythms should try the **Trottoirs de Buenos-Aires** (37 rue des Lombards, 1er) for some mambo, samba, and salsa. **Le Tango** (13 rue Au-Maire, 4e) attracts a sensuous dance crowd. **La Java** (105 rue du Faubourg du Temple, 11e), where Edith Piaf made her name, still seems hung up on the '60s, while **Club Zed** (2 rue des Anglais, 6e) is a prime rock'n'roll venue for all ages. The famed **Le Palace** (3 cité Bergère, 9e), one of Paris's best-known clubs, has been bought by fabled nightclub owner Régine, who is currently remodeling it. Check to see if it has reopened when you visit.

Pubs The number of Paris bars that woo English-speaking clients with a pub atmosphere and dark beer are becoming increasingly popular with Parisians too. The **Académie de la Bière** (88 bis blvd. de Port-Royal, 5e) serves more than 100 foreign brews to accompany good french fries and *moules marinière* (mussels cooked in white wine). The **Bar Belge** (75 av. de Saint-Ouen, 17e) is an authentically noisy Flemish drinking spot, while the **Mayflower** (49 rue Descartes, 5e) is a classy, Left Bank spot, British-style. The **Micro-Brasserie** (106 rue de Richelieu, 2e), just off the Grands Boulevards, brews its own beer. Quaff Guinness in an Irish mode at **Kitty O'Shea** (10 rue des Capucines, 2e) or at the animated **Finnegan's Wake** (42 rue des Boulangers, 5e) in the Latin Quarter. The somewhat snooty **Bedford Arms** (17 rue Princesse, 6e) is open until dawn for draft beer and darts, while the **London Tavern** (3 rue du Sabot, 6e) offers piano and jazz. In the Bastille area, pubs are popping up at a rapid rate. The doyen is the seedy but colorful **Café de la Plage** (59 rue de Charonne, 11e).

Casinos The nearest public casino, **Casino d'Enghien** (tel. 34–12–90–00), is by the lake at Enghien-les-Bains, 10 miles to the north of Paris.

For Singles and Gays **Chez Moune** (54 rue Pigalle, 18e) is a cabaret and disco for lesbians. Upscale **Katmandou** (21 rue du Vieux Colombier, 7e) is Paris's best-known lesbian nightclub. Gay men can try the popular **Le BH** (7 rue du Roule, 1e) or **Broad Connection** (3 rue de la Ferronerie, 1er).

All-night Restaurants Chances are that some of your nocturnal forays will have you looking for sustenance at an unlikely hour. If so, you might find it handy to know that the following restaurants stay open round the clock:

Alsace (39 av. des Champs-Elysées, 8e, tel. 43–59–44–24), a stylish brasserie-restaurant, serves seafood and sauerkraut to famished night owls along the Champs-Elysées.

Au Pied de Cochon (6 rue Coquillière, 1er, tel. 42–36–11–75), near St-Eustache church in Les Halles, once catered to the all-night workers at the adjacent Paris food market. Today, its Second Empire decor has been restored, and traditional dishes like pig's trotters and chitterling sausage still grace the menu.

Au Chien Qui Fume (33 rue du Pont Neuf, 1er, tel. 42–36–07–42), open until 2 AM, has a chocolate mousse worth waiting up for.

Le Congrès (80 av. de la Grande-Armée, 17e, tel. 45–74–17–24), a lesser-known haunt beyond the Arc de Triomphe, is worth checking out if you're in search of a late-night T-bone steak.

Le Grand Café (4 blvd. des Capucines, 9e, tel. 47–42–75–77), whose exuberant turn-of-the-century dining room matches the mood of the neighboring Opéra, provides excellent oysters, fish, and meat dishes at rather hefty prices.

For more suggestions, *see* Dining, Chapter 5.

8 Excursions

Chantilly and Senlis

Romantic Chantilly, with its faux Renaissance château, eye-popping art collection, splendid Rococo stables, classy race-course, and vast (nearly 16,000-acre) forest, lies just 30 minutes north of Paris, yet it attracts far fewer sightseeing hordes than Versailles or Fontainebleau. It is a perfect setting for a day away from the capital. A trip here can easily be combined with a visit to Senlis, 6 miles to the east, whose maze of crooked streets is dominated by the soaring spire of its Gothic cathedral.

Getting There

By Car Highway A1 runs just past Senlis; Chantilly is 6 miles west along the pretty D924.

By Train Chantilly is 30 minutes from the Gare du Nord; a shuttle bus links Chantilly to Senlis.

Tourist Information

Office du Tourisme, 23 av. Maréchal-Joffre, 60500 Chantilly, tel. 16/44–57–08–58; pl. du Parvis Notre-Dame, 60300 Senlis, tel. 16/44–53–06–40.

Exploring

While the lavish exterior of the **Château de Chantilly** may be overdone—the style is 19th-century Renaissance pastiche—the building itself houses the Musée Condé, an outstanding collection of medieval manuscripts and European paintings, including masterpieces by Raphael, Watteau, and Ingres. *Admission: 35 frs. Open Wed.–Mon. 10–6, 10:30–12:30 and 2–5 in winter.*

Les Grandes Ecuries (the stables), near the château and adjoining the racecourse, are majestic 18th-century buildings housing the **Musée du Cheval** (Museum of the Horse). The spacious stables were built to accommodate 240 horses and more than 400 hounds for stag and boar hunts. *Admission: 42 frs. Open Wed.–Mon. 10:30–6:30 in summer; 2–4:30 Wed.–Fri., 10:30–5 weekends in winter.*

The **Cathédrale Notre Dame** in Senlis (place du Parvis) dates from the second half of the 12th century. The superb spire—arguably the most elegant in France—was added around 1240. This is one of France's oldest (and narrowest) cathedrals.

The **Musée de la Vénerie** (Hunting Museum), across from the cathedral, within the grounds of the ruined royal castle, claims to be Europe's only full-fledged hunting museum, with related artifacts, prints, and paintings (including excellent works by 18th-century animal portraitist Jean-Baptiste Oudry). *Château Royal. Admission: 12 frs, (grounds only, 6 frs). Open Wed. 2–6, Thurs.–Mon. 10–noon and 2–6. Closed Tues. and mid-Dec.–Jan.*

Paris Environs

Dining

Chantilly **Relais Condé.** Although this is probably the classiest restaurant in Chantilly—pleasantly situated across from the racecourse—there's a reasonable fixed-price menu (180 francs) that makes it a suitable lunch spot. The new chef has enlivened the menu with such dishes as lobster terrine and duck breast with honey and spices. *42 av. du Maréchal-Joffre, Chantilly, tel. 16/44–57–05–75. Reservations essential. Dress: informal. AE, DC, V. Closed Mon., Tues., evenings in low season, and Feb. Moderate.*

Senlis **Les Gourmandins.** This is a cozy, two-floor restaurant in old Senlis, serving some interesting dishes and offering a fine wine list. The 120-franc fixed-price menu is a good bet for a weekday lunch. *3 pl. de la Halle, Senlis, tel. 16/44–60–94–01. Reservations advised. Dress: informal. AE, MC, V. Closed Mon. eve., Tues., and 3 weeks in Aug. Moderate.*

Chartres

Although Chartres is chiefly visited for its magnificent Gothic cathedral with world-famous stained-glass windows, the whole town—one of the prettiest in France, with old houses and picturesque streets—is worth leisurely exploration.

Worship on the site of the cathedral goes back to before the Gallo-Roman period; the crypt contains a well that was the focus of Druid ceremonies. The original cult of the fertility goddess merged into that of the Virgin Mary with the arrival of Christianity. In the late 9th century, King Charles the Bold presented Chartres with what was believed to be the tunic of the Virgin. This precious relic attracted hordes of pilgrims, and Chartres swiftly became—and has remained—a prime destination for the faithful. Pilgrims trek to Chartres from Paris on foot to this day.

The noble, soaring spires of Chartres compose one of the most famous sights in Europe. Try to catch a glimpse of them surging out of the vast golden grainfields of the Beauce as you approach from the northeast.

Getting There

By Car The A11/A10 expressways link Paris to Chartres (55 mi). To get to Rambouillet from Paris, take A13 toward Versailles, then A12 N10 (33 mi). D906 continues to Maintenon (15 mi), then to Chartres (12 mi).

By Train There are hourly trains from Paris (Gare Montparnasse) to Chartres (travel time is 50–70 minutes, depending on service), many of which stop at Rambouillet and Maintenon.

Guided Tours

Paris Vision (214 rue de Rivoli, tel. 42–60–31–25) and **Cityrama** (4 pl. des Pyramides, tel. 42–60–30–14) can arrange guided visits to a number of sites in the Paris region. Both feature half-day trips to Chartres on Tuesday and Saturday afternoons (250 frs); and combined excursions to Chartres and Versailles (395 frs) on the same days. Additional trips are scheduled in summer; call for information.

Tourist Information

Office du Tourisme, pl. de la Cathédrale, 28000 Chartres, tel. 16/37–21–50–00.

Exploring

Today's **Chartres cathedral** is the sixth church to occupy the same spot. It dates mainly from the 12th and 13th centuries, having been erected after the previous, 11th-century building burned down in 1194. A well-chronicled outburst of religious fervor followed the discovery that the Virgin's relic had miraculously survived unsinged. Reconstruction went ahead at a breathtaking pace. Just 25 years were needed for Chartres cathedral to rise again, and it has remained substantially unchanged ever since.

The lower half of the facade is all that survives from the 11th-century Romanesque church. (The Romanesque style is evident in the use of round, rather than pointed, arches.) The main door—the **Portail Royal**—is richly sculpted with scenes from the Life of Christ. The flanking towers are also Romanesque, though the upper part of the taller of the two **spires** (380 feet as against 350 feet) dates from the start of the 16th century, and its fanciful flamboyance contrasts with the stalwart solemnity of its Romanesque counterpart. The **rose window** above the main portal dates from the 13th century. The three windows below it contain some of the finest examples of 12th-century stained glass in France.

The interior is somber, and your eyes will need time to get used to the darkness. Their reward will be a view of the gemlike richness of the stained glass, with the famous deep "Chartres blue" predominating. The oldest window, and perhaps the most stunning, is *Notre Dame de la Belle Verrière* (literally, Our Lady of the Beautiful Window), in the south choir. It is well worth taking a pair of binoculars to pick out the details. If you wish to know more about stained-glass techniques and the motifs used, visit the small exhibit in the gallery opposite the north porch. The vast black-and-white medieval pattern on the floor of the nave is the only one of its kind to have survived from the Middle Ages. The faithful were expected to travel along its entire length (some 300 yards) on their knees.

Guided tours of the crypt start from the Maison de la Crypte opposite the south porch. The Romanesque and Gothic chapels running around the crypt have recently been stripped of the 19th-century paintings that used to disfigure them. You will also be shown a 4th-century Gallo-Roman wall and some 12th-century wall paintings. *Admission: 10 frs adults, 7 frs children and students. Guided tours of crypt: Easter–Oct. daily 11, 2:15, 3:30, 4:30, 5:15; Nov.–Easter daily 11, 4.*

Just behind the cathedral stands the **Musée des Beaux-Arts,** a handsome 18th-century building that used to serve as the bishop's palace. Its varied collection includes Renaissance enamels, a portrait of Erasmus by Holbein, tapestries, armor, and some fine, mainly French paintings of the 17th, 18th, and 19th centuries. There is also a room devoted to the forceful 20th-century works of Maurice de Vlaminck, who lived in the region. *29 cloître Notre Dame. Admission: 10 frs (20 frs for special exhibitions). Open Apr.–Oct. Wed.–Mon. 10–6, Nov.–Mar. 10–noon and 2–5, closed Tues.*

The museum gardens overlook the old streets that tumble down to the river Eure. Take rue Chantault down to the river, cross over, and head right, along rue de la Tannerie (which becomes rue de la Foulerie) as far as rue du Pont St-Hilaire. From here, there is a picturesque view of the roofs of old Chartres nestling beneath the cathedral. Then cross the bridge and head up to the Gothic **Eglise St-Pierre,** whose own magnificent windows date back to the early 14th century. There is yet more stained glass (17th century) to admire at the **Eglise St-Aignan** nearby, just off rue St-Pierre.

Wander among the steep, narrow streets, with the spires of the cathedral as your guide. Near the station is the striking monument to Jean Moulin, martyred World War II Resistance hero and onetime prefect of Chartres.

The River Eure snakes northeast from Chartres to the town of **Maintenon,** whose Renaissance **château** once belonged to Louis XIV's mistress and morganatic spouse, Madame de Maintenon. Her private apartments are open to visitors. The square, 12th-century keep is the sole vestige of a fortress that once occupied this site. The formal gardens stretch behind the château to the ivy-covered arches of the ruined **aqueduct**—one of the Sun King's most outrageous projects. His aim: to provide the ornamental ponds in the gardens of Versailles (30 miles away) with water from the Eure. In 1684, some 30,000 men were signed up to construct a three-tier, 3-mile aqueduct as part of this project. Many died of fever before the enterprise was called off in 1689. *Admission: 28 frs adults, 20 frs children. Open Apr.–Oct. Wed.–Sat. 2–6, Sun. 10–noon and 2–6, Nov.–Mar. weekends 2–5. Closed Jan.*

Rambouillet, surrounded by a huge forest, was once the residence of kings and dukes; today it is the occasional home of the French president. When he's not entertaining visiting dignitaries here, the **château** and its extensive **grounds** (lake, islands, and flower beds) are open to the public. Most of the buildings date from the early 18th century, but the brawny **Tour François I,** named for the king who breathed his last here in 1547, was part of the 14th-century fortified castle that first stood on this site. *Admission: 24 frs adults, 23 frs senior citizens. Open Wed.–Mon. 10–noon and 2–6 (5 in winter).*

Dining

Chartres **La Vieille Maison.** Situated close to Chartres cathedral, in the same narrow street as Le Buisson Ardent (*see below*), La Vieille Maison is an intimate spot centered around a flower-decked patio. The menu changes regularly but invariably includes regional specialties such as truffles and asparagus with chicken. Prices, though justified, can be steep; the 155-franc lunch menu is a good bet. *5 rue au Lait, tel. 16/37–34–10–67. Reservations advised. Jacket and tie required. AE, DC, MC, V. Closed Mon., Sun. evening. Moderate–Expensive.*

Le Buisson Ardent. This wood-beamed restaurant offers attentive service, fixed-price menus, imaginative food, and a view of Chartres cathedral. Try the chicken ravioli with leeks or the rolled beef with spinach. *10 rue au Lait, tel. 16/37–34–04–66. Reservations advised. Dress: informal. AE, DC, V. Closed Sun. evening. Inexpensive–Moderate.*

St-Symphorien **Château d'Esclimont.** This is a magnificent restored Renaissance château, 4 miles west of the Ablis exit on expressway A11 and about 15 miles from both Rambouillet and Chartres. Set in luxuriant grounds, with lawns and lake, this member of the Relais et Châteaux chain is a regular target for high-profile Parisian businessmen. The cuisine is sophisticated and reliably rich. Quail, hare fricassée (in season), and lobster top the menu. *St-Symphorien-le-Château, tel. 16/37–31–15–15. Reservations essential. Dress: jacket and tie required. MC, V. Expensive.*

Euro Disney

In April 1992, American pop culture secured a mammoth outpost just 32 kilometers (20 miles) east of Paris. Euro Disney Resort, set on 1,500 acres in Marne-la-Vallée, boasts thousands of hotel rooms, a convention center, sports facilities, an entertainment and shopping complex and, of course, the main attraction: Euro Disneyland. Although great fanfare greeted the opening of Euro Disney, the resort has had its share of troubles: image problems, reports of technical glitches, feuds with neighbors objecting to noisy fireworks, and—worst of all—low attendance levels. Europe's economic woes are partially to blame: The devaluation of currency in Great Britain, Italy, and Spain in late 1992 made a trip to Euro Disney a costly venture for many Europeans. But even Parisians have not welcomed their new neighbor with open arms, visiting the park in far smaller numbers than had been forecast. It remains to be seen whether an improved economy among EC countries can bring in the hoped-for crowds.

In the meantime, there's plenty to see here. The theme park is made up of five "lands": Main Street U.S.A., Frontierland, Adventureland, Fantasyland, and Discoveryland. The central theme of each land is relentlessly echoed in every detail, from attractions, to restaurant menus, to souvenirs.

Top attractions at **Frontierland** are the chilling Phantom Manor, haunted by holographic spooks, and the thrilling runaway mine train of Big Thunder Mountain, a roller coaster that plunges wildly through floods and avalanches in a setting meant to evoke Monument Valley. Whiffs of Arabia, Africa, and the West Indies give **Adventureland** its exotic cachet; the spicy meals and snacks served here rank among the best food in the theme park. Don't miss Adventureland's Pirates of the Caribbean, an exciting *mise en scène* populated by eerily human, computer-driven figures. **Fantasyland** charms the youngest park-goers with familiar cartoon characters and attractions featuring the stars of such Disney film classics as Snow White, Pinocchio, Dumbo, and Peter Pan. The focal point of Euro Disney—and its emblem—is Sleeping Beauty's Castle, a 140-foot, bubble-gum pink structure topped with 16 blue-and gold-tipped turrets. Officially known as Le Château de la Belle au Bois Dormant, its design was allegedly inspired by illustrations from a medieval Book of Hours. The castle's dungeon conceals a scaly green, two-ton dragon who rumbles and grumbles in his sleep, and occasionally rouses to roar—an impressive feat of engineering that terrifies every tot in the crowd! Cross the drawbridge from the castle to Central Plaza and walk left to **Discoveryland,** a futuristic setting for high-tech Disney entertainment. Robots on roller skates welcome visitors bound for Star Tours, a pitching, plunging, sense-confounding ride through intergalactic space. In Le Visionarium, blast off on a journey through time and space, presented in wraparound CircleVision by 9-Eye, a staggeringly realistic robot. At CinéMagique, singer Michael Jackson does a star turn as a superhero in *Captain EO*, a 3-D film that pulses with music and amazing special effects.

Euro Disney Resort includes six hotels with more than 5,000 rooms. Predictably, each has a theme, from the pseudo-Victorian splendor of the luxury-class Disneyland Hotel to the make-believe wilderness of Camp Davy Crockett, the resort's cheapest accommodation (also the farthest from Euro Disneyland). For entertainment outside the hotels and theme park, check out Festival Disney, a vast pleasure dome designed by architect Frank Gehry. Featured are American-style restaurants (a crab shack, a diner, a deli, a steak house), a disco, and a dinner theater where Buffalo Bill stages his Wild West Show twice nightly. An 18-hole golf course is open to the public (for information, tel. 64–74–30–00). *Admission to Euro Disneyland: 250 frs adults, 175 frs children under 12; 2-day passport 475 frs adults, 335 frs children; 3-day passport 630 frs adults, 440 frs children. Open Apr.–mid-June, weekdays 9–7, weekends 9–midnight; mid-June–Aug., daily 9–midnight; Sept.–Oct., weekdays 9–7, weekends 9–9; Nov.–Mar., weekdays 10–6, weekends 10–7.*

Getting There

By Bus Shuttle buses link Euro Disney to Roissy (56 km/35 mi) and Orly (50 km/31 mi) airports. Fare is 65 frs.

By Car The Strasbourg-bound A4 expressway leads from Paris to Euro Disney, at Marne-la-Vallée, a journey of 32 kilometers (20 miles) that in normal traffic will take about 30 minutes. The 4-kilometer (2½-mile) route from the expressway to the entrance of the theme park is clearly marked. Disney hotel guests should proceed to their hotel's "resident" parking lot; day visitors must head for the Parking Visiteurs, which costs 30 francs per car and is 600 yards from the theme-park entrance.

By Train Euro Disney's new suburban train station (Marne-la-Vallée-Chessy) is just 100 yards from the entrance to both the theme park and Festival Disney. Trains run every 10 to 20 minutes from central Paris RER-A stations at Charles de Gaulle-Etoile, Auber, Châtelet-Les Halles, Gare de Lyon, and Nation. The trip takes about 40 minutes and costs 66 francs round-trip (including the métro to the RER). A TGV station is expected to open right next to the RER station in June 1994.

Tourist Information

Contact **Walt Disney World Central Reservations** (Box 10,100, Lake Buena Vista, FL 32830-0100, tel. 407/934–7639) or **Euro Disney S.C.A.** (Central Reservations Office, Box 105 F77777, Marne-la-Vallée, Cedex 4 France, tel. 49–41–49–10). For more detailed information, consult *Fodor's Euro Disney*.

Dining

Euro Disneyland is peppered with places to eat, ranging from snack bars and fast-food joints to full-service restaurants—all with a distinguishing theme. In addition, all Disney hotels and Festival Disney have restaurants that are open to the public. But since these are outside the theme park, it is not recommended that you waste time traveling to them for lunch. Be aware that only the hotel and Festival Disney restaurants serve alcoholic beverages. Eateries serve nonstop as long as the park is open. *AE, DC, MC, V at sit-down restaurants; no credit cards at others. Reservations recommended for sit-down restaurants.*

Fontainebleau

Fontainebleau, with its historic château, is a favorite place for excursions, especially since a lush forest (containing the painters' village of Barbizon) and the superb château of Vaux-le-Vicomte are close by.

Like Chambord in the Loire Valley or Compiègne to the north of Paris, Fontainebleau earned royal esteem as a hunting base. As at Versailles, a hunting lodge once stood on the site of the current château, along with a chapel built in 1169 and consecrated by exiled (later murdered and canonized) English priest Thomas à Becket. The palace you see today was begun under the flamboyant Renaissance king, François I, the French contemporary of England's Henry VIII. The king hired Italian artists Il Rosso (a pupil of Michelangelo) and Primaticcio to embellish his château. In fact they did much more: By introducing the pagan allegories and elegant lines of Mannerism to France, they revolutionized French decorative art. Their extraordinary frescoes and stuccowork can be admired in the Galerie François I and the glorious Salle de Bal, which was completed under Henri II, François's successor.

Although Sun King Louis XIV's architectural fancy was concentrated on Versailles, he commissioned Mansart to design new pavilions and had André Le Nôtre replant the gardens at Fontainebleau, where he and his court returned faithfully each autumn for the hunting season. However, it was Napoléon who made a Versailles, as it were, out of Fontainebleau, by spending lavishly to restore it to its former glory. He held Pope Pius VII prisoner here in 1812, signed the second Church-State concordat here in 1813, and, in the cobbled Cour des Adieux, bade farewell to his Old Guard in 1814 as he began his brief exile on the Mediterranean island of Elba.

Another courtyard—the Cour de la Fontaine–was commissioned by Napoléon in 1812 and adjoins the Etang (or pond) des Carpes. Ancient carp are alleged to swim here, although Allied soldiers drained the pond in 1915 and ate all the fish, and, in the event they missed some, Hitler's hordes did likewise in 1940.

Getting There

By Car Take A6 then N7 to Fontainebleau from the Porte d'Orléans or Porte d'Italie (45 miles from Paris). N7 runs close to Barbizon, 5 miles northwest of Fontainebleau. Vaux-le-Vicomte, near Melun, is 13 miles north of Fontainebleau. Take N6 north to Melun, then N36 (northeast), turning right 2 miles out of Melun along D215.

By Train Fontainebleau is about 50 minutes from the Gare de Lyon; take a bus to complete the trip from the station to the château. Barbizon and Vaux-le-Vicomte are not accessible by train.

Guided Tours

Paris Vision and **Cityrama** offer half-day trips to Fontainebleau and Barbizon *(see* Guided Tours in Chartres, *above,* for addresses). Cost: 280 frs. Departures 1:30 Wed. and Sun.

Tourist Information

Office du Tourisme, 31 pl. Napoléon-Bonaparte, Fontainebleau, tel. 16/64–22–25–68.

Exploring

The **château of Fontainebleau** dates from the 16th century, although additions were made by various royal incumbents over the next 300 years. The famous **horseshoe staircase** that dominates the Cour du Cheval Blanc (which later came to be called the Cour des Adieux, or Courtyard of Farewell) was built by Androuet du Cerceau for Louis XIII (1610–1643). The **Porte Dauphine** is the most beautiful of the various gateways that connect the complex of buildings; its name commemorates the fact that the Dauphin—the heir to the throne, later Louis XIII—was christened under its archway in 1606.

Napoléon's apartments occupied the first floor. You can see a lock of his hair, his Légion d'Honneur medal, his imperial uniform, the hat he wore on his return from Elba in 1815, and one bed in which he definitely did sleep (almost every town in France boasts a bed in which the emperor supposedly spent a night). There is also a throne room—Napoléon spurned the one at Versailles, a palace he disliked, and established his imperial seat in the former King's Bedchamber, a room with a suitably majestic decor—and the **Queen's Boudoir,** known as the room of the six Maries (occupants included ill-fated Marie Antoinette and Napoléon's second wife, Marie-Louise). Highlights of other salons include 17th-century tapestries, marble reliefs by Jacquet de Grenoble, and paintings and frescoes by the versatile Primaticcio.

The jewel of the interior, though, is the ceremonial ballroom, or **Salle de Bal,** nearly 100 feet long and dazzlingly decorated with 16th-century frescoes and gilding. It is luxuriantly wood-paneled, and a gleaming parquetry floor reflects the patterns in the ceiling. Like the château as a whole, the room exudes a sense of elegance and style—but on a more intimate, human scale than at Versailles: This is Renaissance, not Baroque. *Admission: 30 frs adults, 19 frs ages 18–25 and senior citizens; 19 frs Sun. Open Wed.–Mon. 9:30–12:30 and 2–5; gardens open 9–dusk (admission free).*

On the western edge of the 62,000-acre Forest of Fontainebleau lies the village of **Barbizon,** home to a number of mid-19th-century landscape artists, whose innovative outdoor style paved the way for the Impressionists. Corot, Millet, Rousseau, Daubigny, and Diaz, among others, all painted here, repairing to **Père Ganne's Inn** after working hours to brush up on their social life. The inn still stands—though it's closed indefinitely for restoration—but you can soak up the arty mood at the houses of Millet and Rousseau farther along the single main street (rue Grande).

North of Fontainebleau stands the majestic château of **Vaux-le-Vicomte,** started in 1656 by court finance wizard Nicolas Fouquet. The construction process was monstrous: Villages were razed, then 18,000 workmen were called in to execute the plans of architect Louis Le Vau, decorator Charles Le Brun,

BOO.

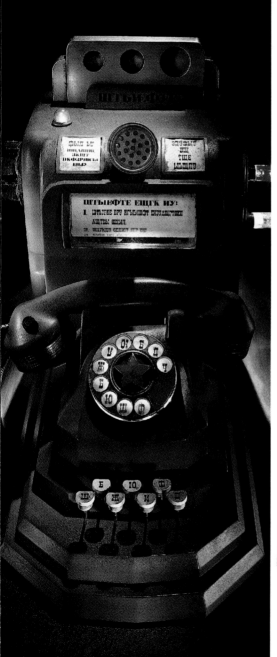

Sprint's WorldTraveler FŌNCARD. The easy way to call from around the world.

Imagine trying to place a call in another country: You have to deal with foreign currency. Alien operators. And phones that look like they're from another planet.

Talk about frightening.

Now imagine making the same call with a Sprint WorldTraveler FŌNCARD™:

To begin with, you'll reach an English-speaking operator just by dialing one easy, toll-free access code. An access code, by the way, that's right on your calling card.

Not only that, you won't have any trouble remembering your card number. Because it's based on your home phone number.

Now what could be easier than that? So call today and find out how you can get a WorldTraveler FŌNCARD.

Because we may not be able to do anything about the phones you'll have to call from. But at least it won't be a ghastly experience.

Sprint.

1-800-347-8989

All The Best Trips Start with **Fodor's**

Fodor's Affordables
Titles in the series: Caribbean, Europe, Florida, France, Germany, Great Britain, Italy, London, Paris.

"Travelers with champagne tastes and beer budgets will welcome this series from Fodor's." — *Hartford Courant*

"These books succeed admirably; easy to follow and use, full of cost-related information, practical advice, and recommendations...maps are clear and easy to use." — *Travel Books Worldwide*

Fodor's Bed & Breakfast and Country Inn Guides
Titles in the series: California, Canada, England & Wales, Mid-Atlantic, New England, The Pacific Northwest, The South, The Upper Great Lakes Region, The West Coast.

"In addition to information on each establishment, the books add notes on things to see and do in the vicinity. That alone propels these books to the top of the heap."— *San Diego Union-Tribune*

The Berkeley Guides
Titles in the series: California, Central America, Eastern Europe, France, Germany, Great Britain & Ireland, Mexico, The Pacific Northwest, San Francisco.

The best choice for budget travelers, from the Associated Students at the University of California at Berkeley.

"Berkeley's scribes put the funk back in travel." — *Time*

"Hip, blunt and lively." — *Atlanta Journal Constitution*

"Fresh, funny and funky as well as useful." — *The Boston Globe*

Exploring Guides
Titles in the series: Australia, California, Caribbean, Florida, France, Germany, Great Britain, Ireland, Italy, London, New York City, Paris, Rome, Singapore & Malaysia, Spain, Thailand.

"Authoritatively written and superbly presented, and makes worthy reading before, during or after a trip." — *The Philadelphia Inquirer*

"A handsome new series of guides, complete with lots of color photos, geared to the independent traveler." — *The Boston Globe*

Visit your local bookstore or call 1-800-533-6478 24 hours a day.
Fodor's The name that means smart travel.

and landscape architect Le Nôtre. The house-warming party was so lavish that star guest Louis XIV, tetchy at the best of times, threw a fit of jealousy. He hurled Fouquet in the slammer and promptly began building Versailles to prove just who was boss.

Entry to the high-roofed château is from the north. Decoration of the cupola, in the **salon,** was halted at Fouquet's arrest. Le Brun's major achievement is the ceiling of the **Chambre du Roi,** depicting *Time Bearing Truth Heavenwards.* The word "squirrel" in French is *écureuil,* but in local dialect they were known as *fouquets;* they appear here (along the frieze) and throughout the château, a sly visual tribute to Vaux's hapless owner. Le Brun's other masterwork here is the ceiling in the **Salon des Muses,** a brilliant allegorical composition painted in glowing, sensuous colors that surpasses anything Le Brun completed at Versailles.

A clever exhibition, complete with life-size wax figures, explains the rise and fall of Nicolas Fouquet. The version is, not surprisingly, favorable to the château's founder—accused by Louis XIV and subsequent historians of megalomania and shady financial dealings, but apparently condemned on little evidence by a court anxious to please the jealous, irascible monarch. The exhibition continues in the **basement,** whose cool, dim rooms were used to store food and wine and house the château's staff. The **kitchens,** a more cheerful sight with their gleaming copperwear and old menus, are also down here.

Le Nôtre's carefully restored **gardens** contain statues, waterfalls, and fountains, and provide fine views. There is also a **Musée des Equipages**—carriages, saddles, and smithy—on the grounds. *Admission: 48 frs adults, 38 frs students. Grounds only: 27 frs adults, 20 frs students. Château open daily 10–6; 11–5 in winter. Closed Dec./mid-Feb. except Christmas/New Year's. Candlelight visits May–Oct., Sat. evenings 8:30–11 (65 frs adults, 52 frs students).*

Dining

Barbizon   **Le Relais de Barbizon.** Solid home-cooked meals are served alfresco. Among the offerings are duckling with cherries and lamb with parsley. Expect crowds in midsummer. The five-course, 135-franc weekday menu is excellent value. *2 av. Charles-de-Gaulle, Barbizon, tel. 60–66–40–28. Reservations advised. Dress: informal. MC, V. Closed Tues. and Wed., last 2 weeks in Aug., and most of Jan. Moderate.*

Fontainebleau   **Le Beauharnais.** Conveniently situated in the Aigle Noir hotel opposite Fontainebleau château, this recently restored restaurant offers classic French fare, including veal sweetbreads with prawns and duck with marjoram, in a grand setting. Set menus are priced at 220 and 300 francs, and there's a tranquil garden for alfresco dining in summer. *27 pl. Napoléon-Bonaparte, Fontainebleau, tel. 64–22–32–65. Reservations recommended. Jacket and tie required. AE, DC, MC, V. Expensive.*

Giverny

This charming village in southern Normandy has become a place of pilgrimage for art lovers. It was here that Claude Monet lived for 43 years, until his death in 1926 at the age of 86. After decades of neglect, his pretty pink house with green shutters, his studios, and, above all, his garden with its famous lily pond have been lovingly restored—thanks to gifts from around the world and in particular from the United States. Late spring is perhaps the best time to visit, when the apple trees are in blossom and the garden is a riot of color; however, Giverny is worth a day trip from Paris at least into mid-autumn.

Monet was brought up in Normandy and, like many of the Impressionists, was attracted by the soft light of the Seine Valley, north of Paris. After several years at Argenteuil, just north of Paris, he moved downriver to Giverny in 1883 along with his two sons, his mistress Alice Hoschedé (whom he later married), and her six children. By 1890, a prospering Monet was able to buy the house outright. Three years later, he purchased another plot of land across the road to continue his gardening experiments, diverting the River Epte to make a pond.

The water lilies and Japanese bridges became special features of Monet's garden and now help to conjure up an image of the bearded brushman dabbing cheerfully at his canvases—capturing changes in light and weather in a way that was to have a major influence on 20th-century art. From Giverny, Monet enthusiasts may want to continue up the Seine Valley to the site of another of his celebrated painting series: Rouen cathedral.

Getting There

By Car Take expressway A13 from Paris to the Vernon exit (D181). Cross the Seine in Vernon and follow D5 to Giverny.

By Train Take the train from Gare St-Lazare to Vernon (50 min). Giverny is a 3½-mile walk or a taxi ride away.

Guided Tours

Guided excursions are organized by **American Express** (11 rue Scribe, tel. 47–77–77–37) and the **RATP Tourist Office** (pl. de la Madeleine), on either a half-day or full-day basis, combined with trips to Rouen.

Exploring

Monet's house has a warm family feeling that may come as a welcome break after visiting stately French châteaux. The rooms have been restored to Monet's original designs: the kitchen with its blue tiles, the buttercup-yellow dining room, and Monet's bedroom on the second floor. You will see the Japanese prints Monet collected so avidly and reproductions of his own works displayed around the house. His studios are also open for viewing. The garden, with flowers spilling out across the paths, is as cheerful and natural as the house—quite unlike formal French gardens. The enchanting water garden, with its lilies, bridges, and rhododendrons, is across the road. *84 rue*

Claude Monet. Admission: 30 frs; gardens only, 20 frs. Open Apr.–Oct., Tues–Sun. 10–noon and 2–6.

Close by is the newly opened **Musée Américain,** endowed by Chicago art patrons Daniel and Judith Terra. On view are works by American Impressionists influenced by Claude Monet. *99 rue Claude-Monet. Admission: 30 frs adults, 20 frs students and senior citizens. Open Apr.–Oct., Tues.–Sun. 10–6; closed Mon.*

Dining

Douains **Château de Brécourt.** This 17th-century brick château, set in extensive grounds, is a member of the stylish Relais & Châteaux chain and lies 7 miles west of Giverny (via D181 at Douains, near Pacy-sur-Eure). Creative dishes in an august setting make Brécourt a popular spot for people who drive to Giverny. The menu includes smoked salmon-and-crab cakes and turbot with caviar, as well as a dessert of pears in a flaky pastry roasted in honey. *Tel. 16/32–52–40–50. Reservations advised. Dress: informal. AE, DC, MC, V. Expensive.*

Giverny **Les Jardins de Giverny.** This commendable restaurant is close to Monet's house, and the old-fashioned dining room overlooks a rose garden. Tourists who lunch here are treated to inventive dishes such as foie gras laced with applejack or seafood terrine with a mild pepper sauce. *Chemin du Roy, tel. 16/32–21–60–80. Reservations advised. Dress: casual. AE, MC, V. Closed Sun. evening, Mon., and Jan. Moderate.*

Reims and Laon

Champagne and cathedrals make a trip to the renowned city of Reims and the lesser-known town of Laon an ideal two-day break from the French capital. Reims is the capital of the champagne industry. Several major producers have their headquarters here, and you will not want to miss the chance to visit the chalky, labyrinthine champagne cellars that tunnel beneath the city. Reims cathedral, one of the most historic in France, was the setting for the coronations of French kings (Charles X was the last to be crowned here, back in 1825). Despite some indifferent 20th-century rebuilding, Reims is rich with attractions from Roman times to the modern era. Laon, which occupies a splendid hilltop site 25 miles northwest of Reims, is known as the "crowned mountain" on account of the many-towered silhouette of its venerable cathedral. This enchanting old town could easily be turned into one of France's leading tourist draws, were lethargic local authorities not firmly locked into the past: Laon was once, after all, the capital of France—almost 12 centuries ago.

Getting There

By Car Expressway A4 goes via Reims on its way east from Paris to Strasbourg. The Belgium-bound N2 links Paris to Laon. Expressway A26 links Laon and Reims—a 25-mile trip.

By Train Scheduled trains cover the 110 miles from Paris (Gare de l'Est) to Reims in 90 minutes. The Paris–Laon route (from the Gare du Nord) takes up to two hours. Trains run daily between Laon and Reims.

Tourist Information

Office du Tourisme, 2 rue Guillaume-de-Machault, 51100 Reims, tel. 16/26–47–25–69; place du Parvis, 02000 Laon, tel. 16/23–20–28–62.

Exploring

The glory of Reims's **Cathédrale Notre Dame** is its facade. Its proportions are curiously deceptive, and the building is actually considerably larger than it appears. Above the north (left) door is the **Smiling Angel,** a delightful statue whose kindly expression threatens to turn into an acid-rain scowl—pollution has succeeded war as the ravager of the building. The postcard shops nearby have views of the cathedral after World War I, and on seeing the destruction, you'll understand why restoration here is an ongoing process. The high, solemn **nave** is at its best in the summer, when the lower walls are adorned with 16th-century tapestries relating the life of the Virgin. The east-end **windows** were designed by Marc Chagall.

With the exception of the 15th-century **towers,** most of the original building was constructed in the hundred years after 1211. A stroll around the outside will reinforce the impression of the harmony and discipline of its lines, which almost belie its decorative richness. The east end presents an idyllic vista across well-tended lawns. There are spectacular light shows both inside (40 frs) and outside (free) the cathedral in July and August.

The **Palais du Tau** next door is the former archbishop's palace and affords excellent views of the cathedral. It contains tapestries, coronation robes, and several outstanding statues removed for safekeeping from the cathedral's facade. *2 pl. du Cardinal-Luçon. Admission: 26 frs adults, 18 frs senior citizens, 6 frs children under 18. Open daily 10–noon and 2–6; 10–noon and 2–5 winter weekdays.*

The nearby **Musée des Beaux-Arts,** Reims's fine art museum, has an outstanding painting collection crowned by 27 Corots and David's celebrated portrait of Revolutionary leader Marat dead in his bath. Nine Boudins and Jongkinds are among the finer Impressionist works here. *8 rue Chanzy. Admission: 10 frs. Open Wed.–Mon. 10–noon and 2–6.*

As you leave the museum, turn right and continue along rue Chanzy/rue Gambetta to the 11th-century **Basilique St-Rémi,** devoted to the 5th-century saint who gave his name to the city. The building is nearly as long as the cathedral, and its interior seems to stretch away into the dim distance. The Gothic choir area has much original 12th-century stained glass. *Rue Simon.*

Several champagne producers run tours of their **champagne cellars,** combining video presentations with guided walks through their cavernous, chalk-hewn, underground warehouses. Few producers show much generosity when it comes to pouring out samples of bubbly, so we recommend you double back across town to **Mumm,** which does. (*34 rue du Champ-de-Mars. Open daily 9:30–noon and 2–5; closed weekends in winter*). If you don't mind paying for samples, however, the most spectacular cellars are those of Taittinger. (*9 pl. St-Nicaise.*

*Admission: 15 frs. Guided 1-hour tours: weekdays 9:30–11:50
(last departure) and 2–4:20; weekends 9–10:50 and 2–4:50.*

Across from the Mumm Cellars is a modern **chapel** decorated by
the Japanese artist Foujita, a member of the Montparnasse set
in the '20s who converted and was baptized in Reims. Head
down rue du Champ-de-Mars toward the railroad station, turn
right onto avenue de Laon, then left onto rue Franklin D. Roosevelt. A short way along is the **Salle de Guerre,** where Eisenhower established Allied headquarters at the end of World War
II. It was here, in a well-preserved, map-covered room, that
the German surrender was signed in May 1945. *Admission: 10
frs adults, 5 frs children. Open Apr.–Sept. Wed.–Mon. 10–
noon and 2–6, Oct.–Mar. Wed.–Mon. 10–noon; closed Tues.*

The **Porte Mars** is an impressive Roman arch that looms up just
across from the railroad station. It is adorned by faded bas-re-
liefs depicting Jupiter, Romulus, and—of course—Remus.

Visitors interested in the history of World War I may want to
visit the **chemin des Dames,** a section of the road between
Reims and Laon. The disastrous French offensive launched
here by General Nivelle in April 1917 led to futile slaughter and
mutiny. Take N44 from Reims to Corbény, then wind your way
for some 17 miles along D18/D985 west, past Cerny-en-
Laonnois, until it meets N2, which heads north to Laon, 12
miles away.

Laon's **Cathédrale Notre-Dame** was constructed from 1160 to
1235 and is a superb example of early Gothic style. The light,
recently cleaned interior gives the impression of immense
length (120 yards in total). The flat ceiling at the east end—an
English-inspired feature—is unusual in France. The second-
floor galleries that run around the building are typical of early
Gothic; you can visit them (and the towers) with a guide from
the Tourist Office on the cathedral square. The airy elegance of
the five remaining towers is audacious by any standard, and
rare: French medieval architects preferred to concentrate on
soaring interiors and usually allowed for just two towers at the
west end. You don't have to be an architectural scholar to appreciate the sense of movement about Laon's west-end facade
compared with the more placid, two-dimensional feel of Notre
Dame in Paris. Also look for the stone bulls protruding from
the towers, a tribute to the stalwart beasts who carted the
blocks of stone from quarries far below.

The medieval **ramparts,** the old fortification walls, lie virtually
undisturbed by passing traffic and provide a ready-made route
for a tour of old Laon. Another notable and well-preserved sur-
vivor from medieval times is the **Chapelle des Templiers,** a small
octagonal 12th-century chapel on the grounds of the town museum. *Admission: 10 frs. Open Apr.–Sept. Wed.–Mon. 10–
noon and 2–6; Oct.–Mar. Wed.–Mon. 10–noon and 2–5; closed
Tues.*

Dining

Laon **La Petite Auberge.** You can expect some imaginative nouvelle
dishes from young chef Willy-Marc Zorn in this 18th-century-
style restaurant close to the station in Laon's *ville basse* (lower
town). Fillet of plaice with champagne vinegar, braised squab,
and frozen nougat are among the choices. The 150-franc menu

is a good lunchtime bet. *45 blvd. Pierre-Brossolette, tel. 16/23–23–02–38. Reservations recommended. Dress: informal. AE, DC, V. Closed Sat. lunch and Sun. Moderate.*

Reims **Boyer.** Gérard Boyer is one of the most highly rated chefs in France. Duck, foie gras in pastry, and truffles (served in a variety of ways) figure among his specialties. The setting, not far from the Basilique St-Rémi, is magnificent, too: a 19th-century château, built for the champagne firm Pommery, surrounded by an extensive, well-tended park. *Les Crayères, 64 blvd. Henry-Vasnier, tel. 16/26–82–80–80. Reservations essential. Jacket and tie required. AE, DC, MC, V. Closed Mon., Tues. lunch, Christmas–mid-Jan. Very Expensive.*

Florence. An old, high-ceilinged mansion is the setting for this elegant and well-run restaurant. Chef Laurent Helleu serves wonderfully light versions of classical French dishes—and at fair prices (two set menus for 220 and 290 francs). *43 blvd. Foch, tel. 16/26–47–12–70. Reservations advised. Dress: informal. AE, DC, MC, V. Closed most of Aug. Moderate–Expensive.*

Lodging

Laon **Paix.** The Paix is a modern, central hotel with stylish rooms and a pleasant little garden. The Drouet restaurant serves up good but not inexpensive cuisine (closed Sun.). *52 rue St-Jean, 16/23–23–21–95. 15 rooms, all with either bath or shower. Facilities: restaurant. AE, DC, V. Moderate.*

Bannière de France. This comfortable old hotel, just five minutes' walk from Laon cathedral, is favored by British travelers, perhaps because Madame Lefèvre speaks English well and offers a cheerful welcome. There is a venerable dining room where you can enjoy sturdy cuisine (trout, guinea fowl) at unbeatable value. *11 rue Franklin-Roosevelt, tel. 16/23–23–21–44. 18 rooms, not all with bath or shower. AE, DC, MC, V. Facilities: restaurant. Closed Christmas and New Year's. Inexpensive.*

Reims **Gambetta.** This hotel near Reims cathedral has small, fairly basic rooms and a decent restaurant, the Vonelly (closed Sun. evening, Mon., and late July–mid-Aug.), which serves a 180-franc menu featuring scallop salad with spinach and roast duck with cabbage. *9 rue Gambetta, tel. 16/26–47–41–64, fax 16/26–47–22–43. 17 rooms with shower. Facilities: restaurant. AE, MC, V. Inexpensive.*

Thoiry

Thoiry, 25 miles west of Paris, is an ideal day-trip destination, especially for families with children. It offers a splendid combination of history and culture—chiefly in the form of a superbly furnished 16th-century château with its own archives and gastronomy museum—and outdoor adventure. Its safari park boasts over 800 animals and is a great place to picnic; drinks and snacks can be bought here, too.

Getting There

By Car Take highway A13 then highway A12 from Paris to Bois d'Arcy, then take N12 toward Dreux. Just past Pontchartrain, D11 heads off right toward Thoiry.

By Train From Gare Montparnasse to Montfort-L'Amaury (35 min), then a 10-minute taxi ride. A special shuttle bus operates to and from the château on Sundays in summer.

Exploring

The **château** was built in 1564. Its handsome Renaissance facade is set off by **gardens** landscaped in the disciplined French fashion by Le Nôtre; there is a less formal Jardin à l'Anglaise (English Garden) for contrast. Owners Vicomte de La Panouse and his American wife, Annabelle, have restored the château and grounds to their former glory and opened both to the public. Highlights of the **interior** include the grand staircase, the 18th-century Gobelins tapestries in the dining room that were inspired by the adventures of Don Quixote, and the Green and White Salon with its old harpsichord, portraits, and tapestries.

The distinguished history of the Panouse family—one member, Comte César, fought in the American Revolution—is retraced in the **Archive Museum,** where papal bulls, Napoléonic letters, and Chopin manuscripts (discovered in the attic in 1973) are displayed side by side with missives from Thomas Jefferson and Benjamin Franklin.

Since 1984, the château pantries have housed a **Museum of Gastronomy,** whose *pièces montées* (banquet showpieces) re-create the designs of the premier 19th-century chef, Antoine Carême (his clients included George IV of England and the emperors of Austria and Russia). One is over 15 feet high and took eight months to confect. Engravings, old copper pots, and early recipe books are also on display.

You can stroll at leisure around the picturesque grounds, stopping off at the Pré Angélique to watch a cricket match (summer weekends) and admiring giraffes, wolves, and—from the safety of a raised footbridge—the world's first *ligrons*, crosses between a lion and a tiger. There is an exploratory play area for children, featuring giant burrows and cobwebs. For obvious reasons, pedestrians are not allowed into the Bear Park or the African Reserve. Keep your car windows closed if you want to remain on peaceful terms with marauding lions, rhinos, elephants, and mega-horned Watutsi cattle. *Château Admission: 25 frs adults, 20 frs children. Château park and game reserve admission: 85 frs adults; first two children 69 frs, thereafter free. Combined admission to all attractions: 108 frs adults, 89 frs children. Open weekdays 10–6, weekends 10–6:30 in summer; weekdays 10–5 weekends 10–5:30 in winter.*

Dining

The château's **self-service restaurant** in the converted 16th-century stables (same hours as the safari park) offers a palatable choice of fixed-price meals. Cold starters include salami, tomato salad, and green salad; the main course may be roast chicken, veal with mushrooms, steak and fries, or *andouillette* (small chitterling sausage). *Inexpensive.*

Etoile. This restaurant, belonging to a three-star hotel, is situated just 300 yards from the château along the main street. There is a special tourist menu as well as a wide choice of à la carte selections. Robust, traditional French dishes are served: steak, chicken, fish, and pâté. *38 rue de la Porte St-Martin, tel.*

34–87–40–21. Reservations advised. Dress: informal. AE, DC, MC, V. Closed Mon. and Jan. Inexpensive.

Versailles

Paris in the 17th century was a rowdy, rabble-ridden city. Louis XIV hated it and set about in search of a new power base. He settled on Versailles, 15 miles west of Paris, where his father had a small château/hunting lodge.

Today, the château of Versailles seems monstrously big, but it wasn't large enough for the army of 20,000 noblemen, servants, and hangers-on who moved in with Louis. A new city—a new capital, in fact—had to be constructed from scratch to accommodate them. Vast mansions had to be built, along with broad avenues—all in an extravagant Baroque style.

It was hardly surprising that Louis XIV's successors rapidly felt uncomfortable with their architectural inheritance. Indeed, as the 18th century wore on, and the taste for intimate, private apartments expanded at the expense of the public, would-be heroic lifestyles of 17th-century monarchs, subsequent rulers built themselves small retreats on the grounds, where they could escape the overpowering formality of court life. The two most famous of these structures are the **Petit Trianon,** built by Louis XV and a model of classical harmony and proportion; and the simple, "rustic" **Hameau,** or hamlet, that Marie Antoinette built so that she could play at being a simple shepherdess.

The contrast between the majestic and the domesticated is an important part of Versailles's appeal, but pomp and bombast dominate the mood here, and you won't need reminding that you're in the world's grandest palace—or one of France's most popular tourist attractions. The park outside is the ideal place to get your breath back. Le Nôtre's gardens represent formal landscaping at its most rigid and sophisticated.

Getting There

By Car Take highway A13 from Porte d'Auteuil then follow the signs to Versailles.

By Train There are three train routes from Paris to Versailles (20–30 min). The RER-C to Versailles Rive-Gauche takes you closest to the château (just 600 yards from it via avenue de Sceaux). The other trains run from Gare St-Lazare to Versailles Rive-Droite (⅔ mile via rue Foch and avenue de St-Cloud), and from Gare Montparnasse to Versailles-Chantiers (¾ mile via rue des Etats Généraux and avenue de Paris).

Guided Tours

Paris Vision and **Cityrama** (*see* Guided Tours in Chartres, *above,* for addresses) offer half- and full-day guided bus tours of Versailles, Fontainebleau, Barbizon, and Chartres. Trips cost from 165 francs (half day) to 435 francs (full day).

Tourist Information

Office de Tourisme, 7 rue des Réservoirs, tel. 39–50–36–22.

Château, **1**
Les Grands Appartements, **2**
Water Terrace, **3**
Orangerie, **4**
Water Mirror Basin, **5**
Latona Basin, **6**
Neptune Basin; Dragon Basin, **7**
Obelisk Basin, **8**
Enceladus Basin, **9**
Apollo Basin, **10**
Grand Trianon, **11**
Petit Trianon, **12**
Hameau, **13**

Exploring

The **château** was built under court architects Le Vau and Mansart between 1662 and 1690; entrance is through the gilt-and-iron gates from the huge place d'Armes. In the center of the building, across the sprawling cobbled forecourt, are the rooms that belonged to the king and queen. The two wings were occupied by the royal children and princes; attendants were housed in the attics.

The highlight of the tour, for many, is the **Galerie des Glaces** (Hall of Mirrors), now fully restored to its original dazzle. It was here that Bismarck proclaimed the unified German Empire in 1871, and here that the controversial Treaty of Versailles, asserting Germany's responsibility for World War I, was signed in 1919.

The royal bedchambers are formal; the **petits appartements,** where royal family and friends lived, are more on a human scale. The intimate **Opéra Royal,** the first oval hall in France, was designed for Louis XV. Touch the "marble" loges—they're actually painted wood. The chapel, built by Mansart, is a study in white-and-gold solemnity. *Admission to château: 31 frs; Sun. 15 frs. Open Tues.–Sun. 9–7 (5:30 in winter); Galerie des Glaces open 9:45–5; Opéra Royal open 9:45–3:30 (tours every 15 min). Closed Mon.*

The 250-acre **grounds** include woods, lawns, flower beds, statues, lakes, and fountains. They are at their best in the fall. The fountains play on several Sundays in summer, making a fabulous spectacle. *The grounds are free and open daily.*

At one end of the Petit Canal, about a mile from the château, stands the **Grand Trianon,** built by Mansart in the 1680s. This pink-marble pleasure palace is now used to entertain visiting heads of state; at other times it is open to the public. *Admission: Grand Trianon: 17 frs; Petit Trianon: 12 frs. Open Oct.– Apr. Tues.–Fri. 10–12:30 and 2–5:30, weekends 10–5:30; May–Sept. Tues.–Sun. 11–6:30.*

The **Petit Trianon,** close by, is a sumptuously furnished neoclassical mansion erected in 1768 by architect Gabriel. Louis XV had a superb botanical garden planted here; some of the trees from that era survive today. Louis XVI presented the Petit Trianon to Marie Antoinette, who spent lavish sums creating an idealized world, the charming *hameau* (hamlet, a handful of thatched-roof cottages) with watermill, lake, and pigeon loft— outrageously pretty and too good to be true. *Hours same as for Grand Trianon.*

The town of Versailles tends to be underestimated. Visitors are usually exhausted from exploring the palace and park, but the town's broad, leafy boulevards are also agreeable places to stroll. The **Cathédrale St-Louis** is an austere edifice built from 1743 to 1754 by Mansart's grand-nephew, and it contains fine paintings and an organ loft. The **Eglise Notre Dame** is a sturdy Baroque monument, built from 1684 to 1686 by the elder Mansart as the parish church for the Sun King's new town, for which Louis XIV deigned to lay the foundation stone. The collection of the **Musée Lambinet,** housed nearby in an imposing 18th-century mansion, is wide-ranging, with a maze of cozy, finely furnished rooms full of paintings, weapons, fans, and porcelain. *54 blvd. de la Reine. Admission: 10 frs. Open Tues.– Sun. 2–6; closed Mon.*

Dining

Les Trois Marches. This is one of the best-known restaurants in the Paris area. It was recently relocated to the sumptuous Trianon Palace Hotel, near the château park. Chef Gérard Vié specializes in creative dishes such as duckling roasted with vinegar and honey. The great style that reigns here can be experienced less expensively by coming for the fixed-price (260 frs) weekday lunch. *1 blvd. de la Reine, tel. 39–50–13–21. Reservations essential. Jacket and tie required. AE, DC, MC, V. Closed Sun., Mon., and Aug. Very Expensive.*

Quai No. 1. Barometers, sails, and model boats contribute to the nautical decor at this small, charming fish and seafood restaurant. Home-smoked salmon is a specialty here, though any dish on the two set menus will prove to be a good value. *1 av. de St-Cloud, tel. 39–50–42–26. Reservations advised. Dress: casual. MC, V. Closed Sun. evening and Mon. Moderate.*

La Grande Sirène. The addition of an appealing 148-franc lunch menu (wine included) served every day but Sunday makes this pretty spot near the château a popular noontime choice. Zesty simmered snails and well-prepared fish are good choices here. *25 rue du Maréchal-Foch, tel. 39–53–08–08. Reservations advised. Dress: casual. AE, MC, V. Moderate.*

Conversion Tables

Distance

Kilometers/Miles To change kilometers to miles, multiply kilometers by .621.
To change miles to kilometers, multiply miles by 1.61.

Km to Mi	Mi to Km
1 = .62	1 = 1.6
2 = 1.2	2 = 3.2
3 = 1.9	3 = 4.8
4 = 2.5	4 = 6.4
5 = 3.1	5 = 8.1
6 = 3.7	6 = 9.7
7 = 4.3	7 = 11.3
8 = 5.0	8 = 12.9
9 = 5.6	9 = 14.5

Meters/Feet To change meters to feet, multiply meters by 3.28.
To change feet to meters, multiply feet by .305.

Meters to Feet	Feet to Meters
1 = 3.3	1 = .31
2 = 6.6	2 = .61
3 = 9.8	3 = .92
4 = 13.1	4 = 1.2
5 = 16.4	5 = 1.5
6 = 19.7	6 = 1.8
7 = 23.0	7 = 2.1
8 = 26.2	8 = 2.4
9 = 29.5	9 = 2.7

Weight

Kilograms/Pounds To change kilograms to pounds, multiply kilos by 2.20.
To change pounds to kilograms, multiply pounds by .453.

Kilo to Pound	Pound to Kilo
1 = 2.2	1 = .45
2 = 4.4	2 = .91
3 = 6.6	3 = 1.4
4 = 8.8	4 = 1.8
5 = 11.0	5 = 2.3

6 = 13.2	6 = 2.7
7 = 15.4	7 = 3.2
8 = 17.6	8 = 3.6
9 = 19.8	9 = 4.1

Grams/Ounces To change grams to ounces, multiply grams by .035.
To change ounces to grams, multiply ounces by 28.4.

Grams to Ounces	Ounces to Grams
1 = .04	1 = 28
2 = .07	2 = 57
3 = .11	3 = 85
4 = .14	4 = 114
5 = .18	5 = 142
6 = .21	6 = 170
7 = .25	7 = 199
8 = .28	8 = 227
9 = .32	9 = 256

Liquid Volume

Liters/U.S. Gallons To change liters to U.S. gallons, multiply liters by .264.
To change U.S. gallons to liters, multiply gallons by 3.79.

Liters to U.S. Gallons	U.S. Gallons to Liters
1 = .26	1 = 3.8
2 = .53	2 = 7.6
3 = .79	3 = 11.4
4 = 1.1	4 = 15.1
5 = 1.3	5 = 18.9
6 = 1.6	6 = 22.7
7 = 1.8	7 = 26.5
8 = 2.1	8 = 30.3
9 = 2.4	9 = 34.1

Clothing Sizes

Men To change American suit sizes to French suit sizes, add 10 to
Suits the American suit size.
To change French suit sizes to American suit sizes, subtract 10 from the French suit size.

U.S.	36	38	40	42	44	46	48
French	46	48	50	52	54	56	58

Shirts To change American shirt sizes to French shirt sizes, multiply the American shirt size by 2 and add 8.

To change French shirt sizes to American shirt sizes, subtract 8 from the French shirt size and divide by 2.

U.S.	14	14½	15	15½	16	16½	17	17½
French	36	37	38	39	40	41	42	43

Shoes French shoe sizes vary in their relation to American shoe sizes.

U.S.	6½	7	8	9	10	10½	11
French	39	40	41	42	43	44	45

Women
Dresses and Coats To change U.S. dress/coat sizes to French dress/coat sizes, add 28 to the U.S. dress/coat size.
To change French dress/coat sizes to U.S. dress/coat sizes, subtract 28 from the French dress/coat size.

U.S.	4	6	8	10	12	14	16
French	32	34	36	38	40	42	44

Blouses and Sweaters To change U.S. blouse/sweater sizes to French blouse/sweater sizes, add 8 to the U.S. blouse/sweater size.
To change French blouse/sweater sizes to U.S. blouse/sweater sizes, subtract 8 from the French blouse/sweater size.

U.S.	30	32	34	36	38	40	42
French	38	40	42	44	46	48	50

Shoes To change U.S. shoe sizes to French shoe sizes, add 32 to the U.S. shoe size.
To change French shoe sizes to U.S. shoe sizes, subtract 32 from the French shoe size.

U.S.	4	5	6	7	8	9	10
French	36	37	38	39	40	41	42

French Vocabulary

Words and Phrases

	English	*French*	*Pronunciation*
Basics	Yes/no	Oui/non	wee/no
	Please	S'il vous plaît	seel voo play
	Thank you	Merci	mare-**see**
	You're welcome	De rien	deh ree-**en**
	That's all right	Il n'y a pas de quoi	eel nee ah pah de kwa
	Excuse me, sorry	Pardon	pahr-**doan**
	Sorry!	Désolé(e)	day-zoh-**lay**
	Good morning/ afternoon	Bonjour	bone-**joor**
	Good evening	Bonsoir	bone-**swar**
	Goodbye	Au revoir	o ruh-**vwar**
	Mr. (Sir)	Monsieur	mih-see-**oor**
	Mrs. (Ma'am)	Madame	ma-**dam**
	Miss	Mademoiselle	mad-mwa-**zel**
	Pleased to meet you	Enchanté(e)	on-shahn-**tay**
	How are you?	Comment allez-vous?	ko-mon-tahl-ay-**voo**
	Very well, thanks	Très bien, merci	tray bee-**en,** mare-**see**
	And you?	Et vous?	ay voo?
Numbers	one	un	un
	two	deux	deu
	three	trois	twa
	four	quatre	**cat**-ruh
	five	cinq	sank
	six	six	seess
	seven	sept	set
	eight	huit	wheat
	nine	neuf	nuf
	ten	dix	deess
	eleven	onze	owns
	twelve	douze	dooz
	thirteen	treize	trays
	fourteen	quatorze	ka-torz
	fifteen	quinze	cans
	sixteen	seize	sez
	seventeen	dix-sept	deess-**set**
	eighteen	dix-huit	deess-**wheat**
	nineteen	dix-neuf	deess-**nuf**
	twenty	vingt	vant
	twenty-one	vingt-et-un	vant-ay-**un**
	thirty	trente	trahnt
	forty	quarante	**ka**-rahnt
	fifty	cinquante	**sang**-kahnt
	sixty	soixante	**swa**-sahnt
	seventy	soixante-dix	swa-sahnt-**deess**
	eighty	quatre-vingts	cat-ruh-**vant**
	ninety	quatre-vingt-dix	cat-ruh-vant-**deess**

	one-hundred	cent	sahnt
	one-thousand	mille	meel
Colors	black	noir	nwar
	blue	bleu	blu
	brown	brun	brun
	green	vert	vair
	orange	orange	o-**ranj**
	pink	rose	rose
	red	rouge	rouge
	violet	violette	vee-o-**let**
	white	blanc	blahnk
	yellow	jaune	jone
Days of the Week	Sunday	dimanche	dee-**mahnsh**
	Monday	lundi	lan-**dee**
	Tuesday	mardi	mar-**dee**
	Wednesday	mercredi	mare-kruh-**dee**
	Thursday	jeudi	juh-**dee**
	Friday	vendredi	van-dra-**dee**
	Saturday	samedi	sam-**dee**
Months	January	janvier	jan-**vyay**
	February	février	feh-vree-**ay**
	March	mars	maars
	April	avril	a-**vreel**
	May	mai	meh
	June	juin	jwan
	July	juillet	jwee-**ay**
	August	août	oot
	September	septembre	sep-**tahm**-bruh
	October	octobre	ok-**toe**-bruh
	November	novembre	no-**vahm**-bruh
	December	décembre	day-**sahm**-bruh
Useful Phrases	Do you speak English?	Parlez-vous anglais?	par-lay vooz ahng-**glay**
	I don't speak French	Je ne parle pas français	jeh nuh parl pah fraun-**say**
	I don't understand	Je ne comprends pas	jeh nuh kohm-prahn **pah**
	I understand	Je comprends	jeh kohm-**prahn**
	I don't know	Je ne sais pas	jeh nuh say **pah**
	I'm American/British	Je suis américain/anglais	jeh sweez a-may-ree-**can**/ahng-**glay**
	What's your name?	Comment vous appelez-vous?	ko-mahn voo za-pel-ay-**voo**
	My name is . . .	Je m'appelle . . .	jeh ma-**pel** . . .
	What time is it?	Quelle heure est-il?	kel ur et-**il**
	How?	Comment?	ko-**mahn**
	When?	Quand?	kahn
	Yesterday	Hier	yair
	Today	Aujourd'hui	o-zhoor-**dwee**

Tomorrow	Demain	deh-**man**
This morning/ afternoon	Ce matin/cet après-midi	seh ma-**tanh**/set ah-pray-mee-**dee**
Tonight	Ce soir	seh **swar**
What?	Quoi?	kwa
What is it?	Qu'est-ce que c'est?	kess-kuh-**say**
Why?	Pourquoi?	poor-**kwa**
Who?	Qui?	kee
Where is . . .	Où est . . .	oo ay
the train station?	la gare?	la gar
the subway station?	la station de métro?	la sta-syon deh may-**tro**
the bus stop?	l'arrêt de bus?	la-ray deh **booss**
the terminal (airport)?	l'aérogare?	lay-ro-**gar**
the post office?	la poste?	la post
the bank?	la banque?	la bahnk
the . . . hotel?	l'hôtel . . .?	low-**tel**
the store?	le magasin?	luh ma-ga-**zan**
the cashier?	la caisse?	la **kess**
the . . . museum?	le musée . . .?	leh mew-**zay**
the hospital?	l'hôpital?	low-pee-**tal**
the elevator?	l'ascenseur?	la-sahn-**seur**
the telephone?	le téléphone?	leh te-le-**phone**
Where are the restrooms?	Où sont les toilettes?	oo son lay twah-**let**
Here/there	Ici/là	ee-**see**/la
Left/right	A gauche/à droite	a goash/a drwat
Straight ahead	Tout droit	too drwa
Is it near/far?	C'est près/loin?	say pray/lwan
I'd like . . .	Je voudrais . . .	jeh voo-**dray**
a room	une chambre	ewn **shahm**-bra
the key	la clé	la clay
a newspaper	un journal	un joor-**nahl**
a stamp	un timbre	un **tam**-bruh
I'd like to buy . . .	Je voudrais acheter . . .	jeh voo-**dray** ash-**tay**
a cigar	un cigare	un see-**gar**
cigarettes	des cigarettes	day see-ga-**ret**
matches	des allumettes	days a-loo-**met**
dictionary	un dictionnaire	un deek-see-oh-**nare**
soap	du savon	dew sa-vone
city plan	un plan de ville	un plahn de la **veel**
road map	une carte routière	ewn cart roo-tee-**air**
magazine	une revue	ewn reh-**view**
envelopes	des enveloppes	dayz ahn-veh-**lope**
writing paper	du papier à lettres	dew pa-pee-ay a **let**-ruh

airmail writing paper	du papier avion	dew pa-pee-ay a-vee-**own**
postcard	une carte postale	ewn cart post-**al**
How much is it?	C'est combien?	say comb-bee-**en**
It's expensive/ cheap	C'est cher/pas cher	say sher/pa sher
A little/a lot	Un peu/beaucoup	un puh/bo-**koo**
More/less	Plus/moins	ploo/mwa
Enough/too (much)	Assez/trop	a-**say**/tro
I am ill/sick	Je suis malade	jeh swee ma-**lahd**
Call a doctor	Appelez un médecin	a-pe-lay un med-**san**
Help!	Au secours!	o say-**koor**
Stop!	Arrêtez!	a-reh-**tay**
Fire!	Au feu!	o fuw
Caution!/Look out!	Attention!	a-tahn-see-**own**

Dining Out

A bottle of . . .	une bouteille de . . .	ewn boo-**tay** deh
A cup of . . .	une tasse de . . .	ewn tass deh
A glass of . . .	un verre de . . .	un vair deh
Ashtray	un cendrier	un sahn-dree-**ay**
Bill/check	l'addition	la-dee-see-**own**
Bread	du pain	dew pan
Breakfast	le petit-déjeuner	leh pet-**ee** day-zhu-**nay**
Butter	du beurre	dew bur
Cheers!	A votre santé!	ah vo-truh sahn-**tay**
Cocktail/aperitif	un apéritif	un ah-pay-ree-**teef**
Dinner	le dîner	leh dee-**nay**
Dish of the day	le plat du jour	leh pla do **zhoor**
Enjoy!	Bon appétit!	bone a-pay-**tee**
Fixed-price menu	le menu	leh may-**new**
Fork	une fourchette	ewn four-**shet**
I am diabetic	Je suis diabétique	jeh swee-dee-ah-bay-**teek**
I am on a diet	Je suis au régime	jeh sweez o ray-**jeem**
I am vegetarian	Je suis végétarien(ne)	jeh swee vay-jay-ta-ree-**en**
I cannot eat . . .	Je ne peux pas manger de . . .	jeh nuh puh pah mahn-**jay** deh
I'd like to order	Je voudrais commander	jeh voo-**dray** ko-mahn-**day**

I'd like . . .	Je voudrais . . .	jeh voo-**dray**
I'm hungry/thirsty	J'ai faim/soif	jay fam/swahf
Is service/the tip included?	Est-ce que le service est compris?	ess keh leh sair-veess ay comb-**pree**
It's good/bad	C'est bon/mauvais	say bon/mo-**vay**
It's hot/cold	C'est chaud/froid	say sho/frwah
Knife	un couteau	un koo-**toe**
Lunch	le déjeuner	leh day-juh-**nay**
Menu	la carte	la cart
Napkin	une serviette	ewn sair-vee-**et**
Pepper	du poivre	dew **pwah**-vruh
Plate	une assiette	ewn a-see-**et**
Please give me . . .	Donnez-moi . . .	doe-nay-**mwah**
Salt	du sel	dew sell
Spoon	une cuillère	ewn kwee-**air**
Sugar	du sucre	dew **sook**-ruh
Waiter!/Waitress!	Monsieur!/ Mademoiselle!	mih-see-**oor**/ mad-mwah-**zel**
Wine list	la carte des vins	la cart day **van**

Menu Guide

English	French
Set menu	Menu à prix fixe
Dish of the day	Plat du jour
Choice of vegetable accompaniment	Garniture au choix
Made to order	Sur commande
Extra charge	Supplément/En sus
When available	Selon arrivage

Breakfast

Jam	Confiture
Honey	Miel
Boiled egg	Oeuf à la coque
Bacon and eggs	Oeufs au bacon
Ham and eggs	Oeufs au jambon
Fried eggs	Oeufs sur le plat
Scrambled eggs	Oeufs brouillés
(Plain) omelet	Omelette (nature)
Rolls	Petits pains

Starters

Anchovies	Anchois
Chitterling sausage	Andouille(tte)
Assorted cold cuts	Assiette anglaise
Assorted pork products	Assiette de charcuterie
Mixed raw vegetable salad	Crudités
Snails	Escargots
Assorted appetizers	Hors-d'oeuvres variés
Ham (Bayonne)	Jambon (de Bayonne)
Cured pig's knuckle	Jambonneau
Bologna sausage	Mortadelle
Deviled eggs	Oeufs à la diable
Liver purée blended with other meat	Pâté
Light dumplings (fish, fowl, or meat)	Quenelles
Dried sausage	Saucisson
Pâté sliced and served from an earthenware pot	Terrine
Cured dried beef	Viande séchée

Salads

Diced vegetable salad	Salade russe
Endive salad	Salade d'endives
Green salad	Salade verte
Mixed salad	Salade panachée
Riviera combination salad	Salade niçoise
Tuna salad	Salade de thon

Soups

Cold leek and potato cream soup	Vichyssoise
Cream of . . .	Crême de . . .
Cream of . . .	Velouté de . . .

Hearty soup	Soupe
day's soup	*du jour*
French onion soup	*à l'oignon*
Provençal vegetable soup	*au pistou*
Light soup	Potage
shredded vegetables	*julienne*
potato	*parmentier*
Fish and seafood stew	Bouillabaisse
Seafood stew (chowder)	Bisque
Stew of meat and vegetables	Pot-au-feu

Fish and Seafood

Angler	Lotte de mer
Bass	Bar
Burbot	Lotte
Carp	Carpe
Catfish	Loup
Clams	Palourdes
Cod	Morue
Creamed salt cod	Brandade de morue
Fresh cod	Cabillaud
Crab	Crabe
Crayfish	Ecrevisses
Eel	Anguille
Fish stew from Marseilles	Bourride
Fish stew in wine	Matelote
Frogs' legs	Cuisses de grenouilles
Herring	Harengs
Lobster	Homard
Spiny lobster	Langouste
Mackerel	Maquereau
Mussels	Moules
Octopus	Poulpes
Oysters	Huîtres
Perch	Perche
Pike	Brochet
Prawns	Ecrevisses
Dublin bay prawns (scampi)	Langoustines
Red mullet	Rouget
Salmon	Saumon
Scallops in creamy sauce	Coquille St-Jacques
Sea bream	Daurade
Shrimp	Crevettes
Skate	Raie
Smelt	Eperlans
Sole	Sole
Squid	Calmar
Trout	Truite
Tuna	Thon
Whiting	Merlan
Fish used in bouillabaisse	Rascasse

Meat

Beef	Boeuf
Brains	Cervelle
Chops	Côtelettes
Cutlet	Escalope
Fillet steak	Filet

Double fillet steak	Chateaubriand
Kabob	Brochette
Kidneys	Rognons
Lamb	Agneau
Leg	Gigot
Liver	Foie
Loin strip steak	Contre-filet
Meatballs	Boulettes de viande
Pig's feet	Pieds de cochon
Pork	Porc
Rib	Côte
Rib or rib-eye steak	Entrecôte
Saddle	Selle
Sausages	Saucisses
Sausages and cured pork served with sauerkraut	Choucroute garnie
Shoulder	Epaule
Steak (always beef)	Steak/steack
Stew	Ragoût
T-bone steak	Côte de boeuf
Tenderloin steak	Médaillon
Tenderloin of T-bone steak	Tournedos
Tongue	Langue
Veal	Veau
Veal sweetbreads	Ris de veau
Casserole of white beans and meat	Cassoulet toulousain

Methods of Preparation

Very rare	Bleu
Rare	Saignant
Medium	A point
Well-done	Bien cuit
Baked	Au four
Boiled	Bouilli
Braised	Braisé
Fried	Frit
Grilled	Grillé
Roast	Rôti
Sautéed	Sauté
Stewed	A l'étouffée

Game and Poultry

Chicken	Poulet
Chicken breast	Suprême de volaille
Chicken stewed in red wine	Coq au vin
Chicken stewed with vegetables	Poule au pot
Spring chicken	Poussin
Duck/duckling	Canard/caneton
Fattened pullet	Poularde
Fowl	Volaille
Guinea fowl/young guinea fowl	Pintade/pintadeau
Goose	Oie
Partridge/young partridge	Perdrix/perdreau
Pheasant	Faisan
Pigeon/squab	Pigeon/pigeonneau
Quail	Caille

Rabbit	Lapin
Thrush	Grive
Turkey/young turkey	Dinde/dindonneau
Venison (red/roe)	Cerf/chevreuil
Wild boar/young wild boar	Sanglier/marcassin
Wild hare	Lièvre

Vegetables

Artichoke	Artichaut
Asparagus	Asperge
Broad beans	Fèves
Brussels sprouts	Choux de Bruxelles
Cabbage (red)	Chou (rouge)
Carrots	Carottes
Cauliflower	Chou-fleur
Chicory	Chicorée
Eggplant	Aubergine
Endive	Endive
Leeks	Poireaux
Lentils	Lentilles
Lettuce	Laitue
Mushrooms	Champignons
Onions	Oignons
Peas	Petits pois
Peppers	Poivrons
Potato	Pomme de terre
Radishes	Radis
Spinach	Epinard
Tomatoes	Tomates
Watercress	Cresson
Zucchini	Courgette
White kidney/French beans	Haricots blancs/verts

Potatoes, Rice, and Noodles

Noodles	Nouilles
Pasta	Pâtes
Potatoes	Pommes (de terre)
matchsticks	*allumettes*
mashed and deep-fried	*dauphine*
mashed with butter and egg yolks	*duchesse*
in their jackets	*en robe des champs*
french fries	*frites*
mashed	*mousseline*
boiled/steamed	*nature/vapeur*
Rice	Riz
boiled in bouillon with onions	*pilaf*

Sauces and Preparations

Brown butter, parsley, lemon juice	Meunière
Curry	Indienne
Egg yolks, butter, vinegar	Hollandaise
Hot pepper	Diable
Mayonnaise flavored with mustard and herbs	Tartare
Mushrooms	Forestière
Mushrooms, red wine, shallots, beef marrow	Bordelaise

Onions, tomatoes, garlic	Provençale
Pepper sauce	Poivrade
Red wine, herbs	Bourguignon
Vinegar, egg yolks, white wine, shallots, tarragon	Béarnaise
Vinegar dressing	Vinaigrette
White sauce	Béchamel
White wine, mussel broth, egg yolks	Marinière
Wine, mushrooms, onions, shallots	Chasseur
With goose or duck liver purée and truffles	Périgueux
With Madeira wine	Madère

Fruits and Nuts

Almonds	Amandes
Apple	Pomme
Apricot	Abricot
Banana	Banane
Blackberries	Mûres
Blackcurrants	Cassis
Blueberries	Myrtilles
Cherries	Cerises
Chestnuts	Marrons
Coconut	Noix de coco
Dates	Dattes
Dried fruit	Fruits secs
Figs	Figues
Grapefruit	Pamplemousse
Grapes green/blue	Raisins blancs/noirs
Hazelnuts	Noisettes
Lemon	Citron
Lime	Citron vert
Melon	Melon
Nectarine	Brugnon
Orange	Orange
Peach	Pêche
Peanuts	Cacahouètes
Pear	Poire
Pineapple	Ananas
Plums	Prunes
Prunes	Pruneaux
Raisins	Raisins secs
Raspberries	Framboises
Red currants	Groseilles
Strawberries	Fraises
Tangerine	Mandarine
Walnuts	Noix
Watermelon	Pastèque

Desserts

Apple pie	Tarte aux pommes
Caramel pudding	Crème caramel
Chocolate cake	Gâteau au chocolat
Chocolate pudding	Mousse au chocolat
Custard	Flan
Ice cream	Glace
Ice-cream cake	Vacherin glacé

Layer cake	Tourte
Sundae	Coupe (glacée)
Water ice	Sorbet
Whipped cream	Crème Chantilly
Thin pancakes simmered in orange juice and flambéed with orange liqueur	Crêpe suzette

Alcoholic Drinks

Straight	Sec
On the rocks	Avec des glaçons
With water	A l'eau
Apple brandy	Calvados
Beer	Bière
Light/dark	*Blonde/brune*
Brandy	Eau–de–vie
Cocktails	Apéritifs
Chilled white wine mixed with blackcurrant syrup	*Kir/blanc-cassis*
Cherry brandy	Kirsch
Cordial	Liqueur
Pear brandy	Poire William
Port	Porto
Wine	Vin
dry	*sec*
very dry	*brut*
light	*léger*
sweet	*doux*
red	*rouge*
rosé	*rosé*
sparkling	*mousseux*
white	*blanc*

Nonalcoholic Drinks

Coffee	Café
black	*noir*
cream	*crème*
with milk	*au lait*
caffein-free	*décaféiné*
espresso	*express*
Ginger ale	Limonade gazeuse
Herb tea	Tisane
Hot chocolate	Chocolat chaud
Lemonade	Limonade
Milk	Lait
Mineral water	Eau minérale
carbonated	*gazeuse*
still	*non gazeuse*
. . . juice (see fruit)	Jus de . . .
Tea	Thé
with milk/lemon	*crème/citron*
iced tea	*glacé*
Tonic water	Schweppes

Index

Fodor's Travel Guides

Available at bookstores everywhere, or call 1–800–533–6478, 24 hours a day.

U.S. Guides

Alaska

Arizona

Boston

California

Cape Cod, Martha's Vineyard, Nantucket

The Carolinas & the Georgia Coast

Chicago

Colorado

Florida

Hawaii

Las Vegas, Reno, Tahoe

Los Angeles

Maine, Vermont, New Hampshire

Maui

Miami & the Keys

New England

New Orleans

New York City

Pacific North Coast

Philadelphia & the Pennsylvania Dutch Country

The Rockies

San Diego

San Francisco

Santa Fe, Taos, Albuquerque

Seattle & Vancouver

The South

The U.S. & British Virgin Islands

The Upper Great Lakes Region

USA

Vacations in New York State

Vacations on the Jersey Shore

Virginia & Maryland

Waikiki

Walt Disney World and the Orlando Area

Washington, D.C.

Foreign Guides

Acapulco, Ixtapa, Zihuatanejo

Australia & New Zealand

Austria

The Bahamas

Baja & Mexico's Pacific Coast Resorts

Barbados

Berlin

Bermuda

Brazil

Brittany & Normandy

Budapest

Canada

Cancun, Cozumel, Yucatan Peninsula

Caribbean

China

Costa Rica, Belize, Guatemala

The Czech Republic & Slovakia

Eastern Europe

Egypt

Euro Disney

Europe

Europe's Great Cities

Florence & Tuscany

France

Germany

Great Britain

Greece

The Himalayan Countries

Hong Kong

India

Ireland

Israel

Italy

Japan

Kenya & Tanzania

Korea

London

Madrid & Barcelona

Mexico

Montreal & Quebec City

Morocco

Moscow & St. Petersburg

The Netherlands, Belgium & Luxembourg

New Zealand

Norway

Nova Scotia, Prince Edward Island & New Brunswick

Paris

Portugal

Provence & the Riviera

Rome

Russia & the Baltic Countries

Scandinavia

Scotland

Singapore

South America

Southeast Asia

Spain

Sweden

Switzerland

Thailand

Tokyo

Toronto

Turkey

Vienna & the Danube Valley

Yugoslavia

WHEREVER YOU TRAVEL, *H*ELP IS NEVER FAR AWAY.

From planning your trip to providing travel assistance along the way, American Express® Travel Service Offices* are always there to help.

PARIS

11 Rue Scribe, 9th
47-777-707

5 Rue de Chaillot, 16th
47-237-215

83 Bis, Rue de Courcelles, 17th
47-660-300

38 Avenue de Wagram, 8th
42-275-880

155 Avenue Victor Hugo, 16th
47-274-319

Euro Disney®
Disneyland Hotel
Marne la Vallée
60-456-520

INTRODUCING

Fodor's
WORLDVIEW
TRAVEL UPDATE

AT LAST, YOUR OWN PERSONALIZED LIST OF WHAT'S GOING ON IN THE CITIES YOU'RE VISITING.

KEYED TO THE DAYS WHEN YOU'RE THERE, CUSTOMIZED FOR YOUR INTERESTS, AND SENT TO YOU BEFORE YOU LEAVE HOME.

EXCLUSIVE FOR PURCHASERS OF FODOR'S GUIDES...

Introducing a revolutionary way to get customized, time-sensitive travel information just before your trip.

Now you can obtain detailed information about what's going on in each city you'll be visiting <u>before</u> you leave home—up-to-the-minute, objective information about the events and activities that interest you most.

This is a special offer for purchasers of Fodor's guides – a customized Travel Update to fit your specific interests and your itinerary.

Travel Updates contain the kind of time-sensitive insider information you can get only from local contacts – or from city magazines and newspapers once you arrive. But now you can have the same information before you leave for your trip.

The choice is yours: current art exhibits, theater, music festivals and special concerts, sporting events, antiques and flower shows, shopping, fitness, and more.

The information comes from hundreds of correspondents and thousands of sources worldwide. Updated continuously, it's like having your own personal concierge or friend in the city.

You specify the cities and when you'll be there. We'll do the rest — personalizing the information for you the way no guidebook can.

It's the perfect extension to your Fodor's guide and the best way to make the most of your valuable travel time.

Your Itinerary:
Customized reports available for 160 destinations

Reg
The
in th
domai
tion as
worthwhil
the perfor
Tickets are u
venue. Alter
mances are canc
given. For more
Open-Air Theatre,
NW1 4NP Open Air
Tel: 935-5756. Ends: 9-
International Air Tattoo
Held biennially, the wo
military air displa
demostra
tions,
ba

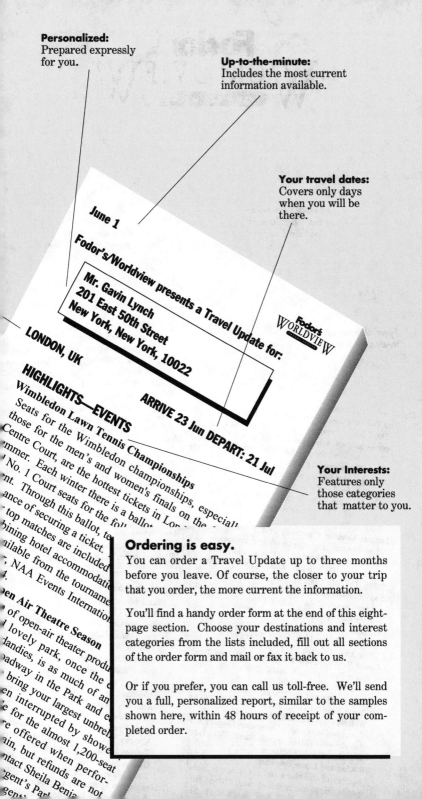

Personalized:
Prepared expressly for you.

Up-to-the-minute:
Includes the most current information available.

Your travel dates:
Covers only days when you will be there.

June 1

Fodor's/Worldview presents a Travel Update for:

Mr. Gavin Lynch
201 East 50th Street
New York, New York, 10022

Fodor's
WORLDVIEW

LONDON, UK

ARRIVE 23 Jun DEPART: 21 Jul

Your Interests:
Features only those categories that matter to you.

HIGHLIGHTS—EVENTS

Wimbledon Lawn Tennis Championships

Seats for the Wimbledon championships, especiall
those for the men's and women's finals on the
Centre Court, are the hottest tickets in Lon
mmer. Each winter there is a ballo
No. 1 Court seats for the foll
nt. Through this ballot, te
ance of securing a ticket.
top matches are included
ailable from the tournam
; NAA Events Internatio

en Air Theatre Season

of open-air theater produ
lovely park, once the
landies, is as much of an
adway in the Park and e
bring your largest unbre
en interrupted by showe
e for the almost 1,200-seat
e offered when perfor-
ain, but refunds are not
ntact Sheila Benja
gent's Par

Ordering is easy.

You can order a Travel Update up to three months before you leave. Of course, the closer to your trip that you order, the more current the information.

You'll find a handy order form at the end of this eight-page section. Choose your destinations and interest categories from the lists included, fill out all sections of the order form and mail or fax it back to us.

Or if you prefer, you can call us toll-free. We'll send you a full, personalized report, similar to the samples shown here, within 48 hours of receipt of your completed order.

**Special concerts—
who's performing
what and where**

**One-of-a-kind,
one-time-only events**

**Special interest,
in-depth listings**

Children — Events
Angel Canal Festival
The festivities include a children's funfair, entertainers, a boat rally and displays on the water. Regent's Canal. Islington. N1. Tube: Angel. Tel: 267 9100. 11:30am-5:30pm. 7/04.
Blackheath Summer Kite Festival
Stunt kite displays with parachuting teddy bears and trade stands. Free admission. SE3. BR: Blackheath. 10am. 6/27.
Megabugs
Children will delight in this infestation of giant robotic insects, including a praying mantic 60 times life size. Mon-Sat 10am-6pm; Sun 11am-6pm. Admission 4.50 pounds. Natural History Museum, Cromwell Road. SW7. Tube: South Kensington. Tel: 938 9123. Ends 10/01.
Childminders
This establishment employs only women, providing nurses and qualified nannies to

Music — Jazz & Blues
Tito Puente's Golden Men of Latin Jazz
The father of mambo and Cuban rumba king comes to town. Royal Festival Hall. South Bank. SE1. Tube: Waterloo. Tel: 928 8800. 8pm. 7/15.
Georgie Fame and The New York Band
Riding a popular tide with his latest album, the smoky-voiced Fame and his keyboard are on a tour yet again. The Grand. Clapham Junction. SW11. BR: Clapham Junction. Tel: 738 9000. 7:30pm. 7/07.
Jacques Loussier Play Bach Trio
The French jazz classicist and colleagues. Kenwood Lakeside. Hampstead Lane. Kenwood. NW3. Tube: Golders Green, then bus 210. Tel: 413 1443. 7pm. 7/10.
Tony Bennett and Ronnie Scott
Royal Festival Hall. South Bank. SE1. Tube: Waterloo. Tel: 928 8800. 8pm. 7/11.
Santana
Royal Festival Hall. South Bank. SE1. Tube: Waterloo. Tel: 928 8800. 8pm. 7/12.
Count Basie Orchestra and Nancy Wilson Trio
Royal Festival Hall. South Bank. SE1. Tube: Waterloo. Tel: 928 8800. 8pm. 7/14.
King Pleasure and the Biscuit Boys
Royal Festival Hall. South Bank. SE1. Tube: Waterloo. Tel: 928 8800. 6:30 and 9pm. 7/16.
Al Green and the London Community Gospel Choir
Royal Festival Hall. South Bank. SE1. Tube: Waterloo. Tel: 928 8800. 8pm. 7/13.
BB King and Linda Hopkins
Mother of the blues and successor to Bessie Smith, Hopkins meets up with "Blues Boy" ... ... Hall. South Bank. SE

Music — Classical
Marylebone Sinfonia
Kenneth Gowen conducts music by Pu... and Rossini. Queen Elizabeth Hall. S... Bank. SE1. Tube: Waterloo. Tel: 928 8... 7:45pm. 7/16.
London Philharmonic
Franz Welser-Moest and George Benj... conduct selections by Alexander G... Messiaen, and some of Benjamin's own ... positions. Queen Elizabeth Hall. South ... SE1. Tube: Waterloo. Tel: 928 8800. 8p...
London Pro Arte Orchestra and Forest C...
Murray Stewart conducts selection... Rossini, Haydn and Jonathan Willcocks... Queen Elizabeth Hall. South Bank. ... Tube: Waterloo. Tel: 928 8800. 7:45pm...
Kensington Symphony Orchestra
Russell Keable conducts Dvorak's ...

Here's what you get . . .

Detailed information about what's going on — precisely when you'll be there.

Show openings during your visit

Reviews by local critics

Exhibitions & Shows—Antique & Flower
Westminster Antiques Fair
Over 50 stands with pre-1830 furniture and other Victorian and earlier items. Thu-Fri 11am-8pm; Sat-Sun 11am-6pm. Admission 4 pounds, children free. Old Royal Horticultural Hall. Vincent Square. SW1. Tel: 0444/48 25 14. 6-24 thru 6/27.

Royal Horticultural Society Flower Show
The show includes displays of carnations, summer fruit and vegetables. Tue 11am-7pm; Wed 10am-5pm. Admission Tue 4 pounds, Wed 2 pounds. Royal Horticultural Halls. Greycoat Street and Vincent Square. SW1. Tube: Victoria. 7/20 thru 7/21.

mpton Court Palace International Flower Show
Major international garden and flower show king place in conjunction with the British

eater — Musical
Sunset Boulevard
In June, the four Andrew Lloyd Webber musicals which dominated London's stages in the 1980s (Cats, Starlight Express, Phantom of the Opera and Aspects of Love) are joined by the composer's latest work, a show rumored to have his best music to date. The 1950 Billy Wilder film about a helpless young writer who is drawn into the world of a possessive, aging silent screen star offers rich opportunities for Webber's evolving style. Soaring, aching melodies, lush technical effects and psychological thrills are all expected. Patti Lupone stars. Mon-Sat at 8pm; matinee Thu-Sat at 3pm. In-person sales only at the box office; credit card bookings, Tel: 344 0055. Admission 15-32.50 pounds. Adelphi Theatre. The Strand. WC2. Tube: Charing Cross. Tel: 836 7611. Starts: 6/21

Leonardo A Portrait of Love
A new musical about the great Renaissance arti and inventor comes in for a London premier tested by a brief run at Oxford's Old Fire Stati
utumn. The work explores the relations
Vinci and the woman '

Spectator Sports — Other Sports
Greyhound Racing: Wembley Stadium
This dog track offers good views of greyhound racing held on Mon, Wed and Fri. No credit cards. Stadium Way. Wembley. HA9. Tube: Wembley Park. Tel: 902 8833.
Benson & Hedges Cricket Cup Final
Lord's Cricket Ground. St. John's Wood Road. NW8. Tube: St. John's Wood Tel: 289 1611. 11am. 7/10.

usiness-Fax & Overnight Mail
Post Office, Trafalgar Square Branch
Offers a network of fax services, the Intelpost system, throughout the country and abroad. Mon-Sat 8am-8pm, Sun 9am-5pm. William IV Street. WC2.

Alberquerque • Atlanta • Atlantic City • Ne
Baltimore • Boston • Chicago • Cincinnati
Cleveland • Dallas/Ft.Worth • Denver • De
• Houston • Kansas City • Las Vegas • Los
Angeles • Memphis • Miami • Milwaukee •
New Orleans • New York City • Orlando •
Springs • Philadelphia • Phoenix • Pittsburg
Portland • Salt Lake • San Antonio • San Di
• San Franc   Seattle • St Louis • Tamp
Oslo • Wash   St. Louis • Tamp
Hawaii • Kauai • Maui • Abacos • Bimini
lu • Island
Ber   a Countryside • Hammon   slan
Antigua & B   uilla
Gorda • Barbados • Dominica • Gren
cia • St. Vincent • Trinidad &Tobago
ymans • Puerto Plata • Santo Doming
Aruba • Bonaire • Curacao • St. Ma
ec City • Montreal • Ottawa • Toron
Vancouver • Guadeloupe • Martiniqu
elemy • St. Martin • Kingston • Ixta
o Bay • Negril • Ocho Rios • Ponce
n • Grand Turk • Providenciales • S
St. John • St. Thomas • Acapulco •
& Isla Mujeres • Cozumel • Guadal
a • Los Cabos • Manzinillo • Mazatl
City • Monterrey • Oaxaca • Puerto
do • Puerto Vallarta • Veracruz • a

Fodor's
WORLDVIEW
TRAVEL UPDATE

Interest Categories

For <u>your</u> personalized Travel Update, choose the categories you're most interested in from this list. Every Travel Update automatically provides you with *Event Highlights* – the best of what's happening during the dates of your trip.

1.	**Business Services**	Fax & Overnight Mail, Computer Rentals, Photocopying, Secretarial , Messenger, Translation Services

Dining

2.	**All Day Dining**	Breakfast & Brunch, Cafes & Tea Rooms, Late-Night Dining
3.	**Local Cuisine**	In Every Price Range—from Budget Restaurants to the Special Splurge
4.	**European Cuisine**	Continental, French, Italian
5.	**Asian Cuisine**	Chinese, Far Eastern, Japanese, Indian
6.	**Americas Cuisine**	American, Mexican & Latin
7.	**Nightlife**	Bars, Dance Clubs, Comedy Clubs, Pubs & Beer Halls
8.	**Entertainment**	Theater—Drama, Musicals, Dance, Ticket Agencies
9.	**Music**	Classical, Traditional & Ethnic, Jazz & Blues, Pop, Rock
10.	**Children's Activities**	Events, Attractions
11.	**Tours**	Local Tours, Day Trips, Overnight Excursions, Cruises
12.	**Exhibitions, Festivals & Shows**	Antiques & Flower, History & Cultural, Art Exhibitions, Fairs & Craft Shows, Music & Art Festivals
13.	**Shopping**	Districts & Malls, Markets, Regional Specialities
14.	**Fitness**	Bicycling, Health Clubs, Hiking, Jogging
15.	**Recreational Sports**	Boating/Sailing, Fishing, Ice Skating, Skiing, Snorkeling/Scuba, Swimming
16.	**Spectator Sports**	Auto Racing, Baseball, Basketball, Football, Horse Racing, Ice Hockey, Soccer

Please note that interest category content will vary by season, destination, and length of stay.

Destinations

The Fodor's/Worldview Travel Update covers more than 160 destinations worldwide. Choose the destinations that match your itinerary from this list. (Choose bulleted destinations only.)

United States (Mainland)
- Albuquerque
- Atlanta
- Atlantic City
- Baltimore
- Boston
- Chicago
- Cincinnati
- Cleveland
- Dallas/Ft. Worth
- Denver
- Detroit
- Houston
- Kansas City
- Las Vegas
- Los Angeles
- Memphis
- Miami
- Milwaukee
- Minneapolis/St. Paul
- New Orleans
- New York City
- Orlando
- Palm Springs
- Philadelphia
- Phoenix
- Pittsburgh
- Portland
- St. Louis
- Salt Lake City
- San Antonio
- San Diego
- San Francisco
- Seattle
- Tampa
- Washington, DC

Alaska
- Anchorage/Fairbanks/Juneau

Hawaii
- Honolulu
- Island of Hawaii
- Kauai
- Maui

Canada
- Quebec City
- Montreal
- Ottawa
- Toronto
- Vancouver

Bahamas
- Abacos
- Eleuthera/Harbour Island
- Exumas
- Freeport
- Nassau & Paradise Island

Bermuda
- Bermuda Countryside
- Hamilton

British Leeward Islands
- Anguilla
- Antigua & Barbuda
- Montserrat
- St. Kitts & Nevis

British Virgin Islands
- Tortola & Virgin Gorda

British Windward Islands
- Barbados
- Dominica
- Grenada
- St. Lucia
- St. Vincent
- Trinidad & Tobago

Cayman Islands
- The Caymans

Dominican Republic
- Puerto Plata
- Santo Domingo

Dutch Leeward Islands
- Aruba
- Bonaire
- Curacao

Dutch Windward Islands
- St. Maarten

French West Indies
- Guadeloupe
- Martinique
- St. Barthelemy
- St. Martin

Jamaica
- Kingston
- Montego Bay
- Negril
- Ocho Rios

Puerto Rico
- Ponce
- San Juan

Turks & Caicos
- Grand Turk
- Providenciales

U.S. Virgin Islands
- St. Croix
- St. John
- St. Thomas

Mexico
- Acapulco
- Cancun & Isla Mujeres
- Cozumel
- Guadalajara
- Ixtapa & Zihuatanejo
- Los Cabos
- Manzanillo
- Mazatlan
- Mexico City
- Monterrey
- Oaxaca
- Puerto Escondido
- Puerto Vallarta
- Veracruz

Europe
- Amsterdam
- Athens
- Barcelona
- Berlin
- Brussels
- Budapest
- Copenhagen
- Dublin
- Edinburgh
- Florence
- Frankfurt
- French Riviera
- Geneva
- Glasgow
- Interlaken
- Istanbul
- Lausanne
- Lisbon
- London
- Madrid
- Milan
- Moscow
- Munich
- Oslo
- Paris
- Prague
- Provence
- Rome
- Salzburg
- St. Petersburg
- Stockholm
- Venice
- Vienna
- Zurich

Pacific Rim Australia & New Zealand
- Auckland
- Melbourne
- Sydney

China
- Beijing
- Guangzhou
- Shanghai

Japan
- Kyoto
- Nagoya
- Osaka
- Tokyo
- Yokohama

Other
- Bangkok
- Hong Kong & Macau
- Manila
- Seoul
- Singapore
- Taipei

Order Form

THIS TRAVEL UPDATE IS FOR (Please print):

Name

Address

City	**State**	**ZIP**

Country	**Tel #** ( ) -

Title of this Fodor's guide:

Store and location where guide was purchased:

INDICATE YOUR DESTINATIONS/DATES: Write in below the destinations you want to order. Then fill in your arrival and departure dates for each destination.

		Month Day		Month Day
(Sample) **LONDON**	From:	**6** / **21**	To:	**6** / **30**
1	From:	/	To:	/
2	From:	/	To:	/
3	From:	/	To:	/

You can order up to three destinations per Travel Update. Only destinations listed on the previous page are applicable. Maximum amount of time covered by a Travel Update cannot exceed 30 days.

CHOOSE YOUR INTERESTS: Select up to eight categories from the list of interest categories shown on the previous page and circle the numbers below:

1   2   3   4   5   6   7   8   9   10   11   12   13   14   15   16

CHOOSE HOW YOU WANT YOUR TRAVEL UPDATE DELIVERED (Check one):

❑ Please mail my Travel Update to the address above **OR**

❑ Fax it to me at **Fax #** ( ) -

DELIVERY CHARGE (Check one)

	Within U.S. & Canada	Outside U.S. & Canada
First Class Mail	❑ $2.50	❑ $5.00
Fax	❑ $5.00	❑ $10.00
Priority Delivery	❑ $15.00	❑ $27.00

All orders will be sent within 48 hours of receipt of a completed order form.

ADD UP YOUR ORDER HERE. *SPECIAL OFFER FOR FODOR'S PURCHASERS ONLY!*

	Suggested Retail Price	Your Price	This Order
First destination ordered	$13.95	$ 7.95	$ 7.95
Second destination (if applicable)	$ 9.95	$ 4.95	+
Third destination (if applicable)	$ 9.95	$ 4.95	+
Plus delivery charge from above			+
		TOTAL:	$

METHOD OF PAYMENT (Check one): ❑ AmEx   ❑ MC   ❑ Visa   ❑ Discover
                                    ❑ Personal Check   ❑ Money Order

Make check or money order payable to: Fodor's Worldview Travel Update

Credit Card #   **Expiration Date:**

Authorized Signature

SEND THIS COMPLETED FORM TO:
Fodor's Worldview Travel Update, 114 Sansome Street, Suite 700, San Francisco, CA 94104

OR CALL OR FAX US 24-HOURS A DAY
Telephone **1-800-799-9609** • Fax **1-800-799-9619** (From within the U.S. & Canada)
(Outside the U.S. & Canada: Telephone 415-616-9988 • Fax 415-616-9989)

(Please have this guide in front of you when you call so we can verify purchase.)

Offer valid until 12/31/94.